This second edition of John Ross' *Time for Favour* is a most welcome addition to the library of anyone interested in Jewish missions. Packed with detailed history and lively biography; based on solid research; drawing out the theological implications of it all – this snapshot of a fourteen-year period in Scottish Jewish missions' history is as relevant today as it was in the mid-nineteenth century. Some may think the detailed account to be of interest only to a small swath of scholars; but to the contrary, I found myself wanting to follow up many of the items in the extensive bibliography. Just who were these people who prayed for Israel and worked for her salvation, sometimes at the cost of their own health and lives? Who journeyed on ship and land to discover Jewish communities and ascertain their openness to the gospel? Who intermingled with Jews, Muslims, and others, learning as they went and committed to a cause greater than themselves? Get a copy today and find out for yourself! You'll be glad you did.

RICH ROBINSON
Senior Researcher, Jews for Jesus, San Francisco, California

The Church today is in dire need of recovering the hope-filled burden for the Jewish people expressed by the apostle Paul, who had 'great sorrow and continual anguish' over Israel's plight, and confessed, 'My heart's desire and prayer to God is for Israel's salvation' (Rom. 9:1-5; 10:1). Such expectation – such theology – is grounded in God's clear, infallible promises in Scripture, and once propelled the Scottish church into one of the greatest eras of missions in church history. Current confusion over the Bible's teaching concerning Israel – and, worse, a warped theology whereby the church has replaced Israel – has led not only to a lack of charity toward Jewish people, but to such indifference one seldom hears prayers for Israel ascending from the gathered church. John Ross's book, *Time for Favour*, aside from detailing the wondrous works of God in the 19th century, demonstrates, too, from what heights especially the Reformed and Presbyterian churches have fallen, and should be required reading for every pastor. May the LORD use *Time for Favour* to spark a renewed interest and burden for the salvation of Israel. May Ross's book also lead to a renewal of the theology that once fed the church's hope, causing her to prioritize the blessing of Israel for the sake of the nations.

L. MICHAEL MORALES
Professor of Biblical Studies, Greenville Presbyterian Theological Seminary, Greenville, South Carolina; author, *Exodus Old and New*

T0278996

Zeal for evangelism to the Jewish people has a long pedigree in Reformed doctrine and practice. For example, the *Westminster Larger Catechism* lists the end-times conversion of the Jews prophesied in Romans 11 as integral to the second petition of the Lord's Prayer. In this masterful work of church history and missiology, John Stuart Ross surveys the historical development, cultural and theological stimuli, and enduring impact of mid-nineteenth-century Scottish Presbyterian missions to the Jews, particularly through the work of the Committee on the Conversion of the Jews to the Faith of Christ. With God's blessing, this excellent work will ignite prayer for and evangelism to the Jewish people, impel twenty-first century believers to reincorporate strategic missional initiatives to the Jewish people in the grand project of the Great Commission, and inspire rising generations of missionaries to become part of what God is doing among the Jewish people today. A delightful and edifying read!

JOEL R. BEEKE
Chancellor, Puritan Reformed Theological Seminary, Grand Rapids, Michigan;
author, *Knowing and Growing in Assurance of Faith*

John Ross' now updated superb exploration into the historic connection between the Scottish church and Jewish mission is an important addition to the corpus of quality material that should make up the library of serious students of Scottish church history. It will also dispel the myth that mission to the Jews was either irrelevant or misplaced. But this book will do more than even that. Ross' infectious passion for Jewish evangelism will draw readers into a greater awareness of their place on the church's radar and the obligation of the believing world to bring the good news to where it originally came from.

IVER MARTIN
Principal, Edinburgh Theological Seminary, Edinburgh

The often-asked question, 'Why are you here?' disturbs the easy equilibrium of what can become an all-too-settled life in ministry. It challenges the person of faith to refocus on the why, the what, the where and the who of mission. At a time of great disruption in the Scottish church, those who first set out to live and serve amongst the Jewish communities in Iasi and Budapest knew exactly why they were there – they were there at God's calling. John Ross's theological and Christological reflection on the sense of calling behind the establishment of a Scottish mission to the Jews, is born of thorough research. A truly engrossing read.

KENNETH I. MACKENZIE
Minister, Braemar and Crathie parish;
domestic chaplain, HM King Charles III;
previous minister, Scottish Mission in Budapest

From Robert Murray McCheyne, the Bonar brothers and John Duncan to martyr Jane Haining, the remarkable story of those Scots who served the Jewish people and shared the Messiah with them is both heart-warming and challenging. John Ross's account of the Scottish Mission and the Jewish disciples of Jesus, such as Adolph Saphir Alfred Edersheim and many others is essential reading to all who have a concern for the Jewish people and the sharing of the Good News of the Messiah. This revised and updated version of his doctoral thesis fills in the gaps, tells the stories and brings alive the encounters, challenges and developments which rightly show the importance of the Scottish Mission to the Jews. As both a mission leader and student of history, John Ross is ideally placed to tell this story, and he does so with passion, detail and due respect for the inspiring legacy to which we are indebted today. Enjoy this book!

RICHARD S. HARVEY
Independent Researcher and a Vice-President of the
International Messianic Jewish Alliance (IMJA)

It is a delight to welcome and commend the publication of this second edition of *Time for Favour*. In telling the story of 'The Scottish Mission to the Jewish People: 1838–1852', Dr Ross provides us with an historical sketch of a vital moment in the life of the Scottish missionary movement. He also does much more than this, by engaging us in a discussion of the reasons and motives for the mission (not least through the additional chapter in this edition). Having previously worked for Christian Witness to Israel, he is well-equipped to discuss the significance of Israel in the plan and purpose of God, in a day when opinions on Israel vary significantly. It was a privilege to supervise the PhD thesis from which this book evolved, although John writes so well that I had to keep stopping myself from becoming so immersed in the story that I forgot the academic task before me!

A. T. B. McGOWAN
Former Director, Rutherford Centre for Reformed Theology, Dingwall;
Professor Emeritus University of the Highlands and Islands

'The Sister on the Hill': Archduchess Maria Dorothea of Württemberg by Anton Einsle, 1843.

TIME FOR FAVOUR

Scottish Evangelism among the Jewish People
1838–1852

John Stuart Ross

CHRISTIAN
FOCUS

Copyright © John Stuart Ross 2024

ISBN 978-1-5271-1135-6

E-book ISBN 978-1-5271-1182-0

10 9 8 7 6 5 4 3 2 1

Published in 2024
by
Christian Focus Publications Ltd,
Geanies House, Fearn, Ross-shire,
IV20 1TW, Great Britain.

www.christianfocus.com

Cover design by
Daniel van Straaten

Printed and bound by Bell & Bain, Glasgow

CONTENTS

For Elizabeth

Thou shalt arise, and mercy yet
Thou to mount Zion shalt extend:
Her time for favour which was set,
Behold, is now come to an end.

PSALM 102 (2):13, *Scottish Psalter*

Abbreviations

Annals	*Annals of the Free Church of Scotland*
BSPGJ	British Society for the Propagation of the Gospel Among the Jews.
CMR	*Children's Missionary Record of the Free Church of Scotland*
DSCHT	*Dictionary of Scottish Church History and Theology*
DNB	*Dictionary of National Biography*
ECI	*Edinburgh Christian Instructor*
Fasti	*Fasti Ecclesiae Scoticanae*
HMFR	*Home and Foreign Missionary Review of the Free Church of Scotland*
LSPCJ	London Society for Promoting Christianity Among the Jews
MBRPC	*Minute Book of the Reformed Presbyterian Church*
MCCH	M'Cheyne Archive in New College Library, Edinburgh.
Memoir	*Memoir and Remains of Robert Murray M'Cheyne*
Narrative	*Narrative of a Visit to the Holy Land and Mission of Inquiry to the Jews*
NAS	National Archives of Scotland
NCL	New College Library
NIDCC	*New International Dictionary of the Christian Church*
NLS	National Library of Scotland
PGACS	*Proceedings of the General Assembly of the Church of Scotland*
RSCHS	*Records of the Scottish Church History Society*
RThJ	*Reformed Theological Journal*

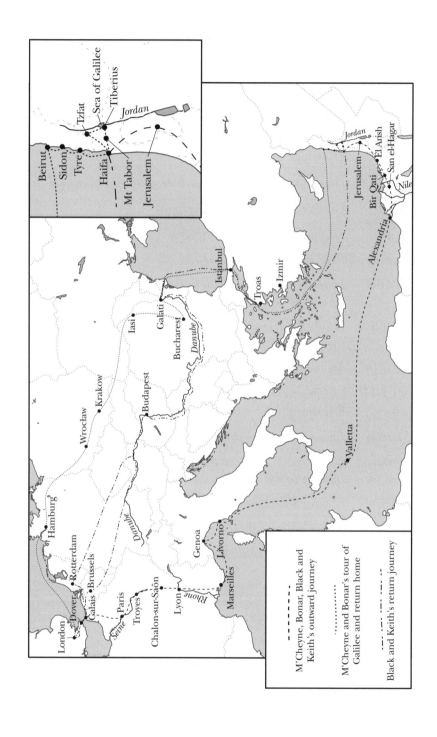

Sea of Galilee
Tzfat
Tiberius
Jordan
Beirut
Sidon
Tyre
Haifa
Mt Tabor
Jerusalem

Jordan
Jerusalem
Bir Qati
San eHagar
El Arish
Alexandria
Nile

Istanbul
Troas
Izmir

Galați
Iasi
Bucharest
Danube

Krakow
Wroclaw
Budapest
Danube

Valletta

Hamburg
Rotterdam
Brussels
Genoa
Livorno
Calais
Paris
Marseilles
Dover
Troyes
Chalon-sur-Saône
London
Seine
Lyon
Rhone

M'Cheyne, Bonar, Black and
Keith's outward journey

M'Cheyne and Bonar's tour of
Galilee and return home

Black and Keith's return journey

Foreword

THIS absorbing book retells the history of Scottish missionary work to the Jewish people in the nineteenth century. Such was its impact on me, when I read the first edition over a decade ago, that I couldn't keep it to myself. I read aloud excerpts to my fellow ministers at First Presbyterian Church, Jackson, Mississippi during our regular weekly meeting, and again to university students gathered for a conference. Since that time, I have recommended it countless times to pastors, seminarians, and church members.

The author, Dr John Stuart Ross, brings a half-century of experience in mission work and pastoral ministry. John has served in the Christian mission in Nigeria and South Africa, and in international Jewish evangelism, as well as pastoring congregations in Belfast, and the Highlands of Scotland. This background affords him, I think, both a unique depth of understanding and vantage point of the subject. His expertise and personal insights enrich the narrative, and his pastoral and missionary heart shows throughout the book.

Having enthusiastically devoured the first edition of *Time for Favour: The Scottish Mission to the Jews 1838–1852*, I am delighted to have the privilege of writing a foreword to its second, updated and expanded edition. The book is theology, history, evangelism, and missiology, all wrapped up together, and introduced with Ross's riveting account of Jane Haining's tragic, heroic, and moving story of courage, self-sacrifice, and faithfulness unto death. Reading it will not only prove informative and inspiring, but devotional.

Time for Favour provides us with best available full account of the mid-nineteenth-century Scottish mission to the Jews, and helps us better to understand its origins, motivations, and influences. Dr Ross offers new insights into an important but relatively unknown chapter of church history, all based on his meticulous research. He engages carefully and critically with existing literature on the subject, challenging controversial views, and offering in-depth analysis, thereby aiding and enriching the future study of the topic.

The book traces the roots of the mission, its formation, and the diverse influences that shaped its trajectory. Chapters three to five provide a nuanced analysis of the mission's strategies and objectives, while subsequent chapters explore the broader impacts and legacies of the mission, including its influence on evangelical spirituality and the establishment of Jewish missions in other Presbyterian churches.

There are many features of the book that I personally appreciated. In the first chapter Ross overviews general and Christian attitudes in England towards the Jews from the thirteenth to nineteenth centuries, highlighting (and contrasting) the ancient Scottish affinity for the Jewish people. I found this helpful and enlightening.

He then takes us to the theology of the Scottish Reformation, introducing us to the views of such leaders as Samuel Rutherford and Thomas Boston and their concern for the conversion of ancient people of God, then across the ocean in the American colonies, to Jonathan Edwards, David Brainerd, and John Eliot, who shared the same hopes, and back across the Atlantic again to Claudius Buchanan, Henry Martyn, and even William Carey, whose missions to India were not without a connection to and concern for Jewish evangelism.

Did you know that one of the things that grew out of Claudius Buchanan's ministry was a translation of the New Testament into Hebrew? Do you know about the great Thomas Chalmers' enthusiasm for missions to the Jews? Or the role that Edward Irving played in it? Or how the premillennialism of the Bonar brothers and the postmillennial views of David Brown each fostered it? Did you know that John 'Rabbi' Duncan (later a renowned professor of Old Testament at New College, Edinburgh) was the Church of Scotland's first missionary to the Jewish people in Hungary, and that through his ministry the Lord was pleased to save Alfred Edersheim (who subsequently authored the famed *The Life and Times of Jesus the Messiah*)? This book is full of those kinds of insights and accompanying theological reflection. *Time for Favour* is a historical and spiritual feast. Taste and see.

J. LIGON DUNCAN, III
Chancellor
REFORMED THEOLOGICAL SEMINARY
JACKSON, MISSISSIPPI

Preface and Acknowledgements

IN some parts of the Church there has developed the notion that missionary work among the Jewish people is inappropriate, preposterous, even hostile. Happy to support mission among other peoples, some evangelicals take no interest in, or do not support Jewish missions. Some years ago, Dr Gerald H. Anderson, then director of the Overseas Ministries Study Centre, New Haven, Connecticut, warned a group of international mission leaders that failure to witness to the Jewish people could lead to the collapse of all missionary work. Some thought he was exaggerating, but, Anderson argued, if the gospel is not for the Jewish people then who is it for? Anderson's domino theory is compelling, and simultaneously disturbing and challenging.

The leaders of the nineteenth-century Scottish mission to the Jews would have wholeheartedly endorsed Anderson's comment. Robert Murray M'Cheyne once remarked that it was not enough for an evangelical church to be evangelistic, as Alexander Duff had insisted it ought to be, but it must be evangelistic 'as God would have us be – not only dispense the light on every hand, but dispense it first to the Jew.' Indeed, the mood was such that, as the Scottish Church of that period sang the second version of Psalm 102:13, by a remarkable consensus, they felt that Zion's 'time for favour' had indeed come, and along with it the conviction that Israel's spiritual restoration would give worldwide mission an impetus sufficient to impel it to its ultimate conclusion. The story this book sets out to tell is that of the first phase of the Scottish mission to the Jewish people, between 1839 and 1852, a period rich in important principles for present mission.

This second edition of *Time for Favour* differs from the first by some amendments, corrections, updates, and alterations, including endnotes based on my original PhD research, plus a new and important chapter (chapter five) which explores the principles and convictions that motivated the mission. Where appropriate I have used current place names rather than their nineteenth-century equivalents.

In writing this book I am obliged to many people. Reverend Professor Andrew McGowan and Rabbi Professor Dan Cohn-Sherbok painstakingly supervised my original PhD research. The Council of Management of Christian Witness to Israel (now International Mission to the Jewish People) generously underwrote many of the costs entailed. Of my former CWI colleagues I would especially mention Mrs Sally Hutson, my indefatigable personal assistant, and Rev. Mike Moore, my successor as General Secretary. I owe a great debt to helpful librarians at the Robinson Library in Armagh, Westminster College library in Cambridge, the Edinburgh libraries at the Free Church College (now Edinburgh Theological Seminary), New College, the National Library of Scotland, as well as the National Archives of Scotland, Edinburgh.

When the first edition went out of print, American friends successfully laid siege to Christian Focus Publications asking for a second edition. To Willie Mackenzie, Director of Publishing, Colin Fast, Editorial Manager, and the staff of CFP I again express my thanks. I am greatly indebted to my editor, Anne Norrie, for her meticulous discovery of my errors and helpful suggestions to improve the text.

I am very grateful to my friend Rev. Dr Ligon Duncan III, Chancellor and CEO of Reformed Theological Seminary, for writing the foreword.

I offer my sincere thanks to those who have endorsed this new edition – Dr Rich Robinson, Prof. Michael Morales, Dr Joel Beeke, Rev. Iver Martin, Rev. Kenneth MacKenzie, Dr Richard Harvey, and Prof. Andrew McGowan – encouraging readers to explore the pioneering, but still relevant, work of the Scottish Jewish mission.

To my wife, Elizabeth, I owe an incalculable debt. Throughout many years of Christian mission and ministry, research and writing, she has lovingly kept me at it, encouraging and supporting, whilst patiently tolerating my absences from home and distractions from the affairs of family life. To her this book is dedicated.

When drafting these comments I glanced at the date and noted that it was 6th October, the last day of the Feast of Sukkot, the celebration of God's protection and care of Israel in journeying from slavery in Egypt to freedom in its Promised Land. Sukkot is also a celebration of harvest, that all is safely gathered in. Little did I realise how unsafe Hamas terrorists would make peaceful communities close to the Gaza Strip feel, and how soon the region would again be enveloped in violence and war. As we pray for wickedness to be defeated and peace to be restored to Arabs and Jews alike, we do so paraphrasing the words of Yeshua the Messiah in Mark 8:36: 'For what does it profit a nation to gain secure borders, material prosperity and national integrity and forfeit its soul?'

This book comes with the hope that it might enthuse a new generation to engage in and support witness to the Jewish people, and join their prayers with those now gone from this world that the sovereign Lord would send His Spirit to gather Israel to the Messiah and so renew its mission to the world. Such a prayer was movingly uttered by George Herbert in his poem *The Jews*:

> Poor nation, whose sweet sap and juice
> Our scions have purloin'd, and left you dry:
> Whose streams we got by the Apostles' sluice,
> And use in baptism, while ye pine and die:
> Who by not keeping once, became a debtor;
>   And now be keeping lose the letter:
>
> Oh that my prayers! mine, alas!
> Oh that some Angel might a trumpet sound:
> At which the Church falling upon her face
> Should cry so loud, until the trump were drown'd,
> And by that cry of her dear Lord obtain,
>   That your sweet sap might come again!

JOHN S. ROSS
DRUMNADROCHIT
7th October, 2023

Introduction:
On the Road to Heaven

Konzentrationslager Auschwitz, German occupied Poland, July 1944

THEY lied about her death. The death certificate said she had died in hospital, but the sketchy details were suspicious. The cause of death was said to be 'cachexia, following intestinal catarrh' or, to put it in layman's terms, she had suffered a chronic infection of the bowel resulting in a fatal and irreversible loss of weight, muscle wastage, fatigue and death. Had she been deliberately starved to death? It is quite possible. Many were. In fact, a short time before her death she had written to a friend about craving apples, fresh fruit, and bread. But she probably did not die of starvation. It is likely that on 17th July, 1944, prisoner 79467 found herself among a group of Hungarian Jewish women herded into the gas chamber in Auschwitz. They were not the first and they would not be the last. The tally of Jews liquidated with heartless industrial efficiency at Auschwitz-Birkenau is estimated to have exceeded a million, perhaps almost a million and a half, of whom it was said five hundred and sixty-five thousand, one in three, was a Hungarian.

Though despised as worthless sub-humans by the Nazis, all who died in that and other fearful extermination camps, were special. All bore the image of God. Each had their own dignity. Everyone was someone's father or mother, husband or wife, uncle or aunt, brother or sister, lover or friend. United in their human dignity, they were individual in their sufferings. Forty-seven-year-old prisoner 79467 certainly did not look very different to those who died along with her. Her soft dark hair framed a warm, sympathetic, bespectacled

17

face, not unlike other Jewish women of her age. A few weeks earlier you might have passed her in a Budapest street and, except for her piercing blue eyes and her different accent, thought she was Jewish herself. But she wasn't. She was a Scot. So what was it that brought middle-aged Jane Haining from the security of Scotland first to Hungary, and then to this place of death in Poland?

The short answer is that the Germans had sentenced her to death as a spy. Whilst working as matron of the girl's school of the Church of Scotland Mission on Vörösmarty utca, in Budapest, Jane had been anonymously denounced to the Gestapo, who raided the mission and arrested her.[1]

As they searched her office and bedroom, Jane was given fifteen minutes to get ready before being driven off, the car's siren blaring. She was charged on eight separate counts, including listening to the BBC, which the Nazi's had made a criminal offence punishable by jail, hard labour, or death. And just as Jesus had refused to defend Himself before Pilate, so Jane did not deny their charges, apart from the political accusations, as it was undeniable that she had worked with Jews, and, of course, the heartless indictment that she had wept when sewing the compulsory yellow star on the girls' clothes was perfectly true. It was also true she had dismissed from her employment her Aryan housekeeper. From the Gestapo's grim jail at Fő utca in Budapest she was transported to a holding camp east of the city and from there to the notorious extermination camp of Auschwitz, but death did not come easily. 'Even here on the road to Heaven', she wrote in one of her last letters, 'there is a mountain range to climb.' On Saturday 26th August, 1944, on page five, the *Dumfries and Galloway Standard* carried a brief death notice:

> HAINING. – On 17th July, 1944, died in hospital in Germany, Jane Mathieson Haining, third daughter of the late Thomas John and Jane Haining, of Lochenhead, Dunscore, aged 47 years.

A fuller answer to the question of why Jane Haining died in Auschwitz requires us to start at the beginning: Jane was born in 1897, to Thomas and Jane Haining, at Lochenhead in Dumfriesshire, in southern Scotland. When Jane was only five years old, her mother died giving birth to a fourth baby, a daughter, who did not survive infancy. It was said that the experience of helping care for the ailing infant left its mark on Jane and gave her a capacity for mothering, an instinct that would not find its fulfilment in marriage and motherhood, but in a girls' school.

Jane attended the village school at Dunscore where early on it became clear that she possessed an outstanding mind. When twelve years old, she won a bursary to Dumfries Academy, where she was so academically successful that she carried away the astonishing number of forty-one prizes during her school career, becoming 'dux' (Scottish: top pupil) of the school in 1915. Rather than attend university, Jane preferred to enter the world of business, taking up employment with the well-established and highly successful thread manufacturers, J&P Coats Ltd., of Paisley. Here too her ability was readily recognised by the company secretary, who invited her to become his private secretary, a job which she held for the next fifteen years.

Jane's parents were evangelicals, attending the Craig Free Church of Scotland in Dunscore, where she was baptised. When she was three years old, the congregation entered the union of the Free Church and the United Presbyterian Church to become Craig United Free Church. Situated in the heart of Covenanter country, the Craig's roots lay in a much earlier congregation. Old Dunscore Kirk had been established as a congregation of the Church of Scotland in the mid-seventeenth century and their first minister was Robert Archibald. Shortly after, in 1663, when the Scottish Parliament was supporting King Charles II's anti-Presbyterian polices, Archibald was, on account of his evangelical and covenanting sympathies, denied the use of the church building and forced to leave his comfortable manse. Rather than assent to the imposition of Episcopal government and liturgy, he, with the support of many of his people, and like many another Lowland Presbyterian minister, took to the hills to preach the gospel freely in the open air. These gatherings were fraught with the dangers of persecution which reached its culmination in what became known as 'the Killing Times', when, between 1680 and 1688, Presbyterians who had signed the Solemn League and Covenant were regarded as insurgents and subversives and liable to summary execution.

Dunscore lay within the jurisdiction of the notorious Sir Robert Grierson, laird of Lag, 'Cruel Lag', as he was known. Grierson was a dyed-in-the-wool Stuart loyalist and hater of Covenanters, and is said to have been guilty of many atrocities against local Presbyterians. He was a byword for evil among Dumfriesshire folk, who said his spittle scorched the earth where it fell. Another tradition had it that on the night he died a chariot surrounded by thunder clouds swept him away to hell. A further story alleges that the horses pulling his hearse to Dunscore's old Kirkyard died of exhaustion on the way and a black raven flew down and settled on the coffin, only flying off at the moment of burial. Such accounts, whilst not the stuff of scholarly history, nevertheless vividly illustrate the loathing and fear in which this man was held.[2]

With the Glorious Revolution of William of Orange in 1689, the majority of the members of the Craig, like many stricter Covenanters, found themselves unable to come to terms with the Revolution Settlement or the Church of Scotland and chose rather to associate with the Reformed Presbyterian Church. By the time of the *New Statistical Account* of 1835 the congregation at the Craig numbered about four-hundred and fifty communicants. In 1876, the Craig joined the Free Church of Scotland and their first Free Church minister, Rev. William Barrowman, was ordained and inducted in 1898. Two years later Barrowman took the congregation into the union with the United Presbyterians to form the United Free Church. It was Barrowman whom the young Jane knew as her minister. He died in 1928, having paved the way for the congregation to come full circle by going back with the United Free majority into the Church of Scotland.

Jane lived in the south-side Glasgow suburb of Pollockshields, and during her time with Coats in Paisley was a member of Queen's Park West United Free Church, which, like her home congregation in Dunscore, re-united with the Church of Scotland in 1929. Here she taught in the Sunday School, becoming its secretary, whilst simultaneously working enthusiastically with the Band of Hope, a temperance organisation for working-class children referred to in broad Glaswegian as the 'Bandyhope.'

Aware of the city's infamous reputation for hard drinking, Jane sought not only to keep her children from the bottle, but to win them for Christ. Following *The Band of Hope Manual*, Jane held a Saturday afternoon meeting, commonly called 'the service', at which strict order was maintained.[3] As the children came in they were segregated: the girls to the left of the aisle and the boys on the right. The meeting commenced with the children reciting in unison *The Pledge*. Sometimes a temperance catechism was used as a teaching aid, and an American-produced monthly paper called *Youth's Temperance Banner* was from time to time distributed. We can imagine the room being dimmed for Jane to operate an acetylene-powered 'magic lantern', illustrating Bible stories and Christian teaching with coloured 3¼ inch square slides. These meetings were famous for the hearty singing of songs and hymns characteristic of the movement, including *Father Guide Us,* sung to the simple and stirring tune Vesper Hymn. By today's standards its sentiments may seem quaint and outdated, yet it was an earnest prayer asking God to keep vulnerable young people safe from dangerous habits:

> Fallen is our favoured nation,
> Sunk in sorrow and in shame;
> Speed the Temperance reformation,
> Ev'ry drunkard now reclaim.

> Each a pilgrim and a stranger,
> Keep us Lord, from evil ways,
> Lead us through this world of danger,
> Guide us in our early days.

The Band of Hope was renowned for its annual summer outings when Jane and her helpers took the children on a steamer day trip from Glasgow's Broomielaw 'doon the water' to a Clyde coast seaside town, perhaps Largs, Millport, Rothesay, or Dunoon. The organisers saw these outings not only as pleasure trips but as opportunities for an evangelistic foray. Often accompanied by a band, the children would stand on a street corner, or take up a prominent position on the promenade, vigorously singing songs and hymns and handing out pamphlets as a witness to other day-trippers.

Though successful and well settled in her work at Coats, and busy in her Christian service at church, Jane hardly regarded these as her true vocation, but in 1932 she heard an address by Dr George Mackenzie on the Church of Scotland's Jewish mission that changed all that. She was so moved by his account of the work in Hungary that she became entirely convinced that it was to this cause that God wanted her to commit her energies. She shortly afterwards commented to a friend, 'I have found my life's work'.

Resigning from her comfortable and remunerative job at J&P Coats, she returned to college to take a diploma in domestic science. Then, to gain further experience, she travelled to Manchester to work as matron at the newly opened Holt Radium Institute at Withington, a hospital at the forefront of the application of radiotherapy to the treatment of cancer. An offer of service was accepted by the Jewish committee of the Church of Scotland and thirty-five-year-old Jane found herself matron at the Scottish Mission School on Vörösmarty utca, in Budapest, with the care of fifty, mainly Jewish, boarders.

The Magyar language of Hungary is considered a difficult language to learn and so it may be taken as a measure of Jane's character and commitment that she readily accepted the discipline necessary to master it and, not long after, was able to converse fluently in the language. She also had fluent German. Further evidence of her dedication was her reluctance to leave the girls even for holidays in Scotland. She returned only twice, once in 1935 and again in the summer of 1939.

It was during this second home leave, whilst holidaying in Cornwall with the school's Hungarian headmistress that, following Hitler's invasion of Poland, Britain's Prime Minister – Neville Chamberlain – declared war on Germany. Aware that German ambitions might bring Hungary into the war, but without any thoughts of her own safety, Jane immediately made plans to return to Budapest. The following year, the Jewish committee pleaded with her to return home, but Jane, trusting in God and the 'true-hearted, honourable and chivalrous' Hungarians, politely but adamantly refused, and although other colleagues did heed the summons and returned home to safety, Jane never saw Scotland again.

INTRODUCTION: ON THE ROAD TO HEAVEN

In 1941, as Europe descended deeper and deeper into the Nazi maelstrom, David McDougall, the General Secretary of the Jewish committee, was putting the finishing touches to his book, *In Search of Israel,* published later that year in Edinburgh by Thomas Nelson. Towards the end he movingly remarked that, 'Miss Haining, the matron of the girls' home, stayed on after the others, and she is there still. By roundabout ways we hear from her sometimes.'

In March 1944, as Hungary was invaded. McDougall, on behalf of the whole Church, which was deeply concerned for Jane's safety, once more pled with her to hasten home, but once again she quietly but emphatically refused. In May she was arrested by the Gestapo, charged with espionage and imprisoned in the Fő utca jail. Then, with hundreds of Jewish people from the Budapest ghetto, she was sent to the transit camp for political prisoners at Kistarcsa just outside Budapest, before a final rail journey by cattle wagon to Auschwitz, five hundred kilometres away in Poland. From this dread place she sent a final postcard home, dated 15th July, it was posted just two days before her death.

It may be taken as a measure of the fanatical intensity of Nazi hatred for the Jewish people that in the last year of the war, when the tide had turned against Germany, it nevertheless dedicated its transport resources not to reinforcing its battling troops, but to clearing the Budapest ghetto and the extermination of its occupants. In the inscrutable yet all-wise and all-loving purposes of God, gentle Jane Haining was caught up in these terrible events, murdered for her love of the Jewish people and martyred for her faith in the Messiah of Israel. On the day of her arrest, one of her former charges had been visiting the Scottish mission and witnessed the event. She later shared her recollection:

> I still feel the tears in my eyes and hear in my ears the siren of the Gestapo motor car. I see the smile on her face while she bade me farewell. I never saw Miss Haining again, and when I went to the Scottish Mission to ask the minister about her, I was told she had died. I did not want to believe it, nor to understand, but a long time later I realised that she had died for me, and for others ... her smile, voice and face are still in my heart.

Even this account, however, is far from the whole story. So many questions still remain unanswered: how was it that a Scot should take an interest in the Jewish children of Hungary and be so dedicated to them that she counted her life cheap if their lives might be saved? How was it that the Church of Scotland came to have missionary work in Budapest? Why was it that for centuries Scottish Christians had a special place in their hearts and prayers for the Jewish people? It will take the rest of this book to unfold the fascinating story that provides answers to these questions.

⇜ 1 ⇝

Entering into the Jewish Heritage
Scotland, c.1290–1843

THE grace of gratitude is deeply embedded in the Old Testament and its importance is dramatically emphasised through the thanksgiving rituals of the tabernacle and temple. It is therefore unsurprising that that most Jewish of the Apostles, Saul of Tarsus – rabbinically trained at the feet of Rabban Gamaliel I and steeped in the Hebrew Scriptures – sought to instil in his converts such a spirit, making even the youngest in the faith aware of their utter indebtedness to God, both for eternal salvation and innumerable blessings daily received. Along with a perpetual need to confess our sins, our prayers are never complete without an expression of gratitude. Thankfulness, as a spiritual grace, develops in proportion to our growing awareness of God, His goodness and generosity, and our complete dependence upon Him. In his 1633 poem, *Gratefulnesse*, George Herbert wisely prayed:

> Thou that hast giv'n so much to me,
> Give one thing more, a gratefull heart.

A special focus for Christian gratitude is those persons who, under God, have been the channel of our greatest blessings. So it was then, that, as the centuries passed, the Scottish Church grew to appreciate more and more the part played by Israel in God's plan of redemption, and marvelled that it should include gentiles such as themselves. Gratitude, growing in relation to faith and knowledge, led first to fervent prayer for Israel's salvation and later to actively sharing the Good News of Jesus the Messiah with the Jewish people.

It is possible, though we cannot be entirely sure, that Jews first arrived in Scotland during the time of the Romans.[1] Certainly Scottish contact with Jewish people grew after the expulsion of the English Jewish community in 1290 led to a northwards emigration. Over the previous seventy years English Jews had suffered prejudice and persecution because their forefathers were seen by English Christians as the Christ-killers. Ludicrous and sensational blood-libel allegations circulated of the ritual murder of English children and the mingling of their blood with flour to bake the unleavened bread of Passover. And, just as in Hitler's Europe, English Jews were forced to wear a badge marking them out from others before being financially penalised in 1270, and expelled in 1290 by royal edict of Edward I.

There is scant evidence of Jews in Scotland in the period up to 1290 and whilst it is plausible that refugees from Edward I's expulsion found sanctuary north of the English border and maybe left their DNA behind, the records are unclear and insufficient to infer, as some have done, that some Scottish clans had a Jewish progenitor.[2] As international travellers, Scots probably encountered Jewish people through trade or when on pilgrimage to the Holy Land. Swept off course by a storm, Arculf, bishop and pilgrim, arrived in Columba's Iona around 680 enthusiastically recounting to Abbot Adomnán and the brothers his experiences of the Holy Land with sufficient detail to allow Adomnán to compile his *De Locis Sanctis* (Concerning Sacred Places), complete with one of the earliest maps of Jerusalem. In this work Adomnán says little about the Jewish people of the Holy Land, except to record an implausible dispute between the Jewish Christians and traditional Jews of Jerusalem over the supposed shroud of Christ.[3]

Almost nine hundred years later, John Knox, in his *History of the Reformation in Scotland* tells with greater authority how George Wishart, his mentor and one of Scotland's Reformation martyrs, testified at his trial before Cardinal Beaton how he had met a Jew when he was travelling down the Rhine to Switzerland and how this man had rejected the claim that Jesus was the Messiah because Christian 'temples' were 'full of idols to whom ye pray and ye even adore a piece of bread, calling it God.' Identifying himself with this excoriating Jewish critique of Roman Catholic practices sealed

Wishart's fate. He was condemned to be strangled the next day, and his body burnt.[4]

In 1656, when Oliver Cromwell gave verbal permission for Jews to re-establish a community in England, they still could not study at or teach in any English university unless they first swore a Christian oath. In Scotland, however, there was no such discrimination. Students training for the ministry of the Church of Scotland learned Hebrew from Jewish lecturers such as Julius Conradus Otto, formerly known as Naphtali Margolioth, who taught at Edinburgh from 1642 to 1656, or Paul Shaletti, who lectured at King's College, Aberdeen, from 1669 to 1672.[5]

The minutes of the Edinburgh town council reflect this goodwill in the realm of trade. In 1691 David Brown, a Jewish merchant, applied for permission to live and trade in the city. His request was opposed by some of the city fathers on the grounds that 'no person whatsoever that denies the basis or fundamentals of our Christian religion can have any privilege within the city of Edinburgh or suburbs.' The majority, however, were of a different opinion and granted him the permission he sought. Hugh Blair, the City Treasurer, denounced the opposition as being at variance with Reformed practice elsewhere. Jews, Blair declared, were not to be considered the same as other non-Christians because, firstly, they were the ancient people of God and were, therefore, loved for the sake of their forefathers and, secondly, it was customary, wherever the Reformed religion was professed, to allow Jews freedom to trade.[6]

Blair's attitude was echoed a hundred years later when Sir Walter Scott's medieval novel, *Ivanhoe*, was greeted in the land of its origin with dismay. Sir Walter's Scottish readers felt that the Jewish Rebecca, in their eyes the true heroine, had not been treated fairly when Scott had allowed Ivanhoe to marry Lady Rowena, and Rebecca was left to Wilfred. Indeed, so strong was the clamour for Scott to rewrite the story in Rebecca's favour, that he felt constrained to make a public explanation, justifying his plot in terms of the balance of historical probabilities.

Scott's sympathetic representation of a Jewish woman stands in marked contrast to antisemitic attitudes not uncommon in English literary circles. Indeed, in its address to the Jewish people, the 1841 General Assembly of the Church of Scotland felt justified in lamenting with the Jewish people that 'in England itself you have at times suffered so much from bitter animosity.' Evidence is not hard to find. Two of Scott's contemporaries, William Cobbett and Charles Dickens, to say nothing of England's greatest literary figure, William Shakespeare in his *The Merchant of Venice*, stereotyped Jewish people in strongly negative terms.

Despite Shakespeare's protestation of Shylock's humanity (the 'I am a Jew. Hath not a Jew eyes? Hath not a Jew hands, organs, dimensions, senses, affections, passions' speech) his portrayal of Jews as venial, ruthless, and calculating has long been considered a perpetuation of antisemitic tropes, at once repulsive and fascinating.[7]

Cobbett, with an almost medieval aggressiveness denounced Jews as parasites, murderers of Christ and blasphemous opponents of the Christian gospel.[8] In *Oliver Twist* (1938) the usually socially sensitive Dickens used a form of caricature, even then out of date, to infamously set a Jew as a master criminal, more of a creature than a man, possessed of immense greed and dressed in 'a greasy flannel gown' with 'a villainous-looking and repulsive face.' Dickens later attempted to justify himself – 'I have no feeling towards the Jews but a friendly one' – but his more kindly representations of Jews failed to make amends for the offensiveness of Fagin. Inspired by George Cruikshank's antisemitic 1838 caricatures, and not far from depictions of Jews in Julius Streicher's Nazi paper, *Der Stürmer*, the English movie director, David Lean, outrageously perpetuated the cliche in his 1948 film adaptation by having Alec Guinness play Fagin wearing an absurdly exaggerated false nose. Lean's clumsy insensitivity, if not deliberate offensiveness, is compounded by the fact that the film came out in 1948, only three years after the world discovered the extent of the Holocaust and in the same year as the establishment of the State of Israel.

It would take one hundred and seventy years to attempt to rescue Fagin's reputation and that by someone who also had a name for depravity. In Roman Polanski's 2005 film version of Oliver Twist, Fagin utters a seemingly throw-away line. 'You know what I consider the greatest sin in the world, my dear?' he says. 'Ingratitude.' But the point is made when at the end Oliver visits Fagin in Newgate prison where he is under sentence of death. Instead of following Dickens' implausible storyline by inviting Fagin to pray for pardon, which Dickens predictably makes the old reprobate reject, Oliver simply thanks the old man, 'You were kind to me'. The truth is that neither Dickens nor Polanksi really get the point, which is, of course, that no one is beyond redemption and may be led there by kindness; self-righteousness always repels.[9]

Dickens' disparaging description of Jews as 'greasy' stuck. Anthony Trollope used it of the Jewish Lopez in *The Prime Minister* (1876), and said much the same of his preposterously named Mohomet Moss in his unfinished novel *The Landleaguers* (1883). Hilaire Belloc and G. K. Chesterton kept alive offensive anti-Jewish portrayals until well into the twentieth century.

By contrast, sympathetic Scots played a key role in the struggle for Jewish political emancipation. In 1830, Lord Macaulay's maiden speech as a Member of Parliament was on 'The civil disabilities affecting Jews in England' in which, amongst other matters, he took Corbett to task for his intolerance. And where was the speech first published but in *The Edinburgh Review*. Macaulay was the son of Zachary Macaulay, a Scottish Highlander, and the son's support for the amelioration of Jewish grievances mirrored the father's support for the abolition of African slavery as the great injustice of his day. A year later, almost to the day, on Saturday, 5th April, 1834, both *The Scotsman* and *The Evening Courant* ran lengthy articles approving the decision taken at a meeting held in Edinburgh the previous Thursday, 'to take measures to petition both Houses of Parliament to remove all the disabilities under which the Jews of His Majesty's dominions now labour.'

This generous attitude was sustained until recent times, giving Scotland the enviable reputation of having no history of persecuting Jews. Mistreated and harassed elsewhere in Europe, the *Encyclopaedia Judaica,* published in the early 1970s, was able to record that 'relations between Jews and non-Jews in Scotland have always been harmonious.' But, as the influence of Christianity has waned in Scottish society, so the situation has deteriorated. Among others, two recent studies have shone light on antisemitism in Scotland. In 2016 the Scottish Parliament officially took note of a study by the Scottish Council of Jewish Communities highlighting antisemitism, and in 2022 the Scottish government was forced to investigate antisemitism in higher education.

What was it then that formed the Scots' generosity of attitude towards a people despised and rejected elsewhere? To go back to the nineteenth century, Dr Alexander Moody Stuart, one of the first generation of ministers of the Free Church of Scotland, argued that it could be explained by a certain similarity between the two peoples, which included a love of the Hebrew Bible, patriotism, the simplicity of worship, and devotion to the moral law of God, particularly that of the Sabbath, and adding, tongue in cheek, an 'adaptability in settling in all lands and making money in them'. Robert Murray M'Cheyne agreed. With just a hint of chauvinism, he wrote, 'In many respects, Scotland may be called God's second Israel. No other land has its Sabbath as Scotland has; no other land has the Bible as Scotland has; no other land has the gospel preached, free as the air we breathe, fresh as the stream from the everlasting hills.'

Remarkably, Scottish Jewish opinion largely concurs. Writing of the religious foundation of Edinburgh's Jewish community, Abel Philips maintained that Edinburgh's Christians were free of intolerance because they had learned to respect the teaching and moral principles of the Old Testament. Chaim Bermant, a twentieth-century Jewish writer and commentator, who as small boy from Eastern Europe grew up in Glasgow, argued that the good relations between Scottish Presbyterians and Jews could be attributed to their common devotion to the Hebrew Bible. He doubted if there was a country anywhere in the world where Jews had been more readily accepted and more happily integrated than Scotland, where 'the Jew is regarded as a sort of aboriginal Presbyterian.'[10]

This opinion was shared by Scottish Jewish scholar, Professor David Daiches (1912–2005), who saw post World War II Scotland, 'with its immersion in biblical lore, as a new Jerusalem in which Jews could contribute to the cultural, social, and commercial life of the society around them without impairing their Jewish loyalties.' A further Jewish writer, Stefan C. Reif, added his voice to this consensus, arguing that 'If any nation may justly claim to be fully conversant with and as closely attached to the Bible as the Jewish people, then that nation must certainly be the Scots'.

That the Bible informed and influenced Scottish attitudes towards Jewish people is indisputable. Many Scots were better acquainted with the history and literature of ancient Israel than they were with that of their own land. This was especially so in the Highlands where a high degree of familiarity with the Bible produced an almost unique fusion of Jewish and Highland perspectives. As Prof. Donald E. Meek has pointed out, for Highlanders, the Bible not only revealed their hearts before God, but in it they 'could read about a chosen people whose history ran parallel to theirs, in spiritual, social and even political terms'.[11]

Immersed as they were in the Bible, it was inevitable that before long Scottish Christians would come to see that, under God's blessing, the Jewish people had been the source of their greatest good. Was not the Bible they so cherished, both its Old and New Testaments, written almost entirely by Jewish authors? Did not Bible-reading teach them that God's covenant with Abraham meant that the human ancestry of the Messiah and Saviour, Jesus Christ, was Jewish? Were not the first members of the Church, God's international family of faith, all Jews, who had shared with the gentiles the riches of the gospel? And was it not true that they too were Abraham's children, at least to the extent that his faith was in their hearts, even if his blood did not course through their veins? Compelled by the evidence to answer these questions in the affirmative produced in Scottish hearts a profound sense of indebtedness, which, as we shall see in the next chapter, first found expression in prayer for the Jewish people's spiritual restoration.

This sense of indebtedness to the Jewish people was something seventeenth-century English Puritans and Scottish Covenanters shared and therefore the idea was incorporated in The Westminster Confession of Faith and its catechisms. Question 191 of *The Larger Catechism* teaches that by praying for the coming of Christ's kingdom the Church prays for 'the gospel [to be] propagated throughout the world, [and] the Jews called.' Similarly, *The Directory for the Public Worship of God*, requires ministers to pray each Sunday not only for the general spread of the gospel, but specifically for 'the conversion of the Jews, the fullness of the Gentiles, the fall of Antichrist, and the hastening of the second coming of our Lord.'

The Scottish Presbyterian view of the essential unity between the Old and New Testaments and the Church as God's covenant community, reflected in Westminster theology, was rooted in the origins of Scotland's Reformation. The Genevan reformer, John Calvin, had made this point in his *Institutes of the Christian Religion*, and it was also incorporated by John Knox and his collaborators in *The Scots Confession* of 1560. By the seventeenth century a version of covenant theology was applied to politics in such documents as the National Covenant of 1638 and the Solemn League and Covenant of 1643.

This notion of religious and national covenanting was so deeply embedded in the minds of some Scottish Presbyterians that by the nineteenth century it led to some bizarre comments. Reviewing the history of the Scottish Covenanters and, overlooking the original Middle Eastern location of the history of redemption, Alexander Smellie remarked that it was in Scotland that 'covenants have their native air and most congenial home.'[12] Similarly, Thomas M'Crie held that, 'our ancestors were naturally led, by similarity of circumstances, to imitate the covenants of ancient Israel, when king, priests, and people, swore mutual allegiance to the true God.'[13]

Bearing in mind that not all agreed that Scotland was a 'covenanted' nation, the seventeenth-century national covenanters nevertheless contributed significantly to the growing momentum to take the Good News to the Jewish people. Samuel Rutherford, for one, rejoiced that the day the Jewish people came to believe in Jesus would be the day of the visible unity of the covenant people, a thought that moved him to ecstasy: 'O day! O longed-for and lovely day-dawn! O sweet Jesus, let me see that sight which will be as life from the dead, Thee and Thy ancient people in mutual embraces.'[14] Richard Cameron, one of the militant second generation covenanters who took up arms against King Charles II, sealed his testimony with his blood on the battlefield of Ayr's Moss as an insurgent with a price on his head. Once, when risking his neck by preaching at an illegal outdoor service in Kirkcudbrightshire on 30th May, 1680, he linked the prosperity of the Church to the restoration of Israel as part of a trinity of prayers for the restoration of the Jews, the fall of Antichrist, and 'the hastening of the day when the Stuarts would be swept from the throne.' When drawing up a manual for the guidance of leaders of underground Presbyterian meetings, Walter Smith of St. Ninians, near Airth, in Stirlingshire, made a similar connection. Prayers, he instructed, ought to be made both for 'Scotland where they are members', and also for 'the old offcasten Israel' and its eventual 'ingraffing again by faith'.

James Walker, however, spoke not only for himself when he voiced serious reservations as to the scriptural validity of national covenanting. Although recognising covenanting's Jewish roots, he saw this as more problematic than helpful: 'The seventeenth century divines were greatly hampered by what I might call their Judaic theory of the world's conversion.' He further elucidated the point:

> What our fathers rather thought of was a sort of expansion of nationalism after the Jewish fashion, in which, when God has elect ones among a people to be gathered in, He takes the nation in external covenant with Himself.[15]

Alexander Keith, a member of the missionary deputation to Palestine and first convenor of the Free Church of Scotland's Jewish Committee, agreed with Walker when he argued in a Free Church of Scotland General Assembly that:

> God never made, and never will make, a National Covenant with any people but one – the children of Abraham; and the day that sees this Church recognising any other National Covenant than that, will see me for the last time a member of it.[16]

Keith's brief but trenchant speech drew a line under the matter: the Free Church of Scotland never has endorsed the idea of national covenanting.

Another influence that predisposed Scottish Christians to hold a kindly view of the Jewish people was the use of the metrical psalms in worship. From the Reformation until the last quarter of the nineteenth century, Scottish Presbyterians sang mainly psalms set to simple tunes, without the assistance of musical instruments. In 1564 the General Assembly of the Church of Scotland instructed that all ministers and others leading public worship should be supplied with copies of the recently published Psalm Book, containing metrical psalms, prayers for various occasions (the 1595 version included Anglican-style collects for each psalm), forms for the administration of the sacraments of baptism and communion, and a marriage service. From then on, the Psalms of David took hold of the popular imagination.

When the Westminster Assembly of 1644 commissioned a new metrical version of the Psalms, it instructed the translators that it was to be as close as possible to the Hebrew original. This, with minor revisions, became the Scottish Metrical Version of 1650, used for centuries by Presbyterian denominations, both for public and family worship. Often the only books possessed by poorer families were the Bible and a Psalter bound together as a single volume. James Hogg, the author of *Confessions of a Justified Sinner*, spoke for many when he remarked that as a child he did not have access to any book save the Bible. 'I was', he said, 'greatly taken with our version of the Psalms of David, learned the most of them by heart, and have great partiality for them unto this day.'[17] This deep affection for the Psalms is seen in other Scottish works of literature such as John Brown's 'Jeems the Doorkeeper' in *Rab and his Friends* and, famously, in Robert Burns' poem, 'The Cotter's Saturday Night.' Singing the metrical psalms Sunday by Sunday fused the thoughts and sentiments of ancient Israel with Presbyterian spirituality.

Of a different spirit was the English Dissenter, Isaac Watts, who made what to Scottish Christians would have been an appalling boast, that he was the first to have 'led the Psalmist of Israel into the Church of Christ without anything of the Jew about him.'[18] In Scotland, the Jewish origin of the Psalter, far from being disowned, was celebrated. That great missionary to the Jews, John Duncan spoke for virtually the whole of confessional Presbyterianism when he said, 'It is a great gift to the Church, that Psalter of Israel. I never tire of the magnificent ancient poetry of the Jews. It is a grand thing that God appointed such ... to be sung in the Christian churches in all time to come.'[19]

As well as being the Scottish Church's hymnbook, the Psalter was also its devotional handbook, its words, expressing its deepest religious thoughts and sentiments, were reiterated in its prayers and preaching. Also, when couched in the congenial language of the Authorised Version of the Bible, its allusions and idioms contributed to everyday speech wherever English was used. It is to the Hebrew Bible that we owe such colourful expressions as 'the writing on the wall', 'lick the dust', 'out of the mouth of babes and sucklings', 'the apple of the eye', 'the strife of tongues', 'a drop in the bucket', and many others.

In Scotland, both in the Highlands and Lowlands, in English and in Gaelic, Presbyterian Christians found profit, pleasure and comfort in the words of the Hebrew psalmists and felt well able to refute the specious allegation that the Psalms lacked any distinctive 'Christian' content, even though, it had to be admitted, such Christian content was by way of allusion and inference rather than explicit statement. Nevertheless, when read or sung in a New Testament frame of reference the Psalms spoke eloquently of the Saviour and His redeeming work. It was, therefore, seen as an indescribable tragedy that those who had enriched the Church with its definitive manual of praise were themselves unaware of its Messianic fulfilment in the person and ministry of Jesus of Nazareth.

Then there was the moral law. Both Alexander Moody Stuart and Robert Murray M'Cheyne considered the Scottish commitment to the moral law, especially the fourth commandment with its Sabbath institution, to be another important area of common ground with Jews. The strict observation of the first day of the week as the Christian Sabbath was by no means a clerical imposition on an unwilling people, as it is often represented, but something which from time immemorial had been an integral and cherished part of Scottish life. Indeed, the institution of a Christian Sabbath antedates the clarification and codification of its theology by the Scottish Reformers, having been inherited from the very earliest days of the Church in Scotland.

The Irish Presbyterian historian W. D. Killen suggests that the Celtic Church observed both the seventh-day Sabbath and the Lord's Day. Killen argues that around the end of the sixth century a rigorous ecclesiastical canon relative to Lord's Day observance, remarkably similar in tone to Jewish rabbinic Sabbath legislation, prohibited all labour:

even sweeping or cleaning the house: no combing: no shaving: no clipping of hair and beard: no washing the face or hands: no cutting: no sewing: no churning: no riding on horseback: no fishing: no sailing or rowing: no journeying of travellers: but wherever a man happened to be on Saturday night there he was to remain till Monday morning.[20]

Although the Sabbath was entrenched in the legislation of the Church of Scotland, and, in 1843, by the General Assembly of the Free Church of Scotland, as well as by Acts of the Scottish Parliament, it was essentially a popular institution. Like the Jewish people, Scots held that the faithful keeping of the Sabbath bore a close relationship to the wellbeing of society not only because it was a day for communal worship, but because it was also a day for strengthening family ties. One writer, James Gilfinnan, put it like this: 'On that day the members of a household who are in many cases necessarily separated on other days, can, and do meet together … and family ties are strengthened, hallowed and blessed by family prayer.'[21]

By the nineteenth century new lifestyles and technology challenged the sanctity as well as the tranquillity of the Sabbath Day. The running of Sunday trains, along with the opening of public reading rooms and public houses, was vigorously resisted by evangelical Christians. In his address, 'I Love the Lord's Day', Robert Murray M'Cheyne argued that it was Sabbath desecration that had led God to cast away Israel and that Sabbath-breakers would bring down the same curse on Scotland, because the Sabbath continued as a covenant sign between God and his 'Scottish Israel'.[22]

Despite a growing number of dissidents, the majority of nineteenth century Scots considered the Fourth Commandment to be binding, even if, for some, its observance erred on the side of joyless legalism. Most agreed with John Duncan that the Sabbath was an undeniable benefit for which Christians were obliged to the Jews, moreover one that led them to respect the spirit of the Hebrew legislation. For those who reverenced Israel's laws it was but a short step to desiring Israel's salvation.

And so it was, that by the middle of the nineteenth century, a number of factors combined to impress upon Scottish Christians a sense of common spiritual identity with the Jewish people and their obligation to them. Through this affinity with Israel, reinforced by Bible reading, the development of its distinctive theology, ecclesiastical traditions, and form of worship, the Church of Scotland entered into what may be called its 'adoptive past'. This paved the way to share with Jewish people, as an expression of heartfelt gratitude, the blessings of the salvation it had received through them from God in Jesus the Messiah.

But such a sense of kinship and its consequent obligations ought not to be thought of as unique to Scots, as John Duncan astutely observed:

> We must all become Jews. That nation retains its hold of the world. There is an Israelite naturalisation for us all. Salvation is of the Jews; and metaphorically we must all become Jews – i.e. we must enter into the Jewish heritage, and reverence the channel in which all our great blessings have come down to us.[23]

By 1838, the time had come for the Church of Scotland to look beyond a sense of kinship and gratitude, or even heartfelt prayer for the conversion of Israel: active steps had to be taken to achieve the goal. In his introduction to a series of lectures held in Edinburgh during the winter of 1838/39, Dr Alexander Black incisively summed up the priority:

> The obligations under which we are to the Jews are such as we can never sufficiently repay. We are indebted to them, as the chosen people of God, for all the spiritual privileges that we enjoy .... Such being our debt of obligation, it is but equitable that we should consider what we can do for the descendants of those to whose ancestors we owe so much; and the greatest boon that we have the means of conferring upon them, is our duty to take every measure that can give promise of success to impart to them the blessings of the gospel, that through our mercy, they also may obtain mercy.[24]

John G. Lorimer concurred that the moral obligation of thankfulness must result in mission:

> Does not a grateful soul weary and long for and rejoice in opportunities of testifying its obligations, and is the soul of the Christian Church to be the only exception to the rule, and *that* when remembering the services of God's ancient people?'[25]

In 1839 the General Assembly of the Church of Scotland, therefore, engaged in its first official venture into Jewish evangelism by publishing and distributing a tract: *To the Children of Israel in all the Lands of their Dispersion*. This remarkable document was skilfully compiled by a Glasgow elder called Robert Wodrow. At its heart, he averred, lay a question with an inescapable answer: 'How can we but seek the good of that people, by whose means, at first, our fathers turned from dumb idols to serve the living and true God, and from whom we have received those oracles of truth which everywhere testify of his Anointed?'[26] Conscious of its responsibility to Israel, the Church of Scotland found itself impelled, by the necessity of logic, the force of Scripture, popular sentiment, and much more the dynamic of the Holy Spirit, to engage in missionary endeavour among the Jewish people.

≈ 2 ≈

Claudius Buchanan: the True Pioneer
Scotland, England, India, 1766–1815

IT is generally true that prayer and the rise of evangelical missions are inextricably linked. It was especially true in the case of the Scottish mission to the Jews. During the spiritually confused and uncertain days of the early sixteenth century, even before the first glimmerings of the dawn of the Scottish Reformation radiated from the glow of the martyr fires of Patrick Hamilton and George Wishart, God placed in the hearts of many a desire for better things. This longing found expression in prayer. Who, apart from God, understands how much the Reformation in Scotland may be attributed to the prayers of earnest but otherwise powerless Christians? As John Duncan would later remind the 'fathers and brethren' of the General Assembly of the Free Church of Scotland, the outcome of their deliberations owed far more than they knew to the prayers of some humble Christian woman on the remote island of St Kilda.

In time Scottish Christians came to see that both they and their salvation had been in the faithful prayers of ancient Israel. This idea was typically expressed by two of Scotland's most influential seventeenth-century Christians, Samuel Rutherford and Thomas Boston. Rutherford, when preaching on Song of Solomon 8:8, took the simile of the 'little sister' to refer to the predominantly gentile Church, whereas the 'elder sister' was the Old Testament Jewish community of faith, who, when 'at their Father's elbow', longed for 'the incoming of their little sister, the kirk of the Gentiles.' Because the elder had once prayed for the younger, Rutherford argued, the younger was now duty bound to pray for the elder.[1]

On 11th March, 1716, Boston preached to his people at Ettrick on 'Encouragement to Pray for the Conversion of the Jews', arguing from Zechariah 12:12 that failure on the part of Christians to remember the Jews in prayer, now that they were locked into the idea that Jesus of Nazareth was not the Jewish Messiah, would be as ungrateful as Pharaoh's butler who neglected Joseph in prison:

> All the means of grace, and acceptance through Jesus Christ, that we have now, we had originally from them. They were our masters in the knowledge of God, and first put the book, even the book of God into our hands ... It was their Moses, their prophets, their apostles, (all of them Jews) that wrote in this book, by which eternal life is brought to us. Nay, it is their countryman Jesus, who is the ground of all our hope ... It was the light that came out from among them, that enlightened our dark part of the world. And now that our teachers are blinded, will we not put up a petition for them, Lord that they may recover their sight.[2]

In the next generation, Lachlan Mackenzie, the renowned minister and 'Happy Man' of Lochcarron, encouraged his congregation to remember that the Jewish people had prayed for four thousand years for the coming of the Messiah, and this, he argued, put into perspective the Church's tardiness in repaying its debt. 'We have not been praying half that time for the conversion of the Jews', he said.[3]

This call to prayer transcended church, family, and private worship. It galvanised a movement that established praying societies, informal gatherings of Christians for fellowship and prayer that had their origin in the small groups whose formation John Knox had encouraged at the Reformation, and later, during the 'Killing Times' of the 1680s, went underground in support of Presbyterians harassed and persecuted by the Stuart regime.

At such a time it might seem perfectly justifiable for these groups to turn inwards to focus on their own troubles, but in fact we find that at such gatherings prayers were commonly offered for the redemption of the Jewish people and these petitions were not left to the subjective whims of the participants. Walter Smith's *Rules and Directions* for praying societies, referred to in the previous chapter, required intercession to be made that 'the old offcasten Israel' might experience its 'ingraffing again by faith'.[4] Although seeing no obvious answer in their own day, these Christians nevertheless confidently awaited God's time of fulfilment, believing that intercession retains its force and immediacy because it reaches beyond time and is perpetually before the eternal God. Eventually, faith was amply rewarded in the sending forth of Scotland's first missionary to the Jews. But before that could happen, many pieces of the puzzle of Providence had first to be put in place, including international revival, a cross-Atlantic coordinated prayer movement, and the eccentric search for the Ten Lost Tribes of Israel.

In September 1741, George Whitefield's evangelistic itinerary brought him to the city of Glasgow where he was heard appreciatively by many, including the Rev. William M'Culloch, the minister of Cambuslang, a parish five miles to the southeast of the city. M'Culloch was deeply stirred both by Whitefield's preaching and his reports of the revival in New England. Reenergised in his own faith, and becoming acutely aware that many of his parishioners had little more than a nominal faith, M'Culloch determined to preach to his people about their need of new birth and conversion. This aroused a deep interest in the parish, giving rise to a fresh impetus to corporate prayer. Some of the local praying societies, which had almost ceased to function after the overthrow of the Stuarts, the coronation of William III, the Restoration Settlement, and the consequent reestablishment of a Presbyterian Church of Scotland, were now given a fresh lease of life. Desiring that God do even greater things among His people, M'Culloch persuaded Whitefield to come to Cambuslang at the first available opportunity. Whitefield, who had heard of the stirrings taking place, enthusiastically accepted M'Culloch's invitation to assist at the communion services of the second week in July 1742. His ministry resulted in transformed lives, renewed commitment to Christ, and many conversions.[5]

At a time when Scottish churches usually had only one Communion a year, two at most, M'Culloch's apparently unconventional response was to propose holding another the following month. Apparently eccentric, the proposal was justified by M'Culloch's knowledge of history. He remembered that a number of Scottish revivals, most notably that at Kirk of Shotts in 1630, had been experienced during the celebration of the Lord's Supper. At Shotts, no less than five hundred people had attributed their conversion to a sermon preached by John Livingstone at the Monday Thanksgiving service. At Cambuslang in 1742 history was to repeat itself.

The crowds attending the second Communion exceeded the large gatherings of the previous month, leading M'Culloch to write to the *Glasgow Weekly History* that it was his belief that no one had seen the like at any Scottish communion held since 1689, the year of the reestablishment of Presbyterianism in Scotland. Just precisely how many attended the services he could not be sure, but he thought it credible that an upper estimate may have been forty or fifty thousand, adding that no-one thought there had been less than thirty thousand. He thought perhaps as many as three thousand communicants had partaken of bread and wine on the Sunday and as many as four hundred attributed their conversion to the ministry of that weekend. Behind the raw statistics was an unseen, irresistible spiritual impetus leading to personal godliness and an increased concern for the expansion of the Kingdom of God, both within Scotland and further afield.

To Jonathan Edwards, the New England Congregationalist, such awakenings as that at Cambuslang, as well as those in North America, of which he had first-hand knowledge, were all part of a spiritual continuum, dating back to Pentecost, whereby, from time to time, God renews and reinvigorates the life of the Church. Without in any way denigrating regular preaching and pastoral work, Edwards was led by his reflection on, and personal experience of revivals to believe that the cause of God gained momentum less by the ordinary work of the ministry and more by such extraordinary works of the Holy Spirit as had been witnessed at Cambuslang.

Publishing in 1774 his *A History of the Work of Redemption*, Edwards predicted that the revivals of the mid-eighteenth century were precursors of greater blessings to come throughout the world. His theory was that spiritual renewal would result in a growing commitment to international missions.[6] This was undoubtedly so in the case of Cambuslang, where some people found freedom in prayer only when they ceased to be preoccupied with their own spiritual concerns and prayed instead for the salvation of the wider world.[7]

When, around 1743, the Great Awakening began to lose momentum, Edwards attributed this to a lack of faithfulness in prayer, and was, therefore, inclined to believe that it was a temporary and remediable setback. In order to regain the earlier impetus, he wrote to M'Culloch to propose launching what he termed a Concert for Prayer. This was the reintroduction, on an international basis, of an old Scottish custom whereby Christians covenanted to pray for a common cause. To which William M'Culloch and his colleagues, John McLaurin of Glasgow and James Robe of Kilsyth agreed, adding the distinctive difference that rather than hold a single day of fasting and intercession there should be a regular, recurring day of prayer. The connection between the Concert for Prayer and William Carey's pioneering missionary initiative fifty years later has become a key element in the narrative of modern Christian missions, but what is too often neglected is its link with missions to the Jewish people.

Many Christians in Scotland shared Edwards' conviction, expressed in his *History of the Work of Redemption*, that the spiritual restoration of Israel was crucial to the worldwide expansion of the Christian Church:

> Nothing is more certainly foretold than this national conversion of the Jews ... When they shall be called, that ancient people, who alone were God's people for so long a time, shall be his people again, never to be rejected more. They shall be gathered into one fold together with the Gentiles; and so also shall the remains of the ten tribes, wherever they be ... Though we do not know the time in which this conversion of Israel will come to pass; yet thus much we may determine from Scripture, that it will be before the glory of the Gentile part of the church shall be fully accomplished; because it is said, that their coming in shall be life from the dead to the Gentiles.[8]

If Edward's clear thought and busy pen provided a biblical and theological rationale for Jewish missions, it was his deeply moving account of David Brainerd that set before the Church an inspirational role model of self-sacrificial missionary service. Thought of primarily as a missionary to Native Americans, Brainerd was in fact involved in what his employers considered a mission to Israel.

Strange as it may seem, when viewed from today's perspective, seventeenth and eighteenth-century missions to American Indians had their roots in a desire for the conversion of the so-called Ten Lost Tribes of Israel. The Bible recounts how the Northern Kingdom of Israel lost its independence around 722 B.C. when the Assyrian monarch Tiglath-pileser III stormed Samaria, broke Israel's power and imposed upon them his customary political expedient of deportation and resettlement in other parts of the empire. Partly on the basis of biblical history and partly as a result of a speculative interpretation of unfulfilled prophecies, such as Ezekiel 37:16-17, there grew up a belief that although they appeared to have vanished from the face of the earth the ten tribes had not lost their identity. Edwards shared this perspective, expressing it in his comment: 'the remains of the ten tribes, wherever they be [shall be gathered into one fold together with the Gentiles].' The task of locating these tribes and winning them for the Messiah's kingdom thus became an important aspect of the Church's mandate, but the question of where to start looking posed a great challenge. In the westward expansion of European colonialism and its contact with other peoples, one group, the Native Americans, especially began to intrigue the Christian mind. There was a growing feeling that they just might be descended from ancient Israel. This notion probably had its origin in *The Hope of Israel*, published in 1650 by an Amsterdam rabbi, Menasseh Ben Israel, who had successfully championed the resettlement of the Jews in England. The same year, in a tract called *Jews in America* by Thomas Thorowgood, minister of Massingham in Norfolk and a member of the Westminster Assembly, left his readers in no doubt of what he thought by subtitling his tract, 'Probabilities that the Americans are Jews.' This conjecture was held, with various modifications, by orthodox Calvinists including the pioneer missionary John Eliot, whom we know had read *The Hope of Israel*. Working among the Algonquin people, Eliot thought that he detected in their religion and culture vestiges of Jewish identity, leading him to surmise that the conversion of the Algonquin would presage the conversion of both branches of the descendants of Abraham, the ten tribes of Israel as well as the two of Judah and Benjamin.

Eliot's translation of the Bible in the Algonquin language was published in 1663, in Cambridge, New England, thus giving a curious twist to the apostolic injunction of Romans 1:16, 'to the Jew first.' The first Bible printed in America was for those who were believed, by the translator himself and by his backers, to be the descendants of the very people who had first given God's Word to the world. The first English Bible would not be published in America for another one hundred and twenty years.

Three years after the publication of the Algonquin Bible, during the so-called Apocalyptic Year of 1666, further events fed speculation concerning the lost tribes. Even before it began, the year was considered portentous because of the mystical significance attached to the numerals 666, the 'number of the beast' of Revelation 14:18. Many expected that during that year events would transpire heralding the final battle between Antichrist and the cause of Christ.

In Protestant Britain, few were surprised by rumours that in January the Papal throne had been set above the altar at St Peter's in the Vatican, or that in June the Dutch had defeated the English fleet, or that in July the city of Piteå in Sweden had been razed to the ground by fire. And it was perfectly in line with apocalyptic speculation when in July and August those earlier losses suffered by the English fleet had been reversed with significant victories over the Dutch, and that in September the Great Fire of London destroyed an estimated fourteen thousand buildings including old St. Paul's Cathedral, or that during the same month the false Messiah, Sabbatai Zevi, to whom thousands of Jews had flocked pledging their allegiance, apostatised to Islam.

In such a highly febrile atmosphere and among an increasingly credulous people, gossip started to circulate that on 23rd October an unusual ship had been driven by bad weather to seek shelter at Aberdeen in Scotland. It was alleged that the only food carried on board was rice and honey. In days when mystical or allegorical significance was attached to various colours, it was considered significant that the sailors on board wore blue clothing, their ship's ropes were of white silk and the sails of white satin, on which was emblazoned an inscription in strange red characters, deciphered by the cognoscenti to mean, 'THESE ARE OF THE TEN TRIBES

OF ISRAEL.' The mystery only deepened when no one could discover from whence the ship had come.

Furthermore, it was said that when a professor of languages from one of the Aberdeen universities visited the crew he discovered that they were bound for Amsterdam and spoke only 'broken Hebrew.' Their purpose, he concluded, was to make contact 'with their brethren there,' leading to the conclusion that they had been sent to invite fellow Jews to some great 'Sanhedrin' at an undisclosed location. In due course the ship left Aberdeen and nothing more was heard of it.

At the time, there were few attempts to follow up the connection between the ten tribes and the Native Americans, but about eighty years later, in 1742, a young man from Haddam, Connecticut, called David Brainerd, commenced evangelistic work among them. His employer was the Society in Scotland for Propagating Christian Knowledge, which had been established in 1709. Its origins lay in the praying societies, but by 1730 it had branched out into missionary work among the indigenous people of America, employing both David Brainerd and his brother John. Jonathan Edwards, Brainerd's biographer, also an erstwhile missionary to the Indians, was more cautious than the SSPCK with identifying Native American, with the tribes of Israel, vaguely referring, as we have noted, to 'the remains of the ten tribes, wherever they be.'[9]

The link between the attempted evangelisation of the lost tribes of Israel, John Eliot, David Brainerd, Jonathan Edwards, George Whitefield, the Great Awakening, the Cambuslang revival, and the Concert for Prayer and modern missions to the Jews, was the life and work of Claudius Buchanan.[10] Buchanan was born in 1766 at Cambuslang and baptised by the Rev. William M'Culloch, by then seventy-five years old but still the minister of Cambuslang. Buchanan's maternal grandfather was Claudius Somers, a convert of the 1742 revival who by the time of his grandson's birth was one of M'Culloch's elders at Cambuslang parish kirk and congregational treasurer. If, on the day he baptised the infant Claudius, M'Culloch could have seen into the future he would have felt his prayers amply answered by the contribution this child would make to building God's kingdom in India among the Bene

Israel of Mumbai and the Jews of Cochin, as well as contributing to wider missions to the Jews, through his translation of the New Testament into Hebrew.

Buchanan's parents – his father was a school master – entertained the hope that their son would enter the ministry of the Church of Scotland, but he had other ideas. After studies at Glasgow University, he planned to explore the Continent but his plans misfired and he did not get beyond London. Whilst there he was greatly influenced by reading Phillip Doddridge's autobiographical *Rise and Progress of Religion in the Soul* and by personal acquaintance with John Newton, then rector of St Mary Woolnoth in the City of London, who added the twenty-five-year-old Buchanan to a coterie of young men he advised and mentored. Their relationship was as close as that of a father and son, with Buchanan signing his letters to the older minister as 'Your affectionate son.'[11] Though penniless, Buchanan's ability was soon recognised and he was enabled to complete his education at Queens College, Cambridge, owing to the generous patronage of the Christian philanthropist, Henry Thornton.

Thornton's father, John, had supported both Newton and William Cowper, enabling them to live in considerable comfort in Olney, Buckinghamshire, and when Newton felt the need of a change of parish, it was Thornton who presented him with the living of St. Mary Woolnoth. Cowper celebrated their benefactor's largesse in his anti-slavery poem *Charity*:

> These have an ear for *his* paternal call,
> Who makes some rich for the supply of all;
> God gifts with pleasure in his praise employ;
> And THORNTON is familiar with the joy.

Henry Thornton was noted for the thoroughness with which he brought his astute Christian mind to bear on matters of economics, banking, and politics. His probity was legendary: he once refused to enter Parliament because the process was corrupted by the necessity of buying votes. As cousin and close friend to William Wilberforce, he had provided the prudence, wisdom, and attention to detail that transformed Wilberforce's fire and vision into practical policy. Some thought he had a cold, hard, and off-putting manner, but Wilberforce testified that underneath the ice was a warm and sympathetic Christian heart.[12]

Thornton's business acumen brought him great wealth, most of which he gave away, at one period living on a seventh of his income and committing all the rest to Christian causes. At his home in Battersea Rise he set up the 'chummery,' a group of friends who became the nucleus of the Clapham Sect, the celebrated evangelical network largely made up of Tories and Anglicans who were at the forefront of social reform in England. Thornton was an ideal patron: interested but not overbearing, his friendship provided the young Buchanan with an introduction into the heart of the gospel party within the Church of England. Here he made many alliances and friendships which would advance God's Kingdom at home and overseas.

At Cambridge, Buchanan became a protégé of Charles Simeon, one of a select group privileged to hear their mentor reading his *Natural and Revealed Religion* in his rooms in King's College, as well as belonging to the famous Sermon Class. It was impossible to belong to Simeon's inner circle and not be exposed to what he himself passionately believed to be 'the most important object in the world,' namely, missions to the Jewish people.

Commitment to this cause was the keenest interest of Simeon's life and, inevitably, he acted upon it by helping to found, in 1809, the London Society for Promoting Christianity among the Jews. His incisive grasp of the issues is well illustrated by an incident that took place at a meeting of the LSPCJ. Hearing Simeon refer to the missionary priority of the evangelisation of the Jewish people put Edward Bickersteth, the assistant secretary of the Church Missionary Society and friend of Thomas Chalmers, in a combative mood. When Simeon sat down, Bickersteth scribbled a brief note suggesting that he had his priorities back to front. Provocatively, the note asked, 'Eight millions of Jews and eight hundred million heathens – which is more important?' Simeon, alluding to Romans 11:15, turned the note over and jotted a succinct rejoinder: 'If the conversion of the eight is life from the dead to the eight hundred, what then?'

Bickersteth was so convinced of the truth of Simeon's comment that he became a fervent supporter of Jewish missions, addressing all eighteen anniversary meetings of the LSPCJ and publishing for The Christian Library an abridged edition of Hugh Pearson's biography of Buchanan. His enthusiasm he passed to his son, Edward Henry (1825–1906), Bishop of Truro, a noted hymn writer and poet.

In 1794, Newton suggested that Buchanan might usefully serve God in India and so, in the summer of 1795, despite a quite brilliant academic career, Buchanan modestly left Cambridge without choosing formally to graduate either in Mathematics or Divinity, feeling this was the most appropriate manner in which to express his indebtedness to Thornton, whom, he thought, should by rights have shared with him the honours. That being impossible, Buchanan quietly turned his back on the plaudits of academia and set his face towards his future work for God.

Plans were laid for his ordination into the Church of England, which was carried out on 20th September by Beilby Porteus, Bishop of London and chaplain to King George III. Unusual among such highly placed ecclesiastics, Porteus was sympathetic towards Evangelicals, an enthusiastic social reformer, and a supporter of Christian missions. Rev. J. W. Cunningham, preaching to members of the LSPCJ in 1815, said he remembered 'the late venerable Bishop Porteus, not long before his death … use his expiring strength to stimulate his countrymen to become apostles to the land of Israel'.

After a brief period as Newton's curate at St. Mary Woolnoth, Buchanan was appointed the first chaplain of the British East India Company. The company had, hitherto, determined to avoid employing chaplains or missionaries to the Indians within its sphere of activity, but, through the persuasion of Charles Grant – a native of Glenurquhart in Highland Scotland, and a member of the company's board of trade – working with Wilberforce and Simeon, this policy was reversed and Buchanan was appointed the first of the company's five chaplains. Sailing in September 1796, Buchanan arrived in Calcutta on 10th March the following year. Here, through his linguistic interests, he became a friend of William Carey, who also shared his belief in the restoration of the Jews.[13]

Henry Martyn, junior to Buchanan by some fifteen years, became in 1803 Simeon's curate, also developing a keen interest in the Jewish people. Three years later he followed Buchanan to

India as an East India Company chaplain and in 1811 commenced travelling through Persia, where he met Sephardic Jews from Basra, Isfahan, and Shiraz who, like the 'Jewish Mullah' Abdulghanee, had embraced popular Islam. This challenged Martyn, and he sought to devote his failing strength to attempt to win them to Christ. In 1812, on his thirty-first birthday, the last before his death, Martyn met two of Abdulghanee's acquaintances who quizzed him regarding their spiritual welfare 'in another world.' Much moved by this, he reflected on their anxiety and spiritual insecurity, recording in his journal his sorrow for their plight:

> Feelings of pity for God's ancient people, and the awful importance of eternal things impressed on my mind by the seriousness of their enquiries as to what would become of them, relieved me from the pressure of my comparatively insignificant distresses. I, a poor Gentile, blest, honoured, and loved; secured for ever by the everlasting covenant, whilst the children of the Kingdom are still in outward darkness! Well does it become me to be thankful.[14]

Six years earlier, as Martyn had sailed up the Hoogly river to commence his work in India and Central Asia, Buchanan was making his way down river on his first journey to the west coast to visit the ancient communities of Cochin Jews of Malabar and the fabled Bene Israel of Mumbai. Descended from the Cochin Jews, the Bene Israel maintain to this day the tradition that their ancestors either left Galilee subsequent to the persecutions of Antiochus Epiphanes in the years 175–163 B.C., or following the destruction of Jerusalem in A.D. 70. According to Bene Israel tradition, a group of seven men and seven women survived shipwreck on the Indian coast to establish the community.

En route to Cochin, Buchanan lingered, visiting the ancient Mar Thoma Syrian churches, reputedly founded by the Apostle Thomas himself, and meeting with the staff of various mission stations. But, much as he enjoyed all this, it troubled his conscience that he had forgotten 'the poor Jews.' Arriving in Cochin in December 1806, he formally introduced himself to Colonel Colin Macaulay, the British Resident at Travancore and an acquaintance of Henry Thornton. In Macaulay, Buchanan found not only a warm-hearted and likeminded Christian, but also a most useful ally. Macaulay was a son of the Rev. John Macaulay, the Church of Scotland minister of Inveraray, a brother of Zachary Macaulay, the abolitionist and governor of Sierra Leone, the colony founded in West Africa as a home for emancipated enslaved Africans.

Colonel Macaulay was keenly interested in the work of Bible translation and a supporter of the recently established British and Foreign Bible Society. Fully appreciating Buchanan's literary and spiritual interest in the Jewish community, he brought to him a copy of certain chapters of the Hebrew Scriptures and used his good offices to obtain other important Hebrew manuscripts. Following conversations with the Cochin Jewish leaders, Buchanan, buoyed by a sense of real accomplishment, re-embarked on his ship to return to Calcutta, from where he continued correspondence with Macaulay, discussing the technicalities of Hebrew texts and sharing anecdotes of the colonel's conversations with a Jewish friend called Levi. Not only did Buchanan arrive back with a marvellous collection of Hebrew manuscripts, which Carey is said to have 'beheld with veneration,' but he was also accompanied by two Cochin Jews, one was a Hebrew *munshi*, or secretary, the other, Judah Misrahi, a highly proficient translator.

Buchanan made a final visit to Cochin in December 1807 while sailing to England, and discovered the community was so agitated by questions of the interpretation of biblical prophecy that they had called a meeting to discuss the matter in detail. Buchanan entered into the debates with enthusiasm, stating in a letter:

> The Jews at Cochin are very unsettled in relation to the prophecies. They wonder at the attention paid by the English to these subjects for the first time. You will read in the Bombay Courier an account of a ceremony in the synagogue at Cochin, which took place at Christmas last, a few days before I arrived. Some Jews interpret the prophecies aright, and some in another way; but all agree that a great era is at hand.[15]

And again:

> I am about to call another Sanhedrin on the subject, before I go. It is a strange event. I am happy I have visited this place a second time. May God direct all these things to his own glory and the good of men! ... Tell H. that the poor Jews, blind, lame, and halt, are come this

morning, exclaiming as usual, 'Jehuda Ani' [poor or afflicted Jews]. I wish I could impart a better gift than silver or gold.[16]

On 18th August 1808 Buchanan arrived in London to learn that his friend and mentor John Newton had died, being buried on 27th December the previous year, the very day he had arrived in Cochin. There then followed a visit to Scotland to see his elderly mother where he discovered with delight that the rigours of old age – she was seventy-two years old – had diminished neither her intellectual or spiritual faculties one whit. Buchanan's wife, too, was astonished and amused by her mother-in law's excellent recall of the Bible 'which she utters in hard words [Scots dialect], without [adopting] at all the English language'.

Like his parents, Buchanan had been brought up speaking English with the Scots dialect but, whilst preparing for the Anglican ministry at Cambridge, he seemed to have suffered a minor crisis of identity which led him to reject his native tongue and take elocution lessons to assist him to adopt a conventional English mode of speech. It is likely that Charles Simeon, who had very decided views on elocution, had a hand in this cultural transformation, but whatever the stimulus of change, the fact that Buchanan was willing to alter his speech in so radical a fashion reflects an apostolic willingness to be 'all things to all people, that by all means I might save some.'

Returning from Scotland, Buchanan visited Cambridge in April 1809, where he deposited in the university library his collection of manuscripts, including the 'Buchanan Bible', a very ancient and beautifully illuminated version of the Old Testament, with the Apocrypha and the New Testament with six books of Clement all handwritten in Syriac. There too was a one hundred and fifty-year old Hebrew New Testament, translated by a rabbi from Travancore who had, in the course of his work, become a Christian. Buchanan told the rabbi's story at the first annual public dinner of the LSPCJ, noting that it was this man's close attention to Scripture which had subdued his unbelief and opened his mind and heart to Jesus the Messiah. Buchanan had this New Testament manuscript transcribed at his own expense, with the intention that it should form the basis of a translation of the New Testament into Hebrew.

This work he hoped would expedite the LSPCJ's attempts to evangelise the people from whom the world had received God's Word. We may, therefore, readily understand his strongly expressed regret that the society had allowed a whole year to pass without any significant progress in this work. As reported in the *Edinburgh Christian Instructor*, Buchanan urged the swift implementation of the project, because, he said, 'How can you find fault with a Jew for not believing the New Testament if he has never seen it?' Adding:

> How strange it appears that, during a period of eighteen hundred years, the Christians should never have given the Jews the New Testament in their own language! By a kind of infatuation they have reprobated the unbelief of the Jews, and have never, at the same time, told them what they ought to believe.[17]

In fact, at the time of Buchanan's remonstrance there were three Hebrew translations of the New Testament in existence: Hutter's, Robinson's, and Cradick's. However, all three were either inadequate, unobtainable, or incomplete. His reproof was taken to heart and the work entrusted to a Jewish scholar, Judah d'Allemand, who, with a gentile colleague, completed Matthew's Gospel in 1814, with the remaining books appearing in rapid succession to great critical acclaim.

On 6th December 1814, Buchanan was surprised to be visited at his home in Broxbourne, Hertfordshire, by two men, a Mr S. and a Mr B. sent by the LSPCJ to invite him to become the society's secretary. He was, however, unable to accede to their wishes, not because of any lack of commitment to the cause – far from it – but because he held radical objections to the way in which the society had been established. The delegation returned on 24th December. This time Mr B. had been replaced by the persuasive Lewis Way, one of the founders of the LSPCJ, but Buchanan could not be prevailed upon.

Indeed, he used the occasion to further elucidate arguments against the LSPCJ's constitution. First, he regretted what he believed to have been the undue haste with which the society had been formed, without adequate consultation with 'good and eminent ministers' in the country. Secondly, he thought the name of the society was all wrong: it ought not to have used the words 'for the conversion of the Jews', as these were deeply offensive to Jews and would prejudice their efforts. Lastly, he believed the society ought not be a joint venture with nonconformists, but exclusively Anglican, a branch of the Church Missionary Society whose goal of world mission was the same.[18]

Although he refused to take up office in the society, Buchanan was supportive of it as well as being greatly influential in forming its policy. His opinion regarding the name was accepted. His view that the society would best achieve its aims as a voluntary society within the Anglican communion prevailed, being justified by the withdrawal of the Scottish Presbyterian and English Nonconformist members after strong disagreement on the validity of baptisms conducted by non-episcopally ordained ministers. Buchanan was right to conclude that other irreconcilable ecclesiastical differences would create tensions, exhausting the strength and trying the patience of all the members. This bitter division, however, eventually became God's multiplication with the formation in 1842 of the British Society for the Propagation for the Gospel among the Jews, thus putting into the field two highly effective agencies, though unable to work harmoniously in the same cause.

Buchanan, now in the last months of his life, still had his thoughts and prayers focused on India. One day, when the plight of two Cochin Jews stranded in London was brought to his attention, he promptly sought advice from his old friend Colin Macaulay, who did not fail him, offering a satisfactory solution to the dilemma. Just three weeks later, on 9th February 1815, Buchanan died, aged forty-nine years, his mortal remains being laid to rest in the cemetery at Ouseburn, between Ripon and York.

Fifteen years later the Jewish adventurer and Christian missionary Joseph Wolff visited the Bene Israel at Pune, and met John Wilson whose work among the Bene Israel of Mumbai owed much to the work of Buchanan. It greatly amused Wolff to observe gentiles from Scotland as God's instruments for teaching Indian Jews their native language of Hebrew and through it introducing them to their Messiah and Redeemer.[19]

3

From Voluntary Societies to Church Mission

Scotland, 1810–1838

MODELLED on contemporary political journals and influenced by William Hay's successful monthly review, the *Christian Observer*, Andrew Mitchell Thomson founded *The Edinburgh Christian Instructor* in 1810 to communicate 'evangelical content in a cultured and intellectual style.' Thomson's forceful editorial policy made the paper the dominant nineteenth-century Scottish religious periodical and the voice of what was rapidly becoming the most dominant grouping within the Church of Scotland, the Evangelicals, thus placing Thomson beside Chalmers as the greatest influencers within the Church of Scotland during the first decades of the nineteenth century.[1]

Throughout its thirty-year life, *The Instructor* was deeply committed to supporting Jewish missions, in almost every issue carrying relevant articles, book reviews, and news reports of the work of various societies and individuals. Through his much-appreciated articles, combined with regular reports of the proceedings of the LSPCJ, Claudius Buchanan, although an Anglican, continued to influence Scottish missionary thinking. A parting of their ways, however, came in 1815 when Thomson took sides in the dispute that led to the reconstruction of the LSPCJ as an Anglican Church society. Thomson, no bland, unbiased reporter, but a ready controversialist, used *The Instructor* to support the Presbyterian members of LSPCJ against what he saw as the prejudices of the Anglican members who, like Buchanan, refused to accept the baptism of Jewish converts unless administered by a minister episcopally ordained.[2]

Such discord, it is worth noting, perplexed and embarrassed Jewish Christians, who saw it as an impediment needlessly put in the way of Jewish people, deterring them from believing the gospel. One such was 'A.D.S' whose comments were recorded by Ridley H. Herschell:

> I was impelled by duty and affection to confess the Lord Jesus, in every possible way before men. Whom was I to join? The Churchmen vehemently railed against the Dissenters, and the Dissenters railed against the Churchmen; I had neither curiosity nor inclination to enquire into that, which I satisfied myself, could be but a frivolous contention; and of a militant, or fighting church of Christ, save against spiritual foes, I had no conception. I recollected how these very dissensions once confirmed me as to the truth of the Jewish faith; I again reflected on the increased stumbling-blocks in the way of my brethren, caused by these dissensions. I determined to join no party …[3]

The furore led to a shift in the editorial focus of *The Instructor,* from supporting the LSPCJ it now drew its readers' attention to work by the Edinburgh Missionary Society amongst two ancient and highly interesting Jewish communities. The first was the small community at Astrakhan, near the Caspian Sea in southern Russia, served by the society's workers, John Dickson, John Mitchell, and William Glen. The second was the more numerous Kai-fung-fu Chinese Jews of Hunan province, who had been visited by Robert Morrison of the London Missionary Society.[4]

The strength of Thomson's support for Jewish missions can be ascertained by a random sample from the three volumes covering the two year period 1822–24, which contain reports from forty-three different Scottish auxiliaries and local societies, plus numerous articles on the qualifications of missionaries to the Jews, the importance of such missionary work, as well as an extensive correspondence defending missions to the Jews, but including an intriguing view from the 'other side', in *An Address from an Israelite to those who attempt to promote Christianity among the Jews.* There were book reviews too, including titles for children, and sermons, such as Chalmers' *The Utility of Missions,* preached in 1814 for the Society in Scotland for Propagating Christian Knowledge. By disseminating information, engaging in controversy and providing support for frontline missionaries, *The Edinburgh Christian Instructor* helped pave the way for a distinctive Scottish Church mission to the Jews.

Before Thomson's withdrawal of support, the most practical way for ordinary Scottish Christians to become directly involved in missions to the Jewish people was by supporting the work of the LSPCJ through its many auxiliary societies, some of which were known as Penny Societies, because the subscription was one penny each week. In 1811, *The Instructor* reported the formation of a large number of such auxiliaries not only in Scotland but also in England, Ireland, and Wales. Some of these, such as that of Leith, also supported other forms of missionary work, including that of the British and Foreign Bible Society.[5]

It was customary to hold an annual fund-raising meeting or a dinner at which speakers representing the parent society would give a talk on the progress of the work and at which local ministers might be invited to preach on a relevant subject. The Scottish auxiliaries were much valued for the strength of their financial support and as a result were invited to send a representative to London to attend the LSPCJ annual dinner and meeting held in June, 1811.

There were women's societies too, one rejoicing in the name of the 'Biggar Female Auxiliary Association for Promoting Christianity among the Jews', Biggar being a town in Lanarkshire. It too was a Penny Society. The proprieties of the day meant that the funds of women's societies had to be administered by a man 'accustomed to the transaction of business,' who attended all the meetings of the committee but did not have a vote, so preserving its integrity as a female society. The weekly, monthly, or quarterly contributions of the members of the Penny Societies were gathered up by collectors visiting the homes of supporters, and were forwarded each quarter to the LSPCJ's treasurer.

Some auxiliaries, such as that at Kilmarnock, had their origins in the praying societies of the seventeenth century or the gatherings held during the Concert for Prayer of the eighteenth. Others, such as Leith, were new and met not only to pray and raise money, but also to undertake direct missionary work amongst the Jewish people in their districts.

On 25th June 1818, an Edinburgh Society for Promoting Christianity among the Jews was founded in support of the work of the LSPCJ, although it was not an auxiliary of that society but an independent organisation sharing the same objectives. Nor, indeed, was it a Penny Society: its considerably larger subscriptions reflected the prosperity of the Scottish capital as each full member contributed half a guinea annually, with life membership at five guineas (approx. £400 in today's values). The constitution stated: 'That this society shall use its best endeavours to promote [mission to the Jews], either by aiding other societies, or by using direct efforts, as circumstances may suggest.' By 1820 it employed two continental missionaries, Mr Bozzart from Switzerland and Mr Besner of the University of Tubigen in Germany.[6]

Similar to the Edinburgh Society was the Aberdeen Association for Promoting Christianity among the Jews, whose first joint secretaries were Gavin Parker and John Duncan. John Duncan's report to the first annual meeting picked up a now familiar theme, lamenting the failure of Christians to evangelise the Jewish people, to whom they were deeply indebted for their spiritual blessings, and even more deploring the malign influence of Christian antisemitism:

> Christians, who are under the greatest obligations to them, have ... not only neglected the Jews, but, in general, loaded them with reproach and persecution. How, then, could they be expected to embrace the religion of those who treated them after this sort? ... how could God be expected to crown with a blessing the wishes which Christians professed to offer up for their conversion, while he beheld them entirely neglecting those means which he has appointed for that purpose? Had Christians properly exerted themselves in their behalf; had they been sufficiently fervent in prayer to God for them; and sufficiently diligent and liberal in giving them instruction, and in furnishing them with the New Testament, in their own venerated language, there is reason to believe that the Lord would have commanded his blessing on such exertions, and rendered them effectual for the conversion of many of the house of Israel. By us in this quarter of the world, their interests have been totally disregarded.[7]

Throughout the nineteenth century as the Jewish communities in Leith, Edinburgh and Glasgow grew, so local auxiliaries sought to reach out to them. Some, notably the Leith auxiliary, failed to make any headway at all, coming up against insuperable difficulties, but others fared better. The Edinburgh and Glasgow societies pooled resources to employ as a missionary a Jewish Christian, Mr Maurice Mark Cerf, who divided his energies between the two cities. Regrettably, little has come down to us of the details of Cerf's work, though he gets a passing mention when Bonar and M'Cheyne met one of his relatives in what was then Gleiwitz in Prussia and is now Gliwice in Poland.[8]

The spread of auxiliary societies throughout the rest of the country was patchy and there are no records of their establishment in the Highlands. Nevertheless, the following story, originally published in the *Christian Instructor*, demonstrates the remarkable generosity and goodwill of the Gaels. The Rev. Leigh Richmond, Rector of Turvey in Bedfordshire and author of the widely read devotional book, *The Dairyman's Daughter*, was itinerating on behalf of the LSPCJ and, arriving in Callander, Perthshire, spoke to a group of children about needy Jewish children in the East End of London. In a few minutes a collection had been taken up which amounted to thirty-five shillings, which Richmond considered 'illustrative of the Christian feeling of these Highland children', and which, he added, he would not fail to mention to his London friends on his return.[9]

It was the voluntary societies, rather than the churches, that at this time played the primary role in the progress of Scottish Jewish missions, combining a commitment to prayer, the dissemination of information, the raising of financial support and, where possible, direct missionary work among Jewish neighbours. And not only did such societies spearhead the work, it was elders rather than ministers who provided the leadership. One of the most influential was the Glasgow merchant Robert Wodrow, a grandson of the famous Scottish church historian of the same name and a descendant of William Guthrie, the author of the spiritual classic, *The Christian's Great Interest*. Writing in 1843, Robert Lorimer summarised Wodrow's biography as follows:

Robert Wodrow, son of Robert Wodrow, Esq., of Viewfield, was born in his grandfather's house, the manse of Tarbolton, on 3rd December 1793. Educated at Mauchline and subsequently at the Academy of Ayr, he was early sent to mercantile business in his native county. He afterwards removed to Glasgow, where for many years, he was engaged in the same pursuits. Retiring from the active care of these in indifferent health a few years ago, he spent the remainder of his life in private study and public benevolence, to which indeed every leisure hour which could be spared from business had been previously devoted. He died at Brodick, in the isle of Arran, in June 1843, in his 50th year. Mr Wodrow married in 1823. His widow survives him.[10]

The depth of Wodrow's commitment in the spiritual welfare of Jewish people can be judged by his assiduous study of Hebrew, Jewish history and culture, and his generosity in supporting needy Jewish people. He was an indefatigable promoter of an international Prayer Union, his imagination fired by the thought of thousands of congregations and tens of thousands of private Christians all engaged in prayer for the Jewish people. Wodrow devoted whole days to fasting and prayer on behalf of Israel. In recognition of his dedication to the cause, he was given the honour of moving in the General Assembly the celebrated memorial of 1838 that led directly to the establishment of the Committee for the Conversion of the Jews, and was appointed one of the first members.

In recognition of his commitment, the General Assembly chose him to be a member of its deputation to visit the Jewish communities of Europe and Palestine. Unhappily, ill health forced Wodrow to stand down. It is deplorable that modern historians tend to overlook Wodrow's contribution to Jewish missions. Not so his contemporaries, who never underestimated his role. Gavin Carlyle saw him as the true father of the Scottish Jewish mission. John Duncan referred to 'the excellent Robert Wodrow'. David Brown enthused over his 'enlightened zeal for the conversion of Israel [which] burned like a flame for many years'. And William Wingate said, 'The Jewish Mission of the Church of Scotland originated with one of the sweetest and most beautiful specimens of Divine Grace I have ever known, Robert Wodrow, of Glasgow.'[11]

Among Wodrow's very many contributions, his greatest was that most remarkable compilation we have already referred to, a document addressed *To The Children Of Israel In All The Lands Of Their Dispersion*. This was not only the product of the diligent application of Wodrow's scholarship and ability, but was marked by a very great warmth and empathy towards those to whom it was addressed. It is essentially an expression of the profoundest gratitude, lovingly and graciously commending the Saviour whom Wodrow believed was the long hoped for but hitherto neglected Messiah.

Commending Wodrow's work to the General Assembly, Robert Candlish said it was quite beyond any plaudits he could bestow upon it.[12] David Brown wholeheartedly concurred, remarking that for 'scriptural character, elevated biblical strain, and unction, it has probably never been surpassed by any human composition.'[13] Published in English and Hebrew, in most European and some Oriental languages too, the address was sent to all known Jewish communities throughout the world by the express authorisation of the 1841 General Assembly under the signature of its moderator, Robert Gordon. After Wodrow's death in 1843 his wife visited many parts of Europe to personally distribute copies of the address.

By 1837 Wodrow and his many associates judged the time ripe for support for Jewish mission to be channelled no longer through non-denominational voluntary societies and auxiliaries but through an official Church of Scotland mission. To convince the Assembly that the mood in the Church was in favour of such a project, Wodrow encouraged congregations, presbyteries, and provincial synods all over the country to send up to the General Assembly ecclesiastical petitions, or 'overtures' as they as are technically known, asking for the establishment of a committee to organise a Jewish mission from the Church of Scotland.

The *Summary of Printed Overtures* included in the papers for the General Assembly of 1838, lists twelve such appeals from the congregations in the presbyteries of Edinburgh, Glasgow, Hamilton, Dumbarton, Dundee, Aberdeen, and Fordoun, as well as Perth, Auchterarder, and Dunblane. With the exception of the southwestern synod of Dumfries, no Lowlands or Borders presbyteries presented overtures, nor, for that matter, did any Highland presbyteries.[14]

The result was, nevertheless, a quite astonishingly unanimous decision, with both Evangelicals and Moderates, for long adversaries on most issues, agreeing on a church mission to the Jewish people. At the time the boast was proudly made, and has often been repeated, that this was the first time that any Christian church, as a *church*, had dedicated itself to missionary activity among the Jewish people. Whilst it is easy to understand the flush of zeal which lies behind such an assertion, the claim is quite unfounded. As was so often the case, it was the Moravian Church which had got there first. One hundred years earlier it had organised evangelism among the Jews with the hope of establishing distinctive Jewish Christian congregations, something the nineteenth-century missions either failed to do, or refused to do on principle.[15]

As if a corroboration of the popular mood, before the Assembly of 1838, Mrs Henrietta Smith of Dunesk, a sister of the Earl of Buchan and the wealthy daughter of Henry Erskine – the famous Whig lawyer, politician, and celebrated wit – brought to Dr Alexander Moody Stuart a donation of over £100. This was, she said, for the use of the Church of Scotland's Mission to the Jews, but Moody Stuart had to remind her that no such thing yet existed. Mrs Smith was not so easily deflected. Confident that the Church would soon take action, she instructed Moody Stuart to lodge the money in the bank 'till the Lord has need of it for that mission.' Her confidence was well placed, as a few weeks later the Church of Scotland established its mission to the Jews.[16]

The Assembly's decision was perhaps more strategic than was immediately obvious to many. The fact that the Moderates had also voted in favour of a mission to the Jews demonstrated that the Evangelicals had won the argument that the aim of Christian preaching was the eternal salvation of men and women, rather than their moral improvement and cultural advancement. No longer would the Assembly stand for the nonsense which had marked out its infamous 1796 meeting when John Erskine had famously stifled Moderate opposition to missions by asking, 'Moderator, rax [reach] me that Bible' and, reading from Acts 28, demonstrated that Paul had preached the gospel to the people at Malta before educating or civilising them, even if a clever Assembly clerk could perpetuate in the minutes an ambiguity that both approved of missions and, at the same time, prevented any action being taken and so strangled the scheme at birth. After 1838 Moderatism would not recover its lost ground until its spirit morphed into the theological liberalism of the latter part of the century. The Act that created the new committee, whose official title was the Committee for the Conversion of the Jews, also set out its responsibilities. They were:

> to receive, and prudently expend, any contributions which may voluntarily be made by individuals, associations, or parishes, towards this object: Appoint the committee to collect information respecting the Jews, their numbers, condition, and character, – what means have hitherto been employed by the Christian Church for their spiritual good, and with what success, – whether there are any openings for a mission to their nation, and where these are most promising, – and generally with full power to take all prudent measures, both at home and abroad, for the advancement of the cause; and report to next General Assembly.[17]

The committee, altogether numbering one hundred members, both ministers and elders, brought together an astonishing array of wise, talented, and godly people, including some of the ablest theologians of the day. Dr Stevenson MacGill was appointed convener, with W. G. H. Laurie as clerk. William Cunningham, 'Scotland's finest theologian' was a member, as was George Smeaton, an outstanding scholar with a brilliant mind and a deep love for Christ. David Brown, considered one of the foremost theologians of his generation also had a seat, as had Robert Smith Candlish, reputedly the ablest churchmen of the day. In addition, there were those who had already, or would in the course of time, play a more or less direct role in the missionary task itself, including Robert Wodrow, Alexander Keith, Alexander Moody Stuart, Andrew Bonar, and Robert Murray M'Cheyne, to name just five.

The minutes of the committee indicate that few of its one hundred members ever attended its meetings, or those of two subcommittees established in Glasgow and Edinburgh to facilitate attendance; most members lived too far from either city to make attendance expedient. In any case such committees would have been unwieldy in practice, though they did provide for representation, and therefore involvement, of all the presbyteries and synods in the church, and thus affirmed the committee's importance and national status.

The Act of Assembly, accompanied by a letter from the convenor stressing the challenges faced by the committee, was sent to every minister of the church, including those in England and the overseas colonies, as well as to ministers of the Presbyterian Synod of Ulster. MacGill's letter asked for the church's prayers, patience, and financial commitment. Eager to glean as much information as possible, he invited ministers to communicate to him any 'facts of importance, or hints that might be useful.'

At this point, all the existing Scottish voluntary societies merged their own operations with those of the committee and none objected to the loss of their independent identities, the Glasgow society requesting only that their school in Posen might continue to be supported and Mr Cerf, their missionary, be employed by the committee.

❧ 4 ❧

Thomas Chalmers: Enthusiast for Jewish Mission

Glasgow, St. Andrews, Edinburgh, 1818–58

FEW motorists or pedestrians negotiating the junction of Edinburgh's George Street and Castle Street give much thought to the man whose imposing statue stands on the traffic island. For most, the sculpture is just another monument to a long dead great and good citizen of the capital. Yet, clearly, he must have been a person of great consequence to be deemed worthy of a memorial sculpted by Sir John Steell, the most eminent Edinburgh sculptor of his day, whose work includes the statue of Sir Walter Scott on the Scott Monument in Princes Street Gardens and the fine equestrian bronze of the Duke of Wellington outside Edinburgh's General Register House, 2 Princes Street. His attire, however, tells us he was neither novelist nor soldier. Clad in a clerical gown, with one of his preaching bands seeming to catch the breeze, and with a Bible in his hand, the indomitable but sensitive face of Thomas Chalmers looks out across the city that he knew and loved and served faithfully as a church leader, professor of Divinity, social activist, political economist, and gifted preacher.

Thomas Carlyle considered Chalmers 'the chief Scottish man of his time.'[1] Charles Haddon Spurgeon's friend and biographer, William Fullerton, went further. For him Chalmers was simply, 'the greatest man that Scotland has ever produced', and he quoted with enthusiasm Lord Rosebery's commendation of Chalmers' Christian character: 'If ever a halo surrounded a saint it encompassed Chalmers.'[2] Spurgeon did not consider himself to be in the same

65

league as Chalmers as a preacher and as a church statesman Chalmers was without peer. Bishops and cabinet ministers jostled each other in the aisles like schoolboys to get a seat to hear him speak in London on the Establishment principle. Lamenting his death, Dr John Brown, great-grandson of John Brown of Haddington, said of him, 'It is no small loss to the world, when one of its master spirits – one of its great lights – a king among the nations – leaves it'.[3] As Sidney Smith said of him, Chalmers was not one man; he was a thousand. His undisputed leadership was a multiplicity of immense organisational skills, towering intellect, and extraordinary oratory, all fuelled by an unremitting commitment to God and close communion with Him. Whatever demands were made upon him, Chalmers always left time for prayer. His great passion for spiritual revival, the evangelisation of Scotland, the revitalisation of the parish system, the care of the poor, the defence of the Establishment principle and the spiritual freedom of the church made him God's man for the day. His influence was colossal and his opinion on just about everything mattered.

By 1838, Chalmers had been Professor of Divinity at Edinburgh University for a decade and it was almost inevitable that he would be appointed a member of the Committee for the Conversion of the Jews and yet the committee's minute books never record him as present at any of their meetings and it seems just as unlikely that he attended the Edinburgh subcommittee, which inevitably prompts the question as to the level of his commitment to mission to the Jewish people.

Indeed, some modern authors, writing of Chalmers' enthusiasm for missionary activity in general, have, either explicitly or by inference, concluded that his commitment to Jewish mission was so slight as to be undeserving of mention.[4] Furthermore, an entry in Chalmers' diary in June 1818 seems to endorse such a conclusion, suggesting that he was not in sympathy with missions to the Jews. The entry recorded his exasperation that he had wasted his time agreeing to speak in Glasgow on behalf of the London Society for Promoting Christianity Among the Jews, irritably remarking, 'this Society in fact has lost me two complete days. You will see how utterly this distraction is at variance with my best and dearest and,

I think, most valuable objects.'[5] Yet, in his *Lectures on the Epistle to the Romans*, published between 1837 and 1842, he describes Jewish mission as nothing less than the primary object of church policy.

So just what did Chalmers think of Jewish mission? It would indeed seem strange if, as a member of the 1838 Assembly, he had voted for a scheme which was quite the most popular missionary venture of the day, but one for which he had no sympathy. It is also difficult to imagine how any scheme, let alone a mission to the Jewish people, could have flourished if Chalmers had considered it unimportant. How then are we to reconcile his irascible comment in 1818 with his later unambiguous commitment to Jewish missions in his *Lectures*?

First, we must separate Chalmers' attitude to the LSPCJ from his opinion of Jewish mission itself. It must be remembered that in 1818 Scottish memories were still raw after the tensions over baptism administered by non-episcopally ordained ministers had led to the withdrawal of the Scottish Presbyterians and the English Nonconformists. Largely due to Andrew Thomson's reports in the *Edinburgh Christian Instructor,* the tide of Scottish public opinion was running strongly against the LSPCJ; therefore an invitation to speak at one of their meetings might well have given Chalmers pause, leading him to accept, but reluctantly.

Secondly, Chalmers as minister of the Tron Church in Glasgow was incredibly busy at the time and may well have considered involvement with the LSPCJ a distraction. His biographer, Hanna, tells us he faced almost intolerable demands on his time and energy in the course of his ordinary parish ministry, to say nothing of other activities important to him. On the Sunday of the week in which he was to speak for the LSPCJ he preached twice and conducted fourteen baptisms. Starting his day's work at seven o'clock on the Monday, he conducted at eight a marriage in his own home, as was customary, (it took half-an-hour); he then breakfasted with a group of preachers, students, and teachers, and afterwards walked with them in the botanic gardens. On Tuesday morning he finished his preparation for the LSPCJ and in the afternoon he visited or, as Hanna put it, 'went through', two hundred and thirty people in the district of Mr Brown, one of his elders. At 8.00 p.m. he preached to eighty-five in a house in the district. Wednesday saw him leave town to visit Mr Falconer's home in the country, where he enjoyed an overnight break, indulging in strawberries and cream. On Thursday, he continued visiting in Mr Brown's district, where he spoke to another group of about eighty people and went to bed by ten o'clock. In the light of such activity, it is scarcely to be wondered at if he had little time, energy, enthusiasm, or patience to spare for any demands over and above his parish duties.[6]

Thirdly, in 1818 Chalmers' interest in missionary causes was at its earliest stage of development. It would not be until five years later, when he was appointed to the Chair of Moral Philosophy at the University of St. Andrews, that his interest in missions would gather momentum to become the passionate commitment that characterised the mature man.

Chalmers' arrival at St. Andrews was a moral and spiritual watershed. Prior to his time, the students were notorious for their hostility to anything religious and, ironically, theological students had the worst reputation of all. Chalmers' influence changed all that: in a spirit of compassion rather than censoriousness and out of a desire to introduce them to a living faith in Christ, he invited a small group to his home on Sunday evenings. These gatherings became so popular that almost against his nature, for he was essentially a shy and retiring man who disliked crowds, he welcomed more and more into his home. The direct outcome was the establishment of the St. Andrew's University Missionary Society. At least four of its members became Church of Scotland missionaries and each was, to some extent, involved in witness to Jewish people. They were Alexander Duff, William Sinclair MacKay, David Ewart, and Robert Nesbit. Duff, the pioneer missionary to India, cooperated enthusiastically with the Jewish committee, as did his colleagues MacKay and Ewart. Nesbit also went to India, where he worked with John Wilson and was directly involved in witness to the Jewish community in Bombay.

Fourthly, to return to Chalmers' *Lectures on the Epistle to the Romans,* published in four volumes between 1837–1842, we see from his remarks on chapters 9–11 how he had come to consider the importance of the evangelisation of the Jews in the overall missionary strategy of the Church. Quite in keeping with the mood of the times, he considered it as, 'the first and foremost object of Christian policy.'[7] Regrettably, however, he had to say that because of its 'sad imperfection' the Church had failed to 'provoke Israel to jealousy,' and instead had become a barrier, actually hindering Jews from coming to faith in Jesus as their Messiah. This made 'the task of a Christian missionary among the Jews all the more arduous.' Nevertheless, he argued, 'we have a task and a duty laid upon us for the fulfilment of their restoration.' This duty was to be performed with Christian integrity and sympathetic witness:

> We should make Christianity the object of emulation and desire to the Jews ... Let us not wonder that this influence has hitherto come so little into play. This is not altogether owing to Jewish insensibility. The failure is ours – at least as much, if not more, than theirs. ... The light of our religion has not so shone upon them as to make it glorious in their eyes.[8]

Notwithstanding past failures, Chalmers believed that missionary witness would ultimately bring about definitive change in the nation of Israel: it would become predominantly Christian. Commenting on Romans 10:26 – 'And so all Israel shall be saved' – he remarked that the word 'all' should not be reduced to the superficial observation that all the elect were to be saved; that was obvious. Rather, he argued, the word 'all' 'signified 'a great corporate change from Judaism to Christianity.'

Although Chalmers' convictions regarding Jewish mission had evolved over the years through a sober reading of the Bible, they were not held as dispassionate theoretical or theological propositions. In his *Sabbath Scripture Readings* he sets this duty in the context of desire for a deeper spiritual life. These short meditations commenced somewhere around 1841 and continued until the time of his death in 1847 and, at one point, his thoughts concerning the Jews are couched in the form of a prayer, where he confessed his earlier inadequate commitment to their salvation: 'And let me also be more considerate of the Jews than before, and of their many claims on the sympathy and service of Christians.'[9]

Finally, Chalmers' personal account books for the years 1838–40, provide eloquent testimony to his commitment to this cause. Although his handwriting is often barely legible, the following entries are clear: 'Nov. 19th 1839 – Jewish collection 23 shillings; 27th March; 1840 – Jewish collection 20 shillings; 26th June 1843 – Jewish collection £1.; Feb. 26th 1845 – Jewish collection 20 shillings; Dec.23rd – Jewish collection £1; 24th June – Jewish collection £1.' These sums compare very favourably with the donations Chalmers made to other missionary causes, and it seems reasonable to conclude, judging from the dates, that these contributions were over and above anything he may have contributed through the Assembly's prescribed annual collection for the Jewish mission on the fourth Sunday of August.[10]

Nor was Chalmers' interest in Jewish missions inward and private: it was abundantly clear to others. Robert Murray M'Cheyne considered that Chalmers was wholeheartedly in support both of the Jewish mission itself and of his own personal participation in it. Throughout his journeys in Egypt, Palestine, and Europe, M'Cheyne carried a small pocket book containing a list of those who had assured him of their support and prayers. Along with Thomas Guthrie, Alexander Moody Stuart, and Robert Candlish, we find the name of Thomas Chalmers.[11]

The evidence leads to the inescapable conclusion that Thomas Chalmers' interest in and support for Jewish missionary work grew from a low point in 1818, where he saw his involvement with the LSPCJ on one occasion as a distraction, to a deep theological, personal, financial, and prayerful involvement, as well as an open advocacy on its behalf. Because of his towering significance during this era it is important that Chalmers' interest in the evangelisation of the Jewish people be seen for what, in fact, it was: an enthusiastic commitment to what he considered 'the first and foremost object of Christian policy.'[12]

※ 5 ※

Motivating the Mission:
Gratitude or Eschatology?

Scotland: 1830s & 40s

ONE of the earliest and most influential discussions of the question
of Israel and the fulfilment of biblical prophecy came from the
pen of one who was to be a member of the survey party sent out
by the General Assembly of 1839 to report on the most suitable
locations to commence the mission to Jews: Dr Alexander Keith.[1]
In his *Evidence of the Truth of the Christian Religion Derived from
the Literal Fulfilment of Prophecy; Particularly as Illustrated by
the History of the Jews, and by the Discoveries of Recent Travellers*
Keith expounded how prophecy and its fulfilment not only had
motivational implications for missions, but important applications
for apologetics and evangelism too. The mere existence of prophecy
was in itself no evidence of the truth of Christianity; everything
hinged on its credible fulfilment. Prophecy's contribution was limited
to the extent that its 'numerous and distinct predictions ... have
been literally accomplished.'[2]

There was nothing at all novel about this or the exegetical
method by which Keith arrived at his conclusions. It was, in
essence, a reiteration of the hermeneutic of the Reformation that
insisted that Scripture be understood in a plain and straightforward
manner, avoiding all unnecessary allegorisation or spiritualisation.[3]
As Keith argued, spiritualising the text would, to the degree that it
is exercised, diminish the value of prophecy as an evidence of the
truth of Christianity. What mattered were 'the facts of history.'[4]

Keith's brilliant younger colleague, Robert M'Cheyne, also believed that the literal or, as he put it, the grammatical, interpretation of prophecy, was essential for all who would be missionaries to the Jews.[5] To Keith's readers, there was little that was controversial in what he said as the majority of Evangelicals expounded Scripture along such lines.[6] Patrick Fairbairn had no gripe with literal interpretation, but was concerned about a perverse selective literalism, common then as now, which takes literally the prophecies of Israel's judgement but sees its promises of restoration as merely figurative:

> When I see that God has magnified his faithfulness in giving the dark side of the prospective history the most literal and complete verification, shall I think so harshly of his character, or so meanly of the consistence of the prophetic word, as to suppose that he will not also verify *to the letter* the other and brighter side, but allow it pass away into some vague generality?[7]

Believing such a balanced and sane interpretation of Scripture was universal in the nineteenth-century Scottish church is, however, to reckon without the eccentric influence of Edward Irving. In May 1828 Irving, the minister of Regent's Square Church of Scotland in London, organised a series of twelve lectures on prophetic themes to take place in Edinburgh during the week of the General Assembly.[8] Like much about Irving, these controversial meetings became a flamboyant spectacle, attracting huge crowds, and making it necessary to switch to the West Church, the largest in Edinburgh.

Alexander Thompson's *Edinburgh Christian Instructor* carried a devastating critique of Irving's performances:

> If Calvin, mighty though he was in the Scriptures, thought himself not qualified to comment on this book of mystery [Revelation] ... we, in these days, will show at least some prudence in not thrusting upon the reluctant belief of others the *ipse dixit* [unproven statements] of our own dogmatism.[9]

The *Instructor* nevertheless somewhat pulled its punches by commending Irving for raising 'a subject of great interest ... for all Christians' who ought to be 'alive and awake' to the matter.[10] The following year Irving gave a second series of lecturers, but the *Instructor* refrained from further comment.

Having been impressed by Irving's oratory at the 1828 meetings, Andrew and Horatius Bonar, then divinity students, asked their mentor, Thomas Chalmers, if it would be advisable for them to attend the next year's meetings. According to Andrew Bonar, Chalmers unhesitatingly replied, 'Oh, gentlemen, there is no harm in studying that subject [premillennialism]; go on, and make up your mind. I have not arrived at a conclusion yet; I am looking into it.'[11] This counsel must not, however, be taken as Chalmers' imprimatur on his former assistant's opinions or his approval of his ostentatious style, but ought rather to be understood as a comment intended to encourage two theological students to stretch their minds and cultivate their critical faculties. In fact, Chalmers found his former assistant's beliefs thoroughly distasteful:

> For the first time heard Mr Irving in the evening. I have no hesitation in saying it is quite woful [sic]. This is the impression of every clergyman I have met, and some think of making a friendly remonstrance with him upon the subject.[12]

Returning to hear another address in the series, he was no better pleased, remarking that it too was 'unsatisfactory and obscure.'[13] His caution was not shared by the Edinburgh crowd. As Mrs Oliphant commented, Irving's 'wonderful popularity was higher at the conclusion than at the beginning.'[14]

Chalmers' sanguine view of Irving's influence was misplaced; by the end of the week Irving had won over both Bonar brothers, who would become the strongest advocates of premillennialism in the Scottish church.[15] Andrew Bonar confided to his diary, 'I have been hearing Mr Irving's lectures all week, and am persuaded now that his views of the Coming of Christ are truth'.[16] What clinched it for him was Irving's handling of Matthew 24. Years later he recalled, 'That chapter decided me on the subject. I could not see a foot-breadth of room for the Millennium before Christ comes in the clouds.'[17] Irving's influence on Andrew's brother, Horatius, was no less profound, reinforcing his tentative hold on premillennial views so that it became a solid conviction, which he held unshakeably and advocated enthusiastically for more than sixty years until his death in 1889.[18]

Chalmers may not have been impressed by his former assistant's 1828 lectures, but that ought not to obscure the possibility that he himself harboured a sympathy towards premillennialism, traces of which may be detected in some of his expository comments, for example those on Psalm 50:1-6 and 68:18-35.[19] Indeed, Andrew Bonar was so bold as to claim that at the end Chalmers came down on the side of the premillennialists, something he never claimed for his close friend Robert M'Cheyne.[20] So, before proceeding to explore the thirty-year long controversy that ensued, it is important to approach the matter with a due sense of proportion and remind ourselves that most of the protagonists were directly involved in the Jewish mission and enjoyed the most cordial relations with each other.

If the main advocates of the premillennial approach were the Bonar brothers, on the postmillennial side was David Brown, convenor of the Jewish committee from 1854 to 1857, and Patrick Fairbairn, who whilst dismissing as whimsical premillennial expectations of Jewish territorial restoration and what he took to be its corollary, 'a revived Judaism,' nevertheless supported and encouraged Jewish missions, speaking on their behalf in the 1839 Glasgow lecture series and writing enthusiastically of the work in *The Interpretation of Prophecy*.[21]

By the time the controversy broke out, the Jewish mission was well established and in 1843 had entered its second phase as an integral part of the missionary enterprise of the Free Church of Scotland, to which all the protagonists belonged. In 1845 David Brown made a strong defence of postmillennialism in a long article he wrote for the *Free Church Magazine*.[22] Holding their premillennial view with great tenacity, and arguing with considerable ability, the habitually irenic Bonars considered Brown's robust attack on premillennialism as unfortunate. In his preface to *Prophetical Landmarks*, Horatius wrote, 'I have striven to avoid the attitude of disputation as much as possible, and to treat with respect the judgement of brethren in Christ who differ from me.'[23] In *Redemption Drawing Nigh*, Andrew sternly counselled against those, 'on both sides … who have employed a bitter and dogmatic tone. Why, then, should we break out into harsh words, and cast unkind imputations on each other?'[24]

As an able and practised expounder of the Bible, Horatius Bonar recognised the existence of different literary forms in Scripture. It was, he asserted, necessary to judge carefully what was literal and what was figurative, and then to determine how best to interpret what was figurative. The problem lay most, he believed, with the figurative material, and he held to the idea that the literal was foundational and primary, the figurative being exceptional and secondary.[25] Only if a literal reading was utterly indefensible should a figurative or spiritual reading be preferred.[26] He held fast to this principle throughout his lengthy ministry, still insisting in 1879 that the 'LITERAL, if possible, is ... the only maxim that will carry you right through the Word of God, from Genesis to Revelation.'[27]

Against Brown, he argued that it was necessary to renounce the idea that a 'whole chapter is one scene' or a passage contained but 'one grand idea.' Instead, he called for a more intricate and surgical approach to the text, 'interpreting verse by verse and clause by clause, and affixing an exact and definite sense to each.'[28] Handling the biblical text in this way, however, raised the question of how a literal fulfilment of the prophecies in regard of Israel could be consistent with the promises of the Gospel and the teaching of the New Testament. His answer was succinct and clear:

> We believe the literal accomplishment of the prophecies regarding the Jews, in which there appear to be many temporal blessings as well as spiritual: but we lay no further stress upon these than the Word of God lay, – we admit spiritual blessings to be the highest and noblest.[29]

Among the promised temporal blessings for which Bonar contended, one seems to have been key to his thought: the Messiah would one day sit on 'the throne of David'. But what precisely did that mean? Bonar neatly sashayed around 'a literal and visible occupation' of a physical throne in Jerusalem, but insisted that the promise did, at least, mean 'the peculiar sovereignty of Messiah over the literal Israel.'[30] He rejected the conventional view that 'the throne of David' alluded to the lordship of Christ over His people or was synonymous with Christ as 'the King and Head of the Church.' Undeniably Christ was Lord over His Church, but in relation to Israel He also was their unique Davidic king. Christ's rule over His

Church was a present reality, whereas His enthronement over Israel lay in the future and would take place more or less concurrently with the fulfilment of a cluster of other prophetic temporalities, including the restoration of the people to the land of promise, the land being restored to productivity and prosperity, and the city of Jerusalem rebuilt.[31]

Likewise, consistent with their growing persuasion that to some degree Israel and the Church were two distinct peoples of God, brother Andrew objected to the tendency of Christians to appropriate certain terms such as 'Israel', 'Zion', or 'Jerusalem', that he believed were titles or names of Israel, or, as he called it, 'the Jewish Church.' Bonar could hardly do less that readily admit that the New Testament itself used the very same language to denote the Church of Christ and he could not therefore totally oppose such use, but the problem with it, he thought, was that the use of such terms as '… figures of the spiritual and not of the Jewish Church, occasioned much confusion in the interpretation of prophecy.'[32]

The way the New Testament used this language, argued Andrew Bonar, was highly complex. At times it used such terms 'spiritually', but, he thought, 'most frequently' in a literal sense.[33] It could at least be said of the New Testament that: 'It *preserves*, instead of changes the former meanings of these familiar terms. It does not, indeed, preclude us from using them in a spiritual sense; but it plainly shows that such is not their natural and scriptural meaning.'[34] But Bonar felt he must go further still, and insist that there 'is no New Testament authority for spiritualizing the name of Israel, Judah, Jerusalem, Zion.'[35]

For the Bonars, consistent literalism had missionary and evangelistic implications. As we have seen, the matter was plain. What credence could 'a stout hearted Jew' possibly give to any attempt by a Christian to convince him of the truth of the Gospel if the Christian insisted, as many did, and still do, on a literal belief in the judgement of Israel and its banishment from the Land, but insisted on a spiritualised fulfilment of the promises of restoration?[36]

The Bonar brothers' approach was accepted by some as a welcome corrective to an overly spiritualised interpretation of biblical prophecy, whilst others found a number of serious flaws in their scheme. First was the relentless drive for rigid hermeneutical consistency that failed to allow for an adequately dynamic fulfilment of Old Testament promises in the New Covenant, such as we find in some of the Old Testament prophets' anticipation of a spiritual fulfilment of some of their predictions, and also by the way the New Testament does not easily accommodate itself to inflexible literalism.[37]

The error in such an approach may be illustrated by the father who promises his young son that on reaching maturity he would buy him a horse and buggy, but in the intervening years the car is invented, the old technology is made redundant, and so the son is presented with a motor car instead. Was the fulfilment of the father's promise merely figurative and not literal? No reasonable person could argue that it was; indeed the fulfilment exceeded expectations, being over and above anything that the son could have asked or thought.

Secondly, and perhaps more troubling, the Bonars increasingly came to represent Israel and the Church as two distinct peoples of God, thus challenging the identity of the Church as a unified covenant community made up of both Jews and Gentiles, throughout all ages. As if that was not enough, their narrow literalism led them to shift the emphasis away from the communication of the gospel to the return of Christ and what they saw as its effects. Remarkably, neither Andrew nor Horatius Bonar, stalwarts of evangelism and supporters of missions that they were, held out any hope that the preaching of the Gospel would be successful in turning the Jewish people to their Messiah. Horatius thought that the gospel might draw Jewish individuals to faith, but as a nation Israel's salvation was 'reserved for the coming of their Messiah.' It would take place 'then and not till then …'[38] Andrew was similarly inclined, asserting, 'There is not to be any national turning of Israel to the Lord till that day.'[39] Evangelistic mission was thereby demoted to being a sign of the imminence of Christ's return: it would not achieve the conversion of the world, but only call the elect.[40] That, however, is a truism, expressing the inevitable and saying nothing new, yet carrying a clear inference that the elect were few.

Andrew also made the startling claim that the work of conversion among the hitherto unevangelised nations as well as the Jewish people would continue after the return of Christ. By this he meant that in the Millennial Age there would still be scope for repentance and faith. At Christ's return, he argued, 'all Christendom', those who had heard but had not responded to the gospel, as well as those who had made a fraudulent profession of Christian faith, would find 'the door … finally and for ever shut'. But, 'the Heathen', those who had never heard the gospel, as well as 'the mass of outcast Jews' who had 'never pretended to honour Christ,' would be afforded a fresh opportunity to believe and be saved.[41]

The ultimate effect of such views would be to dampen zeal for missions and quash all hope of their success. If a second chance were available, would it not be preferable to leave people in ignorance for as long as possible, in the hope that a clearer and more powerful revelation, at the return of Christ, would elicit a positive response? The issue is of great contemporary relevance. The doctrine of a second chance, common among those on the edge of religious universalism, holds a fascination for some evangelicals today seeking an alternative to the doctrine of eternal punishment.

Advocates of premillennialism, with their pessimistic view of the success of gospel witness and a belief in an imminent return of Christ, and imagining themselves to be the last generation on the earth, denied the Church any meaningful future and Christian missions any significant outcome.[42] With his deep commitment to missions in general and the Jewish mission in particular, such charges of demoralising missionary endeavour stung Andrew Bonar into claiming that it was the postmillennialists who had done most to undermine confidence in missions, but he hardly established the case.

So, having entered our caveats against premillennialism, we must acknowledge that Bonar was perfectly correct in asserting that there were, and are, premillennialists who were zealous and faithful witnesses to the Jewish people. These included some of the founders of Jewish missions, such as John Wilkinson of the Mildmay Mission to the Jews (London: 1876), David Baron of Hebrew Testimony to Israel (London: 1893), William Blackstone of the Chicago Hebrew Mission (Chicago: 1887), and Gideon

Lederer, an important independent missionary (New York c.1860–80). Arguably, Thomas Chalmers held premillenarian views, and Adolph Saphir and Alfred Edersheim, converts of the Scottish mission in Budapest, certainly did.

So before we turn to the claims of postmillennialism, it needs to be said that some arguments used by opponents of premillennialism are spurious. Most notably of these is the view espoused by A. A. Hodge that dismissed the attempts of those who, as he put it, tried 'to convert the world directly by units', rather than by planting 'Christian institutions in heathen lands, which will, in time develop according to the genius of the nationalities.'[43] The success of Christian missions in the twentieth century has largely discredited this 'trickle down' approach, not only because of its undue dependence on the support of now defunct colonial structures or the rare existence of sympathetic national governments, but by the very facts of the case. Despite the twentieth century being marked by successive waves of bitter anti-Christian persecution, the growth of the Church in that century, continued into the twenty-first, has been unprecedented and very largely the result of the kind of atomised personal evangelism denigrated by Hodge.[44]

What then of the other side of the argument, the postmillennial literalism promoted by David Brown and Patrick Fairbairn? Strange to say, Brown was also a convert to premillennialism through his contact with Edward Irving, under whom he had served as an assistant at the Regent Square, National Scotch Church, London, from 1830 to 1832. By 1845 he had renounced the theory, giving expression to his opposition in the very article in the *Free Church Magazine* that attracted the Bonars' response. This he followed up the following year by the publication of *Christ's Second Coming: Will it be Premillennial?*, and then in 1861 by a slim volume entitled *The Restoration of the Jews*.[45] *Christ's Second Coming* is to be ranked alongside Patrick Fairbairn's *The Interpretation of Prophecy* as perhaps the most able defence of old-school Scottish postmillennialism. Both books had, and continue to have, relevance to Jewish mission.

According to John Macleod, Principal of the Free Church College from 1929–43, Brown was 'among the foremost theologians of his generation.' In 1857, after a period in pastoral ministry, he became Professor of New Testament Exegesis, Church History, and Apologetics at the Free Church College in Aberdeen, where he was appointed Principal in 1875.[46] Brown stoutly defended the view that not only was the national conversion of the Jews clearly predicted by Scripture, but so too was their return to their forfeited land, challenging the views held by some highly esteemed contemporary scholars, including Patrick Fairbairn, his contemporary at Aberdeen, and J. A. Alexander of Princeton Theological Seminary, as well as two Anglicans, one evangelical, E. W. Hengstenberg, the other High Church, Thomas Arnold.[47]

The Restoration of the Jews shows Brown differing not only from premillennialists, but also many postmillennialists, and thereby, by implication, from amillennialists, who were then a rarity in Scotland. He strongly disapproved of the undue spiritualising tendencies of some postmillennialists, and deplored the confusion of premillennialists who insisted that a return of the Jewish people to their Promised Land would mean the rebuilding of a Third Temple and the resumption of the Jewish sacrificial system, an idea that was deplorable as it would result in the diminution of the finality of Christ's sacrifice on the Cross. Against the spiritualising inclination, he called for a more rigorously literal interpretation of prophecy.[48] But his regard for literalism did not carry him to adopt the inflexible hermeneutic of the Bonars. If a literal reading of a prophecy tended to eclipse the clear prescriptive teaching of the Bible, he counselled his readers to 'let the literalities go.'[49]

Like the Bonars, Brown sought to do justice to the various genres evident in the Bible, but unlike them his approach was dynamic and flexible, citing with approval a passage from J. A. Alexander's commentary on Isaiah:

> whether any prophecy is general or particular, literal or figurative, can only be determined by a thorough independent scrutiny of each case by itself, in reference, form, and substance, text and context, without regard to arbitrary and exclusive theories, but with a due regard to the analogy of Scripture.[50]

By following such an approach, Brown embarked on the interpretation of a number of crucial texts in both Old and New

Testaments, in order to demonstrate that the restoration of the Jews entailed both their conversion to Christ and their literal return to the land of their fathers.[51] The return to the land would not by itself constitute the fulfilment of prophecy, for did not Ezekiel 37:21-28, for example, link a return to the land with a return to the Lord? The promise, said Brown, is of 'the final resettlement of the whole nation in their own land, *under Christ, as their King.*'[52]

Brown's commentary on Romans, published as part of the famous Jamieson, Fausset and Brown *Critical and Explanatory Commentary* was influential. Writing on Romans 11:12-16, 26-31, he demonstrated that the future restoration of the Jews is a consequence of the Abrahamic covenant and is inseparably linked to missionary activity.[53] Whatever the claims of Andrew Bonar, postmillennialism had not diminished Brown's commitment to the Jewish Mission nor had it undermined his role as a member of the committee. Indeed, on his death in 1897, a letter of condolence from the Jewish Committee to his daughter, bore testimony to his devotion to the cause:

> In common with the whole church, they gratefully remember Dr Brown's eminent services, and his personal worth, but in a special manner they recall his early devotion to the cause of the Conversion of the Jews *long before the Church of Scotland formally took any action in the matter.*[54]

Brown's contribution on behalf of the Jewish mission is further seen in his biography of his friend John Duncan, the pioneer missionary to the Jews of Budapest. Doubtless, Brown might have been pleased to claim Duncan as a fellow postmillennialist but, in fact, he shows Duncan as ambivalent by recording an amusing anecdote telling how he was once accosted by a lady who pressed him to take sides in the debate. Too wise to be trapped, Duncan replied:

> I am neither 'pre' nor 'post'. I am willing to hear what the Pre-millennialists have to say, provided it does not take from the glory of the Pentecostal dispensation. Can you tell me any system that reconciles the literal taking of Ezekiel's temple with the Epistle to the Hebrews? When parting from her, he said, 'Now mind there must be no more slain beasts.'[55]

The complexities of the millennium aside, Duncan, like Brown, believed that the Jewish people would one day be restored to their Promised Land. Rev. Robert Sandeman, a nephew of Duncan's housekeeper, recalled Duncan's remark on the extent of the land promised to Israel in Deuteronomy 11: 'They have never got that in verse 24, and Dr Keith says in his book that therefore they must get it yet.'[56]

Although the millennial controversy heightened awareness of unfulfilled biblical prophecy relevant to the conversion and restoration of the Jewish people, we ought not exaggerate its influence or imagine that eschatology was the primary motivation behind the mission, when, in fact, the motivation was a cluster of more general theological, moral, and spiritual obligations, above all gratitude to the Jewish people and obedience to Christ.

The development of Jewish missions in Scotland had been broadly parallel to those of England. The LSPCJ had been established in 1809, during the upheavals of the Napoleonic wars, when prophetic expectations had been greatly aroused and when many believed they could detect portents of the rapidly approaching end of the age, but the compilers of the first annual report sought to draw attention away from End Times speculations:

> If nothing peculiar appeared in the aspect of the times – if neither Jews nor Christians believed the future restoration of Israel – if no exposition of prophecy had awakened attention or excited expectation in men's minds – if it were possible to place things as they stood many centuries ago – still your committee would urge the importance and propriety of establishing a Jewish Mission.[57]

It was not unfulfilled prophecy that drove English Jewish missions, it was deep gratitude to Israel, coupled with obedience to the gospel mandate. It was likewise in Scotland, and as in these pages the story of the Scottish mission to the Jewish people unfolds, we will not tire of saying it. The point was repeatedly made in the many Overtures sent up from Church of Scotland Presbyteries to the 1838 General Assembly requesting the establishment of a mission. The overture from the Presbytery of Edinburgh stated that the Jewish people had 'an equal claim to the sympathy and exertions of Christians and the Church at large ... in seeking the conversion of those descendants of Abraham to the faith.' Glasgow Presbytery insisted that the Jews had 'strong claims on our gratitude and sympathy.' Perth was thankful for having, 'by the divine appointment, received all their spiritual privileges through the medium of the Jewish nation.' Likewise Fordoun Presbytery, in Aberdeenshire, understood that 'salvation is of the Jews, and all spiritual blessings, which we as a Church of Christ enjoy, have been derived through them.'[58]

Robert Murray M'Cheyne agreed. Despite his keen interest in the 'literal fulfilment' of prophecy and his close friendship with the Bonar brothers, his only published sermon on missions to the Jews says little about prophecy, but much about moral obligation, as its title, *Our Duty to Israel,* makes clear. The mission for which M'Cheyne argues is not self-consciously eschatological, but driven by compassion and thankfulness.[59]

The same emphasis is found in the 1838/39 Glasgow series of lectures. In the final paper on the *Immediate Duties of the Christian Church in Relation to Israel,* J. G. Lorimer believed unfulfilled prophecy nurtured the hope of a Jewish return to the land of Palestine, with a glory exceeding the most brilliant days of Solomon, but he added, '... what would this avail if the Jew retained his alienation and ungodliness, and after a few brief years of outward show, died the enemy of God, and of all that is spiritually good?'[60] For Lorimer, the Christian work amongst the Jews must aim not at the fulfilment of prophecy, but at their personal reconciliation to the Messiah. From that all else would flow.

The Edinburgh lectures were specifically held to 'show the obligations on Christians to earnest prayer and renewed efforts on [the Jewish people's] behalf.'[61] Those obligations were not derived from eschatological considerations. Even Andrew Bonar's lecture, *The First Captivity and Restoration of the Jews Viewed in Reference to the Coming of Messiah,* insisted that obedience was a key motivation for mission – 'we are to go as his witnesses to Judea and Samaria, and the ends of the earth' – and that their 'conversion, shall be in them the same process as with us, produced by the same truth and the agency of the same Spirit.'[62]

To the printed version of the Edinburgh lectures was appended a statement from the Jewish Committee, prepared by Dr Alexander Black, which takes us beyond the claims of duty as the primary motivating force, to a powerful spiritual compulsion working in a healthy Christian Church.

> Christianity contains within itself the germ of its own expansion; for wherever its power is felt, wherever its blessings are rightly appreciated, there will be a corresponding desire and endeavour to impart to others the possession of so valuable a gift.[63]

Despite the emphases found in Jewish missions based on Fundamentalist Dispensationalism, there is scant evidence that the Scottish Jewish mission ever set out deliberately to fulfil predictive prophecy. Their missionary agenda was the prescriptive teaching of Scripture, driven by a Spirit-induced gratitude to Israel and obedience to the will of Christ. What belief in the fulfilment of prophecy provided was confidence that their proposed work was not in vain. To be sure, pre- and post- understood that fulfilment differently, but there was more than sufficient consensus as well as a generous brotherly love that allowed followers of both schools to work together in harmony.

In 1843, after fifteen years of gruelling service in India, John Wilson of Bombay was returning to Scotland accompanied by the young Parsi convert, Dhanjibai Naroji. Their nine months journey took them by sea to Aden and on to Suez, then, by a circuitous overland route through Egypt, Palestine, and Syria, they reached central Europe via Cyprus, Turkey, the Black Sea, and the River Danube.[64] They had been requested by the Jewish Committee, at some inconvenience to themselves, to visit en route some Jewish communities in order to supplement the research of the 1839 Deputation.[65] They did so willingly, because, as Wilson put it, it was done 'to repay to [the Jewish people] those mighty obligations under which we are placed for the distinguished blessings for which, under God, we are to them indebted.'[66] That very same influence, he believed, lay at the heart of the Church of Scotland's missionary programme, which 'acted only according to the dictates of true philanthropic prudence, when it turned its particular attention to the Jews.'[67]

❧ 6 ❧

'Oh then pray – pray
without ceasing'

Glasgow and Edinburgh, 1838–1839

RESOURCES for the Church of Scotland's newly established
Jewish mission were slender. The committee, therefore, set to work
to stimulate interest, cultivate intelligent and informed prayer, and
encourage financial commitment. One way of achieving these ends
was to invite famous ministers to address a series of public meetings.
The first series was held in Glasgow during the winter of 1838/9,
and the lectures were published almost immediately afterwards by
William Collins as, *A Course of Lectures on the Jews by ministers
of the Established Church in Glasgow*. These documents provide a
helpful insight into the issues that motivated the church's prayers
and stimulated its action. Whilst some speakers chose to address
prophetic and eschatological subjects, they did so only in a very
limited and restrained manner. All the speakers connected the
Jewish mission to the main doctrines of the Christian Faith, such
as the character of God, the person of Christ and the work of the
Holy Spirit, but above every other motive for the evangelisation of
the Jewish people the one that emerges as the pivot upon which
the whole project turned was, predictably, gratitude to Israel. The
concluding lecture was by John G. Lorimer, minister of St. David's
in Glasgow, who argued that the Church was honour-bound to
share the gospel with those from whom it had first been received.[1]

For the Scots, the primary goal of Christian work amongst
the Jews was not what would later be called Christian Zionism

– the rebuilding of a Jewish state in Palestine – but their spiritual reconciliation to their Messiah. Furthermore, as Lorimer maintained, the church had every reason to get on with the task because the past, the present, the future, the honour of God, the honour of Christ, the honour of the Spirit, compassion to souls, justice, gratitude, humanity, all called the church to its obvious duty: evangelistic action. For far too long, the church had been supine, insensitive, and unmoved by the miseries of Israel, as generation after generation had gone down to destruction with no one caring for their souls. With great solemnity he concluded that the time for Christian witness was the present. There was no second chance after death: a soul in eternity is for ever beyond the reach of the gospel: 'We cannot recall them, we cannot retrieve the evil.'

The frequency with which such sentiments are repeated, not only in the lecture series at Glasgow and Edinburgh, but right across the literature of the period, removes every scintilla of doubt that what led Scottish Presbyterians to engage in missionary witness to the Jewish people was not some millenarian vision but, to repeat the oft made point, a deep spiritual awareness of moral obligation towards those who had been the source of their greatest spiritual good. It was a clear echo of the burdened heart of Apostle Paul: 'For if I preach the gospel, that gives me no ground for boasting. For necessity is laid upon me. Woe to me if I do not preach the gospel!'

The Glasgow lecture series was, at first, greeted by the more conservative Edinburgh sub-committee as something of a novelty, but it soon overcame its timidity to hold its own very successful series during the following winter. These lectures were also speedily published with a brief introduction from the pen of Dr Alexander Black, all the more welcome owing to his enthusiasm for the subject and extreme disinclination to express himself in print. Black's introduction outlined the qualifications he considered desirable for missionary candidates, which included the cultivation of language skills, an ability to handle competently the Hebrew Scriptures, and a thorough knowledge of Jewish religious literature. Black did not regard prophetic beliefs to be so very important. What motivated mission above all was love to the Jewish people:

We are indebted to them, as the chosen people of God, for all the spiritual privileges that we enjoy ... it is but equitable that we should consider what we can do for the descendants of those to whose ancestors we owe so much; and the greatest boon that we have the means of conferring upon them, is our duty to take every measure that can give promise of success to impart to them the blessings of the gospel, that through our mercy, they also may obtain mercy.[2]

Dr Black's virtual dismissal of millenarian views and the interpretation of biblical prophecy, stands in contrast to the approach taken by the younger Andrew Bonar for whom premillennial eschatological opinions loomed much larger.

The Edinburgh lecturers covered a similar range of subjects to those addressed in Glasgow. Rev. George Muirhead dealt with the call of Abraham and the uniqueness of the Jewish people. Andrew Bonar spoke on the restoration of the Jews, viewed in reference to the coming of Messiah. Charles Brown considered the history of the Jewish people as preparation for the coming of Christ. Henry Grey drew out the consequences for Christianity and Judaism of the destruction of the Jerusalem Temple in A.D. 70. Robert Elder addressed the perplexing question of the suffering of the Jewish people from A.D. 70 to the nineteenth century.

The penultimate lecture was delivered by Alexander Moody Stuart whose text was Galatians 3:29: 'If ye be Christ's, then are ye Abraham's seed, and heirs according to the promise' (A.V.). Moody Stuart argued that each Christian is by grace a child of Abraham and each Jew is naturally a descendant of Abraham. The logic of this is that the child of Abraham by grace is bound to love and honour the child of Abraham by nature. Moody Stuart saw gentile Christians as returning prodigals, who are warmly received by the Father and on whom is lavished every blessing, but just as God had mercy on the prodigal so too would He have mercy on the elder son. In a strong appeal to his audience, he urged them not only to pray for the Jews, but also to do all possible to share with them the promises of the gospel.

The minister of St. Georges, Robert Smith Candlish, presented the final lecture. Basing his thoughts on Romans 11:12-15, he discussed what might be the implications of the conversion of

Israel for the future spiritual welfare of the Church. His approach was conventional and the audience was hardly shocked by his gloomy analysis of the days in which they lived. Most shared his diagnosis, as well his desire for the revival of the Church of Scotland in order to save it from being torn apart by internal debates over the intrusion by landowners, on unwilling congregations, of their choice of ministerial candidates. Appealing directly to this topical concern, Candlish (a strong Non-intrusionist, like most of his hearers) put it to his audience that their support of the Jewish mission was especially relevant to the needs at the time because 'the return of the Jews should be the occasion of a new and extensive revival in the Church, and should give a new impulse to the cause of God in the world.'

The two Scottish lecture series inspired at least two other similar events in England. In 1841, under the auspices of the London Society for Promoting of Christianity among the Jews, a course of twelve lectures was delivered at St. Brides Church in Liverpool by Anglican clergymen and later published as *The Destiny of the Jews and their Connection with the Gentile Nations.* In 1843, in connection with the newly established British Society for the Propagation of the Gospel among the Jews, a series of lectures was delivered in London, subsequently published as *Lectures on the Conversion of the Jews by Ministers of Different Denominations.*

The seventeenth-century Westminster *Directory for the Public Worship of God* had made prayer for the conversion of the Jews an integral part of Presbyterian worship; therefore, in the last of the Glasgow lecture series, John G. Lorimer reemphasised the importance of prayer for the success of missionary witness. Using a vivid metaphor from contemporary shipping, he argued that all the other means for the evangelisation of the Jews then at the disposal of the Church were little more than limp canvas sails; what was needed was 'the prosperous gale which fills the sails and speeds the vessel to its destination.' Such a prosperous wind might blow, he believed, but only in answer to prayer.

For Lorimer, prayer also served an important subjective purpose: it would 'produce kindness towards the Jewish people.' It was his belief that it would have been impossible for Christians to have mistreated Jews as they did for centuries, often with bitter persecution and at best with cold indifference, if they had only been in the habit of praying for them. Prayer would have crushed cruelty. Lorimer stated that he was most encouraged by the many Christians in England, Ireland, and Scotland who had started to pray for Israel as they had never done before. Then, drawing on an argument used by Samuel Rutherford and Thomas Boston centuries earlier, he maintained that just as the Church had derived great benefit from the prayers of Jews, it was now obligated to pray for them, in order to 'pay back the prayers of the Fathers, in intercession for the children.'[3]

During this period, throughout Scotland, many special public prayer meetings for the Jewish people were held. Often addressed by leading members of the committee, these attracted great crowds. A meeting in St Andrew's Church in Edinburgh was crowded to capacity and the people gave every sign of deep interest. The Glasgow sub-committee organised prayer meetings throughout the city and reports carried in *The Home and Foreign Missionary Record* give us an idea of the topics on which attention was focused: 'Labourers are needed, and the blessing of the God must be sought, that the committee may be directed aright in the selection of the first missionary station, on which they will be called very soon to decide.'

None were left in any doubt as to the importance of prayer. If at times the committee and individuals associated with the mission gave an impression of being indecisive and irresolute, wavering between different courses of action, it was mainly because it was their custom for each alternative course of action and every area of uncertainty to be equally bathed in prayer. Other things were important; prayer was essential. Enthusiasm, ability, knowledge, and activism all had their place, but were inadequate on their own. Without God's blessing there could be no success. At its heart, evangelism was not dependent on human persuasiveness or logic, but on divine energy. John Duncan accurately summed up the prevailing mood in the Church of Scotland:

> Societies may be formed, churches as such may enter into the field, sermons may be preached, inquiries may be made, information obtained, plans organised, funds profusely furnished, missionaries

instructed and sent forth, institutions formed, Bibles and tracts distributed with the most abundant liberality, and discussions upon discussions held interminably, but all in vain without the Spirit. God will not give his glory to another. The residue of the Spirit is with Him, and will be bestowed in answer to believing, earnest, importunate, persevering prayer. Oh then pray – pray without ceasing, that the salvation of Israel may come out of Zion.[4]

Looking to God in a spirit of earnest prayer, the people of Scotland waited with bated breath for the committee's decision concerning the location of its first mission and the identity of its first missionaries. But before those matters could be decided, the work was required to be established on a sound financial basis and substantial sums of money gathered from a generous and supportive people.

7

'A general and cordial support'

Scotland and the Colonial Churches, 1838–1852

WHEN someone remarked that the General Assembly of 1838 exercised towards its new Jewish mission committee 'a caution completely Scottish', they probably meant that the Assembly was cagey either about underwriting the costs entailed in an unproven venture or granting the committee a free hand in raising funds.[1] It was not permitted to actively fundraise, though it was allowed 'to receive, and prudently expend, any contributions, which may voluntarily be made by individuals, associations, or parishes, towards this object.'

In a letter sent to all ministers in Scotland, the committee's convenor, Stevenson Macgill, reported that all the funds the committee possessed amounted to a meagre £200 (maybe £19,000 in current values), considerably less than the cost of a single missionary's stipend and expenses. A year later, however, the Assembly changed its mind about the rather too narrow financial basis on which the Jewish Mission operated, promoted it to being the fifth of its official schemes, and sanctioned it to raise funds for all its objectives.[2] Shortly afterwards, at a meeting of the committee, Robert Candlish confessed that much to his embarrassment he had failed to respond to a notice in *The Missionary Record* intimating the annual collection for the work and assumed that it was unlikely that he was the only one and suggested, therefore, that a circular letter be sent to every parish, informing congregations that the committee hoped shortly to employ several missionaries and needed the finance to do so. An amazingly swift and generous response meant that the committee's report to the General Assembly of 1840 was justifiably buoyant as contributions for the year had amounted to £4,531 (around £325,000 in current values), almost double the previous year's total. Whilst this generosity allowed the committee to commence its plans, it was pointed out that unless support was sustained at this level, present commitments would soon exhaust the funds in hand.[3]

Nervous as the committee was, there was little cause for alarm, as support flooded in from every part of the Church, including far-flung colonial settlements and even from newly established indigenous congregations founded by the Church's missionaries in India and South Africa. In Canada, exiles and emigrants, driven from Scotland by the notorious Highland Clearances, established their own auxiliary societies to support the Jewish work. The pages of *The Home and Foreign Missionary Record* bear testimony to their open-handedness. More than once, the same Canadian worker sent £5. The Rev. J. Clugston of Quebec contributed £1.10, as did the Rev. Thomas Wilson of Perth in Upper Canada. In South Africa, the Rev. John Bennie of Lovedale, the Glasgow Missionary Society station in British Kaffraria on the frontier of Cape Colony, forwarded a further donation of £23 from Xhosa Christians and the missionaries. In 1841–42 the committee's accounts indicate receipts totalling £295.11.3 from 'furth of Scotland', including £143 from England, £21 from Ireland, £38 from Canada; £20 came from India and a staggering £72 from the missionaries, settlers, and Xhosa Christians in Cape Colony.[4]

It has sometimes been erroneously remarked that in Scotland the Jewish missionary work was largely a project of the wealthier city churches and the more prosperous agricultural communities, rather than something close to the hearts of the poorer folk of the Highlands and Islands. It is true that no Highland presbytery had responded to Robert Wodrow's call to petition the General Assembly of 1838 to establish a mission to the Jews, but against this a number of factors must be set.

The first consideration is the presence of Highlanders within Scotland's city churches at the time. Large scale migration from the impoverished Highlands and Islands brought many to seek employment in Glasgow's engineering shops, Dundee's jute mills, and Aberdeen's granite quarries, swelling the population of these cities considerably. It is estimated that by 1835 there were in Glasgow about twenty thousand people who only spoke Gaelic, and by the middle of the nineteenth century the urban Highland community rose to approximately forty-five thousand. In light of the relative poverty of most and the absolute poverty of some, it is remarkable that such urban working people contributed as much as they did.[5]

Inhibiting Highland Christians from engaging directly with the Church of Scotland's Jewish sachem was their suspicion of Lowland activism. Dr John Kennedy, the doughty champion of the North, conceded that whilst Highlanders did not possess that spirit of activity which distinguished Christians elsewhere, their reticence, he maintained, ought not to be exaggerated. The fact was that Highland evangelicalism channeled its missionary support through the Northern Missionary Society, which had been established in 1800 by Rev. Dr Angus Macintosh of Tain and Rev. Alexander Fraser of Kirkhill, along with other ministers of Inverness-shire, Easter Ross, and Sutherland. This together with the Easter Ross Ladies' Missionary and Bible Society, drew widespread support from the northern counties. In 1840 alone the Northern Missionary Society contributed in excess of £700 to the Jewish committee.

Many Highland Christians also held separatist, even anti-clerical tendencies. Suspicious that Moderate ministers had a disproportionate influence within the Church of Scotland and its committees, the Northern Society retained its separate identity until well after the Disruption of 1843. Only when it had gained the Highlanders' confidence was the Free Church of Scotland considered a congenial outlet for Highland missionary zeal.

Such suspicions went far to explain, if not to justify, the disinclination of the Northern members of the Jewish committee to form a sub-committee after the manner of those in Glasgow and Edinburgh. Disappointed by this, and in an attempt to coax more cooperation from the North, the 1841 General Assembly appointed John MacDonald of Urquhart, the so-called, 'Apostle of the North', perhaps the most distinguished minister of the Northern Highlands, to be a member of the Jewish committee.

On every count, it would have been strange indeed if Gaelic-speaking Christians were not keenly interested in the Jews, for they had long felt a special affinity between themselves and the Jewish people, as the enthusiastic interest shown in the baptism of Ezekiel Caspar Auerbach, nine years before the Jewish committee was established, demonstrates. Auerbach was a thirty-five-year-old Jewish man from Warsaw, Poland, who, having been converted to Christianity, was baptised by the Rev. Alexander Clark of the second charge in Inverness on 3rd March 1830. *The Inverness Journal and Northern Advertiser* reported that well before the service commenced, 'the Gaelic Church was crowded to excess, the doors and passages being completely blocked with persons anxious to witness a scene so novel in this part of the country.'[6] The *Journal's* rival, the *Inverness Courier* also commented on the warmth with which Auerbach had been welcomed into the community: 'A collection amounting to about nine pounds [current value approx. £1,200], was made at the church doors, to enable the convert to bring his family from Warsaw to this country.'[7]

Notices in the Church of Scotland's *The Home and Foreign Missionary Record* also bear witness to Highland interest. In November 1839 donations are recorded as coming from Lochgilphead, Kingussie, Duthil, Kincardine, Ullapool, Eddrachilles, Raasay, North Uist and South Uist, and Uig, Lewis. This list includes not only relatively prosperous locations, such as Kingussie, but also seriously deprived areas like Eddrachilles, Raasay, Lewis and the Uists. Indeed, throughout the Western Isles communal poverty was so widespread at this time that it was rare to charge fees for school attendance and often necessary to provide decent clothing for school children. The *Statistical Accounts of Scotland* for both 1791 and 1845 record some Hebridean church buildings as being 'very wretched', or even, in some places, 'a mere hut,' yet, from such congregations there came generous support for the mission.[8]

A letter to *The Home and Foreign Missionary Record* from the minister of the impoverished parish of Knock on the Isle of Lewis testifies to the liberality of his people in sending a donation for

£12.10.2. The sacrificial nature of this gift is all the more evident when just two years previously Knock had been one of the Lewis parishes to receive official famine relief. It is also astonishing that such islanders were able to find cash for donations when the cash economy had virtually ceased to exist and even the modest fees of the heavily subsidised local schools were usually paid in fish, mutton, eggs, fowls, and butter.[9]

It may be true that Highland overtures to the General Assembly were lacking, but Highland hearts were liberal in support of missions generally and the Jewish mission particularly and these donations came with the prayers of the people. Giving us a typical insight of the Highland spirit is the anecdote recorded by Dr John Macleod in *By-paths of Highland Church History* about a man known as Dòmhnull na h-ùrnaigh, or 'Donald of the prayers,' who was so moved after hearing his minister speak of the Jewish mission that he walked a considerable distance from his home to the manse to take a contribution. But on his way home, Donald, reflecting on his contribution, thought he had not been sufficiently liberal and so he retraced his steps to donate a further generous sum.[10]

In the early years of Queen Victoria's reign many women's Christian associations had been established in Scotland for the benefit of a wide variety of educational, social, and missionary causes, including the excellent Female Penny Societies. These grassroots organisations had their counterparts among the wealthy and aristocratic, who were celebrated for their almost brazen zeal in raising money for missions. When someone from Scotland visited the missionaries in India he was concerned to discover there was inadequate money to fund a special project, so he promptly wrote to his sister, a lady of influence living in the Highlands, saying, 'Could not you ladies, who are so good at begging, set to work to get up a subscription?' The response was immediate and £1,000 [approx. £141,000 today] was sent off.[11]

Mrs Henrietta Smith of Dunesk, whose foresight led her to prevail upon Dr Candlish to bank her gift of one hundred guineas for a work that did not then exist, was characteristic of other Christian women of her status. In time she became Lady Henrietta Erskine, following the death in 1829 of her uncle, the Earl of Buchan, but she much preferred to be known simply as Henrietta Smith. Her name occurs frequently in lists of subscribers to the Jewish mission as one of its most generous supporters.[12]

In 1839, she embarked on an imaginative source of funding by purchasing land at Beltana in South Australia, which she let, investing the proceeds in her favourite missionary projects. As well as the Jewish mission, these included donations to the Smith of Dunesk Mission to the aborigines of Beltana, later run by the Australian Inland Mission, whose Rev. John Flynn (1880–1950), minister, missionary and aviator, founded the celebrated Australian Royal Flying Doctor Service.[13]

Amongst Henrietta Smith's many donations was £52 contributed to the expenses of the survey party sent to Palestine. M'Cheyne and Bonar's subsequent published account of the deputation's activities so delighted her that, at her death in 1873, she left a considerable sum for a mission station in Palestine. This legacy also lay in the bank accumulating interest before being used to finance Dr David Torrance's work at Tiberius and Tzfat. Henrietta Smith worked tirelessly to raise funds from her wide circle of acquaintances.[14]

Elisabeth, the sixth and last Duchess of Gordon, was one of the last of a notable group of aristocratic evangelical ladies that had included the Countess of Leven, Viscountess Glenorchy, Lady Jane Nimmo, and Lady Mary Hamilton whose combined contribution to the spiritual life of Scotland is incalculable. As Elisabeth Brodie, twenty four years his junior, she married George Gordon Duncan, the spendthrift Marquess of Huntly, who in 1827 became the Duke of Gordon. She was close to Queen Adelaide, wife of William IV and described by her rather frivolous and fashionable contemporary, Elizabeth Grant of Rothiemurchus, as 'good, and rich, but neither clever nor handsome', with 'upright principles, good sense, and … a first-rate woman of business.' This commendation was spoiled by a fatuous and inaccurate remark that: 'In her later years she got into the cant of the Methodists.'[15]

Not Presbyterian but Scottish Episcopal by upbringing, the Duchess of Gordon, by force of character, obtained from the Bishop of Moray his reluctant permission for the Church of England's Book of Common Prayer, rather than the less acceptable Scottish

Episcopal liturgy, to be used at Gordon Chapel, Fochabers. After the death of her husband in 1836 she became more openly supportive of the Evangelical cause within the Church of Scotland and when it was established in 1843 she joined the Free Church of Scotland.[16]

Although there seems to be no record of any financial contribution to the Jewish mission directly attributable to the Duchess of Gordon, there can be no doubt of her interest in and support for the work. In November 1840, in the midst of the non-intrusion controversy, she received at her Aberdeenshire home, Huntly Lodge, Thomas Chalmers, Robert M'Cheyne, Andrew Bonar, and Alexander Moody-Stuart, who were simultaneously active in the Church struggle and the establishment of the Jewish mission. She invited Bonar to return to give a drawing room lecture on his journey to Palestine.

After 1841, a particularly warm friendship developed between the Duchess and the members of the mission established at Budapest, especially the Duncans and the Wingates. When in 1844 the Wingates returned briefly to Scotland, she invited William to act as her chaplain at Huntly Lodge. Encouraged and probably initiated by the Budapest missionaries, a cordial friendship developed between the Duchess of Gordon and Maria Dorothea, the Hungarian Archduchess. Letters were exchanged, albeit with necessary circumspection owing to Maria Dorothea's exposed position in the higher echelons of staunchly Catholic Habsburg government. On at least one occasion the Duchess of Gordon sent Maria Dorothea gifts as tokens of her prayers and support. In 1846, when Maria Dorothea visited her mother, the Duchess Henrietta of Wurttemberg, the Duchess of Gordon and her nieces, accompanied by Dr Keith were invited to stay with them at Kirchheim in Germany providing for the Archduchess a rare opportunity of Christian fellowship.[17] In October 1848, during a time of political crisis and revolution in Hungary, the Duchess of Gordon wrote to the committee, expressing her deep concern for the welfare of the missionaries and their patroness, 'I feel most deeply interested in all that concerns your Hungarian Mission and our beloved Archduchess. The accounts are really most fearful, but the Lord reigneth.'[18] The Duchess of Gordon is the only woman commemorated in James Wylie's *Disruption Worthies: A Memorial of 1843*.

Another aristocratic benefactor of the Jewish mission was Lady Janet Colquhoun of Luss, who also subscribed £50 towards the expenses of the deputation to Palestine, collected further funds for that venture, and made other generous donations. An anonymous lady made it known through Robert M'Cheyne that she was ready to fully fund a school for Jewish children on the continent; she may have been the Mrs Baxter through whose gift the Edinburgh Ladies Association on Behalf of Jewish Females established a school at Posen in Prussia (now in Poland).

Not only adroit at fund raising, such women boldly brought to the attention of the committee and the wider church the particular concerns of Jewish women, ardently championing the social and religious rights of their Jewish sisters, particularly those living in traditional closed orthodox communities. Arguing that 'the case of the Jewess in all countries where the Talmud holds its dominion is indeed a very sad one', they protested against discriminatory traditions that denied women the opportunity of studying the Torah, considering that such exclusions were a 'haughty contempt for the female mind.'

They vociferously complained about the traditional disqualification of Jewish women as legal witnesses and were outraged by their exclusion from the synagogue *minyan* – the quorum of ten men required as a precondition of synagogue worship. In their eyes, this tradition was motivated by a 'proud and presumptuous contempt of women.' They abhorred the use of the *Birkot Hashachar* (Morning Blessings), daily recited by Jewish men to bless God for not making them a gentile, a slave, or a woman. All such demeaning of their Jewish sisters, they said, condemned them to lives of illiteracy, superstition, and a preoccupation with trivia such as dress and personal appearance. They took it as nothing less than a calling from God to strive for a greater degree of equality between the sexes, such as they had established at their school at Posen, where Jewish girls were taught the Scriptures along with Jewish boys.[19]

Nor were women of the Edinburgh Ladies Association deferential to the male-dominated church structures and were remarkably robust in their dealings with the Jewish mission committee. For example, they stipulated, as a precondition of their financial support, regular accurate and transparent reports from the committee's secretary. They also expressed their disapproval of what they considered the tardiness of the Jewish committee in arriving at and implementing its decisions. For example, the Edinburgh Ladies Association public report for 1841 testily expressed annoyance that the women they had recruited as teachers, who were ready and eager to take up their posts, were being held back by what they considered the inordinate time taken by the Jewish committee to reach a decision on the most suitable location for its first mission station.[20] The appeal by the Edinburgh ladies for the formation of women's associations throughout the Church met with good success and groups were established in Glasgow, London, Inverness, and in rural Stirlingshire. In consultation with each other, each of these associations adopted particular areas of the work: Edinburgh raised support for Constantinople, Glasgow took an interest in Palestine, and Paisley was involved with Budapest. The Dundee Ladies Association promised to contribute to a mission school a first donation of £40 and then subscribe £35 each year subsequently, but only on condition 'that the Conductor or Conductors of the School communicate directly with the Association furnishing such information as may interest the subscribers.'[21] In the meantime, they all got on with organising prayer meetings, raising financial support, and recruiting women teachers to supervise mission schools overseas.

Women participated directly in mission to the Jewish people, including converts such as Elizabeth Saphir. Unlike the London Missionary Society, whose preposterous rules stipulated that it much preferred 'to avoid all incumbrances of families,' the Church of Scotland saw neither wives nor children as hindrances to missionary endeavour. Although not obliged to be anything other than their husbands' wives, many missionary wives, and sometimes daughters too, voluntarily and enthusiastically took on a full burden of work.

In his biography of his wife, Margaret, John Wilson of Mumbai, praised her commitment and involvement in organising six girl's schools, training teachers, and visiting children and parents at home. She personally taught several Jewish women to read. Wilson appreciatively added:

> During my long journeys she managed, with much fidelity and prudence, the general concerns of the mission, and she always freed me from many secular cares connected with its business ... she ever communicated with me the most valuable counsel, and the most exciting encouragement in my work.[22]

Children also made a distinctive contribution. From earliest days of the mission the pages of *The Home and Foreign Missionary Record* were enlivened with colourful and sometimes poignant accounts of money received from children: three children from Glasgow sent six shillings and sixpence; five shillings came from children in Culross; three and tuppence was the produce of a piggy-bank, and, most touchingly, a mother sent £1, the accumulated pocket money of her recently deceased son, just seven years old. Five boys met weekly for prayer and kept a missionary box which, when full, yielded two shillings and sixpence, which was forwarded to Edinburgh on their behalf by their minister, the Rev. John Bonar.[23]

Moreover, children were encouraged to practice simple acts of self-denial, so that their donations would be from their own meagre funds rather than passed from parent to child to the mission work. One child was commended for accumulating sixpence as a result of 'taking his tea, for a time, without sugar.'

The publication, in 1845, of the Free Church of Scotland's imaginative *Children's Missionary Record* was a milestone in engaging children with missions, arousing and sustaining their curiosity and enthusiasm. This monthly illustrated periodical was attractively produced in a small size, measuring approximately 5¼" x 3½", priced at one halfpenny, and most issues were between twelve and twenty pages long. Young people were enthused by accounts of God's international work from all places where the Free Church had missionary activity, as well as by stories from other parts of the world, and historical articles.

During its first year of production, Dr Makellar, convenor of the Board of Mission and Education, reported that the paper had achieved the amazing circulation of 25,000 copies per month, which by 1846 rose to 32,000. Children were not patronised, but considered serious partners in mission. Articles called them to engage in regular prayer and financial stewardship, thus giving them openings for active involvement in mission, rather than being offered a passive fascination with romantic stories of faraway places.[24] A regular feature was the publication of lists of 'Juvenile Offerings' from Sabbath Schools, children's associations, and missionary boxes. These could be lengthy; one in 1845 covered twelve pages, despite the omission of any contributions from the children of the Highlands and Islands owing to the destitution inflicted during the 'Hungry Forties'. By 1850 there were thirty-five pages of financial statistics, in three columns, acknowledging that children's donations that year totalled over £1,450 from all parts of Scotland: from Coldstream in the south, to Stromness, Orkney, in the north, from the populous central belt to Stornoway in the Western Isles, as well as contributions from the children of emigrant Scots in Australia and Canada. That year thirteen missionary projects benefited and the sum earmarked for the Jewish Mission exceeded £258, making it the best supported missionary project of the Church.[25]

Projects designed to stimulate the imagination of children included calculating the distance that would be covered if their total offerings were paid in half-pennies (each with a diameter of one and an eighth inches) when laid side by side. Using the old measure, one child calculated this very precisely as three miles, two furlongs, thirty-four poles, eight yards, and one and an eighth inches. Young Sandy Moffat informed the editor that the boys in his class had worked out that the sum of all the donations made that year to the Free Church would, if contributed in ha'pennies, stretch from his village, Bridge of Weir in Renfrewshire, to Dr Duff's school in Kolkata, India.[26]

Children were not only encouraged to work, give and pray for overseas missions, they were also persuaded to share the gospel directly with their contemporaries. Some articles give us an insight into why the Free Church spread so rapidly in Scotland: one was entitled 'Children should be Missionaries,' and called upon its readers to be active Christian witnesses at home, whilst another urged that, 'every Christian, old and young, high and low, may be, ought to be, a missionary.'[27]

The magazine informed its readers about Jews and Judaism as well as the Jewish mission itself. One issue carried an account by Dr Keith of the personnel needed for the Jewish mission, and another featured a letter from Elizabeth Saphir in Budapest about her brother starting a girl's school in the city, the same one where, a century later, Jane Haining became matron.

Shortly after the launch of *The Children's Missionary Record*, Dr Makellar expressed his hope that its pages would sow the good seed of the kingdom in young minds.[28] His longing was well founded: the magazine proved to be an investment in the future. By stimulating the missionary interest of its young people, the Free Church of Scotland was able, in later years, both to staff and support its growing missionary work overseas, including its Jewish mission, as well as many evangelistic initiatives at home.

With sacrificial and prayerful giving, the growth of informed interest and widespread popular enthusiasm, the Committee for the Conversion of the Jews had every reason to believe itself well supported by the wider Church. From its leaders in the Assembly to the women of the Church, from the landed gentry and their wives to young children, from the booming industrial Lowlands to the impoverished Highlands and Islands, there was, as William Hanna later put it, 'a general and cordial support'.[29] The committee, with a grateful heart, was well resourced to turn its prayerful hopes into a practical venture.

<⟫ 8 ⟪>

Where in the World?
Scotland, 1838

ONE of the most important tasks now facing the Committee on the Conversion of the Jews was to identify locations suitable for establishing the mission. The first step in the process was to circulate two questionnaires to ministers and church leaders at home and overseas. The first concerned areas where Jewish people lived, asking for estimates of the size of Jewish populations, information about the economic, cultural, and educational circumstances, and if the community might be open to missionary work, and if not, what were the local prejudices against Christianity. It asked if any attempts had been made at evangelism and, if so, what approaches had been used and which had been most successful. Correspondents were asked who they thought might be most suitable to undertake evangelism: gentile ministers or Jewish Christians.[1]

The second, more general questionnaire sought to assess the willingness of the church at home to provide long-term support to the mission: Were there persons in the parish with a special interest in the Jewish people? Was there a local auxiliary or missionary society that could raise funds for the committee's work? Could the minister make any relevant observations? Finally, it posed the financial question, asking if the local minister was willing to press the claims of the Jewish mission upon the liberality of his people.

Many of the correspondents suggested opening missionary work in such places as Tunis, Egypt, and Aden, all with ancient Jewish communities. To us today it might seem bizarre to suggest Jamaica, but at the time it had a sizeable Jewish community which had been established in 1654 when a ship carrying Jews from Recife in Brazil to Holland was waylaid by Spanish frigates and escorted to Jamaica, for its captain and crew to be charged with violating the laws of the Inquisition. Those on board were freed only after convincing their captors that they were not *Marranos*, clandestine Spanish Jews masquerading as Catholics.[2]

Naturally, India was considered. Not only were Scottish Christians well aware, through the pages of the *Edinburgh Christian Instructor*, of the visits of Claudius Buchanan to the Bene-Israel, but had also had the claims of India's Jews pressed on their attention by John Wilson, who directly reminded the committee that the Mumbai community had a strong claim on their attention, not least because of the increasing number of Jewish children attending the General Assembly's English School, many of whom had excelled academically.

In his reports, Wilson separated Bene-Israelites from other Jews on the grounds that the old established Bene-Israel community distinguished itself from the increasing number of Jewish businessmen emigrating to the region. Yet, however they chose to designate themselves, Wilson saw in Mumbai an important field of operation which deserved to be reinforced. The arguments in favour were clear: the community was the largest body of Jewish people in the British Empire; they were very willing to receive instruction in Christianity; the British Government would protect any missionary stationed in Mumbai; and the Assembly's school could be utilised for ministerial and missionary training without incurring extra expense.

As a missionary strategist, Wilson also saw the significance for the surrounding region if Jewish work were to be commenced in Mumbai, from whence the gospel could radiate southwards to the Cochin Jews of the Malabar coast, north-west to the Yemenite Jews on the coast of Arabia, and, following in the tracks of Henry Martyn, reach out to the large Persian Jewish community. The impact on the local Hindu population of the conversion of Bene-Israel would, he argued, be considerable. So, all things considered, there was no place in all Asia, with the possible exception of the Holy Land itself, that appeared to be more suitable than Mumbai as the headquarters of a mission to the Jews. The thought not only appealed to the committee, it unsettled them. Even as it prepared to send delegates to survey the Jewish communities of Europe and Palestine, it continued to seriously ponder Wilson's proposals. In the event, however, no missionary would be sent to work amongst India's Jews until 1844, when the German Jewish Christian, Nathan 'Edward' Laseron went to Cochin as the first missionary of the post-Disruption Church of Scotland.[3] Laseron died in Udhagamandalam (Ootacamund) in December 1868.[4]

As well as Mumbai, Wilson pressed the suitability of the port of Aden, on the southern edge of the Arabian peninsula, as a base for reaching the two-hundred-thousand-strong Yemenite Jewish community, reputedly descended from traders sent by Solomon to Arabia. Aden's potential had recently been greatly enhanced by the Sultan of Lahej ceding to the British Government a large swathe of his territory, including Aden. In 1839, the year after the questionnaire was circulated, the East India Company landed marines to secure the port, thus bringing to an end the piracy which had plagued the Persian Gulf and hindered shipping, and thereby curtailing the influence of the Ottoman Empire.

Aden's claims were supported by both Dr Alexander Keith and the pioneer Indian missionary, Dr Alexander Duff. Robert Candlish, the editor of *The Home and Foreign Missionary Record*, was also enthusiastic, writing: 'We trust, and earnestly pray that God may enable us to take possession of that station ... as soon as it can be considered practicable.' Dr Alexander Moody Stuart of St. Luke's, Edinburgh, informed the committee that a person in his congregation had subscribed £200 towards the support of a missionary there, and their Kirk Session had voted another £150. A public statement was distributed which revealed the committee's mind: 'We feel encouraged to occupy without delay this field which the Lord has given in the hope that it may soon have the fragrance of a field which the Lord has blessed.' Everything now seemed to point in the direction of Aden.[5]

As if to confirm that God was directing the committee towards Aden, two well-qualified ministers now offered themselves for missionary service, both of whom the committee thought eminently suitable for Arabia. They were John Duncan, then minister of

Milton Church, Glasgow, and William Chalmers Burns, later to be associated with revivals at Kilsyth and Dundee before becoming a pioneer missionary to China. The committee was inclined to accept both and so Candlish was instructed to consult officials in London who assured him that the Government and the East India Company would support a mission in Aden and give it every protection possible. [6]

It seemed all sewn up: the two new missionaries would proceed to Mumbai for acclimatisation and thence to Aden to open the new mission station. Yet these plans all came to nothing. The imagined potential of Aden and the assumed ease of reaching the Yemenite Jews had misled the committee; acting somewhat impulsively and imprudently it had allowed Aden a disproportionate place in its planning.

There would be no mission to the Yemenite Jews of Arabia. In 1884 the Free Church sent Ion Keith-Falconer to commence evangelistic mission to the general population of Aden, utilising both medicine and education. After only a brief time Keith-Falconer contracted malaria and died of it in 1887.[7] The Scottish Mission school and hospital he established continued until the ejection of missionaries from the territory in the 1960s, but apart from that tiny beachhead, evangelistic mission never reached the Yemeni hinterland and certainly not the Jewish community. Between June 1849 and September 1950, through Operation Magic Carpet, the Israeli government relocated the majority of Yemenite Jews to Israel.

In 1839, however, the committee had to re-examine the claims of the other possible locations, both exotic and mundane, which included places nearer home. John Duncan saw great potential in London.[8] Other European locations were also suggested, but it was, of course, imperative that the claims of the southern Levant, the region of Palestine, the so-called Holy Land, should be seriously considered. To avoid any further disillusionment to its supporters, the committee decided, at the suggestion of Dr Candlish, to make no statements for the time being, but patiently await the report of the group commissioned to survey Europe and Palestine.

Attention now turned to the task of choosing members for the deputation. The first three selected were Dr Alexander Black of Aberdeen, Robert Murray M'Cheyne of Dundee, and his friend

Andrew A. Bonar of Collace in Perthshire. The great advocate for mission to Jewish people, Robert Wodrow, was also appointed, but as he was unwell, he, with great regret, declined the committee's invitation. Matters were pressing, passages had been booked for the survey team to sail from Dover on 13th April, making it urgent to find a fourth member. Hurriedly, at almost the eleventh hour, the committee invited Dr Keith to take Wodrow's place. This quite literally turned out to be an inspired choice.[9]

Who then were these men who were entrusted with directing the choice of the Church of Scotland's first mission station among the Jewish people? The most senior was Alexander Black, born in Aberdeen in 1789, whose father John was a small-scale horticulturalist owning a few fields near Aberdeen. Possessed of academic gifts, Black studied medicine at Marischal College, before training for the Christian ministry. As a student his intellectual prowess was remarkable, but perhaps even more remarkable was his confidence in his own ability. When, around 1816, a vacancy occurred for the Chair of Divinity at Kings College, Aberdeen, the twenty-seven year-old confidently offered himself as a candidate. He successfully took all the prescribed examinations and, although he was not appointed, his competence attracted the attention of the Earl of Aberdeen who in 1817 introduced him to the charge of Tarves, a small parish near Old Meldrum in Aberdeenshire, where he was ordained and inducted the following year. Black was awarded the degree of Doctor of Divinity in 1831, when only thirty-three years old, and the following year appointed Professor of Divinity at Marischal College.

Apart from knowing that he was shy and retiring yet immensely able, little has come down to us about the man. There is no biography, and not a single sermon of his appears to have survived to give us insight into the man who was so highly regarded in his own day. Hew Scott in *Fasti Ecclesiae Scoticanae* mentions two elusive works attributed to him: *On the Progressive Diffusion of Divine Knowledge* (published Aberdeen: D. Chalmers; 1824) and an *Address at Annual Examination of Merton's English Classes* (Aberdeen, 1838). All we have from his pen that is easily retrievable is the lecture he delivered in Glasgow on behalf of the Jewish mission, but, as we will see,

Black's greatest contribution to the success of the Jewish mission was not academic, it was a fall from a camel.

Black's selection was based largely on his skill as an exceptional Hebraist and linguist, as well as his wide knowledge of Jewish and rabbinical literature. Thomas Guthrie once said of Alexander Black and John Duncan that together they were so competent in languages ancient and modern they could talk their way to the Great Wall of China.[10] He was not exaggerating. Black spoke nineteen languages and could correspond in twelve. Duncan, of whom we shall read more later, spoke and wrote Hebrew and all its cognate languages, was familiar with at least four Indian languages, as well as ancient Sanskrit, had a high degree of fluency in many European languages, and spoke and wrote remarkably elegant Latin.

Dr Alexander Keith was a son of Dr George Skene Keith, minister of Keith Hall, Aberdeenshire. Like Black, he was educated at Marischal College, and licensed to preach in March 1813. He was presented to the parish of St Cyrus, Kincardineshire, by no less a person than the Prince Regent. Ordained in August 1816, in December of the same year, he married Jane Blackie, the daughter of an Aberdonian plumber. Keith was no linguist – as Andrew Bonar remarked he could scarcely speak any language – but nevertheless had such a kind and winning way that he never failed to get what he wanted.

As we have noted, Keith was fascinated by the way in which fulfilled biblical prophecy confirmed the general truth of Scripture and he wrote a number of widely acclaimed books on the subject. The first of these, *Evidences of the Truth of the Christian Religion Derived from the Literal Fulfilment of Prophecy*, was provoked by David Hume's sceptical view of miracles in his work *Of Miracles*, Section X of *Enquiry Concerning Human Reason*, and so established Keith's reputation that it won him his place in the survey party. *Evidences of Prophecy* became a standard text for the study of Christian apologetics and was translated into many other languages, including Arabic and Persian. Thomas Chalmers highly regarded it both as a textbook for theological students and as a work of Christian literature suitable for every Christian home in Scotland.

Published in 1823 and enlarged in 1828, the 1848 edition of *Evidences of Prophecy* was one of the first books to have been illustrated by the use of photographs. When the survey group departed for Palestine, the calotype photographic process was a brand new invention by W. H. Fox Talbot, who had first demonstrated its success to the Royal Institution in January 1839. Although the chemical formula used to prepare photographic paper was a highly guarded secret, Talbot, who had read *Evidences of Prophecy* on holiday in 1834, shared the formula with a few photographic pioneers, including his friend Principal David Brewster of St. Andrews University, Robert Adamson, the first professional to use the process in Scotland, and Keith's sons, George Skene and Thomas, founder members of the Photographic Society of Scotland. Alexander Keith set out on the survey with a cumbersome calotype camera and the processing apparatus in the hope of recording images.[11] Regrettably, perhaps to a lack of patience and the necessary skills to use this process in the field, the supply of light sensitive paper was spoiled and he returned empty-handed. In 1844 he revisited the region with his son, this time using the daguerreotype process, and managed to capture some of the first photographic images ever made of Palestine, from which the engravings illustrating the 1848 edition of *Evidences of Prophecy* were produced.

Amazingly, a copy of *Evidences of Prophecy* found its way into the hand of Maria Dorothea, the Archduchess of Hungary, and contributed very significantly to her kindly disposition towards the mission generally and to Keith and Black personally, especially when Black became dangerously ill in Pesth. But more of that later.

The committee's third choice, was Robert Murray M'Cheyne.[12] In 1838, two concerns were playing upon Robert Smith Candlish's mind, the need to gather information for the committee and the equally pressing needs of his twenty-five-year-old colleague and friend, Robert M'Cheyne. Well-known, even in his own day, for an unfeigned godliness, M'Cheyne had significant additional qualities that recommended him as a candidate for the survey. As a boy he had learned Greek, and at Edinburgh University excelled in Hebrew, being able with some fluency to hold a conversation in the language. He also had theological, pastoral, artistic, musical, and poetical gifts, as well being interested in the fulfillment of prophecy. In 1836 he had been inducted as the first minister of St. Peter's, a new church established in a burgeoning industrial area of Dundee, where grim tenements provided unsanitary and overcrowded housing for many of his congregation. Young, enthusiastic, and somewhat radical, M'Cheyne threw himself into the work, introducing many innovations into his new charge. As a result of his diligent visitation in the impoverished districts in the parish, M'Cheyne contracted typhoid, further weakening an already frail constitution and contributing to his early death in March 1843.

In October 1838 M'Cheyne invited Joseph S. C. F. Frey, a Jewish Christian, to preach at a mid-week meeting at St. Peter's. Frey, a founder of the LSPCJ, had, in the wake of the baptismal dispute, severed his links with that society and by 1816 had taken up work in New York with The Society for Ameliorating the Condition of the Jews. Frey's visit to Dundee made a very deep and lasting impression on M'Cheyne, who recorded in his diary, 'A Jew preached in my church, Mr Frey, to a crowded house. Felt much moved in hearing an Israelite after the flesh.'

Robert M'Cheyne has been typecast as a young man rather more in touch with his feminine side than with his masculinity, a caricature not helped by his reputation for poor health and his untimely death, as well as the few images we have of a rather wan and other-worldly young man, with finely drawn features, a weak mouth, and neatly curled side locks, swept away from a fashionable central parting. The first biography, the highly regarded *Memoir of M'Cheyne*, written by his close friend Andrew Bonar, was admirable in many regards, but perhaps pandered too much to the voracious Victorian appetite for sentimental hagiography. William Garden Blaikie rubbed salt into the wound when he claimed in his *Preachers of Scotland* (1888) that M'Cheyne 'brought to the Scottish pulpit an almost feminine quality.'[13] Alexander Smellie's 1913 biography, sustained the myth by too free a use of epithets such as 'gentle' and 'delicate', until in the 1950's one evangelical author referred to him as 'a perfumed arrow.'[14]

But M'Cheyne's classic Grecian nose gives the lie to the stereotype. In his recent research on biometrics, Dr Adrian Evans, of the University of Bath, has argued that men with Grecian noses, like M'Cheyne, or for that matter, Admiral Lord Nelson, often turn out to be tough, resilient, down-to-earth, and efficient, exactly the kind of people you want to be near in a crisis. As well as possessing artistic flair, moderate competence as an illustrator, and some real poetic skill, M'Cheyne was also athletic, greatly enjoying the outdoors, and little troubled when he and a friend had to sleep rough when lost in the mist in Strathardle.[15]

In his autobiography, Thomas Guthrie confirms that M'Cheyne was no 'ascetic, no stiff and formal man, but ready for any innocent and healthful amusement', and records how, in 1837, he and M'Cheyne had travelled together to Errol in Aberdeenshire to stay with their friend James Grierson, the minister. On arrival, M'Cheyne decided to try out some gymnastic apparatus which had been set up in the manse garden and, exuberantly rushing at the equipment, went through a number of 'athletic manoeuvres.' Hanging upside down by his hands and feet about six feet above the ground, M'Cheyne was throwing out a challenge to Guthrie to do better, when the pole from which he was suspended suddenly snapped and he fell to the ground with an ominous thud. He was carried into the manse, where for some days he lay injured. Although he recovered sufficiently to go about his normal business, it was said he was never the same again.[16] Despite that mishap, two years later, M'Cheyne's vigour and courage would be further demonstrated by finding a way in darkness for himself and Andrew Bonar to escape Bedouin raiders lurking in the woods of Mt Tabor, and again one Sunday afternoon in Poland when he was assaulted by two shepherds and fought them to a standstill, whereupon they ran off empty-handed.[17]

But none of that is to deny an underlying health condition. In 1839, M'Cheyne was suffering heart palpitations which compelled him, under doctor's orders, to lay down his pastoral responsibilities in Dundee and retire temporarily to his parent's home at 20 Hill Street, Edinburgh, for a complete rest. It was during this time he struck up a close friendship with Robert Candlish and his wife, with whom he would often dine. The kindly Candlish, ten years

M'Cheyne's senior, burdened by concern for his young friend, was one afternoon walking through Ainslie Place in Edinburgh's New Town, when he bumped into his former assistant, Alexander Moody Stuart. Years later, Moody Stuart recalled the meeting and their discussing the advice of M'Cheyne's doctor that he go abroad for the benefit of his health. Candlish immediately connected M'Cheyne's need with that of the committee's and suggested to Moody Stuart that both could be addressed by appointing M'Cheyne to the deputation to Palestine. Moody Stuart immediately agreed and, with his usual alacrity, Candlish sped off to follow up the matter and win the committee's approval. He broke the news to M'Cheyne who enthusiastically accepted the invitation.[18]

The thought of missionary involvement was not new to M'Cheyne. As a student, his reading of missionary classics such as the memoirs of Henry Martyn and the life of David Brainerd, challenged him to consider his own readiness to become a missionary. Martyn's life, in particular, led him to examine his willingness to sacrifice everything for the cause of the gospel, leading him to say, 'Would I could imitate him, giving up father, mother, house, health, life, all – for Christ. And yet, what hinders?'[19] Likewise, Brainerd's deep love for Christ and the American Indians also moved M'Cheyne. He wrote, 'Most wonderful man! To-night, more set upon missionary enterprise than ever.' By June 1833, however, M'Cheyne was perplexed as he feared that the motives behind his aspiration to missionary service might not have been the highest, and his interest in mission generated by self-interest, asking himself if he was too much in love with the romance of mission and the popularity a missionary career might give him in the eye of the public.

Mixed motives or not, M'Cheyne was willing to go anywhere he believed God was directing him. So much so, that when invited to become the minister of Collace in Perthshire, before his close friend Andrew Bonar was settled there, he wrote to the Session Clerk, J. M. Nairne, to say that he sought to see his way forward by trusting, if with somewhat naive faith, in his heavenly Father: 'I am willing to move,' he wrote, 'whether it be to Africa or India. I have little courage – little anything – but I just give my hand to him as a little child does, and he leads me and I am happy.'[20] Around about the same time as he wrote these words M'Cheyne heard Dr Alexander Duff, the Church of Scotland's pioneer missionary to India, speak in Stirling and was so moved by the experience that it led him to respond spontaneously with the words, 'I am now made willing, if God shall open the way, to go to India. Here I am; send me!' M'Cheyne's keen interest in the international spread of the gospel and his prayerful commitment to those who were involved in the task remained constant throughout all his life. Andrew Bonar recalled how 'to the last day of his life, his thoughts often turned to foreign lands.' Indeed, one of the last letters he ever wrote was to the secretary of a missionary association in Edinburgh, expressing his interest in their work. [21]

Although some were concerned that M'Cheyne's health might prove insufficiently robust for such an arduous undertaking as a trip to Palestine, others were entirely encouraging. Alexander Cumming, writing to accept an invitation to preach at a St Peter's communion, said he was delighted and earnestly hoped that no obstacles would be put in his way, convinced that if he went abroad he would return to his people with a blessing. And so it turned out to be.

No matter how solicitous they might have been over the wellbeing of their minister, the members of the St. Peter's congregation were also conscious of their own needs, wondering how they might fare in M'Cheyne's absence. Vocalising both their affection and their honest worries, one of their number, Alexander Flemming, touchingly asked him: 'Dearly Beloved Pastor, if it is ordained that you are to leave us what will become of all the sweet Monday evenings that we have spent out of your own loving desire for our spiritual welfare?'[22]

The St. Peter's Kirk Session, however, acceded to the wishes of the committee with all twenty-five elders signing a moving letter of farewell and God-speed to their minister.

> And now, what remains from us but for the present to say, Farewell. May the God of all grace & all consolation be the companion of your journey. May he uphold your soul by rich communications of his love. May he conduct you in safety to the place of your destination: and when your feet stand amid the ruins of the once glorious temple

on that Mount Zion which is 'beautiful for situation, the joy of the whole earth' may the Spirit himself come down upon you 'as the dew of Hermon, even the dew that descended upon the mountains of Zion: There may the Lord command the blessing, even life for evermore!' Again we commend you to the keeping of the God of Abraham, and of Isaac, and of Jacob; and with every expression of affection and esteem, we remain,

Yours most sincerely.[23]

Candlish had also enthusiastically nominated his former parish assistant at St. George's, M'Cheyne's closest friend – later to become his biographer – the twenty-eight year old minister of Collace, Andrew Bonar.[24] Even before he felt able to profess Christian faith, Bonar's interest in the Jewish people had been awakened by the preaching of Thomas Jones, a Welshman, who was minister of Lady Glenorchy's Chapel at Upper Greenside Lane in Edinburgh, where the Bonar family were members and where one of Andrew's brothers, John, served as Session Clerk. His interest was further piqued by the preaching of John Purves, Jones' assistant in Edinburgh. As we have noticed, Bonar was also influenced by the flamboyant and eccentric Edward Irving. As an impressionable nineteen-year-old student, Bonar listened with rapt attention to Irving's lectures on prophecy during the General Assembly of 1828 and in spite of Irving's many foibles and theological aberrations, some of which led to a trial for heresy and his deposition from the ministry of the Church of Scotland, Bonar remained an ardent premillennialist throughout his long life.

As a student in Edinburgh, and later when visiting the city from Jedburgh, Bonar longed to meet some of the city's small Jewish community, and in October 1829 he visited the synagogue in Richmond Court.[25] In 1836, when invited to become Candlish's assistant at St. George's, Bonar took this as a special call from God to witness to Jewish people. As he saw it, he had been sent to the capital 'for the sake of drawing attention to the Jews, and being able to do something for them.' As a parish missionary, working from the Rose Street Hall, he had numerous opportunities to meet Jewish people, and even taught some of their children in the church school.

In June 1837, Bonar engaged in an evangelistic conversation with a Jewish man called Joseph Leo, who asked for further instruction and, to Bonar's great delight, two months later, publicly professed his faith in Christ by being baptised and becoming a member of the St. George's congregation.[26] To Bonar, such personal contacts were highly significant; they were direct answers to his prayers. Writing to Alexander Sommerville he asked, 'Now, Alic, is there not something from God in all this? Is not Christ saying to me that I am right in peculiarly loving Israel?'[27]

Bonar would not himself have the pleasure of baptising a Jewish believer into the fellowship of the Church until more than forty years later, on 2 July, 1882, when he was minister of Finnieston Free Church of Scotland in Glasgow. He recorded the event in his diary: 'In the evening I baptized the Jew, Marcus Buck. I bless God that I have had this privilege in my ministry before its close.'[28]

Convinced that his interest in the Jewish people was the result of God's prompting, Bonar undertook to equip himself for witness. He bought a Hebrew Bible, complete with Rabbinic notes, and prayed earnestly that he might learn to read it with the same facility as he had earlier learned Latin or Greek. It turned out as he hoped and prayed. He progressed rapidly in the language and, with moderate fluency, was able to converse with Jewish people he met in his travels.

Bonar's contact with Jewish people in Edinburgh quickened his hope that their national conversion would speedily become a reality. This led him to become a member of the Edinburgh Society for Promoting Christianity among the Jews and to serve on its committee, becoming secretary in 1838. Like his mentor Thomas Chalmers, Bonar fervently believed that Jewish missions ought to have priority in the missionary programme of the Church and was elated when the Church of Scotland began to take seriously the challenge of Jewish mission. Nevertheless, he was unsettled by Candlish's suggestion that he join the survey deputation.

Candlish's nomination did not go unchallenged. The Glasgow subcommittee questioned Bonar's suitability. Alexander Somerville, who had been present at a meeting when doubts had been voiced, wrote a summary of what had been said for M'Cheyne, admitting he too felt uncertain regarding their friend's place in the group.

The problem, as Somerville saw it was Bonar's obsession with premillennialism, something that he thought was 'going to his head' and which might 'knock the prospect of his going on the head.'[29] Although Sommerville notified M'Cheyne of the committee's reservations, from what remains of their correspondence it is not at all clear that Bonar himself fully understood why his place was in doubt. Writing to M'Cheyne on 8th March 1839, he expressed his suspicion that something was in the air and contrasted M'Cheyne's secure place in the group with his own lack of clarity, feeling bitterly disappointed that he might not, after all, be allowed to go. With a tinge of jealousy colouring his comments, he appealed to M'Cheyne for help:

> Your way is clear – not a cloud upon it. I rejoice for the consolation it must give you under your sore trial of silence, to see that your feet may carry the message of peace in another way than formerly. But, is my way so clear? I do not feel I can sing the song which I have put to your lips. Perhaps if I knew the whole circumstances I might be less doubtful; for as yet I have had no word of the arrangements except what was contained in the hurried line that you and Horace [Horatius Bonar, his brother] wrote. Mr Candlish possibly may write by tomorrow's post.[30]

If only he could receive a simple confirmation, it would sweep aside all lesser problems that stood in his way. If only M'Cheyne would write to Candlish 'without delay and at length', adding, as if fully aware that his frustration was upsetting his spiritual equilibrium: 'I have not forgotten prayer and supplication ... we must "continue in them."' True friend that he was, M'Cheyne sought help from their mutual friend James Grierson of Errol, who, receiving M'Cheyne's letter the following day, responded immediately: 'I shall do all in my power to promote in the Presbytery your views about Mr Bonar, although I see that there may be some difficulty in dealing with it.'[31]

This flurry of panicky activity on Bonar's part proved entirely unwarranted. The committee had met on 6th March, two days before Bonar's letter to M'Cheyne, and decided that Bonar would go. Candlish had written immediately informing Bonar that he had been appointed along with M'Cheyne, Wodrow, and Black and his note arrived on 8th March, the very day that Bonar appealed to M'Cheyne for help, probably arriving by the very same post which took away his letter to M'Cheyne. The incident shook Bonar deeply. He was, after all, an inexperienced young man with an inexperienced young man's exaggerated longings and insecurities. He confided to his diary: 'Got the letter of the committee requesting me to go to the Jews. It is a very solemn matter for me. The arrangements for this parish in my absence will be the most difficult matter ... Spent the forenoon in prayer.'[32]

As Grierson had hinted, the main opposition to Bonar's involvement came not from the committee but probably from his own Kirk Session, maybe from the former minister still resident in the parish who was not always helpful to his successor. Presbytery members siding against Bonar had, through the ministerial grapevine, communicated a negative opinion of the young minister to the Glasgow sub-committee. The disturbance was sufficient to require Candlish to travel from Edinburgh to appear before the Presbytery of Perth on 20th March in order to press them to release Bonar from his congregational responsibilities. His arguments overcame the opposition.

It was hard for Bonar's people to come to terms with what seemed to them to be a strange and exotic journey into the world of the Bible. One old woman asked how her minister would get to Palestine and, on being told he would travel via Egypt, promptly threw up her hands in horror, uttering, 'Oh, then, we'll nae see him again for forty-years!'[33] Bonar, however, relished the adventure that was opening up before him. On the very day he departed from the parish a farmer met him on the road and greeted him in Broad Scots, 'Ye'll be gaun to Pairth the daay, mister Bonar?' to which came the cheery retort, 'No! I'm going to Jerusalem.'[34]

9

M'Cheyne in London

London, 23rd March–11th April, 1839

ONCE the membership of the survey party had been settled, there was little for the committee to do but to get them on their way, support them by their prayers and in whatever practical way was necessary, and patiently await their return and report. But first there were formalities. Official papers, documents, and passports had to be obtained. To demonstrate to any who might doubt that this was indeed a *bona fide* Church of Scotland delegation, an impressive formal commission was drawn up, inscribed on parchment and duly signed by the moderator of the General Assembly and by the convenor of the Jewish committee. Further documentation was provided by the British Foreign Secretary, Lord Palmerston, along with notes of introduction from members of the British aristocracy, including the well-known traveller in the Levant and Europe, Miss Julia Pardoe. Scottish merchants sent introductory letters to their mercantile contacts in places the group might possibly visit, eliciting help and cooperation.

Each member also made their own personal preparations. We don't know how Black and Keith and Bonar managed their affairs, but M'Cheyne's little black notebook survives, and includes lists of the little luxuries he thought desirable for his comfort: tea, biscuits, and brandy.[1] His father, Adam M'Cheyne reminded him that for the success of the venture and for the sake of his health, he needed to be efficient and resourceful in dealing with logistical problems, as well as being faithful in the more spiritual concerns – a balance high-minded young men often find hard to maintain. We detect exasperation in a note M'Cheyne received from his father:

> Your mother is quite distressed that you have no thin clothes with you for the hot climate and to use when travelling. I understand the other gentlemen are all suitably provided in this respect, I really wish you would all meet and overhaul each other's baggage so as to ascertain what each requires in addition to his equipment. I send you this pair of plain trousers which I think you will find pleasant for travelling especially on horseback if you should have occasion to mount anywhere. I also earnestly recommend you also to get a Travelling Bag which you will find quite indispensable for keeping your morning gown, night clothes, foul linen and many other things in constant use. It will prevent your trunks from being over-crowded as they are, and thrown into confusion every time you have to seek for anything. You will find your maps in the other portmanteau.[2]

As well as the trousers sent by his father, M'Cheyne also took a black suit, three pairs of light trousers, a shirt-coat, seven shirts, a nightgown, eight handkerchiefs, two neck cloths, two towels, two night caps, one other cap, as well as three books, and five shillings cash. The reference to a mere five shillings and only three books inclines us to think that this list was an incomplete inventory, for there is no mention of the light clothing his mother wished him to buy and which doubtless he did.[3]

By March 1839, with the departure date looming ever closer, the route to be taken had not yet been finalised. In any case, flexibility was necessary and the travellers had to use their initiative to respond to the vagaries of local circumstances; for example, at one point M'Cheyne suggested travelling to Egypt across North Africa, through Algiers, Tunis, and Tripoli, visiting *en route* some Sephardic Jewish communities and missionaries of the LSPCJ.[4]

Yet again the question of Aden arose. Money had been pledged for a station there, and it was thought appropriate for at least some of the deputation to visit the ancient port and its Jewish community. This matter was resolved, however, when the deputation were attending a dinner in London arranged for them by the diplomat and orientalist Sir John McNeill, British ambassador to Persia. McNeill, a keen supporter of missionary work among the Jews, strongly advised against any attempt to establish a mission station in Aden, or even endeavouring to visit it.[5] Although the territory had nominally been ceded to Britain, the cession had been resisted by the Sultan of Lahej and four ships of the Royal Navy and troops of the East India Company were in action. The region was in turmoil and unsafe for British travellers. Bowing to McNeil's vastly superior knowledge, the deputation eliminated Aden and decided to proceed via France and the Mediterranean to Egypt and from there to Palestine, returning to Scotland via Turkey, the Black Sea, and Central Europe. This, apart from the two separate return itineraries, occasioned by circumstances which would befall Dr Black, was essentially the route that was followed.

It was agreed that Bonar, Black, and Keith would travel to London together by sea, taking the west coast route from Greenock on Friday 5th April 1839 and breaking their journey in Liverpool for a public meeting at Oldham Street Presbyterian Church built by Sir John Gladstone, a friend of Chalmers, and father of Prime Minister, William Ewart Gladstone. Allowing for his less than robust health, it was proposed that M'Cheyne would make a more leisurely journey from Leith, sailing down the east coast to London, where all four would rendezvous in time for a special farewell prayer meeting at the Regent Square Church of Scotland.

History does not recall how the three who travelled via Liverpool fared or what the meeting there was like, but M'Cheyne's records, methodically kept in a little red leather-bound journal, give a detailed account of his journey to London and his time there. Strangely, none of M'Cheyne's biographers made full use of this very interesting material, despite the fact that it casts light on the man himself, his friends, and this period of his life.

On the afternoon of Wednesday 27th March, M'Cheyne embarked on the two-masted, square-rigged *Caledonian* lying at Leith, which sailed at 4.45pm. The evening, he recalled, turned out very pleasant, with a light breeze:

> After a heavy shower came a beautiful evening, North Berwick shore and Isle of May lighted up by the setting sun – the solitary Bass stood immovable in the calm sea – thought of the many godly ministers who had been exiled there and whose prayers had ascended from its rocky

summit. Thought of Him who takes up the isles as a very small thing. Opposite me at dinner observed a Jewish countenance ... he was very gentlemanly – heard afterwards that his name was Tobias. [6]

The following morning, before sitting down to breakfast, M'Cheyne engaged Mr Tobias in conversation, asking if he could read Hebrew. He admitted he could, but then asked how M'Cheyne knew him to be a Jew. When he was told, he quipped that M'Cheyne must be a good 'physiognomist.' Much to M'Cheyne's dismay, Tobias was not at all religious and ridiculed the reading of prayers in Hebrew which, he said, was an unknown tongue that even two thirds of the synagogue could not understand. M'Cheyne was further surprised when Tobias scorned the keeping of two days at the commencement of Passover, saying, 'he would keep one and quite enough.' Furthermore, he denied the inspiration of the Bible, but, like all Jews of a more or less orthodox background, at prayer he wore the *tallit*, or fringed prayer shawl, and *tefillin*, or phylacteries, which he carried, with his copy of the Torah, in his travelling bag.

In this encounter, M'Cheyne came face to face, probably for the first time in his life, with an ordinary, modern, Jewish man not at all like the pious orthodox Jews he imagined. He was disillusioned: 'I suppose this is a genuine specimen of the worldly infidel Jew' he wrote in his notebook, and therefore set himself to 'convince him that he was ignorant of true happiness not knowing how to be forgiven.'

At breakfast on the following morning, M'Cheyne was equally vexed to hear Tobias excuse himself for eating and enjoying bacon, something which judging from his criticism he would not have done himself.[7]

> The Jew ate swine's flesh beside me, saying at the same time 'This is wrong' but evidently not with much feeling. Tried to convince him of inconsistency – had not slept any and asked me if it was from a troubled conscience. Read him part of 1st Psalm in Hebrew and impressed on him the need of 'meditating on God's word' – he seemed more serious and impressed. We may never meet again. Peace be to this child of Abraham. [8]

On this journey, M'Cheyne carried a pocket edition of Lumsden & Son's *Steam-Boat Companion, Or, Stranger's Guide to the Western*

Isles and Highlands of Scotland: Including the Voyages From London to Leith, an illustrated guide, published in 1825, describing everything of interest a traveller was likely to see on the voyage, to which, in his own journal, M'Cheyne added anecdotes and analogies. These notes give attractive insights into his readiness to find spiritual lessons in ordinary things and draw helpful analogies from what he observed.

On the morning of the 28th, they were off Whitby. Lumsden was silent about the place, but M'Cheyne noted, with disappointment, that it was here that the Synod was held at which King Oswiu of Northumberland had rejected the traditions of Iona and the Celtic church and as a result the ancient British Church was subjugated to the See of Rome.

Later, as he walked on deck, M'Cheyne observed gulls wheeling around the stern, commenting, 'Noticed this morning two sea-gulls following the vessel, not straight but flying hither and thither. So my soul follows Christ, not straight as I would desire, for then I should never wander from him – but hither and thither, "faint yet pursuing."'

The calm weather during the voyage, his own poor health, and his knowledge of David Brainerd, led him to ponder on the desirability of a short but fruitful life:

> At midday a complete calm – sails hanging loose or flapping to and fro – Soon the sailors took them in. So may God's ministers when their work is done be taken in. Brainerd used to pray that if it were God's will he might not outlive his usefulness.[9]

The observation is all the more poignant when we know he died just four years later, aged only twenty-nine. Again, in the same place he recorded that he had

> Heard the Captain say when asked if the wind was fair – 'Quite fair but not enough to make sail'. Many Christians seem to have God's Spirit fair enough but not enough to make sail. They do not 'go forward'.

On passing, at night, the recently built lighthouse off Cromer Point, Norfolk, he wrote:

> So may God's ministers be a beacon on the waters casting a steady light, guiding those that are near shipwreck ... shedding light on all within range of their influence.

By 11 o'clock on the morning of 29th March, the *Caledonian* was sailing along the River Thames, passing the gibbets at Blackwall where once hung the remains of pirates and mutineers, and on past the Greenwich hospital, to its berth just short of London Bridge. By 5 o'clock that evening M'Cheyne had settled into his lodging with the Tate family at Hampstead Heath. He wrote immediately to his parents to say that the journey had been entirely refreshing: 'I feel a great deal the better of the voyage – The palpitation has quite left me.' Nevertheless, in the same letter he confessed trepidation at the thought of attempting to negotiate the world's largest city without his three companions: 'I know not how I am to get about London without them.' He managed remarkably well, taking every opportunity during the following days to see the sights of the city, including a pleasurable outing in spring sunshine through Regent's Park with his hostess, Mrs Tate, in her elegant carriage.

On another occasion, frustrated to find that some friends on whom he called were not at home, he decided to see the shops of the West End. Like most ministers, he could not resist a bookseller's and called at James Nisbet & Co., 21 Berners Street, off Oxford Street, afterwards walking through bustling upmarket Burlington Arcade, through the Quadrant, past colonnaded 'shops appropriated to articles of fashion and taste,' and on to Regent Street and Piccadilly Circus, all then at the pinnacle of their fashionability. A delightful contemporary print of the Quadrant, struck in 1838, records the scene that opened up before the young minister: pedestrians walk along John Nash's grand portico, fashionable ladies ride in a smart carriage pulled by two greys, while a troop of mounted soldiers wearing bearskins wheel into Regent Street. Such sights were impressive. It was a heady experience for a young man unused to such grandeur.

M'Cheyne enjoyed it all immensely, and was far from adopting a disapproving or disdainful attitude to what some might have thought 'worldly.' At one point, though, he found the experience somewhat chastening: 'Saw some of the finest buildings in London. Walked up Piccadilly. Found it a lesson in humility. So many better dressed, better looking, wiser, than myself.'[10]

It is worthwhile pausing for a moment to reflect a little on James Nisbet the publisher and philanthropist M'Cheyne visited in the West

End.[11] Nisbet was born in 1785, near Kelso in the Scottish Borders. In 1803, as a young man of twenty-four, he arrived in London to work for Hugh Ussher, a West India merchant, and commenced attending Swallow Street Church of Scotland, where he was converted. In 1809 he began trading as a religious bookseller in Castle Street, later diversifying into publishing and moving his premises to 21 Berners Street. Here he prospered, received the freedom of the City of London, and was elected to office in the Worshipful Company of Stationers, a Livery Company of the City of London.

Like many another, Nisbet had been superficially attracted by the flashy spirituality of Edward Irving, who had been puffed up by George Canning, the Foreign Secretary of the day, as 'the greatest orator of our times.' Not all, however, were so gullible. That shrewd, though cynical observer of vanity, the caricaturist Robert Cruikshank, unflatteringly portrayed Irving in his 1824 series of London characters as the exploding 'puritanical Hatton Garden gasometer.' Likewise, the young Queen Victoria noted in her diary the equally perceptive counsel of her spiritually inert, but theologically informed Prime Minister, Lord Melbourne, that people like Irving who made claims to direct divine revelation, 'should be quite sure ... from what quarter they come!' Having known Irving intimately, when he had served as his assistant in the newly built St John's, Glasgow, Thomas Chalmers deplored both his style and much of his substance; Nisbet came to the same conclusion.

Following Irving to the Caledonian Chapel in Cross Street, Hatton Garden, Nisbet first became a member, then an elder, and finally a trustee, serving on the congregation's building committee. In 1827, the congregation renamed itself the National Scotch Church and moved to its splendid new gothic edifice in Regent Square, specially built for Irving. [12]Nisbet donated the silver communion service consisting of eight goblets, two flagons, and two salvers. However, thoroughly exasperated with the eccentricity and heterodoxy of his minister, he became leader of the opposition to Irving within the congregation, thus contributing to Irving's terminal clash with the London Presbytery over his mistaken belief that Christ's human nature was fallen. In an acrimonious dispute, Nisbet and his fellow trustees barred Irving and his followers from the building. Highhandedly, Irving in turn rejected the presbytery's authority, seceded from the Church of Scotland, and established the bizarrely named Catholic Apostolic Church.

Whatever Nisbet thought we do not know, but, on hearing of Irving's death in 1835, M'Cheyne's comment was characteristically generous: 'I look back upon him with awe, as on the saints and martyrs of old. A holy man in spite of all his delusions and errors. He is now with his God and Saviour, whom he wronged so much, yet, I am persuaded, loved so sincerely.'[13]

Nisbet's commitment to Christian causes was further evidenced when, in 1837, he made a single gift of £1,550, to build and endow the North Kelso Church, where Horatius Bonar was minister from 1837 to 1866. At the Disruption in 1843 he contributed £1,000 to the Free Church cause. He served on the boards of thirty-seven different societies, associations and charities and was especially fond of the eccentric Jewish explorer and missionary Joseph Wolff. He was probably the primary influence in encouraging Wolff's abortive application for membership of the London Presbytery. A plaque erected in his memory in Regent Square Church testified that Nisbet's 'house was the missionary's home.' He died in 1854.

After visiting the sights of the West End, M'Cheyne walked the four or five miles out to Hampstead, at that time a small town of some eight thousand inhabitants, returning to the Tate home enjoyably tired. The next day being the Sabbath, and feeling drained of energy, he decided to worship locally, but found sitting through two services in the dilapidated parish church of St John-at-Hampstead, extremely tedious. Neither service pleased him. He considered both ministers and their sermons to be very feeble indeed, adding that in them was 'little or nothing of Christ.' Nonetheless, he conceded that one of the ministers was 'evidently a very good man, though needing much to be roused up into life and energy.' Nothing he saw or heard in London altered his jaundiced opinion of Anglican ministry. He shared his opinion privately with his parents in uncharacteristically uncharitable generalisations:

> There is very little substance or power in English preaching – the people are all able to bear strong meat. Saw the Baptismal services, far too long, too many kneelings, and the absurd signing with the sign of

the X on the forehead of the child. The sponsors too seemed ignorant clowns. I fear there is a sore evil here.[14]

Notwithstanding, he found St Paul's Cathedral impressive and was much taken by the memorial marble statues, especially that commemorating Reginald Heber, the first bishop of Kolkata. Striking though the architecture and adornments were, M'Cheyne's more reserved Presbyterian taste led him tartly to observe that whilst St. Paul's was undeniably a glorious edifice, it was far better for looking at than for worship. Yet only a few days later he found himself drawn back to hear a service, admitting to being 'much solemnised by its beautiful singing.'[15]

The following days were occupied with procuring equipment for the journey and, in between, continuing to enjoy the sights of London, as well as meeting the friends and influential supporters of the Jewish mission. He visited the LSPCJ at Palestine Place in Bethnal Green and greatly enjoyed meeting its secretary J. B. Cartwright. There forty-five boys read Hebrew to him in unison, whilst a group of little girls sang Psalm 111 in Hebrew. Here too he met Aaron Saul, a Jewish Christian who had opened up a little reading room where enquiring Jewish people could peruse tracts and Christian books and where he could speak to them.

On Friday evening M'Cheyne attended synagogue, probably the imposing New Synagogue in Great St. Helen's Street, to observe the *Erev Shabbat* service. He was much taken with the splendour of the new buildings with their magnificent Hebrew inscriptions, all beautifully lit by fine chandeliers. In contrast to the much slower-paced services back home, he was, however, disconcerted by the speed with which the Rabbi and the two tenor cantors got through the service. Nevertheless, he was so much impressed by a prayer, in the form of an intercession on behalf of the young Queen Victoria, whose coronation had taken place the previous June, that he wanted not only to add his 'Amen', but to record it verbatim in his red notebook:

> May the supreme King of kings, through his infinite mercy inspire her and her counsellors and nobles with benevolence towards us and all Israel, in her days and in ours may Judah be saved and Israel dwell

in safety and may the Redeemer come unto Zion, which God in his infinite mercy grant and we will say Amen.

On Sunday, unable to face once more the tepid services at Hampstead, he walked three and a half miles to Bloomsbury, to worship at St. John's Chapel, Bedford Row, for many years a rallying point for London's evangelicals. Much to his pleasure, he spent the whole day in the company of the minister, the Honourable and Reverend Baptist Wriothseley Noel.[16] Finding Noel's style of ministry much more congenial, he wrote, 'saw the Communion dispensed, with which I was much pleased. It was very simple and solemn. Found Mr Noel a very pleasant man, very kind and interested about our mission.'

On Tuesday 9th April the deputation foregathered to dine at Nisbet's home, afterwards attending a great prayer meeting at Regent Square organised to bid them farewell. The service was attended not only by the ministers of the London Presbytery but also by many Anglican supporters of Jewish missions, English Nonconformists, and a good number of Jewish Christians, including Joseph Samuel C. F. Frey, who had preached for M'Cheyne in Dundee. Enthused, exhilarated and grateful to God, M'Cheyne noted in his red journal:

> Evening prayer meeting of all the Scottish ministers in London and many people in Regent's Square Chapel – to send us away. Very pleasant meeting – many converted Jews present – Frey – Calman – &c Mr MacMorland [Edward Irving's immediate successor at Regent Square] read Ezekiel 36 and prayed – most suitable chapter. Dr Black addressed the meeting – Dr Crombie read Rom XI and concluded with prayer – in a very earnest & feeling manner. Met with many afterwards – Capt. Crawford who had been at Jerusalem.[17]

The final days in London were filled with practical arrangements, including a visit to the Foreign Office to collect their passports, consular letters, and other documents promising safe conduct. The deputation could count on the support of many persons of high rank, great expertise, and significant influence at the very heart of the British Establishment, including Sir John McNeill, whose kindly and invaluable advice had saved the deputation from entangling itself in troubled Aden. McNeill, a native of the island of Colonsay, had risen to high office in the Foreign service under Palmerston, being appointed ambassador to the Shah of Persia in 1836. Despite discouraging them from attempting Aden, McNeill was enthusiastic about their plans and offered helpful information and expert advice regarding the Jewish communities in Persia, which M'Cheyne carefully committed to his journal.

> The number of Jews in Persia are very great. In Isfahan and Bagdad there are several thousands. Would not recommend a mission to Aden until British power be fully established – the Arabs are very jealous of their faith – the hold of Britain on Aden is very uncertain and he would be far from recommending it at present.[18]

McNeill also provided two letters of introduction. One was addressed to Colonel Robert Taylor, the British Resident at Baghdad, should the deputation ever go there, and the other was an open letter of introduction for M'Cheyne personally, which made clear the high regard in which McNeill held him, his colleagues, and the entire project.

> Will you permit me to introduce to you Mr McCheyne a particular friend of some members of my family who is about to proceed with some other ministers of the Kirk of Scotland on deputation from our national Church to enquire into the state of the Jews. Any attention you may have the kindness to pay to him or to them will be conferring an obligation on me.

The deputation also called on the thirty-eight-year-old Anthony Ashley Cooper, seventh Earl of Shaftesbury, a leading Christian politician and philanthropist, who had entered Parliament in 1826 at the age of twenty-five. Amongst his numerous political, social and religious causes, Shaftesbury ardently espoused the right of the Jews to return to their Promised Land, as well as Christian missions to them, and was deeply interested in the Scottish deputation's plans. M'Cheyne very much enjoyed meeting him and his six children.[19]

On the 10th April 1839, the day before their departure, the deputation dined at the home of Sir George Grey, recently appointed by the Prime Minister, Lord Melbourne, to the post of Judge-Advocate-General responsible for administering the court-martial system in the Navy and Army. He was also a Privy Councillor. Grey's mother, Mary Whitbread, of the brewing family, was an ardent evangelical and had been a close friend and staunch supporter of Wilberforce. By her prayers and example, she had impressed upon her son a fervent and simple godliness which never left him.

Grey, although evangelical, followed his tolerant Whig instincts and refrained from dogmatism, both denominationally and theologically. It was around Grey's hospitable table that the deputation met the twenty-five-year-old Liberal member of parliament for Perth, Arthur Kinnaird, the banker and Liberal politician, a close friend of Lord Shaftesbury and a supporter of evangelical and philanthropic causes, including women's suffrage. M'Cheyne thought him 'much interested and kind' concerning their mission.[20]

The deputation slept that night at the Nisbet's home in Hampstead and on the following day called on Lord George Hamilton Gordon, 4th Earl of Aberdeen, Tory politician, who would become Foreign Secretary in 1841. Beyond simply recording the fact, M'Cheyne made no further comment about this visit, which, perhaps, is not so very remarkable in view of the fact that Aberdeen was antagonistic to the position taken by all the delegates regarding the issue of patronage then convulsing the Church of Scotland and which would lead to the founding of the Free Church of Scotland in 1843. Fresh in Aberdeen's mind was the Auchterarder Case, which had been heard in the House of Lords just four days before M'Cheyne left Edinburgh for London. At the time the deputation visited him, Aberdeen was engaged in a discordant correspondence with his now estranged friend Thomas Chalmers. His first letter to Chalmers had been written shortly after the House of Lord's hearing, less than three weeks before the arrival on his doorstep of the deputation. That he deigned to see them at all is eloquent testimony not to any spirit of tolerance in him, for he had precious little, but to the influence which the non-intrusion party within the Church of Scotland had on the Westminster political establishment.[21]

After an early afternoon dinner, in an atmosphere of mounting excitement, the deputation made a few last-minute purchases and packed their bags. At seven in the evening they set off by overnight coach, M'Cheyne noting that the 'thought that we were really on our way raised our hearts'. It was a cold night. The survey party travelled ahead, huddled together inside one coach, and Mr and Mrs Nisbet accompanied them in another. M'Cheyne jotted down their journey through the sleeping Kentish countryside in staccato notes:

We rattled thro' Dartford, Gravesend, Rochester, Chatham, Canterbury – Dover by half past 6 in the morning – 72 miles from London. ... At half past seven we left the white chalky cliffs behind. Mr and Mrs Nisbet bidding us farewell.[22]

❦ 10 ❦

Outward Bound

France and the Mediterranean, April and May 1839

GAZING down at the sparkling wake of the cross-Channel packet-boat Black, Keith, Bonar, and M'Cheyne watched the white cliffs of Dover recede into the distance. The effect on M'Cheyne was sudden and alarming. He became acutely aware of his own fragility, his indifferent health, and the risks inherent in the adventurous journey they were undertaking. He felt exposed and vulnerable. With resignation, he committed his feelings to his journal: 'Who can tell when we shall look upon them again or in what circumstances – or if at all. We may see the shore of a better country – the true home, the heavenly – before then. The will of the Lord be done.'[1]

The packet-boat on which they sailed was a medium-sized vessel that got its name from its task of not only carrying passengers but delivering mail packets and other small articles of freight to the continent. That day the sea was boisterous and the wind contrary, the normally brief crossing of the Straits of Dover to Boulogne took a full three hours. Arriving there, the four travellers, upon disembarking, were not in a good mood and felt outraged when they, her Britannic Majesty's subjects, coming from a country in which proof of identity was never normally required, were expected to show their passports to the French gendarmerie. Furthermore, to add to their annoyance, the lumbering four-wheeled *diligence*, or public stagecoach, in which they hoped to travel to Paris, was delayed and would not now depart until the following morning.

Like many other setbacks they were to experience, this delay worked out for the best by giving them an unexpected opportunity to meet a very interesting Jewish man, whom M'Cheyne described as 'a person of education and agreeable manners, who spoke English fluently.'[2] He immediately piqued their interest by telling them how he had spent a whole year in North America and had lived among the 'Winebegos and Micmacs, learned the Cherokee and Oneida languages, and conformed to their manners, often living almost naked'. He did this, he said, to test the feasibility of the theory that they were descendants of the ten tribes of Israel. The result of his accumulated empirical evidence was that they were not.

As conversation developed, he expressed a general sympathy towards Jesus and the Christian gospel. Moreover, he had heard of Keith's *Evidences of Prophecy* and was delighted to meet the author and even more thrilled when Keith took out a copy from his baggage, autographed it and presented it to him. He left them with judicious words of advice: 'If you wish to gain a Jew, treat him as a brother.' They rejoiced that on the very first day of their mission the Lord had given them an opportunity to speak of the Messianic claims of Jesus of Nazareth with a new Jewish friend. This they took to be a sign, convincing them that God was guiding them in their great adventure.

This encounter not only buoyed their spirits but in this first flush of excitement they reappraised the nature of their task, concluding that they had not been sent by the committee primarily to reconnoitre and collate information – which arguably they had – but to win Jewish people to faith in the Messiah. M'Cheyne noted that from then on, wherever they went, they were intent on carrying the gospel to both Catholics and 'the poor despised Jew.' So, as their lumbering coach slowly overtook pedestrians on the high road, or as they entered villages, they threw evangelistic tracts through the windows, and during halts at various stages handed out books, Bibles, and Bible portions to any they met.[3]

Due to the enforced delay, they did not arrive in Paris on the evening of Saturday 14th April as they had hoped, but on the following morning. Pained by what they saw as a violation of the Sabbath, they attempted to salvage what they could of the day and set out on foot for the Anglican Chapel in the Rue Marboeuf hoping to hear the preaching of Frédéric Monod. The chapel, a picture gallery that had been adapted for worship, was established in 1824 by the Rev'd Lewis Way, Chaplain to the British Ambassador, whom we have met already in connection with the attempt to recruit Claudius Buchanan as secretary of the LSPCJ. Frédéric and his brother Adolphe were pastors of great influence in the Réveil, a strongly orthodox renewal movement in the French Reformed Church, and sometimes preached there. Both were well known and greatly admired in Scotland and the Monods, in turn, held Scotland in great affection, not least because Adolphe's conversion had come about through his contacts with Thomas Erskine and Frédéric's through the preaching of Robert Haldane in Geneva.[4]

Beneath its veneer of fashion and prosperity, Paris was seething as reactionaries and revolutionaries vied with each other for power. In May 1839, barely a month after the arrival of the Scotsmen, there took place a violent workers' uprising, initiated by a secret republican socialist society called the Society of the Season, but in April as the four Scotsmen walked to the Marboeuf Chapel all was calm. Nevertheless, they could not have disagreed more with Lord Melbourne's description of Paris as the European capital of pleasure as he described it to the youthful Queen Victoria. To the eyes of the four travellers the city was the haunt of a flippant, godless, and superficial society totally at odds with their Scottish Calvinist values. They were not at all impressed by what they saw as they walked its streets that Sunday morning and were especially distressed at the utter indifference of the French for the sanctities of the Lord's Day, which they thought was all too apparent. Their opinion was that no city reminded them more of what Sodom might have been before its destruction. M'Cheyne, feeling intensely its uncongenial spirit, jotted in his notebook a sharp critique, 'There is a look of vice about the streets … I do not think it can be lawful to a Christian to live in Paris.'[5]

Glad to escape, they relaxed as their carriage made its way through the beautiful scenery surrounding Troyes, Dijon, Châtillon-sur-Seine, and on through Burgundy to Chalon-sur-Saône, where they embarked on a river steamboat to carry them via Lyons to Marseilles. Captivated by the loveliness of the French countryside in springtime, they compared it not unfavourably with their native Scotland, yet all the while recognising its unique beauty. They also enjoyed being made aware of the great events of church history that had taken place in France. At Lyon they thought of the martyrdom in A.D. 177 of the courageous Blandina and the faithful Pothinus, and of the powerful ministry of Irenaeus, the 'Hammer of heretics'. They found the exquisite beauty of Avignon's ruined palaces and towers, set off against the distant background of the Alps, quite breathtaking. But, in a manner peculiar to their piety, M'Cheyne and Bonar now felt guilty that they were enjoying themselves and concluded that they may have somehow imperilled their souls. Stiffening their resolve and refusing to be distracted, they reminded themselves that they were not tourists and their 'object was not to linger over scenery or enjoy historical memorials' but 'to be self-denied' and focused on their task. It was in such a mood of transcendental other-worldliness that they sailed on through the night, changing steamers at Bauclaire for Marseilles.[6]

The steamboat's engineer, who was English, was very enthusiastic to help them in their evangelistic activity, though he confessed that in ten years he had only been to church twice. Nonetheless, he was recruited as an assistant missionary to distribute tracts to their fellow passengers. Disembarking in Marseilles, where there was reputed to be approximately one thousand Jews, they were disappointed to find the rabbi was a Rationalist, yet were encouraged by his willingness to show them the synagogue and receive their tracts.[7]

On making enquiries in Marseilles, they learned that the steamboat for Malta had sailed the previous day and heard, to their great annoyance, that the next would not depart for another ten days. Marseilles may have been France's oldest town and its 'gate to the Orient' but this burgeoning industrial port held few attractions for them, so rather than waste time there, they resolved to set off for Malta immediately, via Italy, and on the way visit the Jewish community of Livorno.

Called Leghorn by the British, Livorno, in the region of Tuscany, enjoyed the status of a free port, where ships of all nations could export and import goods without paying duty. The travellers appear to have entertained a misguided optimism that a similar liberty might be extended to matters of religion and that the city would be open to the gospel. They, therefore, commenced their witness immediately on arrival, handing out tracts to each of the eight men who carried their luggage from the ship up to their inn, and, as they passed along the street, handing out more to the bystanders as well. But no sooner had they settled into their accommodation when an irate customs official arrived inquiring if they were the ones who had been distributing books. Their tracts and Hebrew books were immediately impounded, and the two senior members of the deputation, Black and Keith, were promptly marched away by the customs officer to appear before the Commissary of Police who proceeded to inflict upon them a long, hostile, and gruelling examination. Eventually, they were told that their books would be sent to the official censor in Florence who would evaluate the case and pass judgement. In the meantime they were dismissed to await the verdict.

About ten thousand Jewish people lived in Livorno, many of whom had found refuge in Tuscany after being hindered from settling in the Papal States. Whilst awaiting the censor's decision, the deputation met and conversed with Jewish leaders, rabbis, and intellectuals in the city. A vigorous yet good-natured dialogue was maintained with scholars at the Jews' library and particularly with a Sephardic rabbi. M'Cheyne, who appears to have had a keen ear for linguistic variants, accurately recorded the rabbi's name as Abuelafi, an observation which confirms that the Livorno Jewish community consisted of the two main blocs of European Jewry, the Sephardim and the Ashkenazim. The name Abuelafi originated in the Ladino-speaking Sephardic community of oriental Jews from Spain, who were, at the time, because off the Inquisition, found mainly in North Africa and the Middle East. The Yiddish-speaking Ashkenazim were largely from Northern Europe.

The easy rapport which they established with the Jewish community was greatly enhanced as a result of the harsh treatment the Scotsmen had received from the authorities. It was agreed by all that Catholicism was equally the enemy of Protestantism and of Judaism, and in that light the travellers came to terms with the idea 'that, in seeking the lost sheep of the house of Israel, we should meet with treatment at the hand of their oppressors.'[8]

The sentence of the censor was that their tracts could be returned to them, but all copies of Keith's *Evidences of Prophecy* would be confiscated, because they were said to contain interpretations of biblical passages at variance with the dogma of the Roman Catholic Church. In addition, the missionaries were immediately and perpetually banished from Tuscany, but this was, they said, a sentence they could easily bear.[9]

Embarking at Livorno on Friday 3rd May, a three-day voyage brought them to Valletta in Malta, where they disembarked from the peaceful order of their ship into the tumult and confusion of the port and the uncomfortable heat of a burning sun. Here they had their first experience of the Orient and the colourful welcome that the eastern Mediterranean then afforded to travellers. They were astounded by the sheer variety of humanity that confronted them. Dockside porters, touting for business, hustled them as they vied with miserable looking beggars for the right to carry the luggage. On the way to their hotel they saw Greeks in their traditional costume, Turks wearing exotic turbans, a monk with a tonsure and, behind him, a 'dismal' priest. They were glad to see a group of uniformed English sailors and their smart officer. M'Cheyne noted a Maltese peasant with an exquisitely embroidered shirt, and a lady wearing a traditional lace mantilla, a garment which he conjectured might be a remnant of an eastern veil.

Although the city and the island were very beautiful and had intriguing connections with the Apostle Paul, they found the Jewish community to be very small and concluded there was little to engage their time and interest. More positively, they gleaned helpful information from the Anglicans stationed on the island, including Rev. C. F. Schlienz of the Church Missionary Society, but especially enjoyed meeting Rev'd William Robert Fremantle, then exercising an evangelistic ministry at West Street Chapel, Seven Dials, London, who was returning from a journey to Jerusalem. Sharing with them his observations of the Jews in the Holy Land, they found Fremantle a kindred spirit, both in his evangelicalism and his love of the Jewish people. On his return he would contribute to the London Anglican lecture series a paper on Romans 11:20, *The Present Dispersion a Moral Warning to the Gentiles, a Literal Fulfilment of Prophecy, and a Sure Pledge of their [Israel's] Future Return*, and also edit the published collection in 1841, as *Israel Restored, or, The Scriptural Claims of the Jews Upon the Christian Church.* Fremantle shared his ardent hopes that Christ Church – the first English Protestant Church at Jerusalem, then in the very earliest stages of construction – would counter the unhelpful misrepresentations of Christianity created by the other churches in the city.[10]

From Malta they sailed north-east via the Greek islands, taking a south-easterly course past the eastern cape of Crete, and arriving at Alexandria on Monday, 13th May. Leaving the stifling heat of their sun-baked cabin, they went on deck from where their sun-dazzled eyes rested on graceful green palm trees and lines of camels moving slowly along the beach. All the evidences of sight, sound and, especially, smell, announced unmistakably that they were truly in the East.

It was said that when Napoleon's armies occupied Italy in 1796, the map of the Grand Tour had been rolled up, it being no longer safe for wealthy young British gentlemen to be packed off for two years to complete their cultural education by travelling through France, Switzerland, and Italy, collecting as they went artefacts, statuary, and paintings. Adventurous aristocratic travellers now needed to find a new destination for their amusement. A decade or two earlier, Lord Byron and his companion Sir John Hobhouse, the Earl of Elgin, and others had made Greece their new playground, a destination logical both in artistic and cultural terms. With the country under Turkish rule, travellers inevitably came in contact with the alluring world of the Levant and it was not long before the 'Franks,' as travellers of Northern European origin were known, pressed beyond Turkey to its Levantine possessions.

In the wake of romantic and dilettante travellers, came scholars attracted not only to Greece and Turkey, but also to Egypt and Palestine, the latter especially because of their connection with biblical history. Such a glut of books had been produced that J. B. Lightfoot in his 1875 commentary on *Saint Paul's Epistles to the Colossians and Philemon*, could list a half-dozen English publications written between 1775 and 1842, plus another half-dozen by French and German travellers. When the American biblical scholar Edward Robinson travelled to Syria in 1838, the year before the Scottish deputation, he took with him a considerable number of recent publications, including copies of the latest maps and, in turn, published in 1841 his *Biblical Researches in Palestine*.

On their return to Scotland, Bonar and M'Cheyne added to this literature their best-selling *A Narrative of a Mission of Enquiry to the Jews from the Church of Scotland in 1839*, which sold over thirty thousand copies in the English edition, as well as a number of American editions and translations into Dutch and French. Another notable Scottish visitor to the Levant in 1839 was the Edinburgh artist David Roberts R.A. whose vivid journal and vast collection of well-observed drawings and watercolour sketches of people and places from Lebanon to Egypt, contributed greatly to the sum of Western knowledge about the area. There is no evidence that he and the survey party from the Church of Scotland met.[11]

By 1839, the number of British travellers arriving in Palestine from Egypt had become so numerous that the recently appointed Consul in Jerusalem, William Tanner Young, a member of the committee of the LSPCJ, wrote to his superior, Col. Patrick Campbell – Commanding General, British Diplomatic Agent, and Consul in Cairo – expressing his concern. Young advised that it might be beneficial for a Vice Consul to be stationed in Hebron because that was the first destination of note for those travelling up from Egypt to Jerusalem. Such a Vice Consulate, he argued, might provide assistance to those having made their 'long and painful journey.' Campbell's tart reply – he was totally unsympathetic towards Young – gives a graphic impression of the increasing number of tourists: 'I do not see the least necessity for it. If agents were named at all places where British Travellers resort, I should have to name agents in every town in Syria.'[12]

At the time the deputation arrived in the East, the days of romantic and adventurous travel in an unspoilt Levant were drawing to a close. A few years after the defeat of Napoleon at the battle of Waterloo, a regular steamer service crossed the English Channel to France and within twenty years the railway network had spread across Europe.

No longer was it necessary to travel the eastern Mediterranean in a Greek *felucca*, though for adventure some continued so to do; now steamships and garish hotels democratised the Grand Tour and aristocratic peregrinations would be replaced in 1869 by Thomas Cook's popular middle class Nile cruises to the Pyramids.[13]

Yet it was precisely this process of modernisation which facilitated the rapid transit of a wide range of travellers, including missionaries, explorers, and biblical scholars. Although primarily engaged in a project related to the spiritual welfare of the Jews, a people who had yet to make their full impact on the region, the four travellers from Scotland were in the vanguard of British Middle East exploration and their researches would add considerably to the little that was then known about the small but growing Jewish colony in Jerusalem and Palestine.

At the eastern end of the Mediterranean there were many differences with which our travellers had to come to terms, not least that they were in a region dominated by Islamic religion, history, and culture. In addition, the region was militarily and politically disturbed because of the hostilities between Mehmed Ali, the Ottoman viceroy in Egypt, and the Sultan in Constantinople, about which they had read in the British Press and discussed around London dinner tables. Now this exotic and somewhat dangerous world formed the immediate environment of their everyday lives.

For over twenty-five years Egypt had been under the rule of Mehmed Ali, an Albanian Muslim, once described as half an illiterate barbarian, half a consummate statesman, wholly a genius. In 1831, smarting at the refusal of Sultan Mahmud II to make him governor of Syria, and encouraged by French *agents provocateurs*, Ali occupied Palestine for a period of nine years, during which he introduced a modernised and centralised administration. His generally benign rule opened up the region to Western influence and in 1824 he permitted the LSPCJ to establish, at the instigation of Lewis Way, its Palestine Mission under Dr George Edward Dalton, whose brief ministry of just one month laid the foundation of the world's first medical mission.[14]

Under Ali's jurisdiction, the region's justice system was reformed and pacified with rebels and bandits made liable to execution.

However, his attempts to curb the encroachments of Bedouin raiders were of limited success and many of these warlike tribes operated unconstrained. More than once they would threaten the security of the Scottish ministers. Nevertheless, compared to former times, the region was relatively safe for travellers leading the American, Edward Robinson, to abandon the general practice of Western travellers wearing disguise.[15]

In 1838 a second war between Mehmed Ali and the Sultan broke out, and as Black and Keith, Bonar and M'Cheyne arrived in Alexandria they saw, and were greatly impressed by, twelve ships of Ali's fleet lying at anchor with their modern equipment and well turned-out marines dressed in white cotton uniforms, red sashes, and bearing shining weapons. At this point, however, it was neither a military buildup nor the underlying political realities that laid hold on the imagination of the deputation. It was the startling news that, coinciding with their arrival in Alexandria, bubonic plague had made its appearance and that would necessitate a significant change to their plans.

11

Journey to Jerusalem

Egypt to Jerusalem, May to June 1839

THE Scotsmen disembarked at Alexandria just in the nick of time, before a quarantine station could be set up. The outbreak of plague meant they could no longer enter Palestine by sea at Jaffa or Beirut, as they had planned to do, because a *cordon sanitaire* was to be established at both of those ports. The best alternative was to travel overland by the ancient coastal route to Gaza, passing through the Egyptian border at El Arish. Even so, this had to be done with great urgency before the Egyptian authorities closed the border crossing.

Unplanned-for housekeeping matters had to be attended to urgently. Although they had purchased light clothes and straw hats in Europe, supplies for a desert journey could only be bought in Egypt and, as most expeditions set off from Cairo, Alexandria was not the best place to obtain an outfit for a desert expedition. With the help of Mustafa, a servant of Major General Patrick Campbell, the British Consul General in Egypt, a visit to the bazaar was organised where tents, carpets, quilts, cooking gear, and provisions could be purchased. Being Scotsmen, they were pleased to get a bargain or two when a gentleman's travel canteen, cooking utensils, and remaining stock of provisions fell into their hands at a cheap rate: two tents cost £3 and the beds, canteen, and general provisions another £14.[1]

Through Mustafa's help they also secured the services of two experienced desert guides, Ibrahim and Ahmed, for three months for the sum of thirty-six Egyptian dollars each. These men turned out to be Mustafa's most significant acquisition on their behalf. Ibrahim was a powerfully built young man who had the previous year travelled with Edward Robinson's American expedition, serving as an assistant to the more experienced *dragoman* Hajji Komeh – whose title *Hajji* indicated he had made the *haj*, or pilgrimage, to Mecca – whom Robinson considered 'a fine resolute fellow, faithful and trustworthy in all he undertook, and ready to stand by us to the last drop of his blood.'[2] The less experienced Ibrahim, however, Robinson dismissed as one who 'answered our purpose well enough as a helper to the other.' But to his new Scottish employers, Ibrahim spoke warmly and generously of Robinson, whom he described as a 'good Christian.'

Due to the excellent tutelage of Hajji Komeh, Ibrahim became to the Scottish expedition what Komeh had been to Robinson's. Moreover, the privations and challenges of desert travel produced a bond of mutual respect and loyalty, indeed affection, between Ibrahim and his clients, particularly with the younger men, Bonar and M'Cheyne, as evidenced by the manner in which they took leave of each other at Beirut two months later:

> Ibrahim exhibited very affectionate feelings. He followed us a little way beyond the gates, then took farewell, burst into tears, and rushed out of sight. We felt it very sad to leave this Arab forever, not knowing how it is with his soul.[3]

Before enduring the rigours of the desert, all four missionaries decided that they would pamper themselves with the exotic luxury of a *hammam* or Turkish bath. In a very entertaining passage in the *Narrative*, M'Cheyne describes the process. After they had disrobed and had towels wrapped around their waists and another wound around their head as a turban, they were laid on their backs, soaped all over and well scrubbed with a rough glove of camel hair. This was followed by a shower of warm water. Next their heads were massaged, their finger joints flexed until they cracked, and their feet scraped. They found themselves rather alarmed, not so much by the experience itself but by the thought they had entrusted themselves to the care of 'Mahometans with shaved heads and black skins.' After hot coffee and cool sherbet they came away 'not a little amused, as well as refreshed.'[4]

This indulgence seems to have conferred spiritual benefit too, M'Cheyne noting a detail that reminded him of John 13:10, said, in his own translation, 'The custom of passing from the bath to the dressing-room, during which the feet might easily be soiled, reminded us of the true rendering of the precious words of our Lord, "He that has been in the bath needeth not save to wash his feet but is clean every whit."'

It may seem odd that M'Cheyne and his companions could think that they were needlessly exposing themselves to moral danger by gazing appreciatively at the French countryside, but could nevertheless enjoy and draw a positive spiritual lesson from a Turkish bath house, which some of their contemporaries considered decadent and discussed only with disapprobation. Queen Victoria's Physician, Sir William Withey Gull, once remarked, 'Turkish baths are probably more adapted to the indolent and luxurious, than to those who toil for their livelihood.'5

The following morning, 16th May, their sleep was rudely broken by the braying of donkeys and the noisy chatter of Ahmed and Ibrahim and ten Egyptian lads busily loading the baggage onto sixteen donkeys. Rising hastily, they dressed and breakfasted and within minutes passed through the city gate in their dash for El Arish.

A week later they found themselves on the other side of the Nile encamped in the vicinity of San el-Hagar, or Tanis, the biblical Zoan, one hundred and twenty miles from Alexandria and with over a hundred miles to go to reach El Arish. San el-Hagar is the most extensive archaeological site of the northeast Nile delta and, rising early to view it in the warm, rosy light of dawn, our travellers were impressed by the remains of temples, royal tombs, obelisks and sphinxes, the architectural treasures of the onetime northern capital of Egypt. Little did they know that directly beneath their feet there lay hidden treasures of gold, silver, lapis lazuli, and finely worked jewellery, surpassed only by those found in the fabulous tomb of Tutankhamen, and which would not come to light until 1939 and the excavations of the French archaeologist Pierre Montet, and later would be fictionalised in the Indiana Jones movie *Raiders of the Lost Ark*. For Black and Keith, Bonar and M'Cheyne, it was notable because 'God performed wonders in the land of Egypt, in the fields of Zoan' (Ps. 78:11-16, ESV).

Returning to their tents they found themselves confronted by much more mundane matters. Their baggage donkeys had now been replaced by eight camels, better suited to the softer going of the sandy coastal desert. As the guides busied themselves arranging the baggage, the four travellers stood talking, anticipating with trepidation the thought of mounting the camels. 'The loading of a camel is a singular scene,' one of them explained later, 'When it rises there is much danger of being thrown over its head, and then of being thrown the other way; and the Arabs are very careless in warning, for they say no one is hurt by a fall from a camel.' In the event, they all mounted safely, if awkwardly, and set off across the desert, borne along by the rocking, rolling, pacing gait of their mounts at a steady three miles an hour.[6]

As for the effect of falling off a camel, their Arab guides were quite wrong. After breakfast on May 25th, they broke camp and at sunrise remounted their camels. That day their route took them deeper into the desert, travelling due east towards the rising sun. The morning was hot, about 90°F (32°C) in the shade, and what with the combination of an early start and the slow, rhythmic, soporific gait of the camels they were all lulled into an irresistible drowsiness.

Suddenly, at about nine-thirty, one of the guides called out that Dr Black had fallen from his camel. The others reined in, couched their camels, slipped from their saddles and ran towards their colleague. Gingerly, not knowing how badly hurt he might be, they carefully administered the restoratives they had brought with them: maybe smelling salts, certainly brandy. They were thankful that Black seemed only to be winded and shaken, not seriously hurt, but it was decided to put up a tent and rest awhile in its shade.[7]

After the worst of the heat had passed, Black was sufficiently recovered to allow them to advance a further few miles before spending that night and all the next day, it being the Sabbath, in a poor Arab village, somewhere near Bir Qatia, marked on their map as Katieh. Indeed, apart from the initial flurry of anxiety it caused, Black's tumble was passed off as trivial, but such are the ways of God, that this fall from a camel by a middle-aged Scottish minister turned out to be the hinge upon which pivoted the entire outcome of their mission, leading to the decision as to the best location for the first mission station.

The vulnerability that had gripped M'Cheyne when crossing Channel, now returned, but this time he found the feelings of isolation and helplessness, heat and thirst, exhilarating. Like so many other British desert travellers before and since, he found something wonderfully bracing in a life reduced to its basic elements. The adventurer in M'Cheyne revelled in the element of risk they were running. He wrote, 'The desert life has its charms – you are alone with God! No object attracts your eye, – there is only one wide ocean of sand, round and round; no sound breaks on the ear, but the plaintive song of the Bedouin, cheering on his slow paced camel.'[8] And to Andrew Bonar's brother Horatius, then the minister at Larbert, Stirlingshire, he admitted that before leaving home he had no idea that desert travel would be so awe-inspiring: the utter solitude was quite fantastic.[9]

Heightened though their emotions were as they travelled up to Gaza, a new, even sharper awareness, amounting almost to an ecstasy, became perceptible from the very moment they crossed the border at El Arish on 31st May, well ahead, as they hoped, of any attempt to establish a quarantine camp. Now they were in the Promised Land itself, the location of the great acts of biblical history and, above all, the theatre of world redemption. Little wonder they considered it most appropriate that their first day in the land was the Lord's Day and they worshipped together in one of the tents, joyfully singing the apt words of the Scottish Metrical version of Psalm 76:

> In Judah's land God is well known,
> his name's in Isr'el great:
> In Salem is his tabernacle,
> in Zion is his seat.
>
> There arrows of the bow he brake,
> the shield, the sword, the war.
> More glorious thou than hills of prey,
> more excellent by far.

This rest day gave them leisure to reflect on Scripture passages, other than Psalm 76, which celebrated the great works that God had accomplished in this land; then, in the cool of the evening they walked out beyond their camp to a little grassy hill which offered a panoramic view. Andrew Bonar, however, recalled another less solemn and more humorous reason for remembering the day. Their tent had been invaded by a colony of ants, and in response M'Cheyne had flicked open his Bible to read aloud Proverbs 6:6 – 'Go to the ant, thou sluggard; consider her ways, and be wise' – and reminded them of the need of untiring diligence in the work of the Lord.[10]

They now faced a delay of three days during which their Arab attendants haggled to obtain fresh camels. Then, once more on their way, they passed through Khan Yunis, circumvented Gaza where the plague was raging, crossed Nahal Sorek, and swung eastwards to reach Latrun, where the road from Jaffa commences its winding and picturesque ascent through the Judean hills to Jerusalem by the Sha'ar Hagai Pass (Bab el-Wad). Surrounded by so impressive and beautiful a landscape, replete with all its spiritual resonances, they could not help but be elated and, when eventually they encamped for the night in the small hamlet of Dayr Ayyub (now destroyed), M'Cheyne wrote:

> The last day's journey to Jerusalem was the finest I ever had in all my life. For four hours we were ascending the rocky pass upon our patient camels. ... the trees and flowers, and the voice of the turtle dove, told us it was Immanuel's land.

Quite evidently, preoccupation with the historical and spiritual associations of the area took their minds off the rigours of their route; seventy-seven years later the rugged troopers of the Australian 9th Light Horse Regiment attributed their slow approach to Jerusalem to the toughness of this country, though it is true they were making their approach in winter.

The next day, a further seven-hour trek brought them within sight of their destination: the city of Jerusalem. Having been brought up from childhood on Bible stories in which Jerusalem featured so prominently M'Cheyne, like thousands of other Christian travellers, found it almost overwhelming to arrive at the Holy City. Impatient with the slow plodding of his mount, on drawing near the city's ancient walls and gates, surmounted by gleaming spires, domes, and minarets, he dismounted and ran eagerly forward to gain his first clear sight of Jerusalem.

Breathless with devotion and almost unable to believe what he was seeing with his own eyes, before him stood the City of David, the place where Jesus had walked and healed and taught and prayed, and into which he rode triumphantly on a donkey and out of which he went to die, and to which without a doubt he would come again. This was quite simply the most wonderful spot in the whole wide-world. Catching up with him, the entire group stood entranced. Speechless and emotional, they moved forward in rapt silence, communicating their pent-up feelings only by whispered, single exclamatory words.[11]

They entered the ancient city from the east through Suleiman the Magnificent's sixteenth-century gate, the Bab el-Khalil, literally 'Gate of the Friend', an allusion to Abraham, the friend of God, but known more prosaically as the Jaffa Gate. Immediately they sought out the British Consul, William Tanner Young, who had taken up his consular post in April, less than two months previously. The Mehmed Ali crisis and the subsequent intervention by the European powers justified an official British presence in Jerusalem, but in relation to the evangelisation of the Jewish community it was wonderfully well-timed. As soon as he had been made aware of a plan to establish a consulate, Lord Shaftesbury had urged the Foreign Secretary, his step-father-in-law, Lord Palmerston, to instruct the consul that an important part of his task was to offer protection to the Jewish community, as well as caring for the needs of British travellers. These sentiments were fully echoed in the official correspondence providing Young with his orders, and he promptly and diligently implemented them as he took charge of this key British initiative.[12]

It was Young's belief that when remote European Jewish communities heard that Great Britain had shown friendship to the Jewish people, it would make them more receptive to British missionaries. And so it turned out to be. Young immediately and very willingly put himself at the disposal of the survey party, warning them that the plague was still in the city and therefore it was inadvisable to camp on the Mount of Olives, as they had planned to do. He promptly found them alternative accommodation consisting of two large rooms, and introduced them to two British travellers who had just arrived in Jerusalem from Petra: Lord Claud Hamilton, Lord Abercorn's twenty-six-year-old son, the Conservative member of parliament for County Tyrone, and his travelling companion, Lyttleton. Hamilton was pleasantly surprised to meet Black, whom he had known during Black's incumbency of the parish of Tarves in Aberdeenshire.[13]

They had not long settled into their rooms when the Danish missionary, Rev. Hans Nicolajsen (known to English readers as John Nicolayson) arrived to welcome them. In 1826 Nicolajsen was sent by the LSPCJ to build upon the work commenced by Joseph Wolff and continued by Dr George Edward Dalton. Until 1833 he had resided outside the city, it being impossible for Protestants to live in Jerusalem, but that year he purchased a property on the edge of the Jewish quarter.

Nicolajsen would not hear of the deputation staying in vermin-infested rented rooms and insisted that they, with Ibrahim and Ahmed, their Arab servants, move immediately to one of houses on Mount Zion owned by the LSPCJ, to occupy apartments recently vacated. They were enchanted by their new accommodation. Its window looked eastwards over the old city where, in the warm glow of the late afternoon sun, they could see before them the Temple Mount with the Dome of the Rock in the middle distance and on the horizon the Mount of Olives rising above the Kidron Valley. Nearby, just within the Jaffa Gate, and beside the so-called Citadel of David, they saw the site that had been purchased on which to build an Anglican 'Hebrew Chapel', with labourers preparing the foundations and masons dressing the stones to be used in what was consecrated a decade later as Christ Church, the first Protestant Church in the Middle East.[14] Nicolajsen, as Rector of the church, was the first Protestant minister to be permanently settled in Jerusalem, holding Christian services there in English, Hebrew, and Arabic until his death in 1856. Nicolajsen is buried in the Mount Zion Protestant cemetery which he had founded in 1848. His epitaph reads:

The Reverend John Nicolayson
Born June 1st 1803
23 years a faithful watchman on the walls of Jerusalem,
fearless in the midst of war, pestilence and earthquake –
a master in all the learning of the Hebrews and the Arabs,
founder of the English Hospital and builder of the Protestant Church.
Lived beloved and died lamented
by Christians, Jews and Mahometans.

As well as Nicolajsen's, the Protestant cemetery contains the graves of four Anglican bishops of Jerusalem, including the first, the Jewish Christian, Michael Solomon Alexander, as well as Joseph Barclay, Samuel Gobat, and George Francis Graham Brown. Horatio Spafford, who wrote the hymn, *It Is Well With My Soul,* is also buried there, as is the Faith Mission evangelist, William Irvine, and the Egyptologist and Archaeologist, Flinders Petrie. The cemetery has often been desecrated, the latest being the destruction of thirty graves in January 2023. Two young men of orthodox Jewish appearance, one fourteen and the other eighteen, were arrested by the police. The attack was condemned as a hate crime by many Israelis, including the Chief Rabbi of Israel, Rav. David Lau.[15]

Of all the scenes that fascinated the survey party during their ten days in the city, it was one of the seemingly most trivial that struck them as most significant. Walking about the city it occurred to them how much of Mount Zion had been given over to agricultural use. Was this not, they asked each other, a precise fulfilment of two identical prophecies in Jeremiah 26:18 and Micah 3:12 (AV): 'Therefore shall Zion for your sake be plowed as a field, and Jerusalem shall become heaps, and the mountain of the house as the high places of the forest.' This spoke strongly to Keith, whose hermeneutical approach in his book, *The Evidences of Prophecy,* was, now with the benefit of firsthand observation, vindicated by what he saw for himself. Zion had indeed, quite literally, become a ploughed field, with the debris of the ages cleared from the ground and standing about the margins of its fields in heaps of stones.

Bonar too was much impressed by this irrefutable literal fulfilment of predictive prophecy. So too was M'Cheyne. But far from taking this bleak prophecy of Jerusalem's ruin as a discouragement, they saw it as a sign for good, arguing that if God had literally fulfilled His promises of judgement, would he not also similarly fulfil His promises of restoration?[16]

The outbreak of bubonic plague in the Jewish quarter of Jerusalem limited their opportunities for gathering impressions of the community, but Nicolajsen proved most helpful by freely sharing his own observations. He spoke of the unique difficulties of attempting missionary work in Jerusalem, asserting that without doubt the Jewish community would subject any of its members who made enquiries about Christianity to a high degree of antagonism. Young had estimated the total Palestinian Jewish community to be in the region of ten thousand persons, similar to his own estimate, but although the community was increasing, most of its members lived in poverty, with as many as one in ten being officially classified as paupers. Suffering from the intolerance and rapacious exploitation of both Muslims and Christians, Jews had to resort to buying protection for themselves by the payment of higher rents. In Young's view they were fearfully oppressed, with the frequently recurring outbreaks of plague being used by unscrupulous landlords to further increase rents and extort money. This, in turn, made Jewish people suspicious of anyone who did not belong to their community.[17]

Both Young and Nicolajsen's estimates of the size of Jewish settlement in the Holy Land were far smaller than the deputation had been led to believe. By 1839 Jewish *aliyah* had slowed down, compared with the preceding six-year period. The Hebrew term *aliyah*, from the final word of 2 Chronicles 36:23, means to 'go up', and had long been used by members of the Jewish diaspora to describe returning to the land of Israel. Many of the pioneer emigrants were followers of a famous Jewish leader Elijah ben Shlomo Zalman Kramer, also known as the Vilna Gaon (1720–1796). Settling first in Tzfat, and later, when permitted, in Jerusalem, his first followers, motivated by a desire to hasten the coming of the Messiah, had participated in the historic Great Aliyah. At the time of deputation, Zionist philanthropists such as Sir Moses Montefiore (1784–1885) and Edmund de Rothschild (1845–1934) actively supported *aliyah*, encouraging Northern European Jews to settle in Eretz Yisrael (the Land of Israel) as *olim*, those who make *aliyah*.

Indeed, it so happened, that Sir Moses was at that very time, plague or no plague, camped on the Mount of Olives and on 10th June the deputation decided to visit him to pay their respects, discuss Jewish resettlement of land and to assure him that the Church of Scotland would encourage every attempt to ameliorate the condition of the emigrants. As well as the hundreds of others who visited him that day, Sir Moses received them with great kindness, offered them cake and wine, and noted the occasion in his diary.[18]

The survey group dutifully, but enjoyably, made visits to many of the famous religious and historical sites within Jerusalem but, like other Christian travellers before and since, were bitterly disappointed by the Church of the Holy Sepulchre. Entering this ancient, forbidding, and austere fourth-century church, built by Constantine reputedly on the very site of Calvary and the Tomb of Christ, many find their idealised expectations dashed and share the sense of disappointment expressed by M'Cheyne: 'Calvary is the only place about Jerusalem which yields nothing but pain and disappointment ... my heart sickened at the view.'[19]

The custodianship of the church, then as now, was shared by Roman Catholic Franciscans, the Greek Orthodox Brotherhood of the Holy Sepulchre, and smaller groups of Armenians, Ethiopians, Syrians, and Copts, all jealously guarding their allotted portion. Distrust is endemic, sometimes breaking out in factional squabbles. This unseemly and unchristian quarrelling has been so intractable a problem that, apart from the century-long interlude of Crusader occupation (1099–1187), the key to the ancient church has, since the days of Caliph Omar in the seventh century, been in the keeping of the Muslim Joudeh family who, with their fellow religionists, the Nuseibehs, one of the oldest Muslim clans in Jerusalem, control access to the church. For the best part of twelve centuries, every morning the key is handed by a representative of the Joudehs to a member of the Nuseibeh family; a Christian priest then passes a wooden ladder through an aperture in one of the massive doors and a Nuseibeh climbs up to unlock them. The keys are then returned to the Joudeh representative. In the evening the door is locked in similar fashion.[20]

The Scottish ministers thought that the Christianity they witnessed at the Holy Sepulchre was a travesty, far removed from the simplicity and truth of the gospel they knew and loved. This for them cast doubt on any claim that this was truly the site of the crucifixion and burial of Christ. Yet they had to admit that they could see no plausible alternative, unless 'on the high ground above Gihon' to the southeast of the city. Edward Robinson, when visiting the Holy Sepulchre the previous year, had been equally disenchanted, and equally prejudiced against its ancient claims. A more attractive though improbable Protestant alternative location for Calvary was suggested some years later by the researches of Otto Thenius from Germany, upon whose notions General Charles Gordon, of Khartoum fame, built his theory that the true site of Golgotha was the rocky escarpment situated to the north of Bab az-Zahra (Herod's Gate). His logic, however, was both superficial and speculative, far too readily influenced by the shape of an outcrop of rock which with its two shallow caves suggested a skull, by a speculative geological link to the Temple Mount (the ancient place of sacrifice), and the existence of an adjacent ancient tomb with a rolling stone, now known as the Garden Tomb. To add some plausibility to his claim, Gordon noted a supposed Jewish tradition that the hill was known as the 'house of stoning,' perhaps indicating an ancient place of execution. Today the rocky hill is crowned by a Muslim cemetery and at its feet lies the East Jerusalem Bus Station.

Though subjectively attractive, Gordon's theory has little historical credence. Writing in the 1907 issue of *Palestine Exploration Quarterly*, with justifiable heavy irony, the Irish archaeologist and Director of Excavations for the Palestine Exploration Fund, Robert Alexander Stewart Macalister, himself an evangelical Irish Presbyterian, accurately summed up the strength of the evidence in its favour.

> In conversation with tourists at the hotel in Jerusalem I constantly hear such a remark as this: 'I came to Jerusalem fully convinced that the Church of the Holy Sepulchre was the true site; but I went to the Church and saw all the "mummery" that goes on there, and I saw the Muhammadan [sic] soldiers guarding the place to prevent the Christians fighting. Then I went to that peaceful garden: and then

I knew that the Church was wrong, and that [General] Gordon had found the real site.' This is the most convincing argument that can be advanced ... and it is obviously quite unanswerable.[21]

Macalister's concern in demolishing specious and sentimental arguments was that the conception they convey is erroneous: the tomb was simply too mean to be that of a rich man like Joseph of Arimathea. He ended his article by slamming shut the door on speculation: 'The true site of the Holy Sepulchre is lost and forgotten, and there is no reason to hope that it will ever be recovered.' But, then, Macalister held no brief for the traditional site of Calvary and the Tomb, within the Church of the Holy Sepulchre. His opinion of that would have reinforced the doubts of the four Scotsmen: the Holy Sepulchre is sited within the walls of Jerusalem and not as recorded in John 19:20 and Hebrews 13:12, and the popular hymn, 'outside the city wall.'

This observation, however, is dismissed by modern historians, including Prof. Dan Bahat, one of Israel's most esteemed archaeologists, who points to the many changes in the alignment of the walls and boundaries of the city, which, combined with clear evidence of six first-century graves in the area of the church, and added to the strength of communal memory retained in venerable tradition, mean that few doubts remain that the area surrounding the Church of the Holy Sepulchre was once outside the walls of Jerusalem, which were expanded to take in that site shortly after the death of Jesus.[22] One wonders what Macalister would make of the current state of the evidence.

Disappointed though they were with the Holy Sepulchre, the deputation found other locations much more congenial, especially Bethlehem, Hebron, and Bethany. Indeed Bethany was Bonar's and M'Cheyne's favourite spot. Twice they walked from the city and around the foot of the Mount of Olives to visit the village.[23]

Notwithstanding the hazardous presence of bubonic plague it was agreed that it was necessary to risk visiting the Jewish Quarter where, out of some five thousand Jews living in Jerusalem, they found only about eighty – all strictly orthodox – resident in the Quarter. Here there were two synagogues, one each for the Sephardi and Ashkenazi members of the community, the poor furnishings of both providing mute evidence of the great poverty which had befallen the community. From a synagogue they stepped into an equally ill-kempt *yeshiva*, or rabbinic training and study centre, and from there into the home of the seventy-year-old Rabbi Haim who, on hearing of their arrival at Jerusalem, had welcomed them with a present of wine sent via Nicolajsen, with whom he maintained a friendly relationship.[24]

A visit was made to the *Kotel*, then commonly known as the Wailing Wall, and now since the 1967 Six-Day War – when it passed to Israeli control – the Western Wall. Here they watched Jewish worshippers uttering audible prayers with their face in close proximity to the wall and witnessed the practice of inserting written prayers in the joints between the Herodian stone blocks. This tradition, which probably commenced in the 18th century, is said to be based partly on the Midrashic teaching that God's presence has never left the Jerusalem temple and partly on Kabbalistic principles that all prayer ascends to Heaven via the Temple Mount, of which the Western Wall is a boundary. Today, the Western Wall Heritage Foundation offers a service whereby people can email their prayers either to be prayed by the continuous daily *minyan* or to be printed and placed between the stones. To make room for others, twice a year the notes are removed and put into safe keeping.

When M'Cheyne later re-visited the area he engaged in conversation with a young Jewish man he saw reading Psalm 22, but, despite friendly attempts to persuade him that the psalm foretold the death by crucifixion of the Messiah, the young man remained unconvinced and 'made the sign with the lip which Easterns [sic] make to show that they despise what you are saying.'[25]

Their last day at Jerusalem was 18th June. They took their farewell of the city by making a final walking tour of its more notable sites, a route which, security considerations allowing, can be followed today:

> We passed through the bazaar and narrow ruined streets, and purchased some articles as memorials of Jerusalem. Issuing forth by St Stephen's Gate, we crossed the Kedron, and once more visited Gethsemane ... we went up the face of the Mount of Olives ... standing on the summit ... [and] once more enjoyed the commanding prospect of

the Dead Sea [and] our last view of the Jordan .... Leaving the summit, we descended, ... upon the 'city of Mary and her sister Martha' ... We left Bethany with regret, and proceeded to Jerusalem by the broad and rocky pathway. Leaving the track, and descending ... we tried to find our way ... through the hanging village of Siloam. [Pausing] at the Pool of Siloam ... [we then] ascended to the wall of the city, and entering by the Zion Gate, once more passed through the Jewish quarters.[26]

Somewhat dragging their feet, they reluctantly left Jerusalem with its rich heritage and supreme spiritual significance, concluding that all they had seen and learned had left them deeply moved and highly motivated. Above all, they were concerned that their impressions would be enduring: 'May we never lose the feelings of intense compassion toward Israel, which these few days spent in Jerusalem awakened; and never rest till all the faithful of the church of our fathers have the same flame kindled in their hearts!'

Then, accompanied by Nicolajsen for a few miles, they headed north out of Jerusalem, following the ancient route through Samaria that traverses the spine of the central highlands, before veering north-west along the ridge of the Carmel to the port of Haifa.

⟨⟩ 12 ⟨⟩

From Galilee to Europe

Galilee, Turkey, and Europe, June to November 1839

A day's journey from Jerusalem brought the travellers to Sychar (possibly the village of Askar), where they set up their tents outside the walls. The following morning, Andrew Bonar, impatient to find Jacob's famous well, set out before sunrise and passing through the already opened village gate searched the streets for signs of a well. Meeting a small Jewish boy he asked him in Hebrew if he knew the way. He did, but he first took Bonar to see a synagogue which was small, clean, and full of worshippers, perhaps fifty or so being present. Handed over to an older guide, Bonar in due course arrived at the well less than two miles away. Surrounded by the ruins of a twelfth-century church, the well was covered by a low-arched stone structure and as Bonar stooped down to enter, his pocket Bible fell from his coat pocket, dropping into the well. His guide shook his head and said, 'Ah, the well is deep', thereby inadvertently using precisely the same words that eighteen hundred years earlier the Samaritan woman used in her conversation with Jesus. Bonar gave up his Bible as irrecoverable.[1]

In 1843, when passing through Palestine on his return to Scotland, John Wilson of Mumbai, having heard of Bonar's loss, hired a young Samaritan, appropriately called Yakub, whom he had lowered on a rope to attempt the recovery of the Bible from the mud and debris at the bottom of the seventy-five foot deep well. Remarkably, Yakub was successful in finding it, or at least what

159

remained of it. Unsurprisingly, after having been steeped in water and mud for four years the Bible was, with the exception of its board covers, little more than a mass of pulp, but Wilson brought back to Scotland what remained. Still recognisably a Bible, it is part of the collection of New College Library, Edinburgh.[2]

The deputation found no further Jewish communities in the hills of Samaria and no more would be discovered until they arrived ten days later at Haifa. Here, a quarantine station was located to attempt to avert the bubonic plague pandemic and here the travellers were detained. The system in place, they were told, was based on the most modern scientific principles and offered two regimes: travellers could remain in isolation and boredom for fourteen days, or if they consented to have all their clothes washed in sea water, they could leave after a week. They chose the former, and here in this sanitary bottleneck again met Lord Claud Hamilton and his companions, and also Sir Moses Montefiore and his entourage. Notwithstanding his dislike of their proselytisation attempts, Montefiore's diary reveals his pleasure at this reunion and the stimulus he enjoyed in conversation with Drs Keith and Black. M'Cheyne and Bonar seem to have been excluded from this aristocratic company as Sir Moses and Dr Keith – Keith being directly related to the Keiths of Aquhorsk, descendants of Alexander Keith, third son of the second Earl Marischal – took long walks together on the beach deep in discussion on how the prophecies of the Hebrew Scriptures had found fulfilment in the general dereliction evident in the land.[3] Sir Moses' considerations had led him to many of the same conclusions as Keith, but he resolutely refused any attempt to be drawn into a discussion of the New Testament.[4]

On his arrival at Haifa, Sir Moses had been pleased to receive from the Superior of the Mount Carmel monastery a gift of Lebanese wine. Lebanese viniculture was renowned as far back as the times of Hosea, who prophesied that when Israel would return to the Lord and to the Land 'they [should] blossom like the vine; their fame shall be like the wine of Lebanon' (Hosea 14:7). Montefiore kindly passed on to the deputation two bottles of this fabled wine, but Bonar and M'Cheyne were not enamoured and were of the opinion that if this was a sample of the famous wine alluded to in Hosea then it had lost much of its excellence with the passing years.[5]

In addition to conversing with the Montefiore and Hamilton camps, the four used this time of enforced idleness to catch up with literary tasks, reworking the notes of their journey, and writing to the committee in Edinburgh, as well as to family and friends.

Their quarantine over, they set sail to Beirut in a large open boat without any kind of shelter. Crossing Haifa Bay, they passed Acre, from where, a few days earlier, they had heard gunfire saluting Mehmet Ali's victory over the Sultan at Nizip in Eastern Turkey. Some hours later, as they sailed past Sidon, they heard drifting across the waves sounds of celebration in honour of the same victory.[6] Twenty-five miles further on, their boat rounded a headland and slipped into Beirut harbour, where they disembarked. Over the ensuing days they took stock of the past phase of their journey and planned for the future. All agreed that it was essential to backtrack and visit Galilee, for they had heard that as many as twelve hundred Jews lived in Tiberias and possibly another two thousand in Tzfat.

Black, however, had that year celebrated his fiftieth birthday, and felt his constitution was not up to any more fatiguing travel. He had no enthusiasm for any personal involvement in further exploration. The fall from the camel in Egypt, followed by the hardships of the journey, the effect of the heat, as well as his depressed mood since being quarantined at Haifa, all conspired to discourage him from further exertion. After discussion and prayer, it was unanimously concluded that he and Keith would set out for home on 7th July, travelling as speedily as possible by steamboat to Istanbul from where another steamer would take them across the Black Sea and then via the River Danube into the heart of Europe. They would then cross Germany and Holland by coach and rail, before sailing across the North Sea to London, from whence a train would carry them back to Edinburgh. Whilst their intention was to get home as rapidly as possible, they agreed to visit on the way as many Jewish communities as they could, especially those of Pesth and Vienna.[7]

It was agreed that M'Cheyne and Bonar would turn southwards again to visit Galilee. As Ibrahim's and Ahmed's contracts terminated at Beirut, they arranged to be accompanied by Erasmus

Scott Calman, a Lithuanian Jewish convert, newly arrived in Beirut from a short visit to Britain. Calman was no stranger, having met M'Cheyne and Bonar at the valedictory prayer meeting that had been held in the Regent Square Church in London, and now after five year's service with Nicolajsen in Jerusalem, Calman was fluent in Arabic and had an intimate knowledge of large tracts of the country through which they would be passing.[8]

On the afternoon of July 8th, after bidding an emotional farewell to Ibrahim and Ahmed, Bonar, M'Cheyne, and Calman, accompanied by newly hired attendants, set out for Galilee. Their route took them southwards along the coast to Sidon, where they visited the synagogue, then to Tyre which they considered a 'wreck of a town.' Two days later they reached what they took to be Cana, the location of our Lord's first miracle, and camped there for the night. The next morning they were rudely awoken by the sound of horses and the alarming appearance at their tent flap of a soldier armed with a rifle and pistols. Much to their relief his purpose was friendly, warning them that Bedouin raiders on the road to Tzfat, to which they now planned to go, had shot and killed a Jew and he and his men were on their way to retrieve the body.

Fully cognisant of the risks, M'Cheyne, Bonar, and Calman decided to continue exactly as planned as they wanted to reach Tzfat that day. Apart from Bonar somehow conspiring to fall off his mule on a steep ascent, without any hurt to himself, their journey was entirely uneventful. Moreover, the Jews of Tzfat were very impressed that, in such a dangerous area and in such troubled times, these young travellers preferred to trust in God rather than carry guns.[9] Not all Christian travellers followed this practice. Some went well armed, whilst others made a show of pretending to be armed. Robinson's American party had, the previous year carried two old muskets and a pair of pistols but without ammunition, trusting that a show of arms would deter potential assailants. It did.

The beautiful hilltop town of Tzfat, with its old stone houses, whispering pines, fruit trees, water pools, and olive groves, is set in a wonderful location high in the Galilean hills and blessed with panoramic views over Galilee and the country to the east. Though the Galilean hills can be cold in winter, the climate is dry and refreshingly cool in the heat of summer. Indeed, the local people summed up the climate of Jerusalem with the single Hebrew word *esh*, 'fire', and that of balmy Tzfat with *ruach*, 'spirit' or 'breeze'. Attractive as the surroundings may have been, in 1839 the population had been greatly impoverished by a destructive earthquake two years earlier. Though friendly towards the three strangers, they thought the people were on their guard against them. This was exactly the case: Montefiore had issued instructions that they were not to have any dealings with the Scotsmen.[10]

Nevertheless, four very enjoyable days were spent reconnoitring the area. The inhabitants were observed, Jewish cemeteries viewed, and ancient synagogues visited. They were especially fond of the picturesque sixteenth-century Sephardic Alsheich synagogue which had survived the earthquakes of 1759 and 1837 undamaged. Ironically, despite Montefiore's attempts to make Tzfat unattractive for missionaries, they reached the conclusion that of all the places they had so far visited in Palestine, it was by far the best location for a mission station.

Reflecting on the possibilities, they concluded that an ideal arrangement would be for missionaries to be based in Tzfat during the heat of summer, decamping to warmer Tiberius in winter. The only real hindrance to missionary settlement was the unsettled state of the region. Marauding Bedouin were taking full advantage of the absence of Mohamed Ali's soldiers, busy at war against the Turks. The passage of time did little to improve the situation: two years later Bonar and M'Cheyne were forced to admit that despite their strong preferences for Palestine, the country was still far too troubled for any missionary community to be safe.

The party descended from Tzfat to the lake-side and, passing through Capernaum, followed the west shore of the Kinneret to arrive later the same day at Tiberius. Here they spent two days visiting biblical locations and meeting the local Jewish community. They enjoyed fresh fish caught from the lake which, from their description, was certainly the bony St Peter's fish or *musht* (Tilapia galilea), which is still fried and served to visiting tourists. They also found that here in Tiberius the threat of Bedouin raiders had so unnerved the local population that the town was home to only around six hundred Jews, Nicolajsen's estimate had led them to expect at least double the number.

From Tiberius, they crossed the plain of Esdralon to the northern slopes of Mount Tabor. Despite none of the Gospels identifying the 'high mountain' of Jesus' transfiguration by name, and although the biblical scholar Henry Alford cast doubt upon Mount Tabor being the location, from as far back as the third century down to the present, the majority opinion has disagreed.

Rising solitary above the Jezreel valley, Tabor is a wonderful viewpoint, with a three-hundred-and-sixty-degree panorama of Galilee. So, having sent their baggage ahead to the village of Daburiyya, on the northwest side of the hill, and it being almost dark, they, in a fit of overconfidence, decided to dispense with the services of a local guide and make a hurried ascent from the north. No sooner had they started out when they promptly lost the path, but, after dragging their mules through scrub and bush up a very steep slope, the party eventually arrived at the summit just in time to watch the sun sink below the Mediterranean in the west. Apprehensive and wearied, they now hastily scanned around, found a path and started their moonlight descent to Daburiyya. Before they had gone far they were surrounded by men armed with clubs who sprang out at them from the bushes, but much to their relief the men turned out to be a search party sent from the village to find them.

Once safely off the hill, they were told that a band of Bedouin had been seen lurking in the woods through which they had passed and, it was rumoured, had killed several travellers the day before. A few days later, when following the long Carmel ridge to Haifa, they had another narrow escape, but their servant Antonio, in retracing his steps to find a lost cloak, was not so fortunate. He was attacked by Bedouin, robbed of his horse, stripped of all his clothes, and left naked at the roadside.[11]

Reaching Haifa with little further excitement, the group then made its way northwards, once more following the ancient road through Tyre and Sidon, to reach Beirut on Saturday 20th July. Finding that the next steamer for Izmir (Smyrna), on Turkey's Aegean coast, would not sail until the following week, they reconciled themselves to the luxurious thought of restful days writing up their journals in Giuseppe's comfortable inn, where earlier they had stayed with Black and Keith. Among the diversions Bonar and M'Cheyne reported enjoying that week was another short visit to Sir Moses Montefiore and his wife, who were said to be waiting for a steamer to Egypt, but the curious thing is, that according to Montefiore's own diary, he wasn't in Beirut on that date; he was in Malta, having arrived there on 18th July, aboard the recently launched HMS *Acheron*, which he had boarded on July 10th, departing Beirut at 7 o'clock in the evening. Apart from consulting the log of HMS *Acheron*, there seems to be no way of reconciling this disparity.[12]

Reviewing their experience to date, M'Cheyne and Bonar felt confident about presenting to the committee in Scotland some conclusions drawn from their investigations of the past months. There were, they argued, five solid arguments in favour of establishing mission stations in Palestine. Firstly, because the Jewish community in the Holy Land was impoverished, oppressed, and vulnerable it responded to those who showed it kindness. Secondly, most Jews in the land were strictly orthodox, believing the Bible to be God's Word and expecting the coming of the Messiah, and this, they thought, would provide a significant area of common ground for intelligent engagement. Thirdly, Jerusalem and Judea were the centre of the Jewish world and whatever happened there would be widely reported across the Diaspora. Fourthly, in the face of Christian anti-Semitism and Islamic hostility, and because of the kindness of the consul at Jerusalem, the Jewish community looked to the British as their friends. Lastly, work established in the Holy Land would probably be well supported by the Christian public. They concluded, perhaps over-optimistically, that, notwithstanding the unsettled nature of Galilee, the Holy Land presented not only the most attractive but also the most significant field for missionary work among the Jews.[13]

Eight days later, M'Cheyne, Bonar, and Calman embarked for Izmir with M'Cheyne suffering from a bout of fever which continued to trouble him when they arrived four days later. In the town they found a British surgeon serving on board a Royal Navy frigate who was able and willing to attend to him, and the very kindly Rev. William B. Lewis and his wife agreed to take on his care, greatly alleviating his condition. Lewis was chaplain to the British Consul in Izmir and incumbent of the English Church at Boudjah, just outside Izmir. He had previously worked with the LSPCJ and introduced the Scottish ministers to John Baptist Cohen, a Jewish Christian from Istanbul who also worked for the LSPCJ. Cohen was a great linguist, who had suffered greatly on account of his Christian faith but whose winsomeness had gained him acceptance in the nine-thousand strong local Jewish community.[14]

Towards the end of their second week at Boudjah, it was clear that M'Cheyne's health was still not sufficiently robust to allow him to continue the journey, so it was decided that he should remain in the care of Mr and Mrs Lewis until able to join the others in Istanbul. Bonar and Calman took farewell of M'Cheyne and boarded the Austrian steamship *Stamboul*, disembarking two days later at Istanbul.

Up to that date, Christian work among the city's Jewish community had been carried on by the LSPCJ through the agency of Rev. S. Farman, who had been appointed to the city five years earlier. Though a faithful worker, Farman had seen only three Jewish people baptised, one of whom was a German Jew called Merkuson. Farman was introduced to Bonar and Calman and shared with them information concerning the size and nature of the community. It turned out that Merkuson had come to Christian faith through the influence of William G. Schauffler, the American missionary to the Jews in the city, who had become so dispirited by the difficulties of evangelism that he had taken the decision to concentrate on translation and the production of booklets. Even that, he discovered, was greatly beset with difficulties. The Ladino version of the Psalms, which he painstakingly prepared and printed, was anathematised by the rabbis of Istanbul, who banded together to denounce him and obstruct its sale.[15]

There were other American missionaries active in the city, but they were all working among the Armenian and Greek Christian communities, rather than among Jews or Moslems. One of them, a Mr Calhoun, accompanied Bonar and Calman on water-borne sightseeing tours of the city, including a visit to the Ayasofya Mosque, the former Byzantine basilica of Hagia Sophia. Much to their disappointment they were frustrated in an attempt to visit the Topkapi Palace and see the Sultan's harem, the famous Seraglio. Instead, they witnessed the Whirling Dervishes, followers of Jalaluddin Rumi, the famous Sufi Muslim mystic. What they understood by what they saw and what Bonar took to be ecstatic cries of 'Ullah, Illah!' sent shudders down their spines, leaving them to reflect somewhat inappropriately on the words of Psalm 74:20, that the 'dark places of the earth are full of the habitations of cruelty.'[16]

The complex Istanbul Jewish community consisted not only of Sephardim and Ashkenazim, but also a sizeable number of Karaites. The distinctive feature of this Jewish sect was its adherence to the Hebrew Scriptures alone as their source of authority. Karaites reject the Talmud, the written record of Jewish oral teaching on biblical texts, ethics, traditions, and history, popularly held by mainstream Jews to be at least as authoritative, if not more so, than the Bible itself. This was the first time the deputation had met Karaites and they were so impressed with their friendliness that they allowed themselves to be misled into thinking that Karaite freedom from Talmudic tradition might open up a frank discussion of evangelical Christian teaching based on the sole authority of Scripture. It was not to be.

On the face of it, the benefits and opportunities of locating a missionary among the eighty-thousand strong Istanbul community seemed obvious, but these had to be offset against the high cost of living in the city and the total lack of protection afforded by the Porte – the Ottoman government – to any Jewish inquirers or converts, who would be fiercely ostracised. Because the Jewish community enjoyed the status of official recognition by the Porte, it was possible for Jewish leaders to obtain the imprisonment of alleged converts to Christianity. Indeed, Bonar and Calman heard of a young Jewish Christian who, after his conversion became public knowledge, was handed over by a rabbi from Izmir to the Turkish authorities to be tortured and imprisoned. In addition, if a Jew embraced Protestantism, both Armenian and Greek Orthodox

Christians might harass him. Unlike the local missionaries, who were perhaps too close to the situation to be objective, the deputation did not find it at all strange that in such an oppressive and intimidating environment Jewish Christians were few.[17]

Planning to leave Istanbul on 26th August, Bonar and Calman were delighted to find M'Cheyne aboard that day's steamer from Izmir fully recovered. A few hours later all three departed for the River Danube aboard the Black Sea packet boat, *Fernando Primo,* whose captain was an Englishman. At midday on 28th they entered the delta, reaching Galati the next day. Here they came up against the elaborate thousand-mile-long European plague *cordon sanitaire* designed to keep the pandemic at bay, and were forced to disembark to endure another tedious quarantine of a week's duration.

In boarding the Danube steamer, they had mistakenly thought they had left privations behind them in the East and had come entirely unprepared for the primitive conditions that now confronted them. Nevertheless, as seasoned travellers, they assured themselves that they were by now 'inured to the rude life of those that live in tents.' They were grateful to Charles Cunningham, the British vice-consul in Galati, who took an interest in them and who provided his *brashovanca* for their onwards journey to Iași. They found travelling by *brashovanca,* a covered carriage without springs, both primitive and unreliable as it transported its four passengers in considerable discomfort.

The importance that they attached to the city of Iași, the capital of Moldavia, may best be judged from the fact that Bonar and M'Cheyne devoted twenty pages of their published record to descriptions of its large Jewish community. They considered both Bucharest and Iași to be of immense significance as potential mission stations. At the time, as a result of extensive Jewish immigration into Moldavia from Russia and Polish Galicia, Iași's Jewish community was burgeoning, its twenty-thousand members accounting for approximately fifty-percent of the city's population. Lodging at the Hotel St Petersburg, owned and run by a baptised Jew who attended the Orthodox Church, Bonar, M'Cheyne, and Calman set out to visit Jewish schools, synagogues and other community meeting places. They were also invited to attend a Jewish marriage ceremony.

In a community made up of so many diverse groups, one sect in particular excited Bonar and M'Cheyne's curiosity: it was the newly established ultra-orthodox 'Chabad'. At the other extreme, they met Jews who were committed to the very liberal interpretation of Judaism characteristic of the Reform movement. It was, however, their opinion that although a missionary stationed in Iași might be given permission to operate, he would undoubtedly face animosity from the Orthodox Church. Indeed, if one were sent to the Jews anywhere in the two principalities of Walachia and Moldavia and succeeded in converting a single Orthodox Christian, that might prove fatal to the mission and every door would immediately be shut to Protestant missionaries.[18]

Leaving Walachia and Moldavia, they now entered Habsburg Poland, and yet another quarantine station on the *cordon sanitaire,* where even the mail was opened cautiously with long tongs and subjected to fumigation. But it was not the country's medical precautions that concerned them; it was the government's equally strenuous attempt to exclude the evangelical message. Habsburg religious intolerance made them feel extremely unwelcome leading them to conclude that the Austrian empire was a realm where ignorance and superstition led souls to hell in peaceful unresisting compliance.

At one point they faced a very hostile policeman, 'a sharp bustling Austrian, with a pipe in his mouth', who took great pleasure in trying to entrap them. Letters purporting to be evidence of illegal activities were produced to show they had been seen in a synagogue, where they had joined in the *Shema* prayer and bought some sets of *tephillin*, or phylacteries. Outraged by what they saw as the sheer impertinence of these allegations, Bonar and M'Cheyne hardly knew how to respond. Feeling both perplexed and amused in equal measure, they decided to stand on their dignity as Protestant ministers from Scotland and explained that all Scottish ministers were taught Hebrew and they had read in the synagogue only to prove to the Jews that they were familiar with their language. As for the *tephillin,* they were merely souvenirs. Their condescending but honest answers thwarted their interrogator. He handed back their passports, but spitefully impounded all their books, including their personal Bibles, sealed them up in a parcel, and forbade them to unwrap it until they had left Austrian territory.

In Lvov their British patriotism was once more ignited when they were asked to fill in a questionnaire, which they found easy enough to do, but were scandalised by the suspicious and tyrannical attitude of their questions. By comparison, they honestly, if chauvinistically, concluded that, in all their experience, no country had the freedoms they enjoyed as British subjects, because, they said, 'no land on earth has had the truth of God so fully preached, and so widely embraced'.[19]

What they saw of the Jewish community in Poland revealed some of the deep communal tensions within the European Diaspora. On the one hand traditionalists held tenaciously to orthodox life and practice; on the other the secularists longed for political emancipation and social integration. Nowhere was this contrast more clearly seen than in two events, separated by just a few days. The first was their experience of a traditional Chasidic synagogue service during the celebration of the feast of Simchat Torah, which marks the completion of the annual Torah reading cycle and is one of the most joyful holidays in the Jewish calendar. As is customary, the Torah scroll was processed through an ecstatic congregation dancing in celebration of the giving of the Law. There is an old Chasidic saying, possibly dating from around this time, which goes something like this: 'we rejoice in the Torah, and the Torah rejoices in us; the Torah wants to dance, so we become the Torah's dancing feet.' All three travellers were greatly moved by the experience, although Bonar and M'Cheyne questioned the necessity of dancing during a service of worship, a response rather more muted than theirs of the Sufi whirling dancers of Istanbul. Afterwards they were warmly welcomed into the rabbi's home for conversation.[20]

By complete contrast, their second encounter was with a group of 'Jews of the New School' who, like most Reform Jews they met in Poland, made it clear that political emancipation and the opportunity to assimilate into the gentile world was the only Messianic hope they entertained.[21]

As they passed through little towns like Brody, five miles from what was then the Russian border and is now the Ukraine border, they discovered not only Jewish communities in the midst of a larger gentile population but to their great interest, entire Jewish villages, or *shtetls*, in which the whole culture was suffused with the ethos of authentic Judaism. At a post-office in one of these villages they were intrigued to see signs and notice boards not only in German and Polish, but in the Hebrew characters of *mame-loshn*, the 'mother tongue', Yiddish.

It was near Krakow, while spending Sunday afternoon in a quiet country district, that M'Cheyne managed to get himself into another scrape. In the afternoon he went for a walk and having travelled about a mile came to a pleasant secluded spot where he sat down to read. Almost immediately he was set upon by two shepherds bent on robbing him and desperately struggled with them for a quarter of an hour until, utterly fatigued, he fell to the ground. His assailants looked at him and, thinking they had done him more harm than they had intended, indeed more than they had actually done, took to their heels and fled into the surrounding woods. When M'Cheyne recovered sufficient strength to return to his colleagues they all acknowledged that yet again 'the hand of God, that had delivered us out of many dangers during our previous wanderings, had been eminently stretched out again.'[22]

Krakow impressed them as a potential centre of evangelistic work, concluding that the vast number of Jewish people may have been made ready to hear the gospel from a missionary by their communal sufferings. But, at the same time, they recognised that the difficulties would also be very great, especially those emanating from a hostile Catholic Government. They crossed from Austria into Prussia, to arrive at the Grand Duchy of Posen (now Poznan in Poland) where, they were told, there lived upwards of seventy-three thousand Jews, offering, they thought, a vast opportunity for a missionary, not least because it was already the location of schools established and supported by the Edinburgh Ladies Association.

They found that a considerable number of Jews were already attracted to the gospel and, when missionaries were in town, were keen to attend special church services. The local missionary, Rev. J. C. Hartmann, told them that as many as five hundred Jews would gather for meetings in the parish church; and in a nearby town, on one occasion, nearly eight hundred had attended a service, at first listening with great interest, but when Hartmann stated that Jesus was the Messiah, they all rose as one and left the church in protest.[23]

In Berlin, they met Rev. C. Becker, an LSPCJ missionary from Dessau, and learned that the city had a Jewish population of five thousand, although other estimates put it as nearer to eight thousand. Between eight hundred and a thousand Jews were said to be receiving Christian instruction. Bonar, Calman, and M'Cheyne attended a Berlin Reform synagogue, visited a museum and went to hear Becker preach a sound but cautious Protestant sermon in the Roman Catholic Kloster-Kirche.

The highlight of their visit to Berlin was an opportunity to attend one of August Neander's lectures at the University. Neander had been born into a Jewish family in 1789 as David Mendel, but as a young man of seventeen he embraced the Christian faith, becoming a Lutheran and changing his name to Neander, meaning 'new man', to which he added the Christian names Johann August Wilhelm. By 1839 Neander was in his prime, an eminent church historian, who had completed the first volumes of his encyclopaedic *Allgemeine Geschichte der Christlichen Religion und Kirche* (General History of the Christian Religion and Church). Neander was, to a certain degree, a disciple of Friedrich Schleiermacher, believing that human emotion was religion's true origin and that sound theology could thrive only in the calmness of a soul consecrated to God, but unlike Schleiermacher, Neander did not consider Scripture to be a fallible record of human feeling about God, but a totally reliable supernatural revelation. He was a strong advocate of Lutheran orthodoxy and an able opponent of rationalism and higher criticism. Although he staunchly defended the place of feeling and devotion in the Christian life, Neander was strongly averse to public displays of piety. M'Cheyne and Bonar, both of a somewhat pietistic bent, noted with surprise and disapproval that his classes neither commenced nor ended with prayer. [24]

The final port of call in Europe was Hamburg, where they were to embark for London but not before meeting with J. C. Moritz, one of the most revered of the early missionaries to the Jews. In 1823 Moritz had responded to a call from Czar Alexander I, who, influenced by the mysticism of Barbara Juliana Freifrau von Krüdener, was concerned to carry on Christian work among Jews in Russia. Moritz later joined the LSPCJ and took up work in Hamburg in 1825.[25]

It was there, on opening a newspaper one morning, Bonar and M'Cheyne were astounded but overjoyed to read a brief and tantalising report of revivals that had taken place under William Chalmers Burns in Kilsyth and M'Cheyne's church, St Peter's, in Dundee. They could delay no longer and hurried homewards. Arriving in London on 6th November, they were met by members of the committee eager to hear of their travels, but they would not be deflected and hastened on to Scotland. Bonar's homecoming to Collace was cool and understated and he made little comment about it. M'Cheyne's reception was altogether different. A prayer meeting was called, attended by a large crowd who warmly welcomed him home.

A few weeks later, both men dutifully reported to the committee in Edinburgh, before travelling from parish to parish telling of all they had seen and heard. Aware of the Scottish Church's affinity with the Jewish people, they found it gratifying to be greeted by the presence of 'aged, patriarchal-looking men of our Scottish peasantry' gathering to hear of 'the seed of Abraham, God's friend – the nation for whose ingathering their godly sires used fervently to pray, as they dropped a tear over the narrative of their miseries.'[26]

⊰⊱ 13 ⊰⊱

Returning to Revival

Dundee, Autumn 1839

NEWS of revival, though it certainly took M'Cheyne and Bonar by surprise, was not, in fact, totally unexpected. For centuries the Scottish church had understood God's promise to Abram, 'I will bless those who bless you' (Gen. 12:3), to mean that if the Church sought Israel's spiritual wellbeing it too would be blessed. Without a moment's hesitation, both men immediately connected the revival with the very task in which they had been engaged since leaving Scotland.

> It appeared also worthy of special notice and thanksgiving, that God had done this in the very year when the Church of Scotland had stretched out her hand to seek the welfare of Israel, and to speak peace to all their seed. And we felt that the same promises that had so often supported us in our trials, had been made good also to our Church at home – 'Blessed is he that blesseth thee:' 'Pray for the peace of Jerusalem; they shall prosper that love thee.'[1]

Besides, there was a general expectation of revival in the air, evidenced by a recent spate of publications on the subject. In 1838 Charles Finney's important though highly controversial, *Lectures on Revivals of Religion* had been published. Thankfully, the year following included more orthodox works, including James Douglas' *The Revival of Religion*, W. B. Sprague's *Lectures on Revivals of Religion,* and the republication by William Collins of Glasgow of Jonathan Edwards' *Narrative of the Revival of Religion in New England.*[2] In the Church of Scotland many fervently prayed that

God would awaken the nation from its spiritual torpor by honouring his promise given to Abram.

Prior to leaving Dundee in March 1839, M'Cheyne had arranged for the twenty-four-year-old William Chalmers Burns to be his locum at St Peter's during his absence. As we noted, in July, whilst still at St Peter's, Burns offered his services to the Jewish committee as a prospective missionary to Aden and an arrangement was made for him to meet with Robert Candlish to explore the possibilities.[3] But in October Burns suddenly withdrew his offer, owing to what he described as 'the peculiar circumstances' in which he was then placed. These circumstances were in fact two revivals that had broken out consecutively: the first was at Kilsyth, where he was assisting his father during the congregation's July communion services, and the second was at St Peters. According to his brother and biographer, Islay, for many weeks previous to the Kilsyth revival William Burns found he could do little other than pray: 'For weeks before he was full of prayer; he seemed to care for nothing but to pray.'[4]

When Burns returned from Kilsyth to Dundee on 8th August he found that news of the revival at Kilsyth had gone before him and the people of St Peter's were caught up in desire for prayer similar to that which had constrained him; indeed their own minister then in Turkey was also praying for their blessing.[5]

While at St Peter's M'Cheyne had taken the then unusual step of establishing small, informal prayer groups. They had flourished in his absence and now began to grow again until around forty such groups met regularly throughout the parish, five, indeed, conducted by children for children. St Peter's was full of prayer: the private prayers of the minister, the prayers of the office bearers, those of the locum minister, and small groups of men, women, and children. The congregation gathered for formal prayer meetings and prayed for revival in their private and family prayers.

Not that the congregation's prayers were narrowly focused on their own inner life or only concerned about revival, rather, encouraged by their minister, they were wide-ranging, un-stereotyped, refreshingly practical, and could at times be overtly political, as would be demonstrated at the Anti-Corn Law meeting in January 1842, when M'Cheyne said that 'if there were twenty praying Christians in Dundee, their application to the Lord would soon set them free from the Corn Laws without going to parliament.'[6] The main burden of their prayers in August 1839 was, however, for revival, and though we ought not to see the relation as simple cause and effect, it is no exaggeration to say that the Dundee revival originated in, and was nourished and promoted by prayer.

Bonar later spoke of that connection: 'Onward from that evening [10 August 1839] meetings were held every day for many weeks; and the extraordinary nature of the work justified and called for extraordinary services. The whole town was moved. Many believers doubted; the ungodly raged; but the Word of God grew mightily and prevailed.'[7]

News of the revival travelled rapidly and within a day or so of the first printed account newspapers all across the British Isles, from the *London Evening Standard* to the *Irish Wexford Independent*, and from the *John O'Groat Journal* in the north to the *South Eastern Gazette* in Kent, all were reproducing this account from the *Glasgow Argus*:

A most universal revival said to have taken place, bearing a striking resemblance to the occurrences at Shotts [1630] and Cambuslang [1741], so much celebrated in history. All worldly business is in a great measure at a stand and public worship is daily, and even oftener, performed by the ministers of the place, and others who have been called from a distance to assist in the services. The most extraordinary scenes have been witnessed on these occasions – people calling out for mercy, groaning, and praying aloud; others fainting from the intensity of their feelings, and hundreds in tears. The excitement is, indeed, altogether remarkable, and is deeply attracting the attention of the religious public.

The local *Dundee Advertiser* was more controlled and rather reticent in its reporting, alluding to but not detailing the unusual phenomena taking place at the meetings:

Symptoms of a change of some kind or other were visible in the course of last week; but all doubt of its character was removed on Sunday night, about twenty two minutes [to/past?] eleven o'clock. It is a matter of delicacy to refer to particulars; but it is not too much to say the demonstrations were striking and startling. Worship has been held in the church every night since, and is expected to continue as long as human nature can sustain the impulse.'[8]

Bonar claimed that for a time the whole town was to some extent moved. Eager to share in the experience or to satisfy their curiosity, a large number of ministers came either to experience or to assist the work, both from neighbouring parishes and also from further afield. Caesar Malan and the seventy-six-year-old Robert Haldane travelled from Geneva, while James Morgan of Fisherwick Presbyterian Church in Belfast crossed the Irish Sea to be present. But the most significant visitor was Dr John MacDonald of Ferintosh in Easter Ross, the so-called 'Apostle of the North.' MacDonald came not out of curiosity but had to be pressed to come 'to witness and assist at a work of revival.' That the repeated invitations came to him from both Kilsyth and Dundee, suggests it was young Burns who sought the sixty-year-old's mature assistance.[9]

MacDonald, a widely respected minister of great maturity, combined considerable personal experience of revivals with a cautious Highland spirituality and the emotional stability needed to consolidate the work in Dundee. Indeed, a little more than a week after the outbreak of revival, the Dundee Press noted that the manifestations were waning and the 'excitement which prevailed at first has, we understand, subsided.'[10] This diminution of the sensational coincided with the arrival of MacDonald who strongly discouraged all such phenomena, later recalling that whilst he was preaching he had not once been aware of any audible expression of emotion, although he had noticed people silently shedding tears or sobbing, which he took as evidence of an awareness of the presence of God.[11]

This difference between the ministry of Burns and MacDonald ought not be exaggerated; there was no divergence of theological conviction. Rather, the difference was one of temperament and maturity and experience. MacDonald was aware of the disparity of their ages as he spoke of 'the young Mr Burns' without in the least patronising him.[12] Nor was Burns unaware of his inexperience and was sufficiently humble to accept criticism and advice. On 23rd September 1839, in the middle of the revival, he recorded in his diary his mother's admonition to avoid the contrived stridency which had crept into his preaching and praying, which she contended had robbed it of its former sweetness and produced an unpleasant sternness. He later added, 'I thanked the Lord for this counsel, and was told by her afterwards that I had been enabled to correct the fault.'[13]

John MacDonald's reputation as a preacher had gone before him and the crowds now exceeded anything previously seen. On the evening of Tuesday 17th September more than two thousand attempted to get into St Peter's, requiring the congregation immediately to move two miles away to St David's High Kirk, the largest auditorium in Dundee.[14] All the following week MacDonald preached almost daily to similarly large congregations, and, as with Burns' ministry, the spiritually seeking remained behind after the service to hear something more from him, whilst others sought help with their concerns from other assisting ministers.

The Dundee and Angus Advertiser had correctly connected the revivals at Kirk of Shotts in 1630, at Cambuslang in 1741, and at Kilsyth in 1839 with the observation of the parish Communion. At Dundee too the revival's zenith coincided with the celebration of the Lord's Supper in October. In Scotland, since the Reformation – first due to a shortage of ministers and then by habit and custom – the Sacrament was observed infrequently, rarely more than twice a year in any congregation, often only once, sometimes less than that. Consequently its consecutive services over a number of days, usually referred to as a Communion season, often intensified spiritual expectations and became a high-water mark in the spiritual life of the parish. Usually, services were held from Thursday to Saturday, leading up to the Table Services on the Sabbath morning, and concluding with Thanksgiving services on the Monday. At these services at Dundee, Burns was principally assisted by Andrew Bonar's two brothers, John, minister of Larbert in Stirlingshire, where M'Cheyne had served as assistant prior to being called to St Peter's, and Horatius, minister of Kelso, Roxburghshire, in the Scottish Borders. Also present were Robert MacDonald of Blairgowrie, Perthshire, and Alexander Flyter of Alness in Easter Ross.

The spiritual tide, now having reached its full flood, began naturally to ebb. Disappointed, the exhausted and emotionally-drained Burns blamed what he considered his recent lack of prayer. Such self-condemnation, however, was extravagant and unwarranted. It was also unhelpful. Distracted by his own foibles, Burns' ministry was robbed of spontaneity and he felt unable to give little more than what he considered an 'exposition of doctrine', though no such failure was alleged by others.[15]

As for the results, Andrew Bonar claimed that about eight hundred people had been moved during the high-water mark of the revival. M'Cheyne agreed. When answering questions from a committee of the Aberdeen Presbytery, he set it a little lower:

> During the autumn of 1839, not fewer than from 600 to 700 came to converse with the ministers about their souls ; and there were many more, equally concerned, who never came forward in this way', adding' the number of those who have received saving benefit is greater than any one will know till the judgment-day.[16]

The cautious MacDonald, however, with a reticence typically Highland, and fearful of dishonouring God and hindering the Holy Spirit by imprudence of language, refused to estimate numbers at all. He simply stated, soon after his arrival in Dundee, that the movement was 'evidently a work of God' and left it at that.[17] John Kennedy, MacDonald's colleague and biographer commented that MacDonald kept his head in those thrilling days, his imagination regulated by the 'strong check of truth', adding that 'It cannot be said that his expectations were realized. Good was done, and abiding fruit remained; but many a bud of promise withered quite away.' Kennedy also made the telling observation, that his experience of revivals had led him to believe that the lasting fruit of an awakening was generally in inverse proportion to any emotional demonstration.[18]

MacDonald, as a good and wise spiritual midwife, was concerned mostly that those born into the kingdom of God were safely delivered and well nourished, and paid scant attention to transient infantile struggles and cries associated with their birth. Although perhaps a little too awed by the accompanying phenomena, Andrew Bonar endorsed MacDonald and Kennedy's restraint by remarking that of the eight hundred or so who had been moved many were spurious, 'impressed only for a time,' and cited with approbation Jonathan Edwards' observation that the result of revivals generally was similar to that of fruit blossom compared to the final crop of apples in the autumn.[19]

M'Cheyne, like a father hastening to meet his newborn children, rushed home from Hamburg as speedily as possible, arriving in Dundee on Thursday, November 23. Believing he had come home to the happy consequences of revival, he found that in fact he was facing a very delicate and complicated predicament. Criticism was being levelled at him from part of the congregation disaffected by an unhelpful address he chose to give immediately on return. Understandably fearful of dissipating the effect of revival, M'Cheyne had decided that on his first night back in his own pulpit he would dampen any expectation of exciting travel stories by pointedly preaching from 1 Corinthians 2:1-5: 'For I determined not to know any thing among you, save Jesus Christ, and him crucified.' This disinclination to utter a single word about his travels was, however, badly misjudged and according to his close friend James Hamilton, who was present, led to some strongly questioning his judgment and his apparent neglect of the congregation's support and prayers. As they had sent him out on the mission with their warmest blessing and had faithfully supported both him and his colleagues throughout with their keen interest and prayers, the least he could have done, they thought, was to give a brief account of his travels, rather than be sidetracked by a revival that had taken place months previously.[20]

The strongest criticisms were vocalised by an already disgruntled faction within the congregation, who, according to James Hamilton scarcely welcomed M'Cheyne's return at all. During his prolonged absence they had, more or less, transferred their allegiance to William Burns, whom they saw as ministering under an uncommon degree of the power of the Holy Spirit and the blessing of God. They now almost resented the return of their own minister, especially if it was to lead, as indeed it must, to the loss of Burns' ministry. In their eyes, the locum was, in almost every sense, the equal of the incumbent. They strongly agreed with M'Cheyne's good friend John

Milne, who was struck by Burns' 'close walk with God, his much and earnest prayer, his habitual seriousness, ... the solemnizing effect ... of his presence, and his success in leading those with whom he conversed to ... heart-searching concern about their state in God's sight.'[21]

Indeed, one of M'Cheyne's loyalest elders at St Peters, who lived long enough to hear Charles Haddon Spurgeon preach, long retained his admiration for Burns, describing him as:

> Gifted with a solid and vigorous understanding, [and] possessed of a voice of vast compass and power, unsurpassed even by that of Mr Spurgeon .... With him there was no oratorical display, but there was true eloquence; and instances are on record of persons, strong in their self-confidence and enmity to the truth, who fell before its power.[22]

And, he further opined, 'Mr Burns wielded an influence over the masses whom he addressed which was almost without parallel since the days of Wesley and Whitfield.' In addition to such invidious comparisons, further unhelpful speculations were aired about the state of M'Cheyne's health, with some doubting he was strong enough to meet the rigours of the duties of a parish minister of a growing congregation situated in an industrial town. Though perhaps meanly stated, such concerns were not altogether without some justification, as events would ultimately prove.

Faced with the looming possibility of a breach in the congregation and, indeed, between the two men themselves, Burns and M'Cheyne were given such a spirit of Christian love towards each other, that they were able to deflect all unhelpful and misplaced partisan spirit. Consequently, the complications melted away, without in any way marring the revival, blunting the edge of the Jewish mission, or leaving any trace of bitterness. Unity was persevered and strengthened and the unhelpful fractiousness soon exhausted itself. As expected, Burns' formal connection with the congregation was severed with M'Cheyne's return, and he left the congregation with mixed emotions. On the one hand, he was delighted to see his friend safely restored to his people and he sincerely prayed that M'Cheyne's future ministry might 'be honoured a hundredfold more in winning souls to Christ' than ever his had been. But, on the other hand, the events of the revival had so firmly united him to the congregation that when he took leave of them he was far too emotional to say anything very much. Empathising with his feelings, the congregation wept as they filed out of the church. As his brother Islay put it, William Burns ended the most eventful period of his ministry in Scotland and his formal connection with the St Peter's congregation in 'the tender bond of sacred affection which still, in part, bound him alike to that people and their pastor.'[23]

In December, M'Cheyne wrote to Burns asking for help to attempt a preliminary evaluation of the revival in which he had been so instrumental. Although much had been accomplished, looking at the parish as a whole, M'Cheyne lamented, 'But O, dear brother, the most are Christless still. The rich are almost untroubled.'[24]

Nevertheless, a considerable number of people had been won to Christ, and Christians had been strengthened in their faith and love to God, and their spiritual experience significantly deepened. As a direct result of the revival the young congregation, barely three years established, had grown into a strong community of vibrant faith, love, and hope to become a bright and shining light in the surrounding darkness of an industrial town.

Important as all this is, our main concern with the St Peter's revival, however, is its connection with God's promise to Abram and the mission to the Jews. To M'Cheyne and Bonar, this was patently obvious and on 17th November, less than a week after his return to St Peter's, M'Cheyne sought to explain it to his congregation. He based his talk on Romans 1:16, a sermon which later was published in *The Memoir and Remains of Robert Murray M'Cheyne* under the title 'Our Duty to Israel.'[25] In its written form it is extremely brief and can be read in as little as ten minutes, but it is very unlikely that in delivery it would have been so brief.

Two things make the address unusual. The first is the amount of illustrative material drawn directly from M'Cheyne's personal experience whilst on his travels, the other the link between obedience in taking the gospel 'to the Jew first' and the bestowal of God's blessing upon the church that does so. M'Cheyne set out four simple arguments to explain why the gospel was 'to the Jew first.'

Firstly, alluding to the parallel phrase in Romans 2:6-10, he sought to draw attention to the vulnerability of the Jewish people to divine judgement. God had specially chosen them; they had received 'more light than any other people' both by being given the Bible and having had the Messiah sent to them, but because 'they have sinned against all this light – against all this love ... their cup of wrath is fuller than that of other men.' The dictates of Christian compassion, therefore, required the Church to respond to the Jewish people with the alacrity of a physician responding to a dying man, or a lifeboat to drowning passengers of a sinking ship. Those most at risk deserve prompt attention.

Secondly, he argued that it 'is like God to care first for the Jews.' Because Christians are to be godly it was imperative that they should cultivate a love for the Jewish people and 'share with God in his peculiar affection for Israel.'

Then, there was the unique accessibility of the Jewish communities in Egypt and Palestine, Wallachia and Moldavia, Austria and Prussian Poland. The Church needed to pay careful attention to what God was saying to it in Providence. The question, therefore, was, 'Do you think that our Church, knowing these things, will be guiltless if we do not obey the call?'

Finally, the Jewish people, he argued, still had a marvellous divine destiny to fulfil. He conjectured, as did so many of his contemporaries, that Jews were likely to prove natural missionaries if they embraced the gospel. Through them God's universal blessing would flow out to the world with increasing power and effectiveness. Not wishing to overstate his case M'Cheyne cautioned against the thought that he was advocating mission to the Jews alone; mission to the Jewish people was but a part of world mission, for Christ had sent the Church to all nations and it is for us to obey His Word 'like little children'.

In drawing his remarks to a close, M'Cheyne reasoned that the evangelisation of the Jewish people, in accordance with biblical principles, would bring a much-needed blessing to the deeply troubled Church of Scotland:

> ... your souls shall be enriched also, and our Church too, if this cause find its right place in your affections. It was well said by one [Dr Alexander Duff] who has a deep place in your affections, and who is

now on his way to India, that our Church must not only be evangelical, but evangelistic also, if she would expect the blessing of God.... May I take the liberty of adding to this striking declaration, that we must not only be evangelistic, but evangelistic *as God would have us be* – not only dispense the light on every hand, but dispense it first to the Jew. [26]

This inspiring peroration alluded to a solution that might heal the discordant strife then dividing the Church of Scotland, if only the church would be united in looking outwards in a spirit of genuine concern for the spiritual welfare of the Jewish people. The festering dispute of 'the Ten Year Conflict' which ran throughout the 1830s, was centred on the question as to whether or not Jesus Christ alone was the Head of Church, or whether to some degree the Church was bound to acquiesce to the will of the State. This seemingly abstract theological debate involved profoundly practical consequences, such as the legitimacy of lay patronage and the intrusion of ministers nominated by landlords into congregations without the consent of the people. Within a few years, the conflict would give rise to the withdrawal from the Church of Scotland of the Non-intrusionists, the supporters of the spiritual liberty of the Church, who would in 1843 form the Church of Scotland Free.

In his address M'Cheyne, who was strongly committed to the overthrow of patronage and, had he lived, would undoubtedly have joined the Free Church, nevertheless he preferred to hope for harmony rather than division, healing through the renewing ministry of the Holy Spirit poured out in revival, rather than cold contention that brought the gospel into disrepute.

> Then shall God revive his work in the midst of the years. Our whole land shall be refreshed as Kilsyth has been. The cobwebs of controversy shall be swept out of our sanctuaries – the jarring and jealousies of our Church be turned into the harmony of praise – and our own souls become like a well watered garden.[27]

M'Cheyne used this material, with very great effect, when preaching in Belfast during his visit in 1840. Bonar claimed it had a marked influence on the Irish Presbyterians, encouraging them also to commit themselves to establishing a mission to the Jews, and noting that after the sermon was over, 'many ministers, as they came out, were heard saying, "How was it we never thought of the duty of remembering Israel before?"[28] Ironically, nineteen years later, Ireland knew revival on a scale which dwarfed even that of Kilsyth and Dundee taken together, although it doesn't appear that any Irish church historian, not Killen nor Gibson nor Hamilton, ever claimed that the 'Year of Grace' of 1859 had any link to the setting up in 1841 of the Irish Presbyterian mission to the Jews, a move so popular that the sheets of the petition by the laity to the General Assembly of that year, when joined together, stretched right around the interior of Belfast's Rosemary Street Church.[29]

❧ 14 ❧

A Door Opens

Budapest, Autumn and Winter, 1839/40

IN all its discussions prior to the departure of the survey group, the Committee for the Conversion of the Jews had taken for granted that the Habsburg government of Hungary was so unfavourably disposed to Protestantism that no plans needed be made to visit the city of Pesth on the north side of the river Danube. Neither the committee nor the deputation knew of a single person in the city. No one had suggested making contact with its large and important Jewish community, or had even inquired if there was a British consul who might give assistance. It seemed a lost cause.[1]

Yet it was to this city, which, with reference to the committee, we might say was 'rejected by men but in the sight of God chosen and precious', that the steps of Black and Keith were extraordinarily directed. On their journey home from Beirut they were unavoidably detained in Pesth long enough to allow them, in ways they could never have foreseen, to establish links with the most unlikely of allies, who would send them on their way with a spring in their step and a promise they would only be too eager to redeem.

Having departed from the Holy Land ahead of Bonar and M'Cheyne, Black and Keith quietly made their way home via the Black Sea and along the River Danube, with little of note taking place until they arrived in Pesth.[2] Here they had to wait for a change of steamers for their onward journey to Vienna and this gave them sufficient time to investigate the extensive Jewish community in the city and establish contact with those they thought able to provide information including rabbis, professors, and Protestant ministers.

187

Keith and Black knew they had to use the very greatest caution, because even the circulation of the Bible within the Habsburg Empire was considered a political threat, a form of subversion to be frustrated at all costs. Much to their delight and greatly to their surprise they found the Jewish community very willing to engage in friendly debate with them. One rationalist rabbi threw down the gauntlet: 'Send us a missionary, and we will reason with him.'[3]

Black and Keith were intrigued, deducing that, notwithstanding the official difficulties, Pesth might after all prove suitable as a mission station. The more he considered the matter, the more he weighed up the positive indications against the many drawbacks, the more Keith came to believe that of all the cities they had so far visited, none was so promising as a place for a Jewish mission. The only thing that seemed to bar the way was the religious intolerance of the Habsburg regime, personified by the vain and ambitious Klemens Wenzel von Metternich, who had once held in his own hand all the main offices of state. By 1839, however, his powers were dwindling, though he still refused to espouse any kind of religious liberty believing it would rapidly undermine the stability and order of the Austrian Empire. The Roman Catholic religion was, he believed, the linchpin holding together the whole fabric of the state. He once wrote, 'Religion cannot decline in a nation without causing that nation's strength also to decline.' Therefore, his legions of spies, and especially his Censorship Commission, were employed to block the propagation of all ideas that, in his opinion, might confound the peace of the state, its interests, and its Catholic order.[4]

So it was, that as Black and Keith walked the streets of Pesth, and glanced across the river to Buda and the palace of the Archduke Joseph, Palatine of Hungary, perched high on its hill, they saw it as an impregnable bastion resisting all progress of the gospel. The religious intransigence of Austro-Hungary was defying them and destroying all their hopes. Yet, remarkable as it may seem, it was precisely from the palace that help came. The forty-two-year-old Archduchess, Maria Dorothea Luise Wilhelmine Caroline of Württemberg, the third wife of the sixty-three-year-old Archduke, was a Lutheran who belonged to the evangelical Württemberg Pietist tradition, a movement whose hallmarks were holy living, a strongly subjective spirituality, reverent biblical scholarship, and missionary endeavour. The death of Maria Dorothea's twelve-year-old son, Archduke Alexander of Austria, two years previously, had sent her to her Bible, which even she was constrained to read in private, but, as she said, it was in these pages that she 'met with Jesus.'[5] The result of this encounter brought a renewal of faith, which, in her sensitive heart, formed a deep spiritual concern for the country and people of Hungary. Keith movingly described her compassion:

> Her private boudoir lay towards the front of the building. There in the deep embrasure of the window, she was accustomed, day by day, to pour out her supplications to God – looking down on the scene below – the city with its one hundred thousand inhabitants, and the vast Hungarian plains stretching away behind in the distance. For about seven years she had been praying to God for the arrival of someone who would carry the gospel to the people around. Sometimes her desire became so intense that, stretching out her arms towards heaven, she prayed almost in an agony of spirit that God would send at least one messenger of the Cross to Hungary.[6]

For some time before the arrival of Keith and Black in the city, the Archduchess had experienced wakeful nights in which she was filled with a strong premonition that something tremendous was imminent. Night after night for two whole weeks she had awoken suddenly in the middle of night and, being unable to sleep, was gripped by feelings of apprehension that she could not define. The pattern was consistent and regular, etching into her mind such a deep foreboding that she considered the only news that could possibly explain these feelings would be that of the death of her mother, and day by day she waited for confirmation of this impression.[7]

Meanwhile, both Keith and Black had fallen ill, suffering early signs of what was popularly called 'Danube Fever', but which was in fact typhus. Caused by the uncontrolled outfall of sewage from the riverside towns and cities, it was considered an almost unavoidable hazard of steamer travel on the river during the hot summer months. Weak though they were from severe abdominal and muscular pains, aching heads and rising fever, they were not daunted from making the most of their time, at least until the day Keith collapsed in the street. Returning to his hotel, he slipped into a coma and soon seemed to be on the threshold of death. Black was so distressed by his friend's illness that it worsened his own condition. His fever took on a fresh virulence until he too was confined to bed. As Keith afterwards put it, 'We were like two dead dogs.' Though in adjacent rooms, fully six weeks passed before they saw each other again.[8]

Despite the application of medical remedies, the only sign of life in Keith was a faint mist on the surface of a mirror placed near his mouth. Partly out of sympathy, and partly out of curiosity, people visited him, including some British travellers whose negative outlook was expressed by one who remarked, 'Nothing can be done but order the coffin.' The hotel staff agreed and they did order a coffin which they parked outside his room. Abandoning up all hope of recovery, they stationed two men at his bedside to carry away his body when death should come. But the pessimists were proved wrong. Keith recovered, though the doctor who attended him later confessed he had never known, heard, or read of anyone else who had come so close to the gates of death without passing through them.

As part of their preparation for travel, the Scottish ministers had taken the precaution of arranging to have letters of introduction from people of position and influence, including one from the renowned traveller, Miss Julia Pardoe, who was acquainted with Archduke Joseph and his Archduchess, Maria Dorothea.[9] By a remarkable coincidence of God's arranging, this warm-hearted, talented and intelligent woman was with her mother in Pesth at this very time. Learning of the infirmity of Black and Keith, she immediately secured an appointment with the Archduchess, informing her of the serious condition of the two ministers. The Archduchess was quite taken aback, replying that the Archduke had only recently given her a copy of Dr Keith's *Evidences of Prophecy*.[10] She now became increasingly confident that her unsettled nights and inexplicable presentiments were a preparation for this meeting and what might flow from it in future. Possessed now of a great sense of purpose, and from that very night having her normal sleep pattern restored, she gave herself to the care of the two ministers. Keith later explained this remarkable change of mood as God's direct intervention:

A motive power compared to which the mere doings of men were as nothing, sprang up that moment in her mind, which was never afterwards obliterated or diminished; which no human being had any part in exciting or anything to do with, which influenced, as it explained, her future actions and unflinching devotedness.[11]

Although no one then realised it, this was the key that opened the door to the mission at Pesth.

As Keith slowly began to regain some strength, he received his first visit from the Duchess, who commenced visiting him every other day. Her deep personal concern was evident in the way she literally cared for him with her own hand. When he was thirsty or exhausted by their lengthy conversations, she would put one hand under his head, raising it gently from the pillows, while with the other offered him something to drink. Moved by her kindness, Keith recorded that she nursed him with the very same cup with which she had nursed her dying son, and that she was Christian kindness itself to him.[12]

Maria Dorothea's extraordinary sympathy included arranging for the patient's main meal to be prescribed by the royal physician and delivered to him hot from the palace kitchen. She also sent to the hotel a bed long enough to allow the very tall Keith to lie comfortably. On another occasion, Keith could not understand why the street outside the hotel had become so unusually quiet and was told that the Archduchess had ordered the road to be covered with straw and given orders that no carriages should use it as a through road, and those having business to be in the street were not to travel faster than walking pace. To ensure her orders were obeyed, she had a soldier posted at each end of the street.[13] Keith hugely enjoyed the irony, and later enjoyed telling the story, commenting with a twinkle in his eye, 'an Austrian soldier too!'

Maria Dorothea found in Keith a wise and tactful spiritual confidante and counsellor. She was able to speak to him freely of the tragic death of her son Alexander and of her deepest spiritual concerns. She shared with him her thoughts regarding a mission to the Jews of the city, for which she was as enthusiastic as Keith himself. And when Keith raised questions as to the legality of such a mission, she stated bluntly that should the Church of Scotland see fit to begin the work, she would place herself between the mission and whatever official threats might harass it.

Nevertheless, her visits to Black's and Keith's hotel, gave her enemies an opportunity to try to implicate her in a conspiracy by circulating the rumour that, with her encouragement, Scottish Protestants planned to establish a mission for the conversion of Catholics. When Keith gently remonstrated with her that she would do well to look to her own security, she dismissed the danger as inconsequential:

> They can only lodge a complaint with Metternich, and all he can do is to present it to the Empress. But I have been beforehand with them, for I have already written to her that I have seen you, and will see you, and nothing shall prevent me; so make yourself easy about me.[14]

The reality, however, was a little different, as we shall see. As the weeks passed, Keith and Black recovered their health and by early November Black, anxious to reach home as soon as possible, felt well enough to travel ahead and take up lodgings in Vienna until the following spring, before proceeding to Scotland. Casting light on this largely undocumented period, there is among M'Cheyne's papers in New College, Edinburgh, correspondence from W. Laurie, the secretary of the Jewish committee, containing an extract of a letter from the London bookseller James Nisbet, urging Laurie to forward some important information to Robert Candlish. Dated 30th November, 1839, Nisbet's letter states that a friend called M'Cann had just returned from the continent where he had met with Black and Keith. He had been with Keith at Pesth on 11th November, and found him in poor health, though a little better than previously. Three days later, at Vienna, he had met Black and was glad to note that he too was feeling better. In his opinion, both were still in a very precarious state of health and it was absolutely necessary for someone to be sent to accompany them home and take care of their practical needs. He did not think that either would be able to travel for some time.

Nisbet told Laurie that Mr M'Cann had left the two ministers a sum of money in case they should run short, and reported that although both had received good care, the companionship of a friend from Scotland would add greatly to their comfort. The efficient Nisbet concluded by peremptorily ordering Laurie to 'pay attention to this immediately and lose no time in seeing Mr Candlish'. Laurie had taken the liberty in forwarding the letter to M'Cheyne because Nisbet had said that either he or Bonar could vouch for M'Cann, having met him at Beirut.[15]

M'Cann's pleas did not go unheeded. One of Keith's sons, George, then a medical student in Edinburgh, was dispatched urgently to Pesth. Not wishing to cast aspersions on the effectiveness of the Buda court physician, he very diplomatically administered to his father a more scientific and effective treatment without which he might not have recovered. Father and son remained in Pesth until the winter was past.[16]

The congenial spring weather encouraged Keith to make the effort and he and his son set off on the journey home. The Archduchess sped them on their way with generous provisions, including a large hamper of food. One of the crested Archducal silver spoons packed with the hamper has survived and is now in the collection of New College Library, Edinburgh.

By the middle of May, Keith's health was sufficiently recovered to allow him to attend a meeting of the committee in Edinburgh. It was with great thankfulness to God and with considerable personal satisfaction, that Keith drew the committee's attention to the strange but kindly providence that secured support from a quarter from which none had been expected. Frequently, both in private conversation and when speaking in public, he would draw attention to the remarkable events in which he and Black had been involved and told how he could trace God's guiding hand in all that had happened to them. The public, of course, knew nothing of these events and the part played by the Archduchess Maria Dorothea, to have publicised them would have placed her in serious jeopardy. Keith's account was not published until 1867, twelve years after the death of Maria Dorothea.[17] Black never wrote an account.

It was only to be expected that Keith remained adamantly convinced that above every other possible location, including Palestine itself, Pesth was by far the most attractive place for establishing the first mission station. Indeed, so resolute was he in trying to gain support for the idea that he admitted that he might have become somewhat tedious in his advocacy of Pesth. He smiled at the witty comment someone made, that the only difference between 'Pesth' and 'pest' happened to be the letter 'h'!

15

On the Brink of a Great Adventure

Scotland, December 1839 to May 1840

THE four surveyors had now fulfilled their task. During their absence the church had followed their progress with imagination, empathy, and faith, closely reading and ardently discussing the reports published in *The Home and Foreign Missionary Record*. Above all, the church had prayed for its deputies. From the Highlands to the Borders, from the Western Isles to Aberdeen, there was throughout all the country a keen sense of anticipation as the Church of Scotland was poised on the brink of a great adventure by which it would attempt to settle its immense spiritual debt to the Jewish people as the channel through which its greatest good had flowed.

In order to capitalise on the prevailing mood of popular interest and secure further support for the mission, even before Black and Keith returned, Bonar and M'Cheyne were sent to visit congregations of the church and report on what they had seen and heard and done.[1] They were told to pay especially close attention to the Scottish universities from which the committee hoped to recruit new missionaries. To prepare for this, Robert Candlish had asked for the full cooperation of the Divinity professors.[2]

Both men also reported to their presbyteries, and despite the Presbytery of Perth's original reluctance to release him, on his return Bonar found the members to be an appreciative and receptive audience. During the last week of 1839, he travelled to Glasgow and Greenock, and in the New Year visited his brother Horatius in Kelso, from where he also made short trips to Ancrum and Jedburgh.

Nineteenth-century missionary meetings, with their heady mix of vicarious travel to exotic places inhabited by seemingly outlandish peoples, were sometimes seen by congregations as interesting entertainment, a welcome diversion for those whose lives were locked into the narrow horizon of a humdrum routine. It was M'Cheyne's fear that the people of St Peter's would allow the romanticism of his exotic journey to the East to detract from the work of revival that made him reluctant to speak about his travels when he first returned to Dundee. Robert Wodrow was equally sensitive to such dangers. Ever keen to avoid any kind of sensationalism, he advised against any excessively colourful retelling of the journey and its experiences. Believing these two young men were in need of wise guidance and counsel, he wrote on behalf of the Glasgow subcommittee to M'Cheyne and Bonar, suggesting how their forthcoming visit to Glasgow might best be used to encourage a thoughtful and prayerful response to the claims of the Jewish mission, urging them to set their reports in the context of worship and remain close to Scripture throughout:

> the Committee here thought it the most appropriate way of introducing to the notice of the Christian public in Glasgow the important information which you and Mr Bonar have to communicate relative to your late Mission, by commencing with Divine worship in the usual manner. You will therefore be prepared to give us *a word of Sermon*. We cannot but think that the more spiritual the way in which we go about this great undertaking, and the more closely we adhere to Scriptural rules and examples, the more likely it is that our efforts will be blessed for the Conversion of Israel.[3]

Whatever the spiritual benefits accrued, the meetings were also beneficial financially, stimulating not only the generosity of the wealthy but also the liberality of ordinary supporters. M'Cheyne, forwarding a sum to the treasurer, added a note indicating that the recent revival in Blairgowrie had stimulated an extraordinary generosity from the poorer members of the congregation, though much less so from the more wealthy:

You know the Lord has been doing great things in Blairgowrie, saving many souls, and refreshing many of his own children. The minister proposed a thanksgiving to God, not of words only, but of substance; none were to give but those who were really thankful. In about four days the above sum [£61] was contributed. Few of the rich gave anything; so you have here the fruits of the praise of the poor of God's people in Blairgowrie. Such offerings are worth £1000 from the world. It is to be devoted to the *first Jewish missionary*. It was presented to me at an immense meeting in the Church.[4]

The round of public meetings and the writing of articles for print were undertaken only by M'Cheyne and Bonar. *The Home and Foreign Missionary Record* communicated the health problems of Drs Black and Keith in Pesth, expressed concern for their safe return, and of course rejoiced on their arrival back in Scotland, but, no letter or report containing their thoughts on the suitability of Pesth as a mission station was ever published in its pages. Dr Keith did not hold the kind of meetings that Bonar and M'Cheyne conducted and retired from his pastoral charge on his return to take up the convenorship of the Jewish Committee, a post he retained until 1847, both in the committee's pre-Disruption form and after 1843 when it went over to the Free Church. Dr Black came home to profound personal sadness finding his wife in the final throes of terminal illness, and only enjoying a very brief period in her company before she died. It was said that he never recovered from this bereavement and, being painfully shy, he almost shunned human company, returning quietly to his academic work. In 1844 he moved to Edinburgh to take up the post of Professor of Exegetical Theology at New College, the Free Church of Scotland's Divinity college.[5]

The notable lack of publicity regarding Budapest was, of course, entirely calculated, being dictated by the sensitivities of attempting covert missionary activity within the sphere of the Habsburg jurisdiction. Shortly after his return, Keith was invited to prepare an article narrating his and Black's experiences in Pesth, but he firmly declined, stating that the object of his journey had not been to satisfy public curiosity, but to establish a mission. Careless publicity would not only compromise the work, but might jeopardise the position of the mission's royal patroness, the Archduchess, Maria

Dorothea. When missionary work was eventually undertaken, it was conducted most discreetly, with equally cautious public reporting until after the expulsion of the missionaries from Hungary in 1852. As Keith pointed out at the time, the missionaries were thrown out of the country in 1852 precisely because of irresponsible journalism in an American periodical.

Only in the 1860s did Keith feel at liberty to explain to the public why such secrecy had been necessary:

> ... wisdom, combined with ... harmlessness, is still needful in the establishment in Roman Catholic countries of Protestant missions, where these are prohibited by law; as the case then was in the Austrian dominions .... Things pertaining to the kingdom of God, which might be done openly and legally in other countries, required to be done, if done at all, in obedience to a higher law than that of mortal man, with circumspection there.[6]

Such discretion did not, however, prevent either man from lobbying Church leaders and members of the committee for a mission at Pesth. In preparation for the General Assembly of 1840, the committee decided to invite Dr Keith and M'Cheyne to prepare the annual report, which would be mainly an account of their researches in Europe and the Middle East, with M'Cheyne presenting the report because he had never before spoken at an Assembly. As well as being published in the official Assembly papers, the report was made available to the general public through the pages of the July, August, and September 1840 editions of *The Home and Foreign Missionary Record*.[7]

What appeared in print was, of course, but a summary, and by no means a full account. Apart from a brief discussion of missionary qualifications, appropriate methodology and the problems that might be encountered by the first missionaries, it consisted of an analysis of the places most suitable for establishing the mission.

Mindful of the work of the LSPCJ station in Jerusalem, and not wishing any conflict of interest, Galilee was cited as the most suitable area for a mission centre, holding, as it then did, approximately half of the Jewish population of the Holy Land. M'Cheyne and Bonar's specific preference for Tzfat was highlighted. The arguments in favour were summarised. First, it was considered most important that the region was under the control of the Egyptian Pasha, Mohammad Ali, who had created a tolerant political climate favourable to Jewish settlement in the land, even allowing Jews to become landowners. Then, it was noted that the harassment and persecution by the Roman Catholic and Eastern Orthodox Christians had made the Jewish communities in Palestine more friendly toward Protestant missionaries.

Thirdly, it was supposed – quite mistakenly as it turned out – that the prevailing orthodoxy of the Palestine Jewish communities would make them open to evangelical missionary work. Fourthly, as Judea was the centre of the Jewish world, it was argued that the impact of the gospel there would have international repercussions. Finally, it was believed that missionary work in the Holy Land itself was best calculated to stimulate the support of the Scottish Christian public.[8]

Alternative locations suggested in the report included Iaşi and Bucharest in Walachia; Hungary was mentioned only cursorily, for obvious reasons; Poznań in Poland, and Izmir and Istanbul, were considered viable, if secondary, possibilities. Iaşi was preferred to Bucharest on account of the Jewish community being seven times larger. Work in establishing schools had already begun in Poznań, where, under the influence of the assimilationist Reform movement, the Jewish community had shed its distaste of Christianity.[9]

Quite apart from any historic connections as the location of one of the 'Seven Churches of Asia' in the book of Revelation and the burial place of the martyred second century bishop Polycarp, Izmir was attractive because of its sizeable Jewish community and the relatively low cost of living. The major drawback was the strength of Jewish influence with the government, which had the potential of directing persecution towards any Jews who showed interest in the gospel.[10]

Istanbul was a good, if challenging, prospect, not only on account of a large and predominantly orthodox Sephardi community, but also because of the many Karaites who rejected the Talmud and followed only the *Tanakh*, the Old Testament. These perceived benefits were offset, however, by noting the minimal impact made by the two resident American missionaries.

References to Hungary, specifically Pesth, were almost buried in the middle of the report, yet, by a subtle use of language, clear allusions were made to its superior suitability owing to its very large Jewish community, the lowest estimate of which was said to be a quarter of a million. That statistic, on its own, was more than sufficient to excite the interest of the church, without any mention of the remarkable providences that had befallen Dr Black and Dr Keith and the wonderful ways in which they had been guided.[11] The openness of many Hungarian Jewish people to Christian influence was mentioned, but government hostility was not.

The second part of the report, responding to the information accumulated from the Assembly's questionnaires, surveyed the lesser claims of a dozen other locations, all of which were deemed to offer some scope, but their Jewish communities were either too small or too inaccessible to warrant further consideration.[12]

Turning to the question of staffing the mission, the Assembly was informed of a number of factors that needed to be carefully weighed. Missionaries should preferably be ordained ministers of the Church of Scotland and ideally a pair should be allocated to each station. Whether missionaries should be Jewish or gentile was, in the opinion of the committee, nicely balanced: in both cases there were clear advantages and disadvantages. In line with an important trend in contemporary missionary thinking, the report promoted 'native agency', the recruitment of lay missionaries, especially nationals of the country, or converted Jewish people, working under the supervision of ordained ministers.[13]

Whether or not Christian schools might also be established as part of the mission was a moot point. The experience of the Poznań schools, where Jewish young people had a better knowledge of Christianity than the children of local Christians, suggested that they might. But the report insisted on the absolute necessity of transparency if schools were attempted. Any education offered to Jewish young people must be clearly and openly Christian, no attempt should be made to conceal missionary motives as the Jewish community was extremely jealous of the welfare of its children and any form of deception was not only unworthy of the gospel, but highly likely to be counter-productive.[14]

Aware of the work at Jerusalem of the pioneering medical missionary Dr George Edward Dalton and his Jewish Christian assistant, the committee had been intrigued by the possibility of entering what was, for them, a new and uncharted area of Christian missions, and one, moreover, that after 1843 the Free Church of Scotland would be reluctant to take up. Dalton's provision of much needed free medical treatment had been very effective in breaking down barriers of prejudice and although the Jerusalem rabbis threatened his patients with excommunication, they disregarded the threat and refused to be intimidated. As justification of a medical mission, the report argued that if the Lord and His apostles had conducted a ministry to the body as well as to the soul, should not the Church of Scotland do likewise? The pragmatic value of a holistic approach was plain to see. In eastern countries especially, the combination of physician and missionary was agreeable both to Scripture and practical wisdom.[15]

Books and tracts were indispensable adjuncts to missionary strategy. The deputation had formed a view that is still regarded as sound today, that in an initial evangelistic approach polemical and doctrinal tracts were unhelpful, as were those specifically directed at Jewish people. Much better were the kind of general tracts that might be given to a nominal Christian.

A missionary in Palestine ought to be able to speak Hebrew and Arabic, and some knowledge of Spanish, Italian, or German might also prove useful. It would be advantageous to be able to speak to European Jews in Yiddish, their mother tongue. In addition to language skills, a missionary should have a competent knowledge of Jewish literature, especially the Talmud and the mystical Kabbalah. Missionaries should be 'wise and scriptural men', and young men offering themselves for service should be helped to cultivate 'persevering habits.'

It was considered highly desirable for missionaries to be able to think on their feet in encounters with quick-witted Jews, and to possess 'a quick invention, and vivid imagination'. Above all, singleness of devotion and purpose transcended all other attainments: 'The grand requisite for a Jewish missionary, as for every other minister of Christ, is, that he be determined to know nothing among the Jews, but Christ and him crucified' and to have 'true love to Israel and … Israel's God in their hearts.'

The Assembly report foresaw that the most challenging problems a missionary might face related to the welfare of Jewish converts. If evangelistic work achieved its aim and Jewish people made a profession of Christianity, and if these converts, as might be expected, were ostracised for their faith by their former friends and family and lost their employment, what might be done to provide economic support for them?

The experience of other churches and societies, such as the LSPCJ, had led to the foundation of training facilities such as the Operative Jewish Converts Institution at Palestine Place in London, where at its commercial printing press and bookbindery new converts were retrained for a self-sufficient life independent of the community to which they formerly belonged. For three years, trainees were supplied with food, lodging, and clothing as they learned their new trades. They were then expected to make their own way in the world and dismissed from the Institute to make room for others.

If the principles operative at Palestine Place were to be transposed to Palestine itself, might it not be possible for converts to trade with the wider population, even if they were boycotted by their fellow Jews? If a young man could be trained, say, to be a tailor, shoemaker, watchmaker, silversmith, or goldsmith, the 'painful trials of poverty and voluntary banishment would no more haunt his mind and deaden his convictions.' Such schemes were already in use in Scottish missions in other parts of the world and had proved particularly successful in the mission at Lovedale in South Africa, where new Christians were taught printing, wagon making, and wheelwrighting.

The very real danger inherent in this approach, attractive as it might be, was that any provision, direct or indirect, of material help could be misrepresented as offering an inducement to secure superficial changes of religious affiliation for perceived material advantage. It might also be taken advantage of, or in the blunt words of the report, it might prove to be 'a bait to all kinds of impostors.'[16] Furthermore, might it not create a community of dependents unable to stand on their feet?

What then might be the environment that is most conducive to the spiritual nurture of new converts? One thing that had to be considered was what to do if Jewish Christians were evicted from their communities or, under pressure, voluntarily moved away from the sphere of the missionary's influence, support, and instruction. This might not only prove harmful to the converts in the early stages of their spiritual development, but might also discourage and hinder the missionary who, at the beginning of his work, could be left alone without a pool of helpers, thus hindering further witness to the community:

> A Jew is awakened – is baptised – and is gone. His brethren see nothing of him – hear nothing, but that he has turned apostate, and denied the faith of his fathers. The Jews that remain are offended, irritated, enraged. And thus one of the most glorious means of awakening and converting them is lost.[17]

In line with the conventional missionary wisdom of its day, the usual solution to the problem was to establish at the 'mission station' an alternative Christian community able to provide personal spiritual nurture as well as economic support. It was argued that even without speaking about his new faith, the life of a new convert would demonstrate that 'by becoming a Christian, he has become a wiser, holier, and better man.' But, not being blessed with the ability to see the future, the committee was unaware of the serious deficiencies of the 'mission station' approach. Heavily dependent for their success upon the existence of sympathetic governments, such communities tended to isolate and sometimes alienate the converts from the surrounding local population, and therefore provided a false sense of security in an artificial spiritual environment. At best, it might be argued, they were a step on the road to indigenisation, but usually they ensured that leadership remained in the hands of overseas – foreign – missionaries. Thankfully, the exigences of working in European urban communities more or less ruled out this solution and saved the Jewish mission from creating an unhelpful culture of dependency.

The final section of the report anticipated the outrageous but commonly held idea that a mission to the Jewish people was bound to be futile because they were lying under a curse of judicial blindness. On the contrary, the report countered, there was every encouragement to undertake such a mission. No less a person than Professor August Tholuck of Halle, an ardent advocate of Jewish missions, had pointed out that more Jewish people had come to believe in the Messiah in the previous twenty years than since the earliest days of the church.[18]

The experience of the deputation corroborated this: they had seen firsthand how God was calling significant numbers of Jewish people to faith in Jesus the Messiah. Had they not met a minister in Berlin who told them that he himself had baptised one hundred and twelve converts? Had the Church not, 'within the last few days received letters from Lyons, Smyrna, Poland, and Jamaica, each bringing the glad tidings of the awakening or conversion of a Jew'? In Iaşi, the Jewish Reform movement was undermining 'the superstitions of Judaism' and, in Smyrna, entire families were receiving instruction. At Württemberg some families had secretly become Christians, but were too fearful to confess their faith openly. Even in Palestine – perhaps especially in Palestine – the door was wide open for the missionary.[19]

There was, however, yet one more objection to be overcome; the report's compilers were very well aware that the Church of Scotland was being torn in two by the ongoing conflict over patronage, so might it not be said that commencing a mission to the Jews at such a time was inopportune and would overtax the church's resources, especially in view of the legitimate demands of the schemes upon which it had already embarked? The report recognised this argument, plausibly masquerading as prudence, but dismissed it as nothing more than narrow self-interest. At heart, it was the hoary old objection, which even today has its stubborn adherents, that it was sufficient to address the needs of the church at home, without engaging in overseas mission. The answer was clear and unequivocal: it was more than prudent to engage as widely as possible in missionary endeavour because it was fundamental to the very continuance of the church. Quite simply, the report argued – in a passage which is pure M'Cheyne – without missions the church would perish. It was not enough to possess the pure light of the gospel; if it was not shared, it would be extinguished. The priority of the Jewish mission over all other missionary endeavour was clearly affirmed:

> But not only must we hold forth the lamp of the gospel; we must hold it forth in the way pointed out by God, if we would expect the blessing from on high; we must let the gospel shine on the 'Jew first,

and also on the Greek'; and whilst we send the Word to all nations, 'begin at Jerusalem.'[20]

The reward envisaged for such a strategy would be God's blessing on the Church of Scotland. It was significant, the report reiterating what had been said countless times before, that the revivals at Kilsyth and Dundee and a number of other places in Scotland had broken out in 1839, 'in the very same year in which God put it into the hearts of the ministers of the Church of Scotland to send out messengers to inquire after Israel and seek their good, – at the very time they were away on their blessed errand, God ... visited his people in Scotland'. The report concluded with an impassioned appeal: 'Shall the Church of Scotland be ashamed to be like Paul, the pattern of all Christian ministers? Shall we not rather ... love as he loved, pray as he prayed?'

After presenting the report to the Assembly, according to the account printed in the leading evangelical newspaper, *The Witness*, M'Cheyne 'sat down amidst great applause.' In expressing the thanks of the Assembly, the moderator, Dr Angus Makellar of Pencaitland, in East Lothian, identified himself fully with 'the claim which you have to the warmest thanks of the house.' The Assembly instructed the committee to take all appropriate steps to send out missionaries and formally elevated the Jewish mission to the status of the fifth of the official schemes of the church, which, in practical terms, meant that the committee now had fund raising powers, and that ministers and Kirk Sessions were required to organise annual collections for the work and to commit it to their own and their people's prayers.[21]

✥ 16 ✥

Narrative of a Mission of Inquiry
Dundee, Collace, and Edinburgh, 1840–1842

THE most significant account of the Mission of Inquiry was not the report to the 1840 General Assembly, nor the articles published in the pages of the Church of Scotland's *Home and Foreign Missionary Record*, but, rather, a book recording the experiences of the survey party, jointly written by M'Cheyne and Bonar and published under the title: *A Narrative of a Mission of Enquiry to the Jews from the Church of Scotland in 1839*. Within a mere five years, over twenty-three thousand copies were sold, not including French and Dutch translations and an American edition.

The work is based largely on M'Cheyne and Bonar's journals and notebooks recording on-the-spot observations and impressions.[1] The importance of keeping a journal had been impressed on M'Cheyne whilst he was staying in London before the deputation's departure for France. One morning he breakfasted with Sir Robert Inglis, a close friend of Henry Thornton and other members of the Clapham Sect of reforming evangelical Anglicans. Rather unflatteringly described as an 'old-fashioned Tory with many prejudices and of no great ability,' M'Cheyne remembered Inglis as very kind and helpful, gladly acknowledging that he had received from him many excellent hints regarding travel in the East, including sound guidance about keeping a journal. It was Inglis' opinion that 'half a line on the spot is worth half a page of recollection.'

M'Cheyne's father, Adam, had also passed on similar advice which he, in turn, had gleaned from Lord Lindsay, the one-time controversial Governor of Jamaica, adding playfully that Robert might be able to make tactical use of a notebook in dealing with truculent Ottoman officials:

> Pull out your Note Book eye the man attentively pretending to write down a minute description of his person – ask his name – which if he refuse to give, no matter – pull out, open and read your firman [Ottoman passport] – make the parchment crackle – talk to your friends about Mohamed Ali or Ibrahim Pasha – with much austerity – and in all probability the man will be your humble servant.[2]

M'Cheyne heeded his father's advice, and both he and Bonar made very good use of their notebooks, recording vivid details of people, places, and events, to which M'Cheyne added a number of naive but charming sketches as well as a few poems he felt moved to write.

Entrusted by the committee to collaborate on the task of producing an officially approved account of their journey, Bonar and M'Cheyne faced the problem of finding sufficient time in which to write it up. Not only were they extremely busy in their own congregations of Collace and Dundee, but as very popular preachers their assistance was sought by ministers in other congregations too, especially where revival had occurred and in particular to share in the duties of communion seasons. In addition, they were often invited to travel further afield to give talks about their journey to Palestine. This placed considerable burdens on both men. The Edinburgh sub-committee was impatient and annoyed by M'Cheyne's delay in completing a revision of Bonar's draft. At one point the members testily chided him, insisting that the work be completed and published by the end of 1841 or else they would burden him with all the costs of publication. Rather more helpfully, they suggested as a solution that he temporarily leave Dundee to go either to Collace, Bonar's parish, or to Edinburgh to complete the work without the distraction of other responsibilities.[3]

M'Cheyne was not unsympathetic to the committee's dilemma, for it was also his own. He had complained to Andrew Bonar that he found it impossible to be a diligent pastor and an author at the same time. Accordingly, to avoid time-consuming parish duties and the necessity of preparing new sermons, he and Bonar agreed to exchange pulpits for a month. The work of writing commenced in earnest in March 1841 and a manuscript, under the working title of *The Church of Scotland's Care for Israel*, was produced by May.

It was a great thrill, in doing the research for this book, to work on the manuscript that Bonar and M'Cheyne had turned from blank paper into their wonderful *Narrative*. The first draft is largely in the hand of Bonar, who constructed an outline by following the chronological account of their journey. To this draft M'Cheyne added many revisions and additions. It is noticeable that throughout the manuscript, M'Cheyne's editorial amendments generally take precedence over the original text, as he embellished Bonar's plainer style with a graphic use of descriptive material. M'Cheyne described scenery particularly well, helping his readers to visualise remote and exotic landscapes, as well as giving detailed, engaging, and colourful accounts of the different peoples they had encountered. His vibrant style caught the emotional effects of their various experiences as, for example, their arrival in the vicinity of Jerusalem. Yet it would be a mistake to conclude that M'Cheyne's contribution was merely editorial, supplementary, and decorative. Large blocks of his own observations and comments indicate a very substantial original contribution to the book.[4]

Out of some eight hundred manuscript pages, few are free from M'Cheyne's crossings out, insertions, or additional comments, with fresh material from his pen being interleaved with Bonar's original work. The final result, despite being a collaborative venture, is a remarkably seamless flow of language with a uniformity of style which, without access to the manuscript, would frustrate any attempt to differentiate each contributor's separate work.

The *Narrative* is a minute description of the delegates' experiences and observations of the various Jewish communities through which they passed. After the decision taken in Beirut for the deputation to separate, allowing Black and Keith to hasten home, the *Narrative* exclusively follows Bonar and M'Cheyne's itinerary. For reasons of discretion, already discussed, no mention is made of Black and Keith at Budapest, nor is there a supplement considering the suitability of that city as a base for missionary operations.

The book's essential purpose was to stimulate interest in the mission and, in spite of Wodrow's strictures about not pandering to any desire for entertainment, the authors knew only too well that an already intense fascination with the land of the Bible could easily be channelled into a deeper interest in the people who 'once possessed it and who still claim it for their own.' A most remarkable feature of the book is its prolific use of Scripture. In his review, the editor of *The Home and Foreign Missionary Record* very wisely regarded an open Bible as indispensable to a proper reading of the *Narrative*.

This, however, has led some modern commentators to observe that the book makes excessive demands on the biblical literacy of readers today. Be that as it may, it was not so for the original readers. The authors could take for granted their readers' wide ranging knowledge of Scripture, substantiating their claim that what they had written was a plain account of their journeys in the land of the Book that any reader familiar with the Book could follow. It is an indictment of a neglectful generation if this proves burdensome to modern readers. As well as thousands of biblical allusions too numerous to count, the authors provided hundreds of biblical references, in addition to which, they expounded about a thousand Bible passages which either cast light on their journey, or might be better understood in the light of what they had seen and experienced.

To an objective presentation of facts and statistics, they also freely recorded their personal impressions, observations, and passionate opinions. The strength of their opinions and their uncompromising descriptions of other denominations and religions may sound intolerant to the point of bigotedness to more tolerant modern readers and, inevitably, in a more liberal age, attempts have been made to explain, mitigate, excuse, or otherwise justify their seeming prejudices against Judaism, Islam, Roman Catholicism, and Eastern Orthodoxy, or to dismiss them altogether as unacceptably bigoted. But, as Jewish scholar, Professor Stefan G. Reif, has generously and correctly pointed out it would be anachronistic to expect these two Scottish evangelicals to display a tolerant attitude towards Rabbinic Judaism.[5]

We must not allow ourselves to fall into the trap of over-simplifying what was, in reality, a complex, subtle and by no means negative attitude to Judaism. Whilst it is true that sometimes *The Narrative* uses derogatory descriptions of some aspects of Jewish religious beliefs and practices, sympathy for what they perceived to be the Jewish people's inestimable loss of their own spiritual destiny is much more characteristic of the work. For Bonar and M'Cheyne, the material poverty in which they found the Jewish inhabitants of Jerusalem symbolised their spiritual condition: 'if we could have looked upon their precious souls, their temporal misery would have appeared but a faint emblem of the spiritual death that reigns within.'[6]

A careful reading of *The Narrative* reveals a considerable ability to draw nice distinctions and see important and subtle differences. For example, whilst the authors criticised orthodox Judaism for its rejection of Jesus as Messiah, its legalistic way of salvation, and its excessive dependence on the authority of the Talmud, it was, they argued, nevertheless untainted by the atheism of France or the rationalism of Germany. In holding the Old Testament to be the Word of God and expecting the coming of the Messiah, they argued that was sufficient common ground for Orthodox Judaism and Christianity to engage in a meaningful dialogue from which an evangelistic conversation might flow.

A similar nuanced view was taken of both the Reform movement and the Karaite tradition. Somewhat surprisingly, they did not consider the influence of rationalism on the Reform movement as an altogether negative phenomenon. Rationalism had produced open-mindedness and that was welcome and was something of which any skilful missionary could take advantage. But openness to change, whilst leading Reform Jews to a welcome denial of the supremacy of the Talmud and a willingness to challenge traditional beliefs, had also led them into an unfortunate rejection of the authority of the Bible. The authors contrasted this to the attitude of the Karaites of the Crimea, whose rejection of the Talmud had not led to a rejection of Scripture. So, whilst being critical about certain aspects in all branches of Judaism, the authors nevertheless saw in every branch some promising opportunities for fruitful contact.

Notwithstanding any criticisms of Judaism, Bonar and M'Cheyne reveal a huge empathy with Jewish people, nowhere more movingly expressed than in their observations of orthodox Ashkenazi worship in the ancient synagogue at Tzfat:

> Several very venerable men were seated all round; more than half of the worshippers had beards verging to pure white, and grey hair flowing on their shoulders. It was indeed a new scene to us. In reading their prayers, nothing could exceed their vehemency. They read with all their might ... from time to time, the tremendous voice of some aged Jew rose above all the rest in earnestness. ... One old man often stretched out his hand as he called on the Lord, and clenched his trembling fist in impassioned supplication. Some clapped their hands, others clasped both hands together, and wrung them as in an agony of distress, till they should obtain their request. A few beat upon their breasts. ... All of them, old and young, moved the body backward and forward, rocking to and fro, and bending toward the ground. ... one young man remained behind prolonging his devotions, in great excitement. We at first thought that he was deranged, and was caricaturing the rest, but were assured that, on the contrary, he was a peculiarly devout man ... often he bent his whole body to the ground, crying aloud, 'Adonai, is not Israel thy people?' in a reproachful tone, as if angry that God did not immediately answer.[7]

The effect of witnessing this scene was profound and lasting:

> We never felt more deeply affected at the sight of Israel. It was the saddest and most solemn view of them that we had yet obtained ... None seemed happy; even when all was over, none bore the cheerful look of men who had ground to believe that their prayers had been accepted. Many had the very look of misery, and almost of despair.[8]

Another important feature of the *Narrative*, which attracted the attention of later Jewish historians, is the authors' detailed recording of the social and religious conditions that prevailed in that period among the Jewish communities in Europe and the Middle East, especially their observations of Jewish attempts to re-colonise the land of Israel. This was understood by all four to be a fulfilment of biblical prophecy. The conversations that Keith held with Sir Moses Montefiore, at both Jerusalem and Haifa, may have focused on very mundane matters such as agriculture and making roads, but in Keith's mind was the thought that these activities might prove to be the beginning of the prophesied national and spiritual restoration.[9]

Typical in this regard was the attitude of the authors to the evidence of the ancient destruction of Jerusalem. They found that the existence of heaps of debris, which they estimated to be some forty and fifty feet deep in places, substantiated the witness of the biblical prophets 'who spoke with divine accuracy when they said that "Jerusalem shall become heaps"' (Micah 3:12) ... And if so, shall not the future restoration foretold by the same lips be equally literal and full? 'The city shall be builded upon her own heap' (Jer. 30:18).

The *Narrative* also casts an important light on the use of Hebrew by nineteenth-century Jewish communities both in the Holy Land and also among the Diaspora. All four of the survey party were at least competent in biblical Hebrew, allowing them not only to read manuscripts and inscriptions, but also to hold conversations in the language. This is all very important, because until recently it was thought that the use of Hebrew by Jewish migrants to Palestine did not take place until the late nineteenth or early twentieth century, subsequent to the revival of the language by Eliazer Ben-Yehuda who made *aliyah* in 1881. The *Narrative* offers undeniable proof that Hebrew was utilised as a vernacular language by Palestinian Jews as early as the fourth decade of the nineteenth century, demonstrating that Ben-Yehuda's work was built upon a pre-existing foundation.[10]

The committee's worry that delay might have an adverse effect on potential sales of the book was supremely ill-founded. *A Narrative of a Mission of Inquiry to the Jews from the Church of Scotland in 1839* (the title underwent minor changes in different editions) was published in 1842, simultaneously in Edinburgh by William Whyte & Co., in Glasgow by W. Collins, in Dundee by W. Middleton, in Hamilton by Adams & Co., in London (predictably) by J. Nisbet & Co., and in Dublin by W. Curry & Co.[11] With three further printings within the first year, the book was a runaway success financially and well on the way to becoming an international best seller. By 1844, eleven thousand copies had been printed. Doubtless M'Cheyne's early death in March 1843 influenced sales, so that by 1878 over thirty thousand copies of the British edition had been sold.[12] As the committee's fears of a financial loss were completely allayed, in grateful recognition of their substantial contribution, M'Cheyne and Bonar were granted the copyright in perpetuity, along with the substantial royalties which flowed from such a lucrative venture.

Despite M'Cheyne's scathing comments about Paris, the *Narrative* was published there in 1843 as *Les Juifs d'Europe et de Palestine: voyage de MM. Keith, Black, Bonar and M'Cheyne, envoyés par l'Église d'Écosse.* The following year the Presbyterian Board of Publication in Philadelphia published an American edition. A Dutch translation by D. Serrurier followed in 1851 as *De Joden in Europa en Palestina, voorgesteld in eene reisbeschrijving van de heeren Keith, Black, Bonar en Mac Cheyne, door de Schotse Kerk afgevaardigd.* A modern Dutch edition of Serrurier's translation was published in 1981 under the inaccurate title: *De zendingsreis van Robert Murray MacCheyne.* A heavily edited modern English edition by Allan Harman was published by Christian Focus Publications in 1996 as *Mission of Discovery.*

It would be utterly inappropriate, however, to conclude on such a commercial and pecuniary note. The spiritual legacy of the book is incalculable. Amongst its earliest reviewers was Thomas Chalmers, who considered it of the greatest value. In 1844, J. W. Alexander reviewed the volume in *The Princeton Review*, giving it a warm welcome and a thorough examination over twenty-one pages, concluding by commending the authors for the:

> rich variety of instructive, entertaining and edifying matter ... The descriptions, though simple, are graphic. ... The great charm of the whole is due to the scriptural piety and evangelical benevolence which glow in every page.[13]

A belated review in the *Jewish Missionary Herald* in 1847 warmly commended it as a 'delightful volume,' which had already claimed the attention of 'all lovers of Israel.' It was 'a well-written book of travels ... affording a very minute account of the state of the Jewish people' but, said the observant reviewer, readers ought not to fall into an all too common trap, that of attempting to understand the biblical world of the ancient Jewish people by comparison with contemporary Arab customs prevalent in the East, a mistake that has continued until the present.[14]

Although unsympathetic to its missionary intentions, modern Jewish scholars have been impressed by the *Narrative's* accuracy in documenting Jewish communities and have appreciated its authors' typically Scottish love for the Holy Land and its people.

Exactly one hundred years after its publication, the European Jewish community, through which the deputation had travelled, found its survival threatened by Hitler's 'Final Solution.' This was followed in 1947 by the survivors of the Holocaust creating the State of Israel. Israel's subsequent wars with its Arab neighbours, the proliferation of Jewish settlements, and the plight of the Palestinian people have radically changed the face of the land traversed by the deputation and has permanently altered the circumstances of the descendants of the peoples they met. It is hopeless to speculate how the authors might have responded to these developments and how they might have fitted them into the prophetic scheme they held. That they would have done is without doubt, believing as they did that biblical prophecy embraces the vicissitudes of the Jewish people in all ages, down to the time of the recovery of their ancient land and, more important, to their return to the God of Abraham, Isaac, and Jacob by belief in his Messianic Son, Jesus of Nazareth.

Today the *Narrative* is not nearly so well known among Christians as it deserves to be and is probably the most neglected of all M'Cheyne's works. This is a strange omission as the book continues to delight, fascinate, and teach, breathing out a spirit of profound and prayerful yearning for the fulfilment of God's covenant promises to the Jewish people and all the blessed consequences that would flow from that to the Church and the world. It also stands as a judgement against the loss of interest in missions to the Jewish people common in modern evangelicalism. Its abiding spiritual significance places Bonar and M'Cheyne's *Narrative* in the very forefront of Christian missionary literature, giving it an even more exalted place than it has rightly earned in the field of early Victorian travel literature.

17

Daniel Edward: Faith and Perseverance at Iaşi

Central Europe, 1841 to 1852

FOLLOWING the return of M'Cheyne and Bonar from Palestine, and Black and Keith from Pesth, the Jewish committee had two strategic issues occupying its attention, both requiring sound decisions to be made with a degree of urgency. The first was the selection of the most suitable missionaries; the second was the choice of the most appropriate location. Due to his heavy involvement in the revivals at Kilsyth and Dundee, William Chalmers Burns, M'Cheyne's locum at St Peter's had withdrawn his previous offer for service in Aden, but, according to Robert Wodrow, John Duncan, the forty-three-year-old minister of Milton Church in Glasgow, was now willing to step into this breach, or for that matter, to serve anywhere the committee wished, at home or abroad. This offer, coming from such a highly regarded minister and, moreover, one who was a gifted Hebrew scholar, was naturally met with general enthusiasm and gave rise to much discussion. With Burns unavailable and with Bonar and M'Cheyne reporting the grave doubts of the Persian Ambassador, Sir John McNeill, over the suitability of Aden, the committee accepted Duncan's offer of missionary service, but in the first instance, only as an instructor of other missionary candidates. On a technicality, therefore, John Duncan was the first missionary to the Jewish people appointed by the Church of Scotland, but he was not the first to see active missionary service.[1]

The committee now turned their attention to where they might locate their new missionary. A forceful letter received from Dr Black indicated his strong preference for the city of Pesth, but Alexander Moody Stuart, the minister of St Luke's, Young Street, Edinburgh, felt inclined to balance this view by putting forward Bonar and M'Cheyne's opinion that Palestine was preferable. Undaunted, Keith once more set out what he considered compelling reasons for Hungary rather than Palestine. The committee, faced with an impasse, deferred a final decision until a meeting could be convened at which, it was hoped, Black and Keith and M'Cheyne and Bonar would all be in attendance.[2]

In the event only Keith and M'Cheyne could attend, the others stating their predictable preferences in writing. After conferring at great length, it was agreed to establish a mission station in Palestine, probably in Galilee, as soon as circumstances allowed, even though the unsettled state of the country at the time made missionary work inexpedient, if not impossible. The European Jewish communities, particularly in Hungary, Wallachia and Moldavia (modern Romania) seemed to offer the best possibility but, yet again, the committee hesitated to specify a precise location, preferring to leave that to the judgement of the missionary on the spot. An important reason for favouring a European location was that a mission could be established by a single missionary and an unordained assistant, whereas two ministers were considered necessary for Palestine. Despite the difficulties already encountered with officials of the Habsburg Empire, the committee continued to entertain the unrealistic notion that no serious opposition to missionary work would arise from any European government. A final point in favour of Europe was that work there would be much less challenging economically.[3]

These competing claims weighed heavily on the committee, and so it was decided to hold in Glasgow and Edinburgh public prayer meetings seeking God's wisdom and guidance in the matter. It was during this time of prayerful deliberation that another name was added to the list of candidates, that of Daniel Edward. Although much less well remembered than the eccentric Duncan, it was Edward who was the true pioneer of the General Assembly's mission to the Jews.

For a while then, the debate became focused on deciding Edward's destination. Robert Candlish, Edward himself, and others proposed that he be sent to Iaşi in Moldavia (Romania). Whilst the committee accepted the logic behind this reasoning, it nevertheless felt thwarted that Palestine and Pesth seemed to be receding even further from reach and in the hope that Pesth might be occupied as soon as possible, the committee appointed Duncan as its missionary there, though no decision could be taken regarding when he might be sent, or who his companion might be. To this meeting the representatives of the Glasgow sub-committee brought encouraging news that another candidate, William Wingate, had offered his services as a missionary and maybe he should be the one to assist Duncan.[4]

Daniel Edward was born in Edinburgh in 1815. Graduating Master of Arts from the University of Edinburgh in April 1836, he immediately commenced studying for a divinity degree. It was at this time that he offered himself for missionary service and therefore the committee thought it prudent to allow him first to complete his course, taking special studies in the Hebrew language, Jewish thought and religion, partly under John Duncan and partly at Berlin. In Berlin Edward found himself in company with William Wingate, both of them taking German lessons from August Ferdinand Carl Schwartz, a young Polish Jewish Christian and licentiate of the Hungarian Reformed Church. Soon after this Schwartz himself became a missionary with the LSPCJ in Constantinople.

Wingate made an immature and unseemly public claim to have had a hand in Schwartz's decision but, if that was so, then his was by no means the only, nor perhaps the main, influence. That honour seems to have belonged to Schwartz's landlady, who one day challenged him by saying, that it was 'all very nice for you to teach these young men foreign languages in order that they may be qualified to preach the gospel to the heathen. Have you thought of your own brethren who live in your own neighbourhood without the light of the gospel?'[5]

Edward completed his studies in Berlin and returned to Edinburgh to graduate Bachelor of Divinity on 10th March, 1841. The following day he was ordained to the Christian ministry by Robert Candlish at St. George's in Edinburgh. In early summer, with the medical missionary Hermann Philip as his assistant, Edward departed for Iaşi, arriving on 16th June. Fifty years later, Edward recalled their arrival in the city:

... after a toilsome journey (but we were young and vigorous and made
nothing of the fatigue), it was with thrilling hearts that we saw, from
the brow of a hill to the south of the town ... Jassy {Iaşi] spread out
before our eyes, glittering with numberless spires and cupolas covered
with polished tin that reflected the rays of an almost tropical sun, the
residence of the prince, with its 25,000 Jews, a third of the population,
and far more than half in importance.[6]

If the journey had proved toilsome, so too would the work into
which the two young men now entered. The committee took the
decision to attempt work at Iaşi well aware that the Orthodox
Church, the majority denomination in the region, would not tolerate
any kind of missionary work amongst their own members. Edward
and Philip discovered early on that opposition could be avoided
only by entirely confining their witness to the Jewish community.
Nevertheless, when they presented the gospel to Jewish people in
the town of Botoşani, the ensuing civil furore almost led to their
arrest and imprisonment.[7]

The main force behind this concerted opposition was the learned
and formidable Rabbi Aaron Moses Ben Jacob Taubes, who had
been appointed to Iaşi and district in 1841, and where he remained
until his death in 1852. Taubes was considered to be the outstanding
rabbinical authority of his time; even famous rabbis turned to him
with their intellectual problems. Much to the distress of Daniel
Edward, Taubes was to prove himself an implacable foe to every
form of Christian missionary work amongst his people.

Early in 1842, the missionaries commenced one of their first
projects, a school for German and Jewish children, but the results
were far from encouraging. The year 1843 was marked in Scotland
by the Disruption of the Church of Scotland and the founding of
the Free Church of Scotland, but in Iaşi Edward and Philip were
casting their net wider and investigating missionary possibilities in
Istanbul where they visited Schwartz, agreeing that Philip should
remain with him as a translator.[8]

In 1844, following the baptism of Benjamin Weiss, a Jewish
merchant, Edward experienced considerable hostility from the
Jewish community in Iaşi. Constantly under attack, the work limped
on. In his report to the Free Church General Assembly of 1845,

Edward said that although five Jewish people had been baptised, opposition from the Jewish community had taken a considerable toll on his health. Such considerations had been entirely overlooked in M'Cheyne and Bonar's over optimistic assessment and, therefore did not register in the thinking of the committee either. After four years of disheartening reports from Edward, the committee should have begun to realise the intractability of the problems of Iaşi, but, preoccupied with Budapest, which had in the meantime been opened as a mission base, they merely instructed Edward to return to Scotland for a few months of rest and recuperation.

It was during this home leave that Edward was introduced to Catherine Grant, a sister of a former college friend, William Grant, Free Church minister in Ayr. In her autobiographical *Memoir of Mrs Edward,* Catherine described herself – doubtless truthfully, though a trifle conceitedly – as 'that friend's sister' whose eligibility to be Edward's wife was enhanced by being 'a kindred spirit, glowing with the same ardent love for the house of Israel, and qualified by natural gifts and acquired attainments to be a help-meet in his home and in his work'.[9]

Meanwhile, Edward, without Catherine, returned to Iaşi to begin his second term of service. In Catherine's somewhat melodramatic imagination, though in fact at the time not all that far removed from reality, Edward was returning to a demanding ministry and a desolate home. But he might not be long alone as they had planned for her to follow him as early as possible, and meet and marry in Germany. Accordingly, their wedding took place in the little principality of Neuwied, according to the rites of the German Reformed Church, on 25th August, 1846, and immediately after they set off for Iaşi, encumbered with a great amount of luggage and household goods, including a piano and a travelling carriage. With regard to the latter, they were doubtless following the advice of Bonar and M'Cheyne, who, because of the appalling condition of the roads and the uncomfortable ride of the local *brashovanca*, considered that some kind of carriage was indispensable.[10]

The two Danubian Principalities of Wallachia and Moldavia, which form modern Romania, were strategically placed at the junction of the Russian, Austro-Hungarian and Ottoman empires. For centuries they had been part of the Ottoman Empire but since the treaty of Adrianople in 1829 the two Principalities had come under Russian protection. The terms of the treaty gave each a degree of autonomy as well as the benefit of free navigation on the Black Sea and the Danube, arrangements that had facilitated the itinerary of Drs Black and Keith in their return from the Holy Land. The generally impoverished state of the region had been accurately reported by Bonar and M'Cheyne.

In the decades leading up to the revolutionary year of 1848, political aspirations and intellectual views in Wallachia and Moldavia developed along different lines. In the Wallachian capital, Bucharest, intellectuals were influenced by French notions of nationality, which meant that they extended a fraternal welcome to any, regardless of their ethnic origin, who were committed to Wallachian culture and who would endorse the goals of the national struggle. Almost anyone could become Wallachian by adoption, except Sephardic Jews, against whom was an intractable prejudice.

In Moldavian Iaşi, by contrast, the prominent thinkers were receptive to the racist ideals and conservative opinions of German romantic nationalism. Some Moldavians, including an influential group in Iaşi, insisted that national identity could not be adopted or learned but only transmitted through blood. In the next century, such evil fruit would ripen to rottenness in German National Socialist ideology. It is odd that during their visit to Iaşi, Bonar and M'Cheyne seemed oblivious to the existence in this city of one of Europe's most virulent strains of antisemitism. In 1839, between a third and a half of the population of Iaşi was Jewish, with around two-hundred synagogues, some very large. The British consul reckoned the number of Jews in Iaşi to be perhaps twenty thousand out of a total population of fifty thousand.

If, during the mid-nineteenth century, conservative Hungary was inclining towards liberalism, democracy, and Jewish emancipation, its southeastern neighbours were moving in the opposite direction. From 1829, under Russian influence, Jews were generally permitted to live only within the restrictions of a specially demarcated area, known as the 'pale of settlement'. At this time, conscious of the liabilities entailed in Jewish identity, a large number of Romanian Jews had renounced orthodox traditionalism to embrace the more assimilationist Reform Judaism.[11]

Others, reacting to the instability of the times, had moved in the opposite direction and were taken up with the new ultra-traditional 'Chabad-Lubavitch' movement ('Chabad' is an acronym for the Hebrew words, *Chochmah*, *Binah*, *Da'at* – 'Wisdom', 'Understanding', and 'Knowledge' – while Lubavitch is from the name of a Russian town where this sect commenced). The movement was introduced into Moldavia from Belorussia in 1842 through the publication, in Iaşi, of the works of its founder and first 'Rebbe', Shneour Zalman of Liadi, whose fundamental maxim was that Torah must be studied with joyous zeal.[12]

Bonar and M'Cheyne had also come across a third discernible minority in Iaşi, not generally acknowledged by Jewish scholars. These were they who were inclined to examine afresh and in careful detail the oft-repeated but hitherto largely rejected claim that Jesus of Nazareth was indeed the Jewish Messiah. Iaşi was, therefore, a dynamic and fluid community, but its apparent openness, which, along with its size and influence, had commended it as a suitable place for the establishment of a mission, turned out to be misleading. There would be no easy pickings in Iaşi.

Returning to the little mission station at Iaşi, conscious of the support of the prayers and goodwill of the church at home, Daniel and Catherine Edward were in an optimistic mood. The Jewish committee had sanctioned their implementation of some of the most modern methods of missionary enterprise which, as well as the malfunctioning school established earlier, included a workshop staffed by Scottish tradesmen to offer training courses, after the style of the LSPCJ Operatives Institute, to new converts who needed to make an independent living. James Bonar, a cabinetmaker, had arrived the previous year and the committee had promised also to send a locksmith by the name of Connacher.[13]

Catherine enjoyed her new home, describing it in a letter to her brother as 'very pretty; the green cotton looks nice, and the tartan divan'. It was, however, she thought, rather too cramped, having to accommodate not only her husband and herself, but two assistants and a number of servants. She commented ruefully that she didn't see how they could go on in that way. They didn't. By the following December they had moved to a larger house, where Catherine still had 'a pretty nice study (green)', but with enough rooms to accommodate all, though they shared a dining room.[14]

In addition to Hermann Philip, now safely returned to Iaşi from Istanbul to take up responsibility for preparing the new converts for baptism, the committee had also appointed the Rev. Alfred Edersheim. From the outset, Edersheim was a lively and energetic addition to the Budapest mission. He had been born in Vienna in 1825, had studied at Budapest and shown himself as unusually able, not least as a linguist. As well as his native German, Edersheim could speak Latin, Greek, Hebrew, English, French, Hungarian, and Italian. In 1842 he met John Duncan and the Scottish missionaries who had commenced work that year in Budapest and through them he had been introduced to the gospel, to which he had opened his heart, committing his life to Jesus the Messiah.

In late 1843, the eighteen-year-old young man was taken by the Duncan family to live in their Edinburgh home and complete his theological study at the Free Church's New College, where Duncan was Professor of Hebrew. In 1844, Edersheim was baptised, and in 1845 licensed to preach by the Free Church Presbytery of Edinburgh. For a few months he served with great acceptance the new Free Church congregation at Makerstoun, in the Presbytery of Kelso in the Scottish Borders. Suspicious that he might have been dragging his heels in Makerstoun, and keen to obtain his services as soon as possible, the committee instructed him to sail for Istanbul and from there travel overland to join Edward in Iaşi, where, on arrival, he was ordained a missionary to the Jews.[15]

Meanwhile, in Iaşi, opposition from Rabbi Taubes continued. Threats of the *herem*, the most rigorous form of Jewish excommunication, were made against any member of the community who dared to go near either the mission or school. Those under the *herem* were excluded from the community for an indefinite period. No one was permitted to teach the offender, work for him, or benefit him in any way, except if he was in need of the bare necessities of life.

Notwithstanding this fierce sanction, the mood of the missionaries was good and the work prospered modestly. Mornings in the mission house were dedicated to study, although Catherine was pleased to report that they were 'continually interrupted by Jews calling.' To both Jewish and gentile enquirers the Edwards hospitably opened their home. Once, Catherine wrote excitedly to her brother, their 'saal was almost full ... upwards of sixty people, and about twenty-five long bearded Jews.'

God blessed the missionaries' faithful witness and during the following months twelve people sought baptism, though they were suspicious that some of the enquirers might be insincere. For some time they had reasons to suspect that ulterior motives were at work, as some Jewish people sought baptism in order to divest themselves of what they considered to be the burden of Jewish identity. In fact, for most Jews, the thought of making and sustaining a Christian profession was daunting, and some who had been baptised, when placed under pressure from members of the Jewish community, had renounced their weak Christian convictions. Others, however, despite all harassment and opposition, remained faithful.

As all the missionaries spoke more or less fluent German, the *lingua franca*, they could easily make themselves understood, but for cultivating a closer acquaintance with individuals and for better access to the community, especially for making contact with women, it was necessary to learn either Yiddish or Hebrew. Perhaps because it gave her a deeper access to Scripture, Catherine preferred the latter and studied it assiduously. She found her new life rewarding and was contented in her missionary career. Her letters home gave the impression of a busy household, fundamentally happy in their work, harassed but not daunted by the difficulties of the task. Catherine seemed to flourish. Writing to a friend, she said, 'I have grown quite fat again; my face is absolutely vulgarly round and my health is, I am thankful to say, very much improved.'[16]

Missionary work is always a spiritual struggle with the forces of darkness and so, in the same letter, indeed in the very next sentence, a different, more ominous note was struck: 'Dr – has raised a storm among the Jews.' The anonymous doctor was John Mason who had served as surgeon and physician to the garrison on the Swedish island of St Bartholomew in the West Indies, and had arrived in Iaşi in early 1846 to open a dispensary and through his medical skill help to break down barriers of suspicion in the community.[17]

Catherine thought Mason rash for taking into his home a young Jewish boy who had quarrelled with his parents and, seeking to ingratiate himself with the missionaries, said he wanted to become a Christian. A riot had ensued and angry Jews had surrounded Mason's home clamouring for the boy to be handed over. But that was not all. Shortly after the riot, Edward, Edersheim, and Philip all found themselves compelled to write to the committee in Edinburgh making complaints about Mason and his family, who 'seemed to entertain views and adopt practices ... inconsistent with the character and objects of the mission.'[18]

It has been suggested that these complaints may have been related to Mason's true status as a doctor.[19] When the Iaşi State Archive was opened to the public after the fall of the Romanian communist regime in 1989, certain documents appeared to cast doubt on Mason's credentials, suggesting that he may not have been a doctor at all, but only a dispenser or druggist.[20] But this allegation can easily be set aside as the Latin list of Edinburgh Medical graduates for 1833 includes a Joannes Abraham Mason, who, two years earlier successfully passed examinations in surgery, anatomy, and pharmacy to became a Licentiate of the Royal College of Surgeons of Edinburgh, a common method of gaining a formal qualification of competency to practice as a doctor.[21] Mason's claim in his book, *Three years in Turkey: the Journal of a Medical Mission to the Jews*, to be a qualified doctor is, therefore, *bona fide*.[22] Furthermore, a paragraph in the *Home and Foreign Missionary Review of the Free Church of Scotland* states that Mason was appointed by the Jewish committee as a doctor, the committee being fully satisfied with these qualifications.[23] Thirdly, after returning to Scotland in 1849 Mason's credentials were accepted by the authorities who allowed him to practice as a doctor both in south west Scotland and later in Northumberland, England.

The doubts his colleagues entertained, and the committee later endorsed, were not over his professional status, but over his family life. So, what were they? Certainly his colleagues objected to Mason's high-handed invitation to his brother to live with him in Iaşi without first obtaining the consent of his colleagues or the Edinburgh committee, but when called to account, Mason was able to explain himself to the committee's satisfaction in 'a pleasing tone and spirit.'[24]

Whatever satisfied the committee did not, however, put Mason's colleagues' minds to rest, nor did they withdraw their allegations. In fact, they pressed them more assiduously, backing them up with sufficient hard evidence to require the committee finally to uphold their complaint and dismiss Mason from service. He was instructed to leave Iaşi forthwith, not to settle with his family in any of the locations where the committee's missionaries resided, nor to consider himself connected with the committee, though they continued to pay his stipend until the agreed time of his service had ended. But much to their annoyance, the disgraced Mason and his family returned to Istanbul where they had lived prior to residing in Iaşi. In April the family began attending the congregation of Rev. Rudolf Koenig and in due course applied for admittance to the Lord's Table but Koenig refused. Feeling obliged to explain, he wrote to the committee alleging 'moral grounds' as the reason.[25]

Once more, Mason was called to account. A minute of 26th December 1848, circumspectly states that the committee was in possession of a letter from Mason, 'explanatory of his conduct with Rebecca.' Rebecca it transpires was Rebecca Bergenstein, a young Jewish domestic servant in her early twenties, who had been born in Poland and resided in the Masons' home, attending to Mason's wife Winifred. Rebecca had been brought from Iaşi because Mason had been given to understand that Turkish servants were more expensive to employ.[26] After Winifred Mason died of fever in November, 1847, his former colleagues at Iaşi suspected he was cohabiting with this young woman half his age, and something like this, though veiled by Victorian euphemism, was also the view of the committee. A letter to Mason by Rev. James Julius Wood, the secretary to the committee, though warm and pastoral in tone, states that Mason's conduct was a 'fall into sin and temptation':

> I hope this unfortunate matter will ultimately turn out beneficial, and I have again to express my regret that it has happened that our correspondence should have taken this direction. I desire ever to feel

for those who fall into sin and temptation as being myself compassed with infirmity. But you will at once see how needful it is that the committee should be strict in these matters.[27]

Mason and Rebecca, with his two teenage children, John and Mary, returned to Scotland in 1849, to take up residence at Gatehouse of Fleet, Kirkcudbright, where he became a doctor in general practice. He and Rebecca married on 11th November 1849, with James Julius Wood participating in the service.[28] The following Sunday Rebecca was baptised by Mason's friend, Rev. W. B. Clark, the minister of Maxwelltown Free Church of Scotland, Dumfries, and received into communicant membership.

Rebecca's mental health deteriorated: as well as enduring the emotional stress of moving from Iași to Istanbul and then to rural Scotland, marrying Mason and being baptised as a Christian and joining a church, it was also alleged that Mason had 'behaved cruelly and harshly to her and had driven her to desperation and insanity.'[29]

Matters came to a head on the morning of 17th August, 1850. As John Mason was washing himself and dressing, Rebecca stealthily stole up behind him and slashed at his throat with a razor, aiming further cuts at his head. Mason shouted loudly that he was being murdered, staggered into the kitchen and collapsed on the floor in a pool of blood. Rebecca was arrested and tried on the old Scottish charge of 'assault to the effusion of blood' at the High Court in Edinburgh in March 1851. Logan, Rebecca's lawyer pled insanity and, after hearing evidence, the jury was directed to find her 'insane and not a proper object of trial.' The court ordered her to be detained indefinitely in the Lunatic Department of the General Prison at Perth, the first specialist unit for the criminally insane in the United Kingdom.[30] It was here in April, 1898, after forty-seven years confinement as a 'prisoner-patient', that she died, aged seventy-seven years old. The *Edinburgh Evening News* of 2nd May reported her passing and added the poignant note, 'she had no friends', a tragic commentary indeed for one who was, at least ostensibly, a convert of the Free Church's Jewish mission and to whom a duty of pastoral care was owed, but who had ended up on the margin and had been allowed to slip from view.[31]

Writing to the Thessalonians, the Apostle Paul once stated that his missionary work had been hindered by Satan: the Iaşi missionaries concluded the same. The follies and foibles of Mason had discouraged them, diverting their energies, unfairly discrediting their work and traducing their witness. Nor was the dismissal of Mason from the missionary team the end of the struggle, another discouragement soon rocked the work as the greatly promising young Alfred Edersheim was removed to Scotland under a cloud of dishonour. The details are vague, but what is clear is that Edersheim had got into difficulties with the committee over what they understood were his confused marriage intentions and although he confessed a fault, he was suspended from the ministry by his Presbytery and had his salary withdrawn by the committee.[32]

The committee and Presbytery, it would seem, had acted rashly and without sufficient evidence, for Edersheim's suspension was lifted the following March, subsequent to his marriage to Miss Mary Bloomfield.[33] It may well be that the real problem lay in the difficult personal relationship that existed between Edward and Edersheim. Concurrent with the allegations concerning his marriage, an acrimonious personal dispute had broken out between the two men concerning financial matters. The committee was appealed to but declined to interfere, advising the parties to refer the matter to some lay friend for arbitration.[34] Aware of a fundamental incompatibility between Edward and Edersheim, the committee declined to reinstate Edersheim as a missionary, although he was entirely vindicated by his Presbytery of any wrong doing. The committee's records state only that it would be 'inexpedient in existing circumstances' for him to return to Iaşi.[35]

In 1849, Edersheim became minister at the Free Church of Scotland charge of Old Machar in Aberdeen, where he remained until health problems forced him to resign. In 1861, he moved to Torquay in Devon, where the English Presbyterian Church of St Andrew was built for him, but declining health and discontent with the English Presbyterian Church led him to abandon pastoral ministry in 1872. For some years he lived quietly at Bournemouth but, in 1882, he joined the Church of England which appreciated, at last, both his academic prowess and spiritual gifts. The last ten years of his life were marked by a series of remarkable appointments, first, from 1880 to 1884 he was Warburtonian Lecturer in Lincoln's Inn, then from 1884 to 1885 preacher to the University of Oxford, and then from 1886 to 1889 Grinfield lecturer on the Septuagint in the University of Cambridge. He died in Menton, France, on 16th March 1889.

Edersheim's literary output was prodigious. *The History of the Jewish Nation after the Destruction of Jerusalem by Titus* was published in 1856; *The Temple: Its Ministry and Services at the Time of Jesus Christ* came out in 1874, followed by the seven volumes of *Bible History*, which appeared between 1876 and 1887. *Sketches of Jewish Social Life in the Days of Christ* was also published in 1876. His Warburton Lectures were published in 1885 as *Prophecy and History in Relation to the Messiah*. In 1890, his most famous work, *The Life and Times of Jesus the Messiah* was offered to a very receptive public and is still much appreciated even though biblical scholarship has somewhat moved on. Finally, in 1890, a miscellany called *Tohu va Vohu, 'Without Form and Void': A Collection of Fragmentary Thoughts and Criticisms* was made available, with a memoir by his daughter, Ella Edersheim.

Thus it was that due to a lack of frankness over a trifling issue, in addition to the strained relationship with his irascible colleague Daniel Edward, and the heavy-handedness of the committee, the Free Church of Scotland carelessly lost the services not only of one of the first fruits of its own mission, but one of the most notable Hungarian Jewish Christian minds of his generation.

Despite Mason and Edersheim's removal from Iași, the storm did not abate. Now Hermann Philip refused to work any longer in the city, alleging he found Edward's attitude intolerably overbearing. He chose therefore to relocate to Istanbul, but the missionaries there either could not, or would not, make use of his services. Supported by William Wingate, the missionary at Budapest, he wrote to the committee indicating his willingness to go anywhere they might send him, except Moldavia. But the committee was unresponsive and the result was a complete impasse. Philip tended his resignation and, without waiting to hear if it had been accepted, took his family to Scotland, informing the committee that he had found alternative employment as a missionary to the Jews in Alexandria on behalf of the United Presbyterian Church.[36] When that station was closed in 1858, he resigned his employment, citing health reasons and in 1866, moved to Rome. In 1871, David Brown refers to him as 'the Rev. Dr Philip at present doing good work among the Jews in Rome.'[37] As well as engaging in evangelistic work, Philip served the beleaguered Roman Jewish community by fighting with them for their civil liberties against oppressive Papal rule. He died in 1878, in his 91st year, and was buried in the Protestant Cemetery in Rome. His tombstone carries the inscription: 'For 40 years missionary to his brethren the Jews; the last 12 years of his life in Rome.'[38]

It would not be unreasonable to conclude that the committee was seriously inept in managing its first group of mission workers at Iaşi, and showed cultural insensitivity to the first generation of Jewish Christian employees. Despite the impossibility of retaining Mason, the loss of both Edersheim and Philip invites a reworking of Lady Bracknell's observation that to lose one missionary may be regarded as a misfortune, to lose three looks like carelessness.

To add to the stress under which he now suffered, Daniel Edward inevitably came under a certain amount of criticism from the committee, partly for his perceived mishandling of the affairs of the station, but mainly for a lack of communication with Scotland. The strong-willed Edward was disinclined to respect the authority of the committee and stubbornly prepared to go contrary to their wishes, especially when he suspected they were attempting to micro-manage his work. As the minutes contained in the second minute book reveal, the committee in its inexperience was responsible for the storminess of its relationship with its staff and then, as its confidence grew, it became overbearing, increasingly inclined to interfere in matters of the day-to-day running of its stations and making decisions it had once more wisely left to the judgement of its missionaries.

However much they sought to sympathise with their workers, the committee, having no direct personal experience of mission, flattered themselves they could find solutions to problems without taking the missionaries fully into their confidence. It was a recipe for disaster. Edward's stubbornness did not help, but in his defence, it must be said, that resolution, strong-will, and a degree of obstinacy were, and still are, essential qualities for a pioneer missionary to possess, if possible in abundance.

To further poison the atmosphere and depress Daniel and Catherine, Samuel Gardner, the British consul at Iaşi, now sent a complaint to Edinburgh, alleging Daniel Edward's overbearing behaviour towards his staff at the consulate. Although previously friendly, Gardner was notorious for his 'variable spirits and capricious temper' and, to their credit, on this matter the committee decided to hold their counsel until such time as Edward had opportunity to defend himself, which, when he did, was entirely to their satisfaction.

Clumsy communication from Edinburgh further served to dispirit the missionaries. When Edward had taken it upon himself to make some cautious inquiry through the good offices of his brother-in-law, Mr Grant of Ayr, the committee fired off a short-tempered missive stating that, 'in future they expect and require that all the communications on the business of the committee, should be made to the committee direct.' Next came notification from the committee that it was considering cutting missionary stipends by £50. This coincided with a tardy response from Edinburgh to a claim from Edwards for the reimbursement of some outstanding expenses which had left him heavily out of pocket. In the event, the committee actually improved its financial support for the mission and the decision to reduce stipends was rescinded, but not before their handling of the matter had disheartened the missionaries and depressed their already flagging morale.[39]

Despite the many struggles and trials they had to endure, Catherine's letters, at this stage were a model of discretion. Apart from the references to Dr Mason, there was nothing in her correspondence to suggest there were any specific problems relating to the functioning of the mission at Iaşi. From time to time, there were vague allusions to unidentified difficulties under which they had to labour, especially as Daniel was the only ordained missionary on the station, but instead of complaining, Catherine prudently described themselves as living 'in the midst of realities', or, surrounded by matters of 'great and deep interest … [not] easily related, especially by writing.'[40]

She was frankest when sharing their sense of bitter disappointment at an all-too-brief meeting with the Duncans who had travelled from Scotland, via Hungary, just as far as Galati, some one hundred and fifty miles from Iaşi, but prevailing quarantine regulations had hindered them from continuing their journey. To Catherine, this unintended failure to visit their little community, 'was a weakening of our hands.' She added: 'Alas! we soon had proofs how much we needed his counsel and support.' Although profoundly discouraged by the inability of the Duncans to reach Iaşi, Catherine expressed no bitterness towards them personally, describing John Duncan as 'dear Dr Duncan' and 'our beloved father.'[41] It is not difficult to appreciate that had he become aware of Catherine's comments, albeit entirely free of all malice, John Duncan's hypersensitive conscience would have been deeply wounded.

The pressures now increased far beyond the point of mere discouragement and turned into a threat to the very survival of the work. In another letter written about this time, Catherine describes a great weight of anxiety that was pressing them into the ground. It was, then, with great relief that they took a brief holiday. On returning refreshed to Iaşi, they found the committee's correspondence both supportive and caring: provision had been made to send the Wingate family from Pesth to join them in Iaşi for the winter of 1847/8.[42]

Despite this small encouragement, it was evident that the Edwards were not managing to cope with their ordeals, and badly needed help. One unmistakable sign of stress was Catherine's increasing bitterness towards the people among whom they worked. Over the years, the attitude of the Edwards, especially Catherine, to the Jewish people had almost imperceptibly shifted. As new recruits, they had been somewhat idealistic in their attitude towards the Jewish people, their customs and traditions. Now, under severe strain, this romanticism turned to self-pitying bitterness, cynicism, criticism, and negativity, which, occasionally, at times of greatest pressure, burst out as racial prejudice.

In May 1848, Catherine wrote to her brother William reporting news of antisemitic outbreaks in Poland and giving vent to her pent-up exasperation. She commented:

That the Jews are hated is certainly not wonderful. They are like horse leeches in a country, adding nothing to its wealth, and sucking out the very heart-springs of wealth from the natives. The cultivators and purchasers doubling the price of the produce, which, instead of going to reward the diligent, is consumed by the indolent, idle population, which is likewise detested for its cunning, fraud and filth. Such are the Jews of Moldavia, and from such are to be gathered the elect ones.[43]

The committee's annual report on the work at Iaşi to the 1848 General Assembly that was based solely on information provided by the Edwards, reflects something of this attitude, referring to the Jewish population of Iaşi as 'oppressed, degraded and semi-barbarous', and 'without the advantages of accompanying civilisation.' It is not altogether clear precisely whom Catherine was trying to describe, but comments about an 'indolent, idle population' hint that she may have had in mind members of the ultra-orthodox Chabad movement. With their stress on intellectuality, the young men of the sect then as today spent little time at ordinary work and much time studying Torah in their *yeshivas*, or houses of Talmudic instruction. Moreover, the Chabad were, and still are, among the fiercest opponents of Christian missionary activity. Rabbi Taubes was resolutely opposed to the mission and all the members of the Iaşi Chabad followed his policy, whilst many, perhaps most, though certainly not all, of the ordinary members of the Jewish population were also inclined to an antagonistic view of the mission.

It was this open hostility, not some vague paranoia, which convinced the Edwards that spies watched the Jewish people who called at their house:

They have got the names of 240 who have visited us in the last fortnight, and upwards of 600 who are known to be guilty of frequenting our premises. In consequence partly of this, partly of events which had previously occurred, the Rabbi has now pronounced another Ban.[44]

This comment, with its reiteration of numbers, shows the immense scale of the work in which the Edwards were engaged. Hundreds of Jewish people of the Iaşi community, knowing nothing of Catherine's hidden bitterness of spirit, found the hospitality, teaching, companionship, and witness of her home so attractive they would risk the censure of the community in order to enjoy it. It is obvious that, despite the unseen spiritual battle raging within the Edwards' hearts, Jewish people, nevertheless, saw the gospel being lived out attractively before them as well as being patiently explained by Daniel, Catherine, and their helpers.

Daniel and Catherine's reports of strong opposition directed against them personally was soon corroborated by stories of harassment suffered by those who had been helped by the mission. A notorious and distressing case was that of Naphtali Horowitz, a young man from Austria whose contact with the missionaries resulted in bogus and vindictive legal charges being lodged against him. The missionaries, having every reason to believe that he had genuinely embraced the Christian faith, planned to baptise him and thus remove him from Jewish legal jurisdiction.

Enraged, members of Horowitz's own community reported him to the police, alleging trumped-up charges of the theft of a silver candlestick. Horowitz was brought to trial for larceny and attempting to escape military service. The plot, however, failed. In answer to the prayers of the missionary community, and much to the chagrin of his enemies, the case was overturned and the accused was acquitted.[45]

Patently, not everything was discouraging, but so fierce was the conflict that the greatest encouragement the missionaries ever experienced turned out to be the catalyst for the fiercest opposition they had to endure. For some time, a rabbi called Nahum Birman had been reflecting on what struck him as the disturbing claims that Jesus was the Messiah and that salvation was obtained from him alone as a free gift of grace. Edward patiently attempted to show Rabbi Birman how the ancient prophecies had been fulfilled in the gospel, and in so doing pressed on him the claims of the Messiah. In due course, and much to the distress of his wife of twenty-five years, he was convinced and presented himself, along with his three children, for baptism.

The following morning, knowing full well that his action would bring down the wrath of the community upon his head, Birman went to open his shop as usual, but it almost cost him his life. On Taubes' orders, more than a thousand Jews assembled to oppose him. Stones were thrown and all manner of abuse was hurled at him. The police intervened and put a guard on his premises. Fearing a riot, the civil authorities issued the regrettable instruction that any Jews found on the streets should be beaten. With the arrival first of two platoons of Cossacks, and then towards evening, a further detachment of soldiers, all the makings of a very ugly incident were in place.

Rabbi Birman eloquently and effectively pleaded that his own people be spared the pitiless attentions of the Cossacks, but no-one was under any illusion as to what would have been his fate at the hands of his own people had the police not intervened. As Daniel Edward put it: 'Could they have gotten him, they would have minced him to shreds.' As Nahum Birman and his daughters moved in with the missionaries, the focus of hostilities shifted from his shop to the mission home, which was surrounded and intermittently stoned. Finally, an attempt was made to break into the mission house at night and although this proved abortive, Catherine's nerves were in tatters as she teetered on the edge of breakdown. Both Daniel and Catherine were lonely, dispirited, and utterly worn out.[46]

In their mind the problems were exacerbated by the suspicion, not without some justification, that neither they nor their work was properly known or adequately supported by the Church at home. This he frankly attributed in part to his own failure to communicate: he had 'hitherto completely failed in setting the station properly before the eye of the Church.' But the committee, preoccupied by the amazing successes concurrently being experienced in Budapest, had failed to be as attentive as it ought to the struggles in Iași. It would not be unfair to remark that Budapest's blessing was in part purchased at Iași's expense.[47]

In November 1847, Catherine discovered she was pregnant and the arrival of the Wingates from Budapest that winter brought the comfort and support of congenial Christian friendship. Wingate found Iași to be exactly as Edward described it, a station that was peculiarly trying. He wrote that it severely tested 'the whole character of the Christian labourer – his energy, his perseverance, his faith, his love.'[48] Nevertheless, he entered into the work with determination and great enthusiasm. Catherine paints a kindly picture of him coming home from visiting Jewish people, marching through the mud and snow with his trousers tucked into his wellington boots, wooden clogs over his boots, clad warmly in a huge Hungarian fur cloak, and with a comforter wound around his neck, his whiskers and even his eye-lashes frozen in the sub-zero temperatures. Enthusiastic and inspiring as he may have been, Wingate nevertheless frankly admitted to his host and hostess that the situation they faced in Moldavia was far more exacting than anything he had ever experienced in Hungary. He said he had never come across such 'bigoted Talmudical Jews' and confided to his journal that the Edwards' morale was very low indeed and their situation frightfully discouraging. The little church was also 'very low in spirituality.'

To help breathe life into the church, Wingate advised Edward to start two fellowship meetings, one on Wednesday and another on Saturday. He also spent much time praying with the Edwards and their colleagues. Forced thus to see the precariousness of their situation through the shocked eyes of her guests, Catherine once more unburdened herself to her brother and sister-in-law:

> When we see these things, *as at first* realized by a stranger, it forces us to look back upon the six years which my husband spent here alone, without one friendly voice to cheer him, without one Christian to help him on, without support from home by letters or visits. I think you will be able to enter into my feelings when I tell you that I have been more tried in spirit since our dear friends have come than I was before. The awful suspense of the former two months kept up a sort of excitement, so that when relief came I *felt* more.[49]

Catherine's words are not to be judged for their objective accuracy or balance. Of course she had discounted the help they had once had from Herman Phillip and Alfred Edersheim, as well as that from the committee, poor as it was, and the prayers of the church at home, to say nothing of the encouragement of the conversion of Jewish people through their ministry, and, of course, there was above all the utter faithfulness of God, His answers to prayer, the Spirit's comfort and the abiding promises of the Word. Hers was not an ungrateful complaint, but a *cri de coeur*, the outpouring of a soul harassed and beleaguered by the powers of darkness, one who was feeling battered and bruised.

On his return to Pesth, Wingate reported that in his opinion his efforts in Iași had not been wasted, but in reality his contribution, helpful as it was at the time, was much too little and far too late.[50] Catherine's first letter of 1848, written to her brother, started on a very low note as she lamented that, 'Satan's blows had been well nigh too strong for us. All loveliness, all joy had fled from us.' It was thus with heavy hearts that they prepared for a celebration of the Lord's Supper, even if their spirits were lifted when a number of Jewish enquirers told them that they too wanted to take their place at the communion table, including Nahum Birman, who brought with him eight Jewish friends, all of whom had been deeply impressed by his commitment to Christ.[51]

As if their cup of suffering was not sufficiently full, to add to all their other woes that winter, Iași was visited by cholera. The Government considered placing the city under quarantine, a move that would have had the most serious repercussions. Catherine considered that had that policy prevailed, in the depths of winter, with few reserves of food available, half of the population would have died of starvation. Although her letters indicated the severity of the weather, she did not comment on the progress of the epidemic, which seems to have been held in check by the sub-zero temperatures.

But as the winter passed and milder weather conditions prevailed, the disease once more took hold on the city with a fresh virulence. The outlook for the work seemed desolate, but in fact the epidemic opened up fresh opportunities for witness.[52] Writing in June to Dr Alexander Moody Stuart, who in 1847 had succeeded Dr Keith as the convener of the committee, Edward informed him that the chaos created by the contagion had opened up many opportunities to share the gospel. It was, he said, the trial of having to stare death in the face daily that led many people to serious spiritual reflection, inclining them to ask questions about eternity and search their hearts in preparation.[53]

And yet another layer of tribulation was about to be added to their complicated and heroic sufferings as the year 1848 brought to Iași the insecurity of the revolutionary convulsions that shook much of Europe and especially the Habsburg domains. In early April, in the Hotel St Petersburg, where Bonar and M'Cheyne had stayed, Moldavian revolutionaries made their proclamation in favour of a moderate liberal political regime and launched their uprising. A little later, as fires broke out, panicking people rushed here and there to secure their valuables. In the Jewish community confusion reigned and the people were uncertain whether to be glad or afraid, screaming out '*die Revoluzy ist gekommen!*' (the Revolution is come!). As with the cholera, so with the revolution: all business ground to a halt and hordes fled the city as the army intervened and imposed martial law. [54]

Unsurprisingly, Catherine's worries were expressed in her correspondence. By June, the question arose as to whether it might not be wisest for the couple to leave Iaşi and attempt to establish a mission in a less troubled area. It was thought that the political upheavals had swept away virtually all the restrictions which once had been considered insurmountable to the organisation of evangelistic work in Galicia, or Austrian Poland. Although the situation was still far too unsettled for itinerant work to be safely undertaken, it was thought feasible to attempt work in a city like Lviv (now in Ukraine).

During the month of June, as such thoughts passed through their minds, yet another outbreak of cholera wracked Iaşi and a renewed bout of revolutionary fervour provoked the Prince to invite the assistance of the Russians, who entered the city in July. The impact on the local economy of thirty thousand Russian soldiers was crippling, inflation soared, and with escalating costs, provisions became increasingly scarce.

On 31st July, amid opposition, revolution, and epidemic, Catherine gave birth to their first child, a daughter. To Daniel, the joy of her birth was mixed with an urgent need to reevaluate his priorities, which he now, rightly, considered to be the welfare of his wife and child. He wrote to the committee informing them that there was no time to spare; he would close up the work in Iaşi immediately, without waiting for their approval, and commence a fresh work in Lviv before the winter would set in. The committee mildly acceded to this *fait accompli*.

The Edward family, however, left Lviv in 1852, expelled by the Austrian government at the same time, and for the same reasons, as the missionaries were driven out of Pesth. Following a brief spell in Scotland, Daniel, Catherine, and their daughter took up a long residence in Wrocław, Poland (formerly Breslau in Lower Silesia). Here they enjoyed many years of fruitful missionary work, from which he eventually retired in 1896, aged eighty-one years old, dying the same year.[55]

Despite numerous difficulties, great discouragements and fierce opposition, the mission in Iaşi was by no means a fruitless venture. Even Catherine, who was disinclined to exaggerate the positive, acknowledged God's faithfulness in the 'many and lasting fruits of the seven and a-half years of labour there.'[56] The reality was that Daniel and Catherine, and their associates, could count as evidence of their faithfulness and Gospel success twenty-nine Jewish Christians who had been baptised during their time in Iaşi. These included the influential Rabbi Nahum Birman, Naphatali Horrowitz, and Weiss and Neuman, who both became unordained missionaries to their own people. Then there was Michael 'B', a young man saved from the cholera and for Christ, who became librarian to the Prince of Moldavia.

Moreover, when others tried to reap where the Edwards had sown, their harvest was very much lighter than that of the pioneers. Around 1850, after the revolutionary wars, the LSPCJ opened a station in Iaşi, but left no record of success, despite the fact that when Theodore Meyer visited the city a decade later he found evidence of the work of the Edwards. Subsequently, when the Berlin Society sent K. J. Gottlieb in 1888 he reported it was 'unresponsive to the missionary's appeals' and his health suffered consequently.[57]

So despite the enthusiastic recommendation of Iaşi by M'Cheyne and Bonar, the early optimism of the committee and the traces of blessing that remained, with its unremitting difficulties and challenges, Iaşi proved to be the counterpoint to the relatively easy success seen at Budapest. Nor could it be claimed that the committee had handled the personal, spiritual, and psychological problems of its embattled missionaries with any degree of competence. When once Dr Keith's illness in Budapest had come to the attention of the committee, assistance was immediately arranged, but apart from very brief visits from the Duncans and William Wingate little pastoral care was provided for the Edwards at Iaşi, especially when disappointment turned to bitterness. Yet it is all too easy, with the benefits of hindsight and long experience, to propose twenty-first century solutions to nineteenth-century pioneer problems. What can fairly be said, however, is that to a very considerable degree, both the iron-willed and irascible Daniel Edward and his fretful but faithful wife Catherine exemplified M'Cheyne's twin *desiderata* for missionaries to the Jews: faith and perseverance.

18

A City and Its Bridge

Budapest, c.1840

REVOLUTION was in the air. Through the powerful influence of music, the visual arts, poetry, and literature, Romantic radicalism was challenging the older rational and conservative forces of the Enlightenment. With its appeal to the subjective, and its visions of the imagination and senses, Romanticism created a hunger for change. Its restless energy made its presence felt not only in the creative arts, but also in politics, where it became identified with the quest for liberty and national independence.

Notwithstanding its apparent solidity, cracks were beginning to show in the antiquated structures of the Habsburg autocracy. The problem was embodied, quite literally, in the inbred Imperial line. The parents of Ferdinand I, reigning at the time the Scottish mission was established, were double first cousins who bestowed upon their son the genetic legacy of hydrocephalus and congenital neurological problems, including epilepsy, a speech impediment, and impotence. Ferdinand is famous for a single coherent but fatuous order: when informed he could not have apricot dumplings because the fruit was not in season, he stormed with infantile petulance, 'I'm the Emperor, and I want dumplings!' This was, according to historian A. J. P. Taylor, 'his only sensible remark.' Adding that Ferdinand actually asked for 'noodles' (knödel), 'But for a noodle to ask for noodles would be in English an intolerable pun.'[1] Nor was the future for the dynasty secured when Ferdinand married Maria Anna of Piedmont-Sardinia to whom he was related. The Austro-Hungarian Empire, knit together through such marriage alliances, lacked vigour, not only physically, but in new ideas. It was unable to construct any effective resistance to the powerful intellectual forces creating strong national identities among Germans, Italians, Magyars, Slavs, and Croats.

Aware of the impending challenge, the Emperor's father, Francis II, called upon his Hungarian subjects to remain loyal, which, in practice, meant accepting the authority of the viceroy, Archduke Joseph of Austria and Palatine of Hungary, whose third wife Maria Dorothea Luise Wilhelmine Caroline of Württemberg, was, as we have noticed, a Protestant island in an ocean of Catholicism, and had become the confidante of Dr Alexander Keith and the enthusiastic, if covert, patroness of the Church of Scotland's plan to establish a mission to Jewish people in Budapest.

Democratic and liberal opposition to Habsburg power was led by the constitutional Magyar national movement, of which Count Istvan Széchenyi and Ferenc Deák were the leaders. Their moderate political objectives opposed violence, and included Hungarian parliamentary reorganisation, tax reform, the abolition of serfdom, free speech, religious freedom, and the replacement of German as the national tongue with Magyar, the Hungarian language.[2] An aristocrat, Széchenyi, believed that national reforms would, through the influence of his peers, gradually evolve without the need for the upsets and destructiveness of revolution.

Quick to see the benefits of technological improvement, Széchenyi promoted the establishment of railway links to the west, steamboats on the Danube and major civil engineering projects such as modern roads, constructed according to the latest theories of the Scotsman John Loudon McAdam, and, significantly, a grand suspension bridge, which was to bear his name. This bridge would form the first permanent link across the Danube between the twin cities of Buda and Pesth, which would not be formally united as Budapest until 1873 and which retained their distinctive characters even after the union. From at least 1841, Széchenyi was well aware of the activities of the Scottish missionaries, identified with their evangelicalism and warmly but quietly approved of them. He could be counted on by Archduchess Maria Dorothea to resist their Roman Catholic adversaries in government.[3]

Széchenyi's political rival was Lajos Kossuth, a lawyer and journalist who had been born into an impoverished noble family in 1802. Opposed to Széchenyi's evolutionary approach, Kossuth would settle for nothing less than Hungary's total political autonomy from Austria, a goal that, as far as he could see, could only be achieved by revolution. In 1837, his radicalism had led to him being jailed for four years for the crime of high treason. But prison did not intimidate Kossuth and he emerged strengthened in his political resolve and in his Calvinistic faith, which he longed to share with others: 'I indeed am a Protestant, not only by birth, but also by conviction. I would delight to see the same shared by the whole world.' His Christian viewpoint would lead him later to tell an audience in St Louis, USA, that:

> the oppressors [need to be told] that there is a God in heaven who rules the universe by eternal laws. The Almighty Father … omnipotent in wisdom, bountiful in His omnipotence, just in His judgment, and eternal in His love … against which neither the proud ambition of despots, nor the skill of their obsequious [lackeys] can prevail – in Him I put my trust and go cheerfully on in my duties.[4]

It was Kossuth's hope that ordinary Hungarians, especially the Protestant adherents of the Lutheran and Hungarian Reformed Churches, could be aroused to patriotic fervour through a popular movement aimed at exposing tyrannical repression and reviving Magyar national loyalties.

Reactionary and powerful, Archduke Joseph was prepared to resist any change, whether evolutionary or revolutionary, that threatened Habsburg rule over Hungary. Through the police and a network of spies and censors, of which Drs Black and Keith had at times fallen foul, the government attempted, largely unsuccessfully, to silence all reformers and repress the work of Nationalist Hungarian painters, poets, and writers.[5] In Hungary, even changes of religious affiliation were only tolerated when Protestant marriage partners became Roman Catholics. With many Hungarians loyal to the Protestant Churches, 'the religious question' was frequently and vigorously debated in the Hungarian Parliament, which began to feel a growing annoyance that any self-respecting country should have to incorporate into its statute books the religious prejudices of an alien power.[6]

Hungary's Jewish population – which maybe dates back to Roman times, it being conjectured that King Decebalus, ruler of Dacia, rewarded Jews who allied with him against Rome with settlements in Transylvania – was in the mid-nineteenth century located largely in Pesth and had been since at least the eleventh century. But like other Jewish communities in the Habsburg Empire, it had for centuries suffered the humiliation of being subject to a discriminatory religious levy, the so-called toleration tax. The 1832–36 Diet of the Hungarian Parliament had debated the legitimacy of this tax and, after a protracted struggle led by the Calvinist Ferenc Deák and the liberal aristocracy, a bill for its abolition was presented to Vienna, but, for allegedly economic reasons it was not ratified.[7]

The Parliamentary Diet of 1839–40, held when Keith and Black were in the country, once more took up the question, arguing that Jews were not a separate nation and ought not to be excluded from the ordinary privileges of Hungarian citizens. The result was an Act extending to Hungarian Jews a package of civil liberties, including the right to establish factories, acquire plots of land and engage freely in commercial activities. Though the new legislation was not as comprehensive as the Jewish community had hoped, it was a step on the road to full emancipation and was widely welcomed as such. Now, at last, Hungarian Jewish people could advance in commercial and professional life. The same year as the Act was passed, Zsigmond Saphir, a relative of the Saphirs, who were among the earliest converts of the mission, became the first Jewish editor of a Hungarian newspaper, the *Pester Tagblatt*.

Perhaps inevitably, the main religious change taking place in the Hungarian Jewish community was the growing influence of the Reform movement, which there, as elsewhere, enthusiastically embraced almost anything that would break the domination of Jewish Orthodoxy and open the door to assimilation. The Pesth Reform Society campaigned for six major changes in Jewish observance. The first two were radical enough: the observance of the Sabbath on Sunday instead of Saturday and the abolition of, what it termed, the 'exceedingly purposeless' dietary laws. It also hoped to reform the Jewish calendar, by reducing what was seen as the burdensome number of memorial observances and, except for Yom Kippur, abolishing all traditional fast days.

Further liturgical changes introduced by the Reform Society, included briefer services and the use of vernacular instead Yiddish. It also wanted to totally abandon symbolic clothing and the covering of the male head. Circumcision was to be non-obligatory, the Ten Commandments alone were core religious principles, and the Talmud (the authoritative written record of the Oral Law on biblical texts, ethics, traditions, and history) and Halakhah (laws, customs, and observances) were to be declared obsolete. Other theological changes included jettisoning belief in a personal Messiah, and the obligation to perform *aliyah* (emigration to Palestine). Church-like trappings, such as organs and choirs, and psalms and hymns sung in Hungarian or German, were introduced into Reform synagogues.

Above all, Reform advocated low profile assimilation into the gentile community, and thereby threatened not only the cohesion and visibility of the Jewish community but, in fact, its very existence as an identifiable entity.[8]

Inevitably, such innovations were strongly resisted by leaders in the Orthodox community, who threatened the expulsion of theological students from *yeshivas* (rabbinic academies) if they so much as touched the new vernacular translations of the ancient texts. This reactionary animosity led to the harassment of reformers such as Mordecai Weisz, who had vociferously criticised the practice of *kashrut*, the Jewish food laws, and had taught that traditional dress was out of date and should be abandoned. But, as so often it does, reactionary opposition overreached itself and as a result of a spate of vitriolic attacks, Weisz abandoned Judaism altogether and professed Christianity.[9]

Mordecai Weisz was by no means the only Hungarian Jewish intellectual who felt crushed between the upper and nether millstones of Orthodox reaction and illiberal Habsburg Roman Catholicism. By rejecting Jewish Orthodoxy and attempting a radical reconstruction of Judaism, Reform sought to offer a viable Jewish alternative to Christianity, but in fact, once assimilation became acceptable and believing in Jesus was no longer seen as a denial of Jewish identity, Reform opened the door into the Church.

Virtually all of the influential converts of the Scottish mission, such as the Saphirs, Alexander Tomory, and Alfred Edersheim came from non-Orthodox backgrounds. Even prior to the arrival of the missionaries, some prominent Hungarian Jews had embraced Christianity, including Moritz Gottlieb Saphir, Leopold Julius Klein, Karl Beck, and, most notably, Moritz Bloch, who in 1847 changed his name to Ballagi Mór. Mór's bilingual, multi-volume translation of the Pentateuch into Hungarian, with detailed philological comments and commentary, was published in 1840 and 1841. These researches shocked some, but pleasantly surprised others by hinting at possible Christological interpretation of passages of the Hebrew Scriptures.[10]

In 1843, he further upset the Jewish applecart by becoming first a Lutheran and then an ordained minister in the Hungarian Reformed Church. His initial commitment to a largely intellectual and nominal Christianity was challenged by his contact with the Scottish missionaries, especially William Wingate, through whose influence he underwent a profound spiritual conversion. Keenly working for the renewal of the Reformed Church, and (probably unknowingly) echoing Alexander Duff's adage that 'missions are the chief end of the Christian Church', he once ventured the opinion that a church's missionary activity is the best thermometer of its spiritual life. In 1855 he was appointed a professor of theology at the Reformed Theological Academy in Budapest, nominated in 1858 to the Hungarian Academy of Sciences, and in 1861 elected a member of Parliament.

In 1836, Löw Schwab was appointed Chief Rabbi of Pesth. Born in Moravia in 1794, Schwab was a brilliant pupil of the famed and pragmatic Rabbi Moses Sofer, who was a champion of orthodoxy but no reactionary. Once established in Pesth, Schwab sought to bring his irenic spirit to bear on the divisive tensions within the community. Although no friend of Reform, he became a strong advocate of 'Magyarisation', often preaching in Hungarian rather than Yiddish because of his conviction that full emancipation would come only if the Jewish community convincingly demonstrated its loyalty to Hungary. Under his patronage students in the city's Jewish school made excellent progress in the Hungarian language. In 1848, Schwab sided with the nationalist revolution led by Lajos Kossuth and when the revolution failed he was imprisoned by the Austrians on the charge that he had preached a seditious sermon advocating independence.

Schwab died in Budapest in 1857 and is remembered as being responsible for the building of the magnificent Dohány Street Synagogue, distinguished both by its size – it is the second largest synagogue in the world – and by its wonderfully flamboyant Moorish Byzantine style. It stands as a testimony to Schwab's pragmatic relationship to orthodox liturgical scruples that the synagogue, which was inaugurated after his death, was equipped with an organ.

Standing almost as symbol to the current of modernisation running through both Jewish and gentile Hungarian society was the challenge of solving the problem of erecting a permanent link between the twin cities of Buda and Pesth. The Danube is prone to heavy flooding and for centuries the best solution appeared to be the use of a temporary pontoon bridge, which was removed each time flooding threatened and then re-erected when the danger passed. From Roman times a permanent bridge was considered impracticable, but in February 1832 a Bridge Society was founded to examine the project in the light of modern engineering solutions.[11]

The same year Count István Széchenyi, in company with the radical Count Gyula Andrássy, then head of the Hungarian government's technical department, travelled to London to seek advice from notable bridge builders including William Tierney Clark and Thomas Telford. Tierney Clark's original design for the Marlow Bridge, which spans the River Thames between Marlow in Buckinghamshire and the village of Bisham in Berkshire, caught Széchenyi's eye as a model for a Budapest suspension bridge.[12]

The English style was adopted even to the extent of the replication of stone lions on the bridge's abutments modelled on Sir Edwin Landseer's magnificent bronze lions that form the base of Nelson's Column in Trafalgar Square. The project, financed by the sale of shares, many of which were purchased by the Austrian-Greek entrepreneur and banker Georgios Sinas, commenced in September 1839. The bridge was officially opened on 20th November, 1849, its incomplete structure having been a battle ground in the Hungarian revolution of 1848.

Whilst most of the manual labourers who worked on the bridge were local Hungarians, they were supervised by skilled craftsmen and engineers from Britain, many in fact from Scotland. At the height of the construction, the British community comprised some sixty-two families. Scottish masons, under the direction of a committed English Christian called James Teasdale, who had worked for Clark some years earlier on the Norfolk suspension bridge over the River Adur in Shoreham-by-Sea, West Sussex, formed the nucleus of a little Presbyterian congregation. It was the spiritual welfare of these people which provided an official reason for the presence in Hungary of Scottish Protestant ministers, making the timely bridge project key to the establishment of the Scottish mission to the Jewish people of Hungary.[13]

Leaving aside the contact with Black and Keith in 1839, the arrival of the Scottish missionaries in Pesth in August 1841 was by no means the first contact between the Hungarian Reformed Church and the Church of Scotland, nor did it mark the origin of the Hungarian Church's interest in the Jews. In the second half of the sixteenth century, Hungarian students in Heidelberg were taught Hebrew and Semitic languages by one of the foremost Hebraists of their generation, the Italian Jewish Christian, Giovanni Emmanuele Tremellio, better known as John Immanuel Tremellius. Converted first to Catholicism in 1540 through Cardinal Pole, a native of England then resident in Padua, and then falling under the influence of the Italian Reformer Pietro Martire Vermigli, better known as Peter Martyr, Tremellius embraced the doctrines of the Reformation.

In 1547 he sought asylum in England, more or less at the same time as his mentor, Peter Martyr, responded to an invitation from Thomas Cranmer, Archbishop of Canterbury, offering sanctuary in England from persecution in Italy. Tremellius taught Hebrew at Cambridge, enjoying the friendship of Cranmer and Bishop Parker. On the accession to the English throne of the Roman Catholic Mary

Tudor, he fled to the Continent and took refuge at Heidelberg, where from 1561 to 1577 he was professor of Old Testament. His chief literary work was a Latin translation of the Hebrew Bible, but he also translated Calvin's Catechism into Hebrew and complied *Sefer inukh Be irei Yah* (Catechism for Enquiring Jews) in Hebrew and Latin, which was reprinted in the nineteenth century in an English translation by the LSPCJ, who provided the English title, and was still in use at the beginning of the twentieth.[14]

Curiously, it was Tremellius' Latin Bible's rendition of Exodus 3:2, rather than that of the more common Vulgate, that provided the Church of Scotland with its Latin motto, *Nec Tamen Consumebatur*. This was unofficially adopted in 1691 when the printer and bookseller George Mosman, impressed at his Glasgow printing works, near the Tron-Church, the symbol of the Burning Bush, surrounded by Tremellius' Latin motto, on the title page of the Principal Acts of the General Assembly.[15]

By the middle of the seventeenth century many Hungarian Calvinist students sought further education in England and Scotland, where they discovered that the Puritan and Presbyterian belief in the restoration of Israel and the conversion of the Jews reflected very similar convictions common at the time in Hungary. In Scotland, some of these students may have also come under the influence of two other central European Jewish Christian Hebrew instructors: Naphtali Margolioth (Julius Conradus Otto), who taught in Edinburgh, and Paul Shaletti, a former Rabbi, who was a lecturer at King's College, Aberdeen.[16]

In Hungary, the doctrine of the restoration of the Jews had been taught at the Reformed Academy at Sárospatak by David Valerius from the late 1630s. Valerius had been converted through contact with Johan Alsted of the academy in Gulyafehérvár. Alsted's international circle of friends included the Scottish minister John Durie, whose postmillennial views he shared. Most of the leading ministers of the Synod of Transylvania shared Valerius' eschatology, and it is not surprising, therefore, that from time to time the Reformed Church in Hungary contemplated missionary activity not only among the Muslim Turks, who occupied the southern part of their country, but also to the Jewish community in their midst.[17]

This inter-communal friendliness was reinforced a century later when, in 1746, Matthew Bohil, a Hungarian Calvinist pastor, who was imprisoned by the Jesuits, was enabled to make good his escape through the generous help of a Jewish rabbi. As the Protestant Churches languished under Roman Catholic Habsburg rule, the story of Bohil symbolised the solidarity in suffering under Habsburg intolerance of both Jews and Protestants, very similar to the solidarity Black and Keith, Bonar and M'Cheyne felt with the persecuted Jews of Livorno.[18]

The advent of Scottish missionary activity in Hungary approximately coincided with the notorious Highland Clearances, when rural Scots were evicted from their land and forced to emigrate to the colonies. Alert to injustice and tyranny wherever it might rear its head, many of Scotland's Christians followed Hungary's struggles for independence with great interest. Christian journalists, such as Hugh Miller, the editor of the evangelical paper *The Witness*, depicted the Highlanders' land struggles and the revolution in Hungary as parallel events, further strengthening the link between the two countries.[19]

The familiarity of Scottish readers with events in Hungary was, however, mostly a by-product of their interest in the missionaries in Pesth, whose activities were widely reported in both the religious and secular press. In Hungary, the Archduchess Maria Dorothea exerted a spiritual influence quite the equal of her Scottish peers, such as Viscountess Glenorchy and the Duchess of Gordon, including among her many interests relief for the poor, support for Bible printing and evangelisation, personal involvement in the nursing of the sick, and the founding of various moral and religious associations.

From 1839 until her husband's death in 1847, Maria Dorothea stood at the very centre of the evangelical life of Budapest. Under her sponsorship there came into existence a remarkable international, interdenominational, and influential coterie of evangelical Protestants that brought together Scottish Presbyterians and Hungarian Lutheran and Reformed ministers. Through this circle, she also brought together the political rivals Széchenyi and Kossuth, both of whom espoused the evangelical cause.

It was the formation of this group that marked the beginning of a new era of spiritual prosperity in Hungarian Protestantism. Little wonder, then, that her circle, with its international Protestant connections and its nationalist and liberal democratic tendencies, was viewed with grave suspicion by Vienna. The Catholic clergy spied on her and constantly intrigued against her, but she bravely dismissed all such dangers as inconsequential.[20]

The Scottish missionaries nevertheless recognised that her situation was not without personal risk and, in their correspondence, in order to guard her interests, they gave her a code name: 'the sister on the hill.'[21] Their suspicions proved well grounded. On the day of her husband's funeral in January 1847, Maria Dorothea was cruelly ordered away from Budapest and obliged to remove to Vienna. In such revolutionary times, to a paranoid regime, a widowed Protestant Archduchess with dubious international Protestant connections seemed too great a threat to Habsburg power. She and her influence had to be marginalised.[22]

Such then, in brief outline, was the religious, political, and social context prevailing in Hungary in August 1841 forming the backcloth to the stage on which the missionaries entered. The supporting cast was made up of Hungarians and Britons, Jews and gentiles, royalty and commoners, clergy and people, politicians and engineers. The leading players were four ministers of the Church of Scotland who were determined, by the blessing of God, to establish, by covert methods if need be, a mission to the Jews of Pesth. Who then were these courageous men and what were their backgrounds?

⤳ 19 ⤳

'He won us all': John Duncan and the Pesth Mission

Hungary, 1841–1852

FOR many people, the words 'pioneer missionary' probably bring to the mind such people as David Brainerd, Henry Martyn, William Carey, David Livingstone, or Mary Slessor. In other words, people not only of spiritual maturity and organisational ability, but also of great initiative, iron self-discipline and, when necessary, raw courage. Many of them devoted a lifetime to God's service and sometimes sacrificed life itself.

On the face of it then, John Duncan was a most unlikely contender for the title of pioneer missionary. He was no born leader of men, in fact he often seemed incapable of controlling himself. Brilliant he was, but also undisciplined, erratic, emotional, eccentric, and easily distracted. He served only temporarily as a missionary, returning to Scotland to become the very personification of the absent-minded professor. Yet, under God's blessing, the benefits of Duncan's brief missionary career in Hungary left an incalculable legacy, not only in the Jewish community, but also for the wider Hungarian church.

As the most senior, Duncan had been appointed leader of the four-man mission group sent by the Free Church of Scotland to Pesth. He was forty-four years old, slightly built, with a thin bony face and long scruffy hair. His unkempt appearance both betrayed his eccentricity and hinted at his preoccupation with the things of the mind and spirit. He was born in 1796 in Old Aberdeen to parents who were members of the Secession Church. Educated at

Aberdeen Grammar School, he showed from the outset an aptitude in languages and philosophy which, along with mathematics, were to be his life-long intellectual passions.[1]

So great was this early interest in philosophy that he was once discovered during class furtively reading a copy of Aristotle hidden under his desk, much as a schoolboy of a later generation might read Marvel Comics in America or *The Beano* in Scotland. In 1810, he entered Marischal College in Aberdeen and four years later graduated Master of Arts. Despite his Christian upbringing, he was attracted to the atheistic teaching of the Jewish philosopher Baruch Spinoza, yet, nevertheless, undertook theological studies, becoming a communicant member of the Church of Scotland in 1816. Under the influence of one of his tutors, Dr Mearns, his scepticism fell away and he felt able, at least to believe in God's existence.

This truth dawned upon him whilst he was crossing the Brig o' Dee in Aberdeen and he danced for joy when he realised he could believe in God and still be intelligent.[2] The removal of his atheism did not lead immediately to Christian conversion, however, and, when, in 1825, he was licensed by the Church of Scotland to preach, it had been, as he later remarked, a regrettable step taken, 'in ungodliness and doctrinal unbelief and heresy.' The following year, however, saw Duncan's conversion under the influence of the Swiss minister, César Malan.

Although conversion brought Duncan immediate peace, a morbid preoccupation with his spiritual state gave rise to deep doubts as to the authenticity of his Christian profession, which eroded whatever assurance he might have had. He rapidly subsided into a mood of profound pessimism, but found help in the works of John Owen, Herman Witsius, and especially his own countryman, John Love, an eloquent preacher and theologian and one of the founders of the London Missionary Society.[3]

Through such reading and the support of his friends, Gavin Parker and James Kidd, Duncan passed through an experience which he called his 'second conversion.' For the rest of his life he retained such a dread of superficiality that, much to the distress of his family and friends, he was never again able to feel completely assured that his faith was genuine and that he was without doubt a true Christian.

As well as a sensitive soul, Duncan possessed a remarkable intellect. Not only was he thoroughly proficient in Hebrew and all the related languages, he also knew at least four Indian languages – Bengali, Hindi, Marathi, and ancient Sanskrit – enjoyed a high degree of fluency in many European languages, and had an amazing facility to express himself in the most elegant Latin. This is illustrated by an anecdote from the period after his time in Hungary. His daughter, Maria Dorothea, named after the Archduchess, completed her education at an international school in Eclépens near La Sarraz, twelve miles north of Lausanne in Switzerland. Duncan's visits to the school were warmly remembered because he always spoke a few words to each girl in her own language as they filed past him to say goodnight.[4]

One of the very few surviving fragments of Duncan's writing also bears testimony to his linguistic skill. It consists of undated, scribbled annotations by way of a response to a student's request for insight on the text of 2 Corinthians 9:6, in the Authorised Version, 'He which soweth sparingly shall reap also sparingly; and he which soweth bountifully shall reap also bountifully,' and comprises of approximately one hundred words: six are Greek, eight are Hebrew, and four are Sanskrit, the remainder being English.[5] Duncan's deep interest in the Jewish people, his profound knowledge of the Hebrew land, his total immersion in Jewish culture and Rabbinic literature, coupled with an eccentric teaching style, resulted in him earning the apt nickname, 'Rabbi'.

Duncan married twice: in 1813 he married Janet Tower of Aberdeen; a daughter, Annie, was born in 1838 the year before Janet died. In 1842, shortly before departing for Hungary, he married Janet Douglas-Torrance, the widow of John Torrance, a military surgeon from Kilmarnock. Duncan's friend Moody Stuart, knowing well his friend's lack of domesticity, once said of Janet: 'None but a most superior woman would ever marry John Duncan.'[6] Janet came to the marriage with two daughters, Annabella who in 1842 married William Allan, one of the Pesth missionaries, and Margaret, who married William Wingate, another of the missionary team. In 1844, in Edinburgh, John and Janet had a daughter, the only child of the marriage, who was named Maria Dorothea, after the Archduchess. Maria married Adolph Spaeth, who, prior to his departure to America, was a tutor of Sir John Douglas Sutherland Campbell (later Marquis of Lorne, Governor General of Canada), afterwards becoming a pastor of St. John's German Lutheran congregation in Philadelphia, and Professor of New Testament Exegesis and Catechetics at the Lutheran Theological Seminary, Philadelphia.[7]

Added to Duncan's deep spirituality and intellectual powers was a charming eccentricity and absentmindedness. There are numerous examples, but to take just one, on the morning of his second marriage he went to his room to dress. As the minutes passed his niece wondered why he was so delayed in his preparations. Going upstairs, she discovered Duncan peacefully asleep in his bed, with an open Hebrew Bible on his chest. The act of taking off his clothes had automatically triggered his night-time routine, which included changing into his night clothes, getting into bed and reading his Hebrew Bible. Such unconventional behaviour had, however, great missionary usefulness, endearing him to the Jewish people of Pesth. One of his fellow missionaries, Robert Smith, spoke of him as 'a child and a giant in one, both characters curiously intermingled. No man ever inspired less awe, nor called forth deeper reverence.'[8]

Next in seniority was Duncan's son-in-law, the thirty-two-year-old William Wingate, the eldest son of Andrew Wingate, a wealthy merchant who resided in Blythswood Square, then one of the most fashionable residential addresses in Glasgow.[9] With all the privileges of his upbringing, William was educated at the Grammar School of Glasgow and studied law at Glasgow University, becoming a partner in his father's business. After a period of religious disinterest, the deep distress he felt at the death of his first wife, Jessie Buchanan, to whom he had been married for only three years, led to his Christian conversion.

Comforted by his newfound faith and enthusiastic for the cause of the gospel, he became a member of the Tron Church, then under the ministry of his cousin, Dr Robert Buchanan, and was shortly after ordained an elder. Through his friendship with Robert Wodrow an interest in the Jewish mission was aroused and in due course he offered himself to, and was accepted by, the committee as a missionary. As we have noted earlier, he was required to undertake further studies in Berlin, in company with Daniel Edward.[10] In September 1843 Wingate married John Duncan's stepdaughter, Margaret Wallace Torrance.

The third member of the team was twenty-four-year-old Robert Smith, a farmer's son, who was born at Benholm, near Montrose on the Aberdeenshire coast, and educated five miles away at St Cyrus during the time when Dr Keith was parish minister. In 1835 he entered Marischal College before becoming a minister of the Church of Scotland. It was during his divinity studies that Smith developed an interest in mission to the Jewish people and offered himself to the committee.[11] On the strength of warm testimonials affirming his suitability, he was accepted in March 1841 and, just prior to his departure to Pesth, was licensed by the Presbytery of Fordoun and placed under Duncan's tutelage in preparation for ordination.

The final member of the group was thirty-three-year-old William Owen Allan. Little has come down to us about Allan's early life apart from the facts that he was born at Torthorwold, Dumfriesshire and studied divinity at the University of Glasgow. After being accepted by the committee in 1841, the General Assembly took the unusual step of waiving his attendance at the final session of Divinity and Church History and authorised his ordination by the Presbytery of Hamilton.[12]

In June 1841 the party, minus Wingate, who was first to be married, made their final arrangements for departure to London in readiness for crossing the Channel. They set off with the great good will of the church and much heartfelt prayer and enthusiastic support. But even as the missionaries assembled in London, there was a fresh attempt to resuscitate the plan for a mission station in Palestine. At this eleventh hour, unwilling to follow reason rather than sentiment, the committee insisted that Duncan should be told to be ready to change his plans and travel to Palestine if and when the instruction was given.[13]

This disarray was exacerbated by a further suggestion that the available forces be split and two stations opened, one in Pesth under Duncan, and the other in Palestine under Dr Keith. Following a frantic consultation between Alexander Moody Stuart, M'Cheyne and Keith, Keith took the initiative and settled the matter once for all by indicating that if his health permitted he might be willing to go to Pesth, but only for a short time to introduce the missionaries to the Archduchess and other friends who might help them. The idea was dropped.[14] Apart from getting wind of a rumour of possibly being diverted to Palestine, it seems that Duncan and his family remained blissfully ignorant of this last-minute disorder and departed on schedule for Hungary.

Crossing the Channel, their route took them through France and Germany, entering Austria at Linz. Having learned from the experience of the survey party and concerned not to betray their purpose to the Austrian police, they considered destroying any incriminating books they possessed, particularly a copy of the General Assembly's tract, *To The Children Of Israel In All The Lands Of Their Dispersion*. Their disinclination to lose this valuable document gave rise to a wonderfully eccentric and very Duncanesque plan: in the event of a challenge, the tract's pages would be divided among the members of the team, who would memorise the contents, destroy the evidence and then reconstruct the document from memory when they were safely on the other side of the border. Mrs Duncan protested that it wouldn't work as she, and perhaps some of the others, did not trust the retentiveness of their memories. For her part, she decided to hide her portion in her shoe. Discovering this after the event caused Robert Smith to grumble that she had been very reckless because if she had been questioned by the authorities her Christian honesty would have obliged her to divulge her secret. In the event, no challenge was offered and the party continued their journey from Vienna to Pesth, arriving shortly after midnight on Sunday 22nd August in the midst of a magnificent thunderstorm.[15]

Their coming to Pesth coincided with the great annual fair. The city was thronged and private rented accommodation was unavailable, so they put up at a hotel, spending the following days searching for suitable accommodation for the mission. Eager to commence their activities as soon as possible, Duncan held services in English at the hotel on the following Lord's Day, where, despite limited publicity, thirty persons attended. Accommodation both for residence and the mission, was found in a side-street called the Bella Gasse, where a basement room was cleaned, whitewashed, and equipped with a reading desk and chairs, and so turned into a serviceable place of worship.[16]

Two services were held each Sunday: the morning service conducted by Duncan and an afternoon service by Smith. For the most part, the congregation consisted of British and Irish workmen engaged in building Széchenyi's bridge, together with their families, plus a considerable number of Hungarians and Germans, including, from the very beginning, some Jewish people, some coming out of genuine religious interest, with others keen to improve their English, the study of which was at the time very fashionable.[17]

Moody Stuart informs us that also present at the meetings was a 'venerable Countess of Brunswick ... a devout Catholic clinging to the hope of reformation in her venerated Church.'[18] This was none other than the sixty-six-year-old Hungarian aristocrat, Countess Therese von Brunsvik, who in her youth had been a friend and very gifted pianoforte pupil of Ludwig van Beethoven and to whom his exquisite 1809 Piano Sonata No. 24, Op. 78, 'à Thérèse', was dedicated. Her younger sister Josephine was said to have been Beethoven's lover, but Therese dedicated her spinster life to promoting nursery schools for the protection and care of young children from poor families, along the lines of those set up in London by Samuel Wilderspin, and in Scotland by the utopian socialist Robert Owen at New Lanark.[19]

Shortly after his arrival in the city, Duncan consented to marry two British subjects. Word of this reached the palace and the Archduke sent for him. He was received very kindly, but left in no doubt that marriage in Hungary was a civil as well as a religious affair to be performed only by clergymen recognised by law. Duncan's actions, the Archduke regretted to tell him, were illegal and were not to be repeated. The usually placid Duncan bridled at this intervention and insisted that as a Church of Scotland minister he was perfectly entitled to conduct a marriage between British subjects. The diplomatic Archduke resolved the matter amicably by asking if in future Duncan would do so only as the representative of a legally recognised pastor. At once Duncan consented to this solution and from that day forward marriages, baptisms, and other ordinances were conducted by the missionaries under the authority of Pastor Pal Török, the evangelical superintendent of the Hungarian Reformed Church in Pesth, with whom a very close and co-operative friendship developed. Very much to the annoyance of their Catholic opponents, but to the delight of his wife, the Archduke's solution both regularised the missionary's activities and strengthened their ministerial standing.[20]

A degree of mastery of the local language has always been considered an important preparation for missionary service, but, as many missionary candidates can corroborate, time for intensive language study is all too easily lost when new work exerts its own pressure. For the most part the Scottish missionaries abandoned the ideal and conceded to the demands of reality, but to a man of Duncan's linguistic aptitude, learning a language 'on the job,' was little challenging and within three months of his arrival he mastered both the vocabulary and the difficult grammar of the Magyar language. Even so, his natural reticence did not permit him to speak it in public, leading Pal Török to comment on his, 'wisdom, modesty, and judicious procedure', adding, 'He thus won us all, and carefully and happily avoided every cause of offence.' And in a further tribute added that Duncan, 'felt it a duty to adapt himself to [our Hungarian] habits, usages and ecclesiastical regulations.'[21]

Clearly, as far as cultural sensitivity and adaptation was concerned, Duncan was far ahead of his time. His close identification with the Magyar people, their culture and cause was so highly developed that when he visited Hungary after the Austrian crushing of the 1848 revolution, he was quite prepared to incur the wrath of the victorious Habsburgs by loudly and publicly applauding the sight of the red, white, and green national tricolour of Hungary and, discarding his silk top hat, seen as a badge of the Austrians, he went bareheaded until he could buy one of the distinctive flat Magyar felt hats worn by Hungarian nationalists.

It was necessary for the missionaries to cultivate friendly relations with as many people of influence as possible, including Reformed, Lutheran, and Roman Catholic clergy, as well as leaders in the Jewish community. Duncan's personal circle of acquaintances included the Chief Rabbi, Löw Schwab, with whom he had much in common, sharing a scholarly knowledge of the Hebrew language and Judaism, as well as delighting in mathematics and philosophy. Duncan took a great interest in the Jewish schools and offered two Hebrew Bibles and two copies of the Torah as prizes, as well as donating an English Bible, complete with New Testament, to the head-master. As their friendship blossomed, Schwab invited Duncan to attend the marriage of his daughter to a young rabbi, Leopold Löw, who was destined to become the outstanding Reform rabbi of nineteenth-century Hungary and a pioneer of Hungarian Jewish journalism. Löw was delighted to make the acquaintance of a man about whom he had heard so much.[22]

Duncan, who was in the habit of spending whole days in receiving visitors, was delighted to bring into play his remarkable conversational and persuasive powers. The family home was open to any Jewish person who cared to visit, and those who did witnessed a very gracious and welcoming form of Christianity without anything being forced upon them. One early convert spoke of Mrs Duncan's involvement: 'She took her full share of the work and the responsibilities. She had a smile and word of counsel for us all. She was beloved by all and very popular. She had an eye upon our comforts, upon our studies, scotticising us and imbuing us with good principles.'[23]

Duncan's Jewish visitors were delighted with all his eccentricities, the homely chat, and his frank, if unconventional, attempts to persuade them of the claims of Jesus. The story of his encounter with a twenty-one-year-old medical student, Sandor Tomori, gives a wonderful insight into Duncan's original but highly effective approach to evangelism. When Tomori first began to show an interest in Christianity he approached a Roman Catholic bishop from Vienna who, feeling unable personally to offer any meaningful help, encouraged him to pay a visit to the Protestant missionaries in Pesth. Tomori vividly recalled the first occasion he and Duncan met:

> Three days later I was introduced to the dear man. In a most syllogistic way, and in fluent Latin, he brought out the truth of the gospel, and urged me to accept Christ as my Saviour. But quite in keeping with

the character of the doctor, with the ruling passion, in the same breath he began to teach me in English. While the tears were yet in my eyes and his, he began to conjugate an English verb, and made me repeat it. After that I saw him almost daily till he left for Italy. This was in the year 1842.[24]

After studying Arts in Kecskemét, and medicine at Pesth, Tomori left Hungary in 1843 with Alfred Edersheim, to go with the Duncans to live in their Edinburgh home and study theology at New College. He later anglicised his name to Alexander Tomory and became a long-serving Free Church of Scotland missionary to the Jewish people of Istanbul.[25]

The spiritual condition of the Protestant churches in Hungary prior to the arrival of the Scottish ministers was at a very low ebb. Pal Török, the leading Hungarian Reformed Church minister in Budapest, complained that German rationalism reigned supreme and unchallenged among Lutheran preachers and Professors of Theology and the situation in his own denomination was very little better. So serious was the general spiritual decline and so dominant unbelieving rationalism that it led Smith, one of the missionaries, to conclude that in Hungary 'the elementary ideas of the Christian life had well-nigh died out.' Israel Saphir, another of the early adherents of the mission, concurred, going so far as to opine that 'there was not a village in all Hungary in which they knew that there was such a thing as evangelical religion.'[26] Alexander Keith, however, held that matters were bad enough, but less desperate than that, although he more or less confirmed that they were by remarking that, 'there were three Evangelical ministers in Hungary.'[27] Such jaundiced impressions must be tempered by the better informed judgement of Georg Bauhofer, the godly Lutheran chaplain to the Archduchess, historian of the Hungarian Lutheran church and friend of the mission, who stated that many of the rural landowners, if not the ministers, had astonishingly 'clear views and evangelical principles.'[28]

Though sent specifically as a missionary to the Jews, Duncan strongly believed that the mission could only succeed as the church in Hungary generally prospered. In this way his missionary strategy reflected that of his Anglican contemporary Henry Venn, who taught that mission was to be subservient to the wider interests of the Church and in this connection coined the graphic but helpful expression, 'the euthanasia of mission.' By this Venn meant that when a mission had fulfilled its task in establishing a properly constituted church, able to support, govern, and propagate itself, the mission, as the servant of the church, was to die well by handing over all control to the church.

In one of his earliest letters to the committee, Duncan expressed similar priorities. Missionaries ought to 'labour for the revival of true religion (both as regards sound doctrine and godly living) in the Protestant Churches of the land' which would then be 'the best instrument for carrying on the work of gathering in the lost sheep of the house of Israel.'[29] This commitment to the primacy of the Church universal over narrow denominational concerns led Duncan, though a Presbyterian with a strong affinity to the Hungarian Reformed Church, to establish a close friendship with Bauhofer, the Lutheran.

In a memorable ordering of his priorities, Duncan once described his personal ecclesiology: 'I'm first a Christian, next a Catholic, then a Calvinist, fourth a Paedobaptist, and fifth a Presbyterian. I cannot reverse this order.'[30] When Duncan heard that the Archduchess planned to build a Lutheran place of worship in the Buda Castle district, the first Protestant church to be built in this royal borough, he put his ecumenical sympathies into practice and appealed to the Free Church of Scotland for financial help, which, with an equally large heart, readily responded and contributed two hundred thousand Austrian florins, two thirds of the total cost of the building, which was erected at the junction of Bécsi kapu tér and Táncsics Mihály utca and still stands. Its first pastor was Bauhofer, and in the vestry hangs a fine portrait of the twenty-two-year-old Maria Dorothea von Württemberg, painted the year before her marriage to Archduke Joseph.

In due course, and with little opposition, the Pesth mission station was successfully established with the missionaries achieving official legitimacy as ministers to the bridge builders. Exceptionally good relations had been established with the palace and through the good offices of the Archduke, with the Archduchess active behind the scenes, a very satisfactory understanding had also been established with government. Friendships had been made with all the local evangelicals and, above all, there was a good rapport with the Jewish community.

The missionaries and the committee had good cause to reflect with amazement and with deep thanksgiving on God's remarkable guidance and provision. With the 1842 General Assembly drawing near, the committee in Edinburgh began to draft its report, warmly acknowledging every evidence of the wise and sovereign hand of God.

Duncan had a tendency to suffer from the cold and during his first mid-European winter his health had deteriorated, the committee, therefore, permitted him to spend the next winter among the Jews of Livorno in Italy, from where the 1839 deputation had been unceremoniously banished. Notwithstanding this intolerance, Duncan thought he might be able subtly to testify to the gospel and at the same time recover his health in a congenial climate. But he was frustrated in Livorno. He sorely missed Pesth, and as soon as spring came he was anxious to get home as quickly as possible. On his return, he found the small congregation blossoming. A point of friction over some unspecified matter of practice had arisen, but the situation had been handled with great wisdom and any crisis had been averted. He was delighted with the diligence of his junior colleagues and how well they had managed the station in his absence. He heaped lavish praise on them, saying they were astonishingly assiduous in meeting and conversing with inquirers, teaching Greek and theology and holding prayer meetings, as well as preaching.[31]

If the mood in Budapest was tranquil, in Edinburgh it was not. In Scotland, the fractious ten years conflict over the question of patronage (the intrusion of ministers on congregations without their consent), and the intervention of secular officialdom had reached its crisis. If the Church of Scotland was now at breaking point, there was no sign of this underlying tension in the measured tones of the committee's minutes of 3rd May 1843. In a very matter of fact, business-as-usual manner, they concluded with the routine remark: 'The committee appoints the Convenor to prepare the report to be laid before the next Assembly.' But no report was ever again placed before a General Assembly of the Church of Scotland by that committee; it and all its missionaries would never again be answerable to the Church of Scotland.

In the early afternoon of 18th May 1843, in a calm and dignified manner, one hundred and twenty-one ministers and seventy-three elders, led by the retiring moderator Dr David Welsh, walked out of the Church of Scotland's General Assembly at St. Andrews in George Street, Edinburgh, to walk the best part of a mile to the Tanfield Hall at Canonmills. Here they reassembled as the General Assembly of the Church of Scotland, Free. These were the vanguard of a total of over four hundred and fifty ministers and many hundreds of elders that formed the leadership of the new church. It was here, in the Tanfield Hall, on the second day of the Free Church Assembly, that the Jewish committee's report was delivered by Dr Keith, and very much to his liking, it was the very first report to be presented to the Assembly. He later took great delight in commenting 'that it was "to the Jew first" that the Free Church of Scotland turned her regards.'[32] In this way, the Jewish committee, its minute books and records and all its work effected a smooth passage from the Church of Scotland to the Free Church of Scotland, through one of the most turbulent and stormy seas to engulf the Scottish Church since the Reformation.

Keith, in delivering the report, noted that, according to a story from Dr Henry Cooke of Belfast, the Disruption had made a positive impact upon at least one Jewish person, who being so impressed by the ministers he saw leaving St Andrew's church in George Street, came to visit him. Cooke asked his Jewish friend if he thought these men truly 'believed that Jesus Christ was King of kings, and that they had the love of God in their hearts' to which came the emphatic reply, 'that is certain.'[33]

A fortnight later, on 31st May, the first meeting of the Free Church of Scotland's Committee for Promoting Christianity among the Jews took place. As well as adopting a more sensitive new name, some of its structures were modernised too, though Dr Keith was reappointed as convenor of the committee which, like its predecessor, remained unwieldy large and broadly representative of the Church's regional diversity. The committee decided, as a matter of urgency, that all serving missionaries must be canvassed regarding their denominational loyalties, assurance being given that if they adhered to the Free Church they would be retained on the original terms and conditions of their engagement. Apart from Ann Petrie, a single lady missionary in India, who held out for the old Kirk, all the missionaries, foreign and Jewish, joined the Free Church.[34] Owing largely to their geographical proximity and use of more sophisticated communications, it was the Jewish missionaries who were the first to affirm their allegiance.

If the Free Church had all the missionaries, it was a very different story concerning the money. The Church of Scotland insisted that all missionary funds were its entitlement, to which the Free Church countered by alleging that the funds had all been subscribed to finance the work in which the missionaries were currently engaged. It should, therefore, by rights, be allocated in proportion to the number of missionaries adhering to either body. This unseemly dispute rumbled on for months but not a single penny was ever made over. The Free Church was forced to raise everything necessary to support the work.[35]

Perhaps the most harmful effect of the Disruption on the Budapest mission was not financial and certainly not inflicted by the Church of Scotland; it was the Free Church Assembly's incredible decision to take John Duncan from Pesth and appoint him to the Chair of Oriental Languages at its New College in Edinburgh. Informed of the Assembly's decision, Duncan acceded to the wish of the Assembly and agreed to accept the Chair, though he did so with much heart searching and not a little regret. Also feeling Duncan's loss to the mission and sensitive to his desires, the committee expressed its regret at the loss of his valuable services, but it hoped he might be able to return to Pesth each summer.

In October 1843, Duncan commenced an unbroken period of twenty-seven years as Professor of Hebrew. Although a brilliant Hebraist, he was a very inadequate teacher of elementary Hebrew, entirely lacking the necessary discipline and application. Both his own minister, Alexander Moody Stuart, and Alexander Whyte, who studied under Duncan at New College in 1862, commented on his inability as a teacher, and his biographer, David Brown, was of the opinion that few of his friend's best gifts 'came out in the Professor's

Chair or in the pulpit.'[36] Duncan was best in informal conversation and, later, with characteristic humility he admitted his failures, and remarked that he really never should have left the Jewish Mission to teach Hebrew.[37]

It ought not be thought, however, that his classes were devoid of some sudden, unexpected, and utterly unconventional flashes of brilliance. Moody Stuart records one of Duncan's students, Robert Boag Watson, of Madeira, being deeply moved by one of these in the winter of 1864, when Dr Duncan was reading part of Isaiah with his senior class:

> The particular passage I cannot remember, nor does it matter, for it only served as a suggestion of the cry in verse 1 of the 22nd Psalm, 'My God, my God, why hast thou forsaken me?' By the time Dr Duncan had reached that point he had left his desk and, bent nearly double, was pacing up and down in front of the students' benches, his snuff box and pocket handkerchief in one hand, a huge pinch of snuff occupying the fingers of the other, but utterly forgotten in the absorbing interest of his subject, our Lord's sufferings for sinners, which he was turning over and looking at, now on this side, now on that, but all with a loving reverence, and as one who spoke in a half-sleeping vision, when suddenly a flash went through him as if heaven had opened. He straightened himself up, his face kindled into a rapture, his hand went up and the snuff scattered itself from the unconscious fingers as he turned to the class, more as it seemed for sympathy than to teach – 'Ay, ay, d'ye know what it was – dying on the cross forsaken by His Father – d'ye know what it was?' What? What?' (as if somebody had given him a *half* answer which stimulated him, but which he had to clear out of his way, a very usual exclamation of his when wrapped in thought.) 'What? What? It was damnation – and damnation taken *lovingly*. And he subsided into his chair, leaning a little to one side, his head very straight and stiff, his arms hanging down on either side beyond the arms of his chair, with the light beaming from his face and the tears trickling down his cheeks he repeated in a low intense voice that broke into a half sob, half laugh in the middle, 'It was damnation – and he took it *lovingly*.' No saying of the many I have heard from him, nothing in all his manner and expression, ever struck me like this.[38]

Notwithstanding his removal to Edinburgh, Duncan maintained a very lively interest in all that was taking place in Hungary, corresponding in French with Archduchess Maria Dorothea and in Latin with his friend and former colleague Pal Török. He also made significant contributions to the cause of Jewish mission in the General Assembly, often speaking with great effect in response to the report from the Jewish committee. Between 1847 and 1867, he delivered six 'highly animated and elevated addresses, marked by genius and spiritual power.' Although strikingly over-optimistic regarding the speed of the realisation of eschatological events – especially the collapse of Roman Catholicism and the triumph of the gospel – his reflections, nevertheless, inspired and motivated the Free Church to maintain its missionary vision.[39] In all these addresses his brilliant use of the English language, generously larded with colourful Latinisms, shows originality, brevity, clarity of expression, and a quite amazing precision of vocabulary, amply justifying Moody Stuart's comment that he had a 'fastidious sense of the music of words.'[40]

Apart from Duncan's removal to Edinburgh, the committee's minutes reveal that it had remarkably little to discuss concerning the work in Pesth during the years 1843 to 1847, but this was certainly not due to any lack of activity in the branch, rather, the reverse. Smith and Wingate were effective in managing a very large volume of work with great efficiency and with little need of assistance from Edinburgh, apart, of course, from funds. Towards the end of that period, the mission in Pesth found itself conducting its work in an atmosphere of increasing political tension and instability which came to a head in 1848, the Year of Revolutions, when the quest for Hungarian independence led to a protracted military conflict.

Lajos Kossuth's Hungarian army, initially successful in the field, was eventually outnumbered by an alliance of Austrians and Russians and surrendered at Világos (now Siria, Romania) on 13th August, 1849. Kossuth and many of the leading 'Forty-Eighters' went into exile, while dissent in the country was ruthlessly suppressed by the Austrians, who ordered a number of political executions, including the thirteen generals executed at Arad, (now Romania). Hungary now entered a period of 'passive resistance.'

On 25th September 1848, at a meeting of the Jewish committee in Edinburgh, the members were unexpectedly joined by William

Wingate and Robert Smith.[41] It was not a crisis in the work that brought them home, but the revolution. Before leaving Pesth, they had placed the oversight of the work in the capable hands of Israel Saphir and Georg Bauhofer. By the end of 1849 the situation in Pesth seemed stable enough for the missionary families to return, and when they did, they found that a sense of profound insecurity weighing heavily on the minds of Jewish people, created many openings to discuss spiritual questions. Enquirers proliferated and there was much work to do.

Then, a little over two years later, a fresh crisis broke. In January 1852, the Austrian Government made allegations that the missionaries had been implicated in political interference during the recent war, and ordered Smith and Wingate to leave Hungary immediately and to take their families with them. The same order was simultaneously served on Daniel Edward in Lviv. At first, the Free Church interpreted this act as part of the vindictive repression of Protestantism and the crushing of the Magyar people.[42]

With so many Scottish Liberal politicians owing their seats in the British Parliament to Free Church votes, it was expected that Lord John Russell's government would be sympathetic to their cause, and so Dr Alexander Moody Stuart was instructed to go to London to discuss the crisis with the Foreign Secretary, Earl Granville. Moody Stuart brought with him a full delegation of ministers and missionaries from Scotland, as well as a deputation from the Protestant Alliance and the Scottish Reformation Society, a notable array of sympathetic supporters which included the Earl of Shaftesbury, the Hon. Arthur Kinnaird, Member of Parliament for Perth, the Rev. Dr James Hamilton of Regent Square, the publisher Mr James Nisbet, and Charles Cowan, the Member of Parliament for Edinburgh, who owed his 1848 election victory to strong Free Church support.

In his discussions with Granville, Moody Stuart insisted that the missionaries had been entirely apolitical, had carried out their work with the knowledge and approval of the Archduke of Hungary, and had engaged in no actions forbidden to Hungarian citizens. All their actions had been open and transparent; indeed their very location was in the same building and beneath the office of the watchful eyes of the military police, yet in ten years no allegation had been brought of illegal activity. Moody Stuart considered that the Austrian government's case had been built around political pique and xenophobia. The missionaries only 'crime' was that they were 'foreign' missionaries and they were being expelled not on the basis of Austrian law, but by the fiat of the Austrian government.

Unfortunately this point of view had already been less than helpfully expressed in a clumsy and insensitive article in a relatively new and naive New York paper, *The Independent,* which blew the missionaries' cover, putting up the backs of the Austrians.[43] *The Independent's* correspondent, unhelpfully exercising his First Amendment right of free speech, and unconstrained by his inexperienced editor, reported:

> The mission has here found a favourable soil. The missionaries have here converted 300 Jews and distributors, who now circulate Bibles throughout the country. They have opened in the neighbourhood of the Chain Bridge an English service, and later by imperceptible degrees, a German one; so that, step by step, working with the greatest precaution, they have gained a considerable influence in Hungary. The greatest marvel is, that they should have been permitted in the heart of the Austrian Monarchy to work. I am expecting, however, the removal of the mission by the Austrian Government.[44]

Well, thank *you* very much indeed! For Lord Granville, the problem was exacerbated by the fact that the Hungarian war generally, and Lajos Kossuth in particular, had both become extremely sensitive political issues. Indeed, he had become Foreign Secretary in Russell's government because his predecessor, Lord Palmerston, had been sacked for expressing hostility to the Austro-Hungarian government, by entertaining Kossuth and a group of political radicals, who made undiplomatic references to the Habsburg emperor.

Unknown to the Free Church, the expulsion of its missionaries had in fact been one of the first diplomatic reprisals the Austrian government directed at Palmerston's actions. Now, facing imminent Parliamentary elections, Granville felt under no pressure to handle this hot potato with any degree of urgency and decided to procrastinate to allow the ballot box to decide his future. Lord

Russell's Liberal government was defeated and by the end of July, Lord Derby's minority Conservative administration appointed Lord Malmesbury to the post of Foreign Secretary.

As Free Church votes had done little to put Malmesbury's Conservatives in power, the new administration felt little sympathy for the plight of the missionaries and refused to support the Free Church's case in the House of Commons. In the ensuing parliamentary debate, a motion seeking 'prompt and earnest measures on the part of Her Majesty's Government' was moved by opposition member Sir Harry Verney and seconded by Arthur Kinnaird, the MP for Perth, but the motion was lost. Vindictively, Malmesbury's government followed up by refusing to make any representation to the Austrians on behalf of the Free Church, asserting that any loss or distress suffered by the missionaries was entirely of their own making. Needless to say, the Free Church's representations to Vienna were of no avail; the Austrian government adamantly refused to reinstate the missionaries and countenanced no claim for compensation.

Back in Scotland, Hugh Miller's evangelical newspaper *The Witness* loosed off intermittent spirited but futile tirades aimed at the government, accusing Malmesbury of ineptitude and a lack of 'promptitude and earnestness.' Miller likewise condemned the British Ambassador to Vienna, General John Fane, the Earl of Westmorland, for failure to obtain any redress, but for all the good it did, Miller might as well have saved his ink.[45]

The Free Church Moderator, Dr Andrew Makellar, and the General Assembly feted their missionaries as heroes, inviting Smith, Wingate, and Edward, who were all in Scotland, to address the house, and John Duncan gave a moving address on the post-revolution state of the Protestant Churches in Hungary.

In an attempt to mitigate failing to achieve any form of redress, the committee proposed a conference to discuss the future of the work, whose membership would be made up of all Assembly commissioners and the missionaries, to be held immediately the Assembly rose. The motion was passed, but, with the usual ebbing of enthusiasm and stamina at the end of any busy General Assembly, the meetings were poorly attended and the consultation flopped.[46]

With its European mission in tatters, the committee, so long accustomed to success and progress, was hard put to devise a new strategy. It also urgently needed to address the question of the maintenance of the Hungarian workers still employed in Pesth, including a band of itinerant colporteurs trained to distribute Bibles, Gospels, and tracts, and to engage in person-to-person witness. In the post-war Austrian clamp-down such work had been declared illegal and the police were encouraged to harass the hardworking colporteurs, so they could not continue. The committee, therefore, decided to cut their losses and offer the colporteurs six month's paid notice of termination of employment. This, however, caused such deep resentment within the ranks of the missionaries that Wingate wrote a very outspoken letter, strongly critical of the committee and managed to get it published in the February 1852 issue of the *Home and Foreign Missionary Record*. This brought down such a storm of protest from the wider church that the committee was forced to back down and offer the colporteurs a further three month's salary.[47]

In August the committee, battered and bruised by its experiences, agreed to send Daniel Edward to Wroclaw, where he remained until his retirement in 1896. Smith went to work with Carl Schwartz in Amsterdam, and later in Frankfurt, but problems with his eyesight led him back, in due course, to conclude his years of ministry in the quiet country parish of Corsock in Dumfriesshire.[48]

Wingate, acting entirely in good faith and with the approval of some of the most influential members of the committee, including Candlish, Cunningham, and the convenor, Moody Stuart, began missionary work in London on the understanding that this was committee policy. But it was not. The majority opposed the idea on the grounds that it might compete with the work of the *British Society for the Propagation of the Gospel among the Jews*. It, however, expressed sincere gratitude to Wingate for his faithful service in Budapest, regretted its inability to sanction work in London, but agreed to pay his salary for a further year. Bitterly disappointed with the decision and deeply embarrassed by the thought that he may have been the cause of unnecessary division, Wingate refused their offer and resigned.[49] He later returned to Bayswater in London to work independently on behalf of the Jewish people. In 1872 he published *The Close of the Times of the Gentiles*. He died on Christmas Eve 1899 in his ninety-first year. His son, Col. George Wingate had a highly distinguished military career in the Indian army, and his grandson, Major-General Orde Wingate, who gained fame as a solider in Palestine and Burma, inherited his grandfather's Zionism, but not his missionary spirit.

For many, it seemed that this first phase of the Scottish mission to the Jews of Europe, which had been launched on such a tidal wave of optimism, prayer, enthusiasm, and unstinted support, had ended in tatters. But had it failed? Judgement must be reserved until the full story is told and an attempt made to assess the effectiveness, overall results, and legacy of this amazing period of pioneer missionary work.

◁⊱20⊰▷

'Hebrew Christians are everywhere'

Europe, Israel, New York, and China: 1841 onwards

THE New York *Independent* may have been blundering in its comments, but at least it was close to the truth. Although evaluating the results of any aspect of Christian ministry or mission is notoriously difficult, the paper's assessment that in the decade to 1852 some three hundred Jewish people had come to faith in Jesus the Messiah would not be far out. Certainly, the foundation was solid.

At the Jubilee celebration of the Free Church of Scotland's Jewish mission, a letter of congratulation was received from the celebrated Hebrew scholar Professor Franz Delitzsch of Leipzig, in which he alluded to the conversion of the Saphir family by way of a pun on Isaiah 54:11, observing that 'Sion's Restorer' had laid the foundation of the Scottish mission in Budapest 'with *sapphires*.'[1] It was true enough. Some of the most influential conversions that took place in the earliest days of the mission were those of members the Saphir family and they were real gems. As we noted earlier, there were three Saphir brothers: Israel, Leopold, and Moritz. The first to embrace Christianity was Moritz (Moses) Gottlieb, the newspaper editor, poet, and caustic satirist who, in 1832, at the age of thirty-seven and seemingly motivated by assimilationist rather than spiritual reasons, was baptised as a Lutheran.

Of Leopold, little is known. It seems he died as a relatively young man and enters into our story through his daughter Elisabeth

277

Johanna. When Leopold's wife remarried, their children, Elisabeth Johanna and Gottlieb Wilhelm, adopted their stepfather's surname of Leitner. Elisabeth Leitner married an Englishman, Charles Amery, and it was their son, also named Leopold, who in due time had a most important role to play in the story of the Jewish people in the twentieth century. But more of that later.

Israel Saphir, like his father before him, made a fortune as a woolbroker and became an influential member of the Budapest Jewish community and a close friend of the Chief Rabbi, Löw Schwab. As an active and generous philanthropist, he founded a school in Pesth for children from wealthy Jewish families. Having acquired a good knowledge of Hebrew, French, and German, in his late fifties he decided to learn English because he wanted to read the works of Shakespeare in their original language.[2] It appears that his first contact with the Scottish ministers was in 1839, when he met Drs Keith and Black, when they were delayed in Pesth. This acquaintance, coupled with his interest in the English language, led him, in the early days of the mission, to occasionally attend the services taken by John Duncan.

On one occasion he was present, as an observer, at a celebration of the Lord's Supper and had brought with him his eleven-year-old son Adolph. Throughout the service, the boy stood between his father's knees, the old man's chin almost resting on his head. The communion service was almost over and Dr Duncan announced as the concluding item of praise the sixty-fourth Scottish Paraphrase of Revelation 1:5-9: 'To Him that loved the souls of men and washed them with his blood.' To the great surprise of the worshippers the voice of the old man rose above all others, and when they looked towards him they saw that his tears were falling freely onto the head of Adolph. Someone who was present that day later understatedly remarked that such days were to be remembered.[3]

Both Adolph and his elderly father already had come to believe that Jesus was the Messiah of Israel and saviour of the world, but both remained reticent about declaring their new faith. Then, on 7th June 1843, much to the amazement of the Jewish community, Israel Saphir and his entire family then resident in Pesth – his son Philipp being at Karlsruhe, in Germany – together with Maria, their twenty-four-year-old servant, were baptised into membership of the Hungarian Reformed Church by Rev. Pal Török. Saphir's address given at his baptism was published soon after and widely circulated in Hungary. For the Jewish community it was beyond belief that their leading layman, a person greatly trusted by all, a very close friend of the Chief Rabbi, and one intimately involved with many charitable causes, should betray the community by becoming a Christian.[4] Shaken and hurt, it fell to Schwab to undertake the distressing duty of publicly denouncing his friend through a Sabbath sermon he preached in the synagogue.

Although Schwab declined to speak the name of the one who had dared to expose his children to harmful influences from outside the community, Saphir was in the synagogue at the time and everyone knew that the sermon was addressed to him. To Schwab's credit, his denunciatory sermon was very mild, and based on his understanding of Isaiah 53 because, he alleged, it was the favourite text of the missionaries, who, from his point of view, seriously misinterpreted it. This mild reproof was about as far as his criticism went. Tipped off, allegedly by Schwab himself, that he would also be expelled as a director of the school, Saphir pre-empted any disagreeable disciplinary action by tending his resignation. After the initial clamour had died down, notwithstanding the harsh criticism circulated by some in the community, the tolerant Schwab openly declared that Israel Saphir was an honourable man. The two remained friends and, it is said, from time to time met clandestinely in the private rooms of a bookseller's shop in Pesth.[5]

Schwab now found himself on the horns of a dilemma. Hitherto, he had held up Saphir as a paragon of Jewish identity, now he was embarrassed to discover that his errant protégé's influence was not disposed of so easily. For the mission, Saphir's conversion and baptism proved to be nothing less than strategic, making it considerably easier for other enquiring Jews to take a similar step of faith. As Gavin Carlyle said, 'A hundred other conversions could not have produced the same impression as his.'[6] From the time of his baptism to his death, Saphir was deeply and openly involved in Christian work in Pesth.

Philipp Saphir, absent from home at Karlsruhe in Germany, at the time of the family baptisms, had, about the same time, also become a follower of the Messiah, through a sermon preached in Pesth by Carl Schwartz. During his time in Karlsruhe, Philipp damaged his foot while on a walking tour and from December 1844 was confined to bed. Returning to Budapest, though bedridden, he was active in establishing a free school for poor Christian and Jewish children and in launching an association for young men based on the principles of the Young Men's Christian Association, founded in 1844 by George Williams, a Scottish tailor and a member of James Hamilton's Regent Square congregation in London. Philipp Saphir's Budapest Association was one of the very first groups inspired by Williams' work.[7]

The Budapest school commenced in the most humble fashion imaginable, with a solitary pupil, the son of a Jewish widow, being instructed at Philipp Saphir's bedside. The Free Church of Scotland held that prudence dictated it would be wisest to leave the operation of the school to Saphir and not make it an official part of the Church's work, although the church provided financial support worth £30 a year. By 1847 the school had grown to one hundred and twenty children. Philipp wrote in his diary, 'The school goes on admirably, most of the children, nearly all, are Jews. My school has been noticed in the Pesth newspapers, and very favourably.' Philipp's *Letters and Diaries*, edited by his brother Adolph, were published soon after his early death in 1852, when, according to a note on the last page, the school was attended by about three hundred and fifty children, almost all of them from Jewish families.[8]

The member of the Saphir family to achieve most prominence was Aaron Adolph, Israel's youngest son, who, whilst a boy of eleven, was probably the first of his immediate family to become a Christian, a short time before his father took that step. He soon became an icon of the success of the Jewish mission in Budapest. In W. O. Hill's famous painting, *The First General Assembly of the Free Church of Scotland Signing the Act of Separation and the Deed of Demission at Tanfield, Edinburgh, May 1843*, which hangs in the Presbytery Hall of the Free Church of Scotland building on The Mound, Edinburgh, twelve year old Adolph can be seen between Drs Black and Keith, pointing to a map of Palestine, as he is held protectively by John Duncan. To the right of this group, Andrew Bonar is depicted holding the manuscript of *The Memoirs and Remains of Robert Murray M'Cheyne*. In this way Hill, anachronistically, includes in the picture all four members of the original 1839 survey group, and others who in fact were not present at the Disruption: M'Cheyne had died some months earlier, and both Saphir and Duncan were in Pesth at the time.

When Duncan was recalled to teach Hebrew at New College, Adolph travelled with him and spent his first college session in their home, together with Alfred Edersheim and, Sandor Tomori. After Edinburgh, Saphir continued his studies in Berlin where he stayed with Carl Schwartz, who by that time was his brother-in-law, and a missionary with the Free Church. In 1848, when Schwartz moved to Amsterdam to establish, with Isaac da Costa, the Scottish missionary seminary, Adolph moved to Aberdeen to take up the post of tutor in the family of a Mr William Brown. In 1854, on completion of his divinity studies, he was ordained by the Belfast Presbytery of the Presbyterian Church in Ireland and appointed a missionary of that church to the Jews in Hamburg. He returned to Britain in 1861 where, despite a more or less constant battle with ill health and general infirmity, he served as minister to a succession of congregations at South Shields in Northumberland, in London at Greenwich, Notting Hill and Halkin Street off Belgrave Square.[9]

Adolph Saphir, always an ardent advocate of Jewish missions, was a prolific author, strongly opposed to theological liberalism and a staunch premillennialist. As time passed, Saphir, rather like Edersheim, shrugged off their commitment to Presbyterianism, but unlike Edersheim who moved over to Anglicanism, Saphir held to an open view of both baptism and church government, first taking on an assistant who held to believer's baptism and then by aligning himself, though rather loosely, with the Plymouth Brethren movement, but he was not happy there either. Troubled by this inability to find a congenial spiritual home he once said, 'You see I am enough of a Plymouthist to make me feel very lonely among the Presbyterians, and yet I could not be a Plymouthist, as I think ... they are unscriptural in their method.'[10] The dawning of the era of

Messianic congregations, with which he may have been happier, was still over a distant horizon.

Indirectly, it was Leopold, the least known of the Saphir brothers who, totally unknown to himself, helped shape the modern history of the Middle East and the creation of the State of Israel.[11] For reasons best known to himself, the British politician Leo Amery, hid the fact that his mother was Elizabeth Johanna Leitner, Leopold's daughter and Adolph Saphir's cousin. The family name changed from Saphir to Leitner when Leopold's wife, Marie Henriette, married Johann Moritz Leitner after Leopold's death. Elizabeth travelled to India, probably in company with her brother, the orientalist, Gottlieb Wilhelm Leitner and there met her husband Charles Frederick Amery, an English officer of the Indian Forest Department. Their son, whom they named Leopold Charles Moritz Stennett, was born in Gorakhpur in 1873. He was baptised the following year by the Rev. Henry Aaron Stern, a Jewish Christian missionary. Stern's romantic and hazardous career led him across Asia, from Istanbul, via Baghdad, to India and ultimately to Ethiopia, where he saw hundreds of Beta Israel or Ethiopian Jews baptised, before being accused by Tewodros II, Emperor of Ethiopia, of insulting his mother. Stern was beaten and condemned to death, but finally imprisoned until rescued five years later, in 1868, by a British expedition under command of Lieutenant-General Sir Robert Napier.[12] He then returned to England to become the director of the LSPCJ.[13]

Leo Amery's additional name, Moritz, was in memory of his uncle, Moritz Gottlieb Saphir, whose adherence to Christianity first awakened the curiosity of his brother Israel. Amery, however, changed this Jewish-sounding name to Maurice. Why, we do not know, but there are a medley of suggestions, including his not wanting to have a foreign-sounding name which made him vulnerable to bullying at school, maybe to evade antisemitic prejudice that could have hindered his career prospects, perhaps to facilitate his assimilation into gentile life and provide him with a degree of cultural anonymity, or to avoid being pressurised by Jewish interests when he became a Member of Parliament.

After a successful career as a correspondent on *The Times*, Amery entered politics and came under the influence of the Coefficients, a dining club founded by the Fabians, Sidney and Beatrice Webb, for socialist reformers and imperialists. As a convinced imperialist, in 1911 Amery stood for the constituency of Birmingham South and was elected to Parliament as a Liberal Unionist (the party would merge with the Conservatives in 1913).[14]

In 1917 Amery, by then a staunch Zionist, became an under-secretary in Lloyd-George's coalition war cabinet and was given the responsibility for drafting the text of a document advocating a Jewish 'national home' in Palestine. That document became known to history as the Balfour Declaration, as it was first made public in a note to Lord Rothschild from the Foreign Secretary, Arthur Balfour.

Balfour was born at Whittingehame in East Lothian, Scotland, and grew up in a home where attendance at the Church of Scotland was routine and where he was surrounded by influences in which the Jewish people, Jewish missions, and a Jewish home in Palestine were recurrent themes, thus influencing him to sympathise with the Zionist cause. Dated 2nd November, 1917, the three sentence Declaration contains perhaps the most explosive one hundred and seventeen words of political exchange in the whole of the twentieth century:

> I have much pleasure in conveying to you on behalf of his Majesty's Government, the following declaration of sympathy with Jewish Zionist aspirations which has been submitted to, and approved by, the Cabinet – 'His Majesty's Government view with favour the establishment in Palestine of a national home for the Jewish people, and will use their best endeavours to facilitate the achievement of this object, it being clearly understood that nothing shall be done which may prejudice the civil and religious rights of existing non-Jewish communities in Palestine, or the rights and political status enjoyed by Jews in any other country.' I should be grateful if you would bring this declaration to the knowledge of the Zionist Federation.[15]

As drafted by Amery, the Balfour Declaration did not propose a Jewish state but a 'national home' where Jewish, Gentile, and Arab cultures could co-exist and flourish with equal rights. It was precisely the impossibility of squaring a 'national home' with the contradictory commitment 'that nothing shall be done which may prejudice the rights of existing non-Jewish communities' that was arguably Britain's most enduringly troublesome legacy of Empire, perhaps shaping the modern world more than any other of its many imperial projects. Today, the Balfour Declaration's terms and their effects are hugely controversial and are endlessly discussed, but in 1917 its immediate effect was that which Balfour intended, to take Zionism from the wings and place it firmly in the centre of the political stage to fight its own cause.

Amery further contributed to Zionism's military capacity by assisting Vladimir Ze'ev Jabotinski to place several thousand volunteers of the Jewish Legion under British command, so contributing to the formation of the Haganah, a Jewish paramilitary organisation and the precursor of the Israel Defence Force. After World War II it became an insurgency against the British, angered by Britain's refusal to lift restrictions on Jewish emigration to Palestine. From here the story takes a most curious twist: Amery's sponsorship of the Haganah provided the setting for his meeting with Orde Wingate, the grandson of William Wingate, who had been so influential in the conversion of the Saphirs.

Orde Wingate was a British Zionist and soldier who, before achieving fame as a leader of the Chindits, a special forces unit in Burma, served with the British army before the war as an Arabist in Palestine. Wingate was eccentric: he never washed but dry scrubbed himself with a brush (as a radio operator in Malaya, my father witnessed him going through this ablution), and he was obsessed with the romantic notion of being, like Gideon and David, the leader of a Jewish army. The closest Wingate ever came to this was forming and commanding the brutal counter-insurgency Special Night Squads, whose members included both Yigal Allon – later a commander of the elite Palmach, a general in the Israeli Defence Forces, and a politician – and Moshe Dayan, the famous but controversial general who later became an advocate of peace with the Palestinians.[16]

Amery, who could hardly have been ignorant of Wingate's ancestry or the contribution it had made to his own personal dilemmas, first met Orde Wingate during the winter of 1939/40 and was immediately impressed with him. It is intriguing to consider what Wingate might have made of Amery if only he had been open about his own antecedents.

In 1918, the year after the Balfour Declaration, Orde Wingate's first cousin once removed, Sir Reginald Wingate, Britain's High Commissioner of Egypt, who helped lay the foundation for his younger relative's military career, wisely cautioned the Zionists to 'feel their way carefully and to do all in their power to show sympathy and goodwill to the Arab and Moslem peoples, with whom their future must lie.'[17] Aspiring nations, however, rarely take advice from representatives of former colonial powers, often to their peril.

At the same 1889 Jubilee celebration at which Franz Delitzsch's letter was read, Adolph Saphir drew attention to another convert of the mission, Gideon Reuben Lederer, and the part he had played in the conversion of Samuel Isaac Joseph Schereschewsky. Lederer was the son of an orthodox rabbi and, for a time, a rabbi himself.[18] He became a Christian at the age of thirty in Pesth; William Wingate's witness had been particularly influential. From the time of his baptism Lederer served in his home city as a lay-missionary and colporteur, and was one of those who were made redundant in 1852 as a consequence of the expulsion of the missionaries.[19] In 1855 Lederer emigrated to New York, became the editor of a periodical called *The Israelite Indeed,* and by 1866 was the New York City Mission's missionary to the Jews of Manhattan where his witness contributed to the conversion of Samuel Schereschewsky.

Born in Lithuania in 1831 Schereschewsky's interest in Jesus was first stirred whilst a student at a rabbinic seminary in Zhytomyr, now in Ukraine, but then Zhitomir in Russian-Poland. At this seminary there seems to have been an 'anything goes' atmosphere, and, as Dr Rich Robinson observes, if any book, then why should the New Testament not find its way there?[20] It was here that Schereschewsky read the 1817 LSPCJ translation of the New Testament published at the instigation of Claudius Buchanan, and given to him by a fellow student unimpressed with its contents. It had the opposite effect on Schereschewsky who was convinced 'that in Jesus the Messianic prophecies of the Old Testament ... had been fulfilled.'[21] As well as this intellectual 'conversion', Schereschewsky's daughter recalled her father standing transfixed in the nave of a German cathedral where a crucifix, illuminated by a stray shaft of sunlight, seemed to glow with an 'unearthly glory.'[22]

Emigrating to the United States in 1854, he met with and was influenced by a group of Jewish Christians which included John Neander and Gideon Lederer. About a year later, whilst attending a Jewish Christian Passover seder, Schereschewsky heard some of those present share their stories of faith in Jesus. His conscience was touched, and the earlier influences on his mind and heart now coalesced into a truly spiritual conversion experience. This led to his baptism, which under Lederer's influence was by immersion.[23] In 1857, Schereschewsky entered New York Theological Seminary after which he was ordained as a minister of the Protestant Episcopal Church. In 1859 he went to China, where he became the outstanding missionary of his church during the second half of the nineteenth century.[24]

In March 1867, while in Beijing, Schereschewsky received a visit from three young Jews from the Chinese Jewish community at Kaifeng in the central Chinese province of Hunan. An earlier abortive attempt by the Jewish community of London to contact the Kaifeng Jews had been channelled through the father of Chinese missions, the Church of Scotland missionary, Robert Morrison who, after ordination in the Swallow Street congregation in London, arrived in China in September 1807. The visit of the three young men, coupled with a previous meeting with a missionary visiting Kaifeng, led to a decision to send Schereschewsky on a reconnaissance mission with a view to establishing a work there. Regrettably, because of the unsettled nature of the region and anti-foreign agitation, it was considered imprudent to proceed with setting up a mission.[25]

Elected bishop of Shanghai and consecrated in 1877, Schereschewsky founded a college where Chinese young men could study Christianity and Western science. He was a remarkable linguist and during his twenty years in China assisted in the translation of the New Testament into Mandarin Chinese, and completed the entire Old Testament himself, as well as the *Book of Common Prayer*, and a Mongolian translation of the Gospel of Matthew. Amongst other projects, he rendered the whole Bible, together with four Christian catechisms, into Classical Chinese, a literary form of Mandarin Chinese. He contracted Parkinson's disease and was forced to resign his bishopric, but, nothing dismayed, he typed the last two thousand pages of the Classical Chinese Bible with his one good finger. Housebound for many years, he once remarked: 'I have sat in this chair for over twenty years. It seemed very hard at first. But God knew best. He kept me for the work for which I am best fitted.'[26]

Whilst it is impossible to quantify the impact of Schereschewsky's Bible translation on China's millions of Christians, one very small part of the story traces a remarkable trajectory. In 1996, Lan Yih-Ming (Grace Lan), influenced by her reading of Schereschewsky's Bible, became, as far as is known, the first Mandarin-speaking Chinese Christian missionary to the Jews. The following year she commenced work with Christian Witness to Israel (now the International Mission to Jewish People) in Wingate's home city of Glasgow, barely five miles from Cambuslang, the childhood home of Claudius Buchanan. She remains there still.[27]

Alfred Edersheim, already noted in some detail as John Duncan's protege and Daniel Edward's missionary colleague, in due course came to live and work in Britain, becoming the only Hebrew Christian clergyman to have been invited by Dean Stanley to preach in Westminster Abbey.

Sandor Tomori, whose conversion was an example of Duncan's unconventional evangelistic methods, was licensed in 1847 and went, for a period of a few months, to work among the Jewish community in Jamaica. In 1858 he was ordained a minister of the Free Church of Scotland and appointed a missionary to Istanbul, where he laboured until his death in 1895.

Among the other Pesth converts was W. Friereich, a rabbinical student who had particularly fond recollections of long discussions with Duncan in 1842 as together they explored the rabbinic writings. An enthusiastic advocate of the Jewish heritage, national identity, language, and religion, Friereich was once invited to write an anti-missionary defence of the synagogue in order to 'silence the new disturbers of the peace of Judaism', the missionaries. He drew up an outline of his defence, in which he argued for the finality of the Hebrew Scriptures and the impossibility of further revelation. Assured of his position, he announced to the missionaries his plans to debate with them the status of the New Testament. This prompted him to re-read the New Testament, with the outcome that not only was he convinced of the value of the New Testament, but felt obliged to inform his friends in the synagogue that he could no longer go through with their anti-missionary project.

For two years Friereich undertook a detailed comparative study of Christianity and Judaism, reading such classic works of Calvinistic theology as *The Westminster Shorter Catechism*, *The Westminster Confession of Faith* and Thomas Boston's *Human Nature in its Fourfold State*. His friends could not but notice the change that was taking place in his thinking. From being a staunch advocate of Orthodox Judaism, he now attempted to defend the Christian gospel as 'the new way of life'.

To some degree he was successful and managed to persuade a few of his friends to attend meetings held by the missionaries. Then one day he read Daniel 7:13-14:

> I saw in the night visions, and behold, with the clouds of heaven there came one like a son of man, and he came to the Ancient of Days and was presented before him. And to him was given dominion and glory and a kingdom, that all peoples, nations, and languages should serve him; his dominion is an everlasting dominion, which shall not pass away, and his kingdom one that shall not be destroyed.

As he meditated on the missionaries' interpretation of the passage and how it speaks of Jesus the Messiah and his kingdom, the impact was dramatic. Friereich suddenly and unpredictably abandoned all outward interest in religion, withdrew from the company of his Jewish friends and the missionaries, and went far away to live in a Hungarian city that had no Jewish population. Here he found employment in the home of a nobleman, but despite all the luxurious perks provided by his new employer, he felt homesick and wanted to return to Pesth. Homesick may have been the way he described it to his employer; gospel hungry he certainly was. He immediately sought out the missionaries to share with them how, during his absence from the city, he had passed through a profound change of heart and mind. He had reassessed his entire life in the light of the claim that Jesus was the Messiah and therefore Saviour and God. This experience challenged what he had previously held and shook him to the core of his being, but it also brought him to profess his faith in Jesus. He was baptised in 1846 by Pál Török in a Hungarian Reformed Church in Pesth.[28]

The same year, in Buda, on the opposite bank of the Danube, a Mr Brown (probably Braun), a humble tradesman, was baptised with his wife and five young children by the Lutheran, Pastor Georg Bauhofer. A congregation of about three hundred Protestants, Roman Catholics, and Jews witnessed the administration of the sacrament and heard Brown make a clear public declaration of his faith and tell how he had been greatly influenced through contact with Israel Saphir and, despite much criticism from his former friends in the synagogue, could not be dissuaded from making confession of his Christian faith. As he told the attentive congregation on the day of his baptism: 'now he felt true peace of conscience, and, though poor, would not exchange his position that day for anything that was in their power to offer him.'

The day following, Brown and his family were shocked when he was summoned to appear before the magistrates on a charge of disturbing the peace. With much trepidation he made his way to court, but his accusers failed to turn up and the magistrates sent him home. The next day he received a fresh summons to answer three charges. The first was that he had been trading illegally. Unknown to any but his former friends in the synagogue, he, a Bohemian Jew, had never obtained official authorisation to carry on his business in Buda. In addition, he had a son of ten weeks who, contrary to law, had been neither baptised nor circumcised. Thirdly, he was suspected of not having paid that year's toleration tax, the poll tax levied on every Jew in Habsburg domains. The magistrate dismissed the first charge, ordered his child to be baptised or circumcised within three days, and instructed him to pay the tax.

The Jewish elders who undertook the collection of the tax vindictively assessed him as owing an extortionate sum, over seven times that for which he was actually liable. The magistrate again intervened and reproved the elders, who lowered the figure but to a still punitive amount, three times more than his true indebtedness. With that, Brown and his antagonists left the court bound for the synagogue, where he paid his tax and obtained a receipt for it. There he was subjected to a further barrage of questions and invective, his opponents finding it inconceivable that any Jew would become a Christian unless lured by material inducements. When pressed on what he stood to gain from professing faith in Christ, he laid his hand on his heart and said, 'God has promised in his Word and I have received what I expect. I have it *here*. I have already received what God in his Word promised. More I ask not. More I expect not.'[29]

Brown's testimony at his baptism, and Bauhofer's testimonial to Brown, deeply moved both congregation and ministers to tears. One of those observed weeping was described as an elderly 'respectable-looking' Jew who, on further enquiry, was discovered to be one of the synagogue elders who had brought the summons against him. Wingate reported that a direct consequence of Brown's baptism was a gathering in Old Buda city of a small group of Jewish men to read and discuss the New Testament.[30]

These and other accounts William Wingate kept as a record of the converts of the mission during his period of nine years service in Pesth between 1843 and 1852. The list contains the names of over seventy people, of all ages, drawn from all strata of society, including students, surgeons, soldiers, musicians, teachers, successful businessmen, society ladies, even a baroness and a rabbi. Their age range runs from children received into the Church with their parents to the seventy-year-old Rabbi Husch. The majority, however, were young men in their twenties. Not all, however, continued in the faith and Wingate was frank about the failures. Four were excommunicated, one 'fell into scandal' and another 'went back to Judaism.'

The most fruitful period of the mission appears to have been 1843–4, when Wingate records twenty-eight adults professing Christian faith and being baptised. But they were not all. Unable, or unwilling, to be preoccupied by statistics, Wingate summarised the results in general terms:

> Hebrew Christians are everywhere. Every class of Jewish society contributes these converts – professors in universities, lawyers, medical men, literary men, musicians, artists, merchants, mechanics, poor and

rich are quickened by the Spirit of all grace, convinced of their sin and guilt. They are at the feet of Jesus, and enabled to say with every believer, 'We have redemption through the atoning blood of Jesus, even the forgiveness of our sins.'[31]

Such evidence challenges the tediously and tendentiously repeated allegations by opponents of Jewish missions that such work enjoys success only at the margins of Jewish society, only catching, as one Jewish leader put it to me, 'the falling leaves of Israel', those who, in pre-emancipation days, could not 'make a living with their minds' within the Jewish community. Though it cannot be denied that superficial changes of religious allegiance, often motivated by social and economic considerations, were common in Hungary at the time, such could not be said, in the main, of the converts of the Scottish mission. Further evidence of the true spiritual conversion of most of those listed by Wingate is afforded by the fact that twelve out of a total of fifty-five either became missionaries or ordained ministers. And although it has been necessary, owing to their influence and future importance, to highlight the lives of some of the more prominent converts, there were many others, ordinary people, whose stories illustrate the dynamics of that spiritual change of mind, heart, and life that are the hallmarks of authentic Christian conversion.

It is also worth noting in this context the very different meanings traditionally given by Jews and Christians to the word 'convert', both as a noun and as a verb. As a noun there is broad agreement that 'a convert' is a one who, either freely or under duress, has decided to change their religious affiliation. But there is a great difference of opinion regarding the meaning of the verb. Jewish writers generally use the active voice, saying that a person has 'converted.' Christians, however, generally – at least in the recent past – use the passive voice, to indicate that a person has 'been converted.' Additionally, when Jewish writers use the term 'to convert' in connection with Jews who have become Christians the word often carries overtones of duress. In evangelical Christian theology, conversion is understood to be entirely voluntary; it is, as theologian Wayne Grudem has put it, 'our willing response to the gospel call, in which we sincerely repent of our sins and place our trust in Christ for salvation.'[32] Christian conversion cannot be considered genuine if it is brought about under any kind of duress or material inducement.

Adhering to the doctrine of *The Westminster Confession of Faith*, the Scottish missionaries moreover believed that conversion is never accomplished by human effort unaided; it is always essentially a work of God's Holy Spirit. John Duncan spoke for them all when he once said: 'I preach a free gospel to every man or I don't preach the gospel at all, but I know that its acceptance without the help of the Spirit is an impossibility.'[33] In fact, the traditional Scottish evangelical tendency was to be cautious of professed conversions, almost to a degree of scepticism, until the credibility of a convert's profession of Christian faith was established by evidence of new life and a changed character. It was adherence to such clear theological principles that generally inhibited Scottish missionaries either from playing the numbers game or exaggerating the tally of new converts.

❧ 21 ❧

'The results have been great and glorious'

Hungary and Poland, 1841 to 1944

FIFTY years after the expulsion of the missionaries from the Hungarian domains in 1852, Gavin Carlyle, a nephew of Edward Irving and the minister of St Andrews English Presbyterian Church, Ealing, London, commented in his biography of Adolf Saphir on the success of the work at Pesth:

> Few missions, either Jewish or other, have had so remarkable a history or so widespread an influence as that of Pesth. It gave an impetus to Jewish missions, the effect of which will never pass away.[1]

It would be tempting to conclude this story by simply taking Carlyle at face value but questions must be asked concerning the reliability of this remark. Was Carlyle too close to the mission to be objective? He was, after all, the friend and biographer of both Adolph Saphir and William Wingate. Was he prejudiced, so that his opinion must be dismissed as partisan exaggeration? There can be no doubt that nineteenth-century missionary propagandists did sometimes embellish the effectiveness of the mission work they sought to advocate and frequently for the lowest of motives, to maintain financial income for their work.

Another Free Church writer of the period, William Garden Blaikie, correctly pointed out that the first phase of the mission contrasted strikingly with the period following in that there was 'no repetition of the brilliant epoch 1843–44, either at Budapest or at any of the other mission stations.'[2] In the light of the wider European context Carlyle's comment does not seem sensational. As well as the work carried on by the Scottish missions, there was a profusion of Protestant missions to the Jews, including the London Society for Promoting Christianity Among the Jews (1809), the Berlin Society for Promoting Christianity among the Jews (1822), the Saxon Mission (1822), the Basle Association of Friends of Israel (1830), the Strasbourg Association of Friends of Israel Society (1835), the Berlin Proselytes Union (1836), the West German Association for Israel (1822), the Irish Presbyterian Jewish Mission (1841), the British Society for the Propagation of the Gospel among the Jews (1842), the Norwegian Jewish Mission (1844), the Holland Auxiliary (1844), the Lubeck Friends of Israel (1844), and the Bavarian Union (1849).

The result of their combined work led the scholar Johannes Friedrich Alexander de la Roi, in his massive three volume study of Jewish baptisms in the nineteenth century, to advance the opinion that, by 1900, as many as a quarter of a million Jewish people may have professed faith in Jesus as the Messiah and been baptised into the Christian Church. Nevertheless, any attempt to accurately quantify results is fraught with difficulty, as W. T. Gidney, the historian of the Anglican LSPCJ, was forced to conclude:

> We know not what standard to set up, or what test to apply. The tabulation of … statistics is always risky, never accurate. The fallacy of argument based on them is proverbial, and when they are brought forward as a test of operations … the fallacy is immensely greater. Mere enumeration … may mean little or much, anything or nothing.[3]

The 1927 publication, *The Findings of the Budapest Conference on the Christian Approach to the Jew*, likewise demonstrates a caution worthy of emulation in a less modest age:

> When a Jew applies for baptism, the missionary should do his utmost to test his profession and observe his life lest there be any ulterior motives in his mind. The aim of missions is not to 'make propaganda'.[4]

The fact is that the available data does not lend itself to accurate analysis. Scottish missionaries kept no detailed statistical records, nor do the surviving committee minute books help. Wingate, who privately recorded details of the seventy or so converts at Pesth during his years of service, did so with great circumspection, not always distinguishing Jewish converts from gentiles. For Scottish Calvinists, keeping a head count of converts was distasteful and contradicted their fundamental belief that, as the work was God's not theirs, its reality was frequently hidden from human sight. In an address to the Free Church Assembly of 1864, John Duncan summarised the success at Pesth with such characteristic reserve:

> Like God's works usually, its beginnings were small, the steps of its increase slow and remarkably providential; it experienced the alternation of cheering blinks of sunshine, and dark and cloudy days. Often apparently about to be uprooted, it was long sustained through the watchful care of its kind, intelligent in both ways, highly exalted protectress. Afterwards when, she having gone home, our missionaries were expelled, the flourishing school which had commenced with a few little Jewish children round the devoted Philip Saphir's bed of sickness, was taken under the fostering care of the Hungarian Reformed Church, and, still retaining its connection with us, has served to prepare the present happy state of things, so analogous in several respects to that which subsisted when I and my younger colleagues had the happiness of preaching Christ's gospel in that city, which we all loved so well, and where we enjoyed so many heart-cheering tokens of our Divine Master's presence.[5]

Duncan much preferred to speak of success simply, even vaguely, as the 'happy state of things' or the enjoyment of 'heart-cheering tokens of our Divine Master's presence', rather than in scientific terms or with mathematical precision.

So, if the missionaries are unable or unwilling to provide reliable statistics, maybe it was that Jewish Christians, wanting to validate their convictions and provide justification for their cause, might be inclined to exaggerate the strength of the believing community. Yet that is not what we find. Reporting to the Jewish Convention held in Mildmay Park in 1889, the Rev. Carl A. Schönberger, brother-in-law of Adolph Saphir and a former Free Church of Scotland missionary in Pesth, was very reluctant to speak about results:

Results. Ah! we cannot perhaps speak so much of results, if by results you mean individual conversions and baptisms. Now I do not regard the work from that point of view at all. I have no sympathy for those who speak of converts as if they were mere commerce, paid for at so much per head. Results are with Him, and not with us; still, the results have been great and glorious.[6]

Nor can reliable help be found from anti-missionary Jewish sources which, depending on mood, are either vaguely dismissive, thus minimising the effectiveness of the mission, or are alarmist, arguing that conversions were 'rampant'. A more careful assessment made by Raphael Patai in his 1996 study *The Jews of Hungary,* suggests there were some hundred thousand 'Jews of Christian Confession' in post-World War I Hungary and the Hungarian-ceded territories.[7] Crucially, however, such sources fail to differentiate between those who experienced a spiritual conversion and those who for largely economic or political reasons simply assimilated with the Christian majority. Nevertheless, it cannot be denied that the numbers of Jewish Christians in nineteenth-century Hungary were very large indeed, making Carlyle's general point about the success of the Scottish mission perfectly credible.

Instead of counting heads, perhaps a more helpful approach to take in assessing the value of the Scottish mission is to consider its influence on the nation of Hungary and its Christian institutions. William Wingate, compiling a report for the 1847 General Assembly of the Free Church of Scotland, added an interesting paragraph in which he contrasts the spiritual state of Hungary before the mission arrived, with that afterwards: 'Those who know the state of things five years ago, will bless the God of all grace for the great and glorious change.'[8]

In the periodical *The Sunday at Home*, Robert Smith described this transformation in greater detail. On arrival in the country in 1841, his first impressions of the spiritual state of the Hungarian Protestant churches were somewhat negative. Only a small minority of ministers, including Török and Bauhoffer in Budapest, were evangelicals, and even they were suspicious of Scottish Presbyterianism. Two years later, the barriers had been broken down and real friendships had been established. In 1842, at the initiative of Archduchess Maria Dorothea, a weekly ministerial fraternal for prayer and the study of Scripture came into being, where fresh approaches to Christian work were discussed, leading to a number of important innovations.[9] On arrival in Budapest, the Scottish workers commenced a Sunday school; this became so popular that it was copied by many Protestant churches throughout Hungary.[10] Even before the fraternal was formed, the Scottish ministers persuaded their Lutheran and Reformed Church friends to collaborate in the production of a Christian newspaper aimed at defending scriptural principals, challenging false doctrines and church abuses, and promoting a missionary and evangelistic outlook.[11] They likewise introduced into the country the idea of using local agents to distribute evangelistic literature.

Wingate saw this latter development as strategic, preparing the Protestant Churches 'for the next important stage in mission work: the evangelisation of Hungary by trained evangelists selected from the best and most experienced of the converts from Judaism.' Then, alluding to Romans 11:15, he remarked that:

> The conversion of the Jews became in this way 'life from the dead' to the professing Protestant Churches greatly needing the testimony of living, earnest Christianity.[12]

Both directly and indirectly, under God's blessing, the strategic influence of the Scottish mission extended variously to theological reform, Bible distribution, Christian social and philanthropic work, the spiritual revival of congregations, and the establishment of a strong Hungarian home missions movement. In addition, a foundation was laid for Hungarian Protestant foreign missions. Long after their departure in 1852, the influence of the missionaries remained strong and the momentum they had established steadily increased.

Around 1887, Aladár Szabó was inspired by the evangelical Calvinism of Andrew Moody, the missionary nephew of Alexander Moody Stuart, to 'establish in the headquarters of the Scottish mission, the Hold Street Fellowship.' Its aim, to promote awareness of foreign missions among Hungarian Christians, led, by the first decade of the twentieth century, to the sending of the first missionaries of the Hungarian Church.

In her extensive, almost exhaustive, study of Hungarian missionary endeavour, Dr Anne-Marie Kool depicts the great mission leader and bishop of the Hungarian Reformed Church, Béla Kennesy, standing for the last time in the old mission building in Hold Street, shortly before its demolition, reflecting on the Scottish influence:

> I received the first truly serious impressions of God's Word there in that big hall ... All this wells up in my memory and fills my spirit with gratitude to those who were instruments in the hands of the Lord for me to see and find my Redeemer, our Lord Jesus Christ.[13]

Then there was the school. When Philipp Saphir died in 1849 the control of the school he had established passed into the capable hands of his father, Israel Saphir. The work had been mercifully preserved through the dark days of revolution, war, and Habsburg repression, and the policy of the Free Church in insisting it was independent of church control had been fully vindicated. Not only did it remain functional, but it had positively flourished. In 1863, after a decade of absence, the Free Church recommenced work in Budapest, sending Andrew Moody to reorganise the school in its new buildings at Hold utca. In 1900, all the Free Church missionaries, including those at Budapest, joined the newly formed United Free Church of Scotland and in 1929 the majority of the United Free Church went into the Church of Scotland. The wheel of the Jewish work in Hungary had turned full circle. The mission, which now consisted largely of the school in Vörösmarty Utca, with its adjacent girl's hostel, was again under the oversight of the Church of Scotland. Just three years later, in 1932, Jane Haining was appointed matron. She alone of all the missionaries paid the supreme cost, laying down her life as a martyr for God, the gospel, and her young charges.[14]

Jane Haining's kindness towards Jewish people was mirrored by many Hungarian Christians. Among both Lutherans and Reformed Christians, sympathy for the Jewish people and a desire to ameliorate their suffering was a long-established habit. Just as in 1848 when the Reformed pastor Pál Török had stood at the gate of his Budapest church with a drawn sword to protect Jews fleeing from a hostile mob, so now Hungarian Christians sought to shield Jews from the Nazi menace.

In the summer of 1942, a Christian organisation was set up to save Jewish Christians from the threat of deportation. Called the Jó Pásztor Bizottság (Good Shepherd Committee), its leading figure was Rev. Jószef Éliás, a resourceful young evangelical Jewish Christian minister of the Hungarian Reformed Church. In March 1944, Germany occupied Hungary, rapidly moving to establish a ghetto in Budapest and commence the deportation of Jews to Auschwitz and other death camps. Jó Pásztor became remarkably adept at saving many Jewish people from deportation and death, but as more and more were taken away, Éliás became frustrated by the failure of the churches to condemn what was happening.[15] He bravely proposed that the government be confronted with an ultimatum: either it must halt the deportations or face popular condemnation by having its anti-Jewish activities exposed in pastoral letters to be read in all the churches, with church bells remaining silent until the deportations ceased.

Éliás' suggestion was rejected by cowardly Protestant and Catholic leaders alike and he was eventually forced into hiding, but not into inactivity. In May 1944, a copy of the *Vrba-Wetzler Report* came into the hand of Éliás. This remarkable document had been compiled in April by two Slovakian Jews who had escaped from Auschwitz with the express intention of alerting the world to the enormous numbers being killed there and to warn that advanced preparations had been made to gas eight hundred thousand Jewish deportees from Hungary. The report was speedily copied by Éliás and others and distributed to government and church leaders at home and abroad. As a result Regent Miklós Horthy halted the deportation of Hungarian Jews to Auschwitz in early July, but this did not save the four hundred thousand who had already been transported going to their deaths.

After the war, it was darkly rumoured that Jó Pásztor had only been interested in saving the lives of Jewish Christians, but such allegations were firmly rebutted both by Éliás and his colleague at the Scottish Mission in Vörösmarty utca, Rev. János Dobos.[16] In a personal conversation with the author, János Dobos recounted how, in attempting to save non-Christian Jews from extermination in Auschwitz, he and his colleagues had freely given away blank baptismal certificates. But, he insisted, there had been no spurious baptisms; the only people to have been baptised were those who made credible professions of faith. As we walked together along Budapest's Karoly körút, we came to the junction with Dohány utca. Standing within sight of the Great Synagogue, at the heart of the area that had been demarcated by the Nazi's as the Budapest ghetto, Dobos turned to me, and with tears in his eyes at the memory of those harrowing days, said quietly: 'And, you know, there were many baptisms.'[17]

Terrible as was Hungary's holocaust, it would be a misreading of history to lay the guilt on the majority of Hungarians. Indeed, in July 1944, Anne McCormick, a foreign correspondent for *The New York Times*, described Hungary as the last refuge of Jews in Europe, declaring that 'as long as they exercised any authority in their own house, the Hungarians tried to protect the Jews.'

As the Holocaust burst upon the Jewish world, it was not only in Hungary that God's saving grace was at work. During the late 1930s in Bialystok, Poland, the workers of the British-based Barbican Mission to the Jews witnessed an extraordinary degree of interest in the gospel. Large crowds of Jewish people attended preaching meetings at the hall in Świętego Rocha 25, which still stands and is used as a cinema, the Teatr 'Arkadia.' Here, night by night, in excellent Yiddish and with a God-given urgency which could only be understood with hindsight, the missionaries set out the claims of Messiah Jesus as the Glory and the Hope of Israel, and men and women were called to a living faith in Him. The response was remarkable and there were so many genuine conversions that, from accounts published in the Barbican mission's periodical, *Immanuel's Witness*, it would not be exaggerating to call the movement a religious revival.

So it was, in the years prior to the Holocaust, through faithful gospel witness, untold numbers of Polish Jewish men and women were encouraged to 'Have regard for the covenant, for the dark places of the land are full of the habitations of violence' (Ps. 74:20, ESV). As indeed they were. In 1939, Bialystok was overrun in the Nazi *Blitzkrieg*. On 27th June 1941, Nazi paramilitary police herded Jewish residents into the Great Synagogue, the largest wooden synagogue in Eastern Europe. Some, accused of moving too slowly, were shot dead on the spot. Others – some estimates say eight hundred, others as many two thousand – men, women, and children, were locked in the synagogue, which was then set on fire. Within a month, five thousand Jewish citizens of Bialystok had been murdered; within a period of two years, some fifty thousand Jewish men, women, and children from Bialystok lost their lives.

Christian faith did not, of course, save people from summary death or the gas-chambers. The Nazis did not distinguish between Jewish Christians, Jews who followed the various sects of Judaism or Jews who were irreligious. Identity was based on the status of one's grandparents: you were Jewish if you had even one Jewish grandparent. This meant that the population of the death camps included not only many first generation Jewish Christians but also those whose parents and grandparents were Jewish Christians, including some who were ministers and pastors and Christian workers. Clearly, even in the camps the Messiah was not without his witnesses. Although, in the years following the liberation of the death camps Jewish Christian survivors told their stories, it is doubtful if we can reconstruct the reality and assess the spiritual impact of the witness of Jewish believers and gentile Christians in the camps. But their testimony, like that of Jane Haining, resonates with the words of an earlier Jewish Christian missionary, prisoner, and martyr, filling our hearts with the hope that the work of God's Kingdom, among Jew and gentile, will always go steadily, indefatigably, onward:

> I want you to know, brothers, that what has happened to me has really served to advance the gospel, ... most of the brothers, having become confident in the Lord by my imprisonment, are much more bold to speak the word without fear.
> PHILIPPIANS 1:12 & 14

Appendix 1

Scottish Influence on the Growth of Jewish Missions

THE Scottish Church first shared its vision for the evangelisation of the Jews with her sister church, the Presbyterian Church in Ireland. Robert Candlish, Alex Keith, and Robert M'Cheyne were sent to Belfast in 1840 as delegates from the Church of Scotland to attend the first General Assembly of a new church formed by the union of the Synod of Ulster and the Secession Synod. They found the Irish Presbyterians very receptive to the idea of missionary outreach to the Jews. Andrew Bonar recalled that when M'Cheyne preached on Romans 1:16, it had a most marked effect; many ministers, as they came out, were heard saying, 'How was it we never thought of the duty of remembering Israel before?'

The Belfast Newsletter was also caught up by the enthusiasm and published many Jewish-related stories, statistics, commentary, and other relevant articles.[1] By 1841 popular support resulted in two appeals being sent up to the General Assembly asking it 'to take into consideration the propriety of adopting measures for the Conversion of the Jews.' One appeal came from the Presbytery of Belfast and was sent through the normal ecclesiastical channels, but the other was from the laity of the town and took the form of a petition subscribed by over one thousand four hundred signatures. According to one account, when the pages of this memorial were joined together as one scroll it reached from the pulpit of Rosemary Street Presbyterian Church, in which the Assembly was gathered, to half way down the aisle. Another account insisted that it encircled the interior of the church.[2]

There could be no denying that Irish Presbyterians were keen to commence a mission to the Jews.

During the Assembly debate, however, some cautious souls expressed reservations: was it wise for such a newly established denomination to immediately undertake such a heavy commitment to new missionary work. The Rev. William Graham of Dundonald, speaking for the more adventurous majority, argued that the Irish church ought indeed to follow the example of the 'gigantic step which the Church of Scotland had made', for Irish Presbyterians also 'owed much to the Jews.'

The Belfast Newsletter reported that Graham had urged that the moral and spiritual claims of the Jewish people 'were stronger than any other – stronger than those of the inhabitants of their native land.'[3] While it was pleasant to converse with the Irish in their own language, as he had done, there was something even more delightful: to address the Jews in Hebrew – for although the language of India was sublime, and the language of the Irish was soft, the Jewish language was sacred. To him there was a deeper theme, a holier subject; it was the blood of a Jew which atoned for the sinner's transgressions; it was upon a Jewish head that the crown of thorns was placed; it was a Jewish heart which was pierced and bled.

Aware of the strength of feeling in the church at large and convinced by the arguments rehearsed in its presence, the Assembly, 'deeply humbled by its former neglect' resolved immediately to form a mission to the Jews. This outcome was attributed largely to the impression left by the delegation from Scotland and especially the effect of M'Cheyne's preaching. Over half a century later, when compiling the history of the union of the synods, the prodigious memory of the Irish Church historian, W. D. Killen, remained highly impressed with the content of M'Cheyne's sermons: 'When here at this time he spoke once and again, and all his addresses produced a marvellous impression.' Killen's testimony is all the more significant because he strongly disliked M'Cheyne's voice production, his mannerisms, and relaxed preaching style.[4]

Over the years the Irish church maintained regular contact with the Scottish committee, seeking advice on practical issues such as the appropriate level of remuneration for missionaries and, on one occasion, offered one of its own missionaries to serve in Palestine. Reciprocally, the Scottish General Assembly recorded its gratitude to the Irish Assembly for its fellowship 'in this field of Christian labour, as well as the assistance rendered by the missionaries of the American Churches.' To cement this relationship, each month the *Missionary Record of the Church of Scotland* was sent free of charge to all Irish Presbyterian ministers.[5]

This cooperation was symbolised in 1854 when Dr Keith recommended that the Presbyterian Church of Ireland take on as its missionary the newly graduated Adolph Saphir. Ordained by the Presbytery of Belfast, Saphir commenced a brief period of service in Hamburg, but not long after resigned over what he considered to be the intolerable restraints imposed upon his work.

The Church of Scotland had long desired to see missionary work established in London and fully supported the initiative taken in 1842 to found the British Society for the Propagation of the Gospel among the Jews (BSPGJ). Although the BSPGJ was an interdenominational society, its story commences in the Church of Scotland. In 1841 an overture from the Newcastle Presbytery was sent to the English Synod of the Church of Scotland held in London in 1841, requesting the Synod take immediate action for 'promoting missionary operations among the Jews and Heathen' in cooperation with the Church of Scotland.[6]

When John Duncan was passing through London on his way to Hungary he met with a Jewish Christian called Ridley Herschell and impressed on him the great potential of London, pointing out that whilst at this time the Scottish Jewish community was in the low hundreds, London was home to around twenty thousand Jews. As well as being made up of new immigrants from Europe, there was also a growing Anglicised, educated, and organised community, with a strengthening middle class.

Herschell himself was an immigrant, having arrived in London in 1825. Born as Haim Herschell in Strzelno, Prussia (now Poland), in April 1807, he had been educated at the University of Berlin. Once, whilst journeying to Hamburg, he had successfully managed to acquire an outside seat on a carriage privately hired by a Herr Heintz, who took a great interest in him. Heintz entertained him at Hamburg, paid his fare to England and gave him letters of introduction to several of his acquaintances in London, including the Duke of Wellington.[7]

After returning to the continent to live briefly in Berlin and Paris, Herschell finally came back to London to take up residence in a home for Jewish converts and inquirers, run by a Jewish Christian called Erasmus Simon. By April 1830, he had come to personal faith in Jesus, and despite threats to his life presented himself to the Bishop of London for baptism. Later that year whilst attending one of Edward Irving's meetings he met Miss Helen Mowbray, daughter of a Leith merchant, and the following September they married. Helen Mowbray was both spiritually mature and intellectually competent. It was her detailed study of the prophetic passages of Scripture that had first attracted her to Irving as someone who took seriously 'the literal interpretation of the Scriptures.'

Desiring fully to support her husband in his work she became competent in Hebrew and familiar with the rabbinic writings. Shortly after their marriage, the Herschells opened and ran a home in Woolwich for destitute Jews. In 1835 Ridley was invited to become a minister of a congregation in Scotland, but preferring to work as an evangelist rather than a pastor, he declined and became a home missionary in the village of Leigh-on-Sea in Essex. Then, in December 1838, he commenced work at the Church of Scotland's Founder's Hall Chapel beside the Bank of England in the City of London.

Among his congregation were many poor Jews who not only showed interest in his teaching and personal beliefs, but also sought relief for their poverty. Concerned 'lest the name of Christ should be dishonoured, through the indifference of Christians to the temporal wants of his brethren according to the flesh,' Herschell established the Jews Benevolent Fund, and also opened a home for inquirers and converts.

Responding to John Duncan's information, in August 1841 the Church of Scotland's Glasgow sub-committee explored the possibility of establishing a mission station in London, asking Rev. James Hamilton of the National Scotch Church, Regent Square, to approach Herschell for his advice. In the meantime, Herschell, acting independently, was busy urging the Edinburgh sub-committee to start missionary work in London. In May 1842, responding to Herschell's approach and Hamilton's advice, both sub-committees pressed the English Synod to implement its decision of the previous year. The London Presbytery likewise recommended that a missionary auxiliary be set up immediately, and the denominational Jewish missionary committee went a step further by suggesting that it should be inter-denominational in character.[8]

The 1842 General Assembly approved these proposals and ordered that they be carried into effect. That year, James Hamilton, of Regent Square National Scots Church, invited his close friend, Robert M'Cheyne, to be the main preacher for his November communion services. On 7th November a well-publicised meeting was held at Regent Square to implement the General Assembly's instruction. Those present included Dr Burder, a Congregationalist minister from Islington; the controversial Secession Church minister, Dr Alexander Fletcher of Finsbury Chapel; Dr Henderson, a lecturer at Highbury College, the Dissenting (Congregational) Academy; Rev. John Cumming of Crown Court Church of Scotland; Rev. James Brown of London Wall Church of Scotland; Rev. William Yonge of Albany Congregational Chapel, Brentford; Rev. Peter Lorimer and Rev. Ridley Herschell of Islington Church of Scotland; and Rev. James Hamilton, minister of the National Scotch Church, Regent Square.[9]

Robert M'Cheyne attended this meeting and was invited to open the proceedings with prayer. The group then proceeded to form themselves into The British Society for the Propagation of the Gospel Among the Jews, electing Hamilton and Henderson to be the first secretaries. Curiously, but perhaps understandably in light of the excitement of the pre-Disruption convocation held in Edinburgh on the 17th of the same month, there is no mention of the formation of the BSPGJ in either M'Cheyne's or Hamilton's biographies, though both refer to M'Cheyne preaching for Hamilton at Regent Square.

The new society was not only endorsed by the Church of Scotland but also awarded a generous grant of £500 (worth about £70,000 in today's values). The relationship between the Church and the society continued for another few months until the Disruption in

May 1843, at which point the English Synod largely threw in its lot with the Free Church of Scotland and formed the Presbyterian Church in England.[10] The society went on to flourish and reflect its increasingly international character, eventually changing its name to the International Society for Evangelisation of the Jews, and again in 1976, after uniting with the Barbican Mission to the Jews, adopted the name Christian Witness to Israel. In the late 1980s to late 1990s as many as nine members of the Free Church of Scotland were actively serving with CWI. It continues to flourish as a witness to the Jewish people under its current name of the International Mission to Jewish People. The link with Scotland is now somewhat tenuous: although no Free Church members currently serve with the society, it remains formally the Free Church's mission to the Jewish people and a representative of IMJP addresses the Free Church General Assembly each year.

In August 1846, three years after the Disruption and the formation of the Free Church of Scotland, a resurrected Church of Scotland mission to the Jews was established at Halkin Street, Belgrave Square. The first missionary was Rev. Henry Douglas. Later this work became better known through its association with the ministry of Adolph Saphir, but terminated in 1866, with the sale of its property.[11]

A third strand of Scottish influence is seen in the Free Church's cooperation with the Reformed Presbyterian Church of Scotland in its attempt to establish a Jewish Mission in London. In June, 1844 *The Free Church Magazine* contained an article announcing, a 'New Mission to the Jews' which reported the intention of the London congregation of the Reformed Presbyterian Church to commence a mission. £100 had been donated to set up the work and in December 1844, Dr William Symington offered himself as a missionary. His offer was accepted, and to help him to gain missionary experience the Reformed Presbyterian Synod recommended that he be seconded to the Free Church of Scotland.[12]

There is no evidence that this plan was ever carried out, rather, the Reformed Presbyterian Church established its own independent Jewish mission the following year. Its first missionary, John Cunningham, was born in Newtonlimavady in Co. Londonderry,

Ireland, but studied in Scotland, graduating from Glasgow University in 1836. In May 1846 he was appointed to preach to a newly formed Reformed Presbyterian congregation meeting in the Presbyterian Chapel in Edward Street in London's Soho district, where, for five months he ministered each Sunday afternoon with great acceptance. In September, however, the congregation was forced to vacate the building and were unable to find a suitable alternative until the following year.[13]

In October 1846 Cunningham started missionary work in London in close cooperation with, and under the direction of, the BSPGJ. The society gave him advice regarding a suitable area of work and suggested the most appropriate methods which he might follow. Around this time Cunningham was ordained by the Reformed Presbytery of Glasgow. On his return to London he rented 6 Burton Street, off Burton Crescent, Bloomsbury, as his home, where each week he accommodated the destitute congregation, to whom he faithfully preached. At first the congregation was enthusiastic for his work among the Jews, and made a generous financial contribution, but either its interest flagged or its numbers declined, so that by 1852 the congregation's financial contribution had dwindled to only half of its initial commitment.

Cunningham continued to work among London's Jewish people for thirteen years. It was said, that although he had diligently sowed the seed, he reaped no harvest. Now and again a gleam of hope appeared, only to be snuffed out by disappointment. Cunningham's lack of success seems quite remarkable in view of the growing number of converts that all the other contemporary Jewish mission agencies were reporting. It is probable that the distinctive Reformed Presbyterian doctrine of national covenanting was objectionable to Jewish thought, which held that the only national covenant God established was with Israel. Perhaps to some extent the problem lay with Cunningham himself, of whom it was once said that although his 'zeal and patience were worthy of all admiration ... some of the methods he pursued were of questionable wisdom.'[14] Just precisely what they were is unknown, but it appears that the combination of national covenanting and eccentric methods of evangelism proved fatal to success. In 1858, Cunningham, hardline Covenanter that he was, dissented from the Reformed Presbyterian Synod's relaxation of the traditional ban on allowing their members to vote in political elections, unless the candidate also upheld national covenanting, resigned as a minister and left the denomination. The Synod, unable to find a suitable successor, abandoned its mission to the Jews.[15]

As early as 1811 the Calvinistic Methodists, later to be known as the Welsh Presbyterians, took an interest in Jewish missions. That year Rev. Thomas Charles of Bala, famous for his work in translating the Bible into Welsh, the establishment of Bible societies, and education for the poor, invited Joseph S. C. F. Frey to speak about his work at a meeting of Calvinistic Methodists in North Wales and to appeal for their prayers and financial support for missions to the Jewish people.[16]

Around 1842, shortly after its formation, the BSPGJ also established links with the Calvinistic Methodists through J. P. Cohen, a Jewish Christian resident in Swansea, who had offered to work in London. The BSPGJ recommended that Cohen train for missionary work under the care and instruction of the Independent minister, Rev. W. C. Yonge of Brentford.[17] He continued with the BSPGJ until 1873, afterwards operating independently.[18]

In March 1845, Dr Keith had been invited as the convenor of the Free Church of Scotland Jewish committee to be present at the meetings of the North Wales Calvinistic Methodist Association held at Ruthin in Denbighshire. In his address he attempted to remind the church of its duty to pray and work for the conversion of the Jewish people. Consequently, Rev. John Mills of Llanidloes in Powys, who was at the time the minister of the Ruthin church, informed friends that he had been very exercised by what Keith had said and felt a strong desire, which he believed to be a call from God, to work among the Jewish people.[19]

In June the idea of a Calvinistic Methodist mission to the Jews was further considered, but immediately ran into difficulties. It is clear from the minutes of the Association Board that there was scant enthusiasm for the work and little transpired other than an inconsequential and arcane debate about whether evangelistic work among the Jews was a department of home mission or foreign missions. Attempting to maintain the weak momentum established in Ruthin, Dr Keith, and others, suggested, with some acceptance, that the Welsh church might commence work in Hamburg, where there was a strong Jewish population and where the Irish Presbyterians had commenced a mission.[20]

The weak momentum, however, stalled, the church declining to allow Mills to operate overseas without first proving himself at home and suggesting that he should gain experience by working for twelve months in London. Mills, keen to prove his calling, moved to London in 1846 and commenced work in connection with the BSPGJ. Although his time in London was considered something of a success, his church procrastinated yet further by demanding he continue there for another year, and the following year the church rescinded its earlier decision to consider commencing work in Hamburg, insisting that Mills remain permanently in London and that the Association's Mission to the Jews should now be regarded as established.

Whatever disappointment Mills might have felt, he patiently submitted and worked tirelessly in distributing tracts and Scripture portions, seeking to get a New Testament into every Jewish home, setting up a small library and holding popular lectures. He did his best to break down prejudice and to show a friendly Christian face to the Jewish people he met. Three years afterward a young Jewish man, Henry Wolf, professed his faith in Jesus, testifying that, 'the veil was taken away from his heart.' On Whit Monday 1851, in Rose Place Chapel, Liverpool, Wolf was baptised, much to the fascination of the large numbers of visitors attending the annual preaching services.[21]

Regrettably, the earlier apathy and inertia among the Calvinistic Methodists now turned to outright opposition. Some said the results were too sparse. Others complained that Mills' methods were too controversial; though it is hard to see why. Reluctantly, he was given permission to continue for another three years, but effectively his denomination declared its lack of confidence in him by insisting he submit to the direction of a London-based supervisory committee. His friends and the faithful supporters of the mission prayed earnestly for a more positive spirit, and for a while the opposition subsided, allowing a more reasonable decision to be taken allowing the work to continue, 'as long as our circumstances permit, and while we have any reason to hope that the missionary's labour, under the Lord's blessing, may prove advantageous.'

The following year Mills enjoyed a visit to Palestine to familiarise himself with the culture and character of the Jews in their own country, coming back with sufficient material for two books of his experiences. The first, in Welsh, was privately published by Mills in 1858 as *Palestina: Sef, Hanes taith i ymweled ag Iuddewon Gwlad Canaan*, the second was published in London by J. Murray in 1864 under the title, *Three Months' Residence in Nablûs, and an Account of the Modern Samaritans.*

A fresh storm of hostility to Mills' work broke out, creating strong divisions in the Monthly Meetings of Calvinistic Methodist Associations all across the Principality, yet, despite everything, the London committee remained enthusiastic, renting a chapel to help the work forward. By 1859, however, the tide of antagonism became too strong to be resisted. Just when the decision to abandon the work was about to be made by the denominational authorities, the forbearing but broken Mills took the initiative and forestalled the decision by resigning. Ironically, it transpired that his work was not as unproductive as his critics had imagined, through his witness a good number of Jewish people were brought to faith in their Messiah.[22]

Although the Scottish work was not the first British Jewish mission, that honour belonging to the LSPCJ which was founded in 1809, it has a legitimate claim to be considered as a truly pioneering work, providing a lead which others followed. Various denominational and interdenominational Jewish missions welcomed the Scottish Church's guidance and allowed themselves to be influenced through contact with its work. Not only so, but its innovative approach to mission proved to be enduring, providing a repertoire of missionary methods still in use today. Indeed, almost ninety years after the Scottish work was established, the report of the 1927 Budapest conference on *The Christian Approach to the Jew* reads like an inventory of the methods of the Scottish missionaries.

Apart from personal evangelism, it listed Christian education, medical missions, philanthropy and community centres, and the production and widespread distribution of the Bible and Christian literature. At the heart of the Scottish strategy, however, lay not methodology but theology, the deep conviction that Jesus of Nazareth was the fulfilment of Hebrew Messianic expectations. The challenge to which mission sought to rise was how best to present this highly controversial, if not overtly offensive claim in such a way that, on the one hand, it did not antagonise Jewish people, nor, on the other, encourage only a spurious change of religious affiliation. As we have seen, there is no doubt that both the mission's direct work and indirect influence was used by God to bring large numbers of Jewish people to faith in Christ.

The mission's foundational motivations of gratitude to, and love for, the Jewish people were epitomised in missionaries like John Duncan, who once deliberately allowed himself to be cheated out of £5 by two poor Jews, saying, that he wanted thereby to 'gain an opportunity of slyly stealing away a prejudice or two, and insinuating a word for him who is the Gentile's light and Israel's glory.'

Appendix 2

To the Children of Israel in all the Lands of their Dispersion

THIS remarkable missionary document is an evangelistic address to the Jewish people from the 1841 General Assembly of the Church of Scotland. It takes the form of a tactful and irenic appeal, citing only the text of the Hebrew Bible. Prepared under the auspices of the Committee for the Conversion of the Jews, its author was Robert Wodrow, an erudite Glasgow elder and pioneer of the Jewish mission. Published in English, Hebrew, most European languages, as well as some Oriental languages, the address was sent to all known Jewish communities throughout the world under the signature of Robert Gordon, Moderator of the General Assembly. This version has been minimally edited mainly by restoring the full names of the books of the Bible.

To the Children of Israel
in all the Lands of their Dispersion,
the General Assembly of the Church
of Scotland
Sendeth Peace.

MEN AND BRETHREN, BELOVED FOR THE FATHERS' SAKE, – The God of glory appeared to Abraham, when he dwelt in Ur of the Chaldees, and promised to make of him a great nation, and that in him all the families of the earth should be blessed. This promise, which was again and again renewed to him, was confirmed to Isaac and to Jacob; Genesis 12:1-3; 13:14-17; 15; 17; 21:12; 22:15-18; 24:2-5, 24; 27:26-29; 28:10-15; 32:24-30; 35:9-12; 46:2-4. As it is also said in the 105th Psalm, 'He hath remembered his covenant forever, the word he commanded to a thousand generations; which he made with Abraham, and his oath unto Isaac; and confirmed the same unto Jacob for a law, to Israel for an everlasting covenant.' Within the ample bosom of this covenant, the glorious charter of all the blessings which, as a nation, you have ever possessed, or yet hope to receive, we, sinners of the Gentiles, as well as you, the men of Israel, find ourselves embraced; for so it is written, Genesis 28:14, 'In thee, and in thy seed, shall all the families of the earth be blessed.' Of this promise we, in this distant island of the sea, and after the lapse of almost 4000 years, can attest the truth. In Abraham and his seed we have been blessed. In Him who was to be the Desire of all nations, Haggai 2:7, our souls have found a secure refuge. Through Him have we been brought to the knowledge of that God whom your fathers worshipped. In Him have we found peace to our consciences, hope and joy to our hearts; even in the Man who, as the prophet foretold, Isaiah 22:2, would be an hiding-place from the wind, and a covert from the tempest; as rivers of water in a dry place; and as the shadow of a great rock in a weary land.

Men and Brethren, having thus obtained mercy ourselves, how can we but be deeply moved by the unhappy condition of those from whose stock has sprung that branch of the Lord, beautiful and glorious? Isaiah 4:2; under whose wide-spreading shadow we have been made to sit with great delight? Song of Solomon 2:3. How can we but desire that they, too, might come and find rest from their weary wanderings under the shelter of that wonderful name, Jehovah our Righteousness? Jeremiah 23:6. How can we but seek the good of that people, by whose means, at first, our fathers were turned from dumb idols to serve the living and true God, and from whom we have received those oracles of truth which everywhere testify of His Anointed?

Moved by these considerations, our Church, as many of you know, sent forth, two years ago, four of its ministers to seek the welfare of the children of Israel. These brethren, full of love to your nation, traversed many lands and brought us word again. They have been at Jerusalem, and have seen the Jew at his mournful devotions beside its ruined wall. They have been through the land once flowing with milk and honey, and have seen the thorns and the briars which now cover it; Isaiah 22:13. They have seen your holy cities a wilderness, Zion a wilderness, Jerusalem a desolation; Isaiah 64:10. They have been in your synagogues; they have visited your families; they have observed your religious services; they have conversed with your people; and, grateful as they have felt for the kindness received, they have been pained, though not surprised, to witness your wide departure from the ordinances of God, and the ignorance which prevails of His life-giving Word; Deuteronomy 8:3.

Knowing, as we do, that the Lord, in His sovereign grace, has persuaded us, the sons of Japhet, and caused us to dwell in the tents of Shem, Genesis 9:27; enjoying, as we do, the fullness of the provision of our Father's house, we would seek, in our turn, to persuade you, saying to you, as Moses to his father-in-law, Numbers 10:29, 'Come with us, and we will do you good.' We cannot think of possessing alone the privileges and honours of adopted children, while you, the natural heirs, are outcast and destitute. We feel it to be a reproach to us that it should be written, 'This is Zion whom no man seeketh after;' Jeremiah 30:17. We would rather desire to be employed, under the Shepherd of Israel, in seeking out His sheep, and delivering them out of all places where they have been scattered in the cloudy and dark day; Ezekiel 34:12. We have therefore thought of sending you this Letter. May the Lord incline your hearts to receive it from our hands, and lead many among you soon to call to mind the blessing and the curse among the nations whither the Lord your God hath driven you; Deuteronomy 30:1.

And because we know that, by the Jews, the very name of Christian is oftentimes regarded with aversion, from the idea that those who bear it are the adherents of a false religion, and have been the authors of the calamities they endure, we consider it needful, at the outset, to declare that, in our opinion, none who call themselves Christian deserve that name whose religion is not founded on the Word of God.

We are well aware what a stumbling-block it has been to the Jewish mind to observe the idolatry and other corruptions which prevail in many countries which profess the religion of Jesus. But we wish you to understand that such things are forbidden by the precepts of the gospel as much as by the commandment of the law. Those who worship saints or angels, or bow down before graven images, show themselves to be, not Christian, but anti-Christian; belonging; not to Jesus, but to that great apostasy from the faith, which both the Old and New Testament declared would take place in the latter days; Daniel 11:36-39.

Nor are the cruelties and oppressions to which you have been so often and so grievously subjected less repugnant to our holy religion, which teaches us to do to others as we would have others to do to us. We lament to think that in England itself you have at times suffered so much from grasping avarice and bitter animosity; but we bid you remember that these things were done during the reign of that iron superstition which persecuted the true followers of Jesus Christ as well as the Jews; Daniel 7:8, 20, 21, 24, 25.

And now, Men and Brethren, permit us to inquire whether every visible mark which the Scripture gives of the advent of the Messiah, may not be seen in connection with Jesus of Nazareth? Your father Jacob foretold, Genesis 49:10, 'The sceptre shall not depart from Judah, nor a lawgiver from between his feet, until Shiloh come, and unto him shall the gathering of the people be.' The sceptre did depart when Jesus appeared, and to Him the Gentiles have come. You have, therefore, here a double mark that Jesus is the Christ. Again, the Prophet Haggai, when the second temple was a building, foretold, in Jehovah's name, Haggai 2:7, 'I will shake all nations, and the Desire of all nations shall come, and I will fill this house with glory.' All nations were shaken as the Persians gave place to the Greeks, and the Greeks to the Romans. The second temple is no more, having been destroyed not long after Jesus came to it. You have, therefore, a double mark again that Jesus is the Christ. Isaiah foretold that Messiah would be rejected by the Jews, but believed on by the Gentiles, as may be seen from his Book of Prophecy, Isaiah 42:1-12, 22-25; 49:1-6, 13-15; 53; 54:1-3; 55:1-5; 65:1, 2. This has been largely fulfilled in reference to Jesus of Nazareth, and furnishes another proof again that He is the Christ. Daniel, one of the greatest benefactors of your race, who, like another Jacob, had power with

God and with man, to procure their release from Babylonish and Persian thraldom, Daniel 9:1-3, 20,23; 10:1-3, 10-14, 19,20; 11:1, foretold, that, in a given time, the Messiah the Prince would appear, and be cut off, though not for Himself; and that afterwards the city and the sanctuary would be destroyed by war : the sacrifice and oblation would cease; and a flood of desolations would continue till an appointed period; Daniel 9:24-27. All this has been accomplished in connection with Jesus of Nazareth. Seventy prophetic weeks, or 490 years, elapsed from the time when Ezra restored the law, Ezra 7, to the time when your fathers put Jesus to death. Not long after, as you know, Jerusalem was destroyed, and you have remained ever since, as another prophet declares, without a king and without a prince, and without a sacrifice; Hosea 3:4; your land left desolate, yourselves aliens in a strange land, and everywhere pursued by the manifest tokens of the Divine displeasure. You have, therefore, here manifold proofs that Jesus is the Christ.

We wish we could persuade you to read and examine the New Testament for yourselves. You might then, by the teaching of God's Spirit, discover that it is not the evil thing you have hitherto imagined, but is in truth the Word of God. You might find that it is no new revelation, but rests on your own beloved Scriptures, and is full of references to them. You might see that the doctrine of the Apostles is the same as that of the Prophets, and its system of morality nothing else than the Ten Commandments enlarged. You might find, with admiration and joy, that the long-promised Saviour has already come; the Rod from the stem of Jesse, Isaiah 11:1; and yet David's Lord, Psalm 110:1; the Child born, the Son given, whose name is Wonderful, Counsellor, the mighty God, the everlasting Father, the Prince of Peace, Isaiah 9:6; whose birth-place should be Bethlehem Ephratah, yet whose goings forth have been from of old, from everlasting, Micah 5:2.

Surely you will allow, that everything in your circumstances as a people calls for consideration. Is it not the case, that ever since the time when your fathers crucified Him who declared Himself to be the Messiah, sent of God, and rejected the salvation preached by His apostles, your nation has been under the perpetual rebuke of a frowning Providence? Your civil and sacred institutions have been entirely broken up. The holy and beautiful house where Jehovah was praised, has been burnt up with fire, and all your pleasant things laid waste; Isaiah 64:11. Your cities have been wasted without inhabitant, and your houses without man, and the land made utterly desolate. And the Lord has removed you far away, and there has been a great forsaking in the midst of the land; Isaiah 6:11, 12. The Lord has scattered you among the heathen and dispersed you through the countries; Ezekiel 36:19. And among those nations you have found no ease, neither has the sole of your foot had rest; but the Lord has given you there a trembling heart, and failing of eyes, and sorrow of mind; and your life has hanged in doubt before you, and you have had fear day and night, and have had none assurance of your life; Deuteronomy 28:65, 66.

We write not these things to add to your affliction, but from love to your souls. Surely you, as well as we, may put the question, 'What meaneth the heat of this great anger?' Deuteronomy 29:24. 'Why is it that the Lord has covered the daughter of Zion with a cloud, and cast down from heaven to earth the beauty of Israel?' Lamentations 2:1. It is not enough to say that you have sinned. Your fathers oftentimes sinned, and were led into captivity by their enemies. But where, in all their history, will you find a captivity like this? Even when carried to Babylon, the desolations of Jerusalem lasted only seventy years; Daniel 9:1. But now, for eighteen hundred years, the Holy City has been trodden under foot, and you banished from the land of your fathers. If it be alleged that the ten tribes have been longer in captivity than the Jews, and that they had no hand in putting Jesus to death, we answer, that seeing the Messiah was to spring from Judah, Genesis 49:10, seeing that Jerusalem was the place which the Lord had chosen to put His name there, 2 Chronicles 6:6, and seeing the temple which was there, with its priesthood and sacrifices, prefigured Him who was to come Psalm 110:4; 40:6-10; 51:7; 2 Chronicles. 6:18; 7:12-16, it follows, that the separation of the ten tribes from Judah, and the erection of another altar at Bethel, 1 Kings 22:25-33, was nothing else than the rejection of the promised Messiah Himself. When Israel said, 'We have neither portion in David, nor inheritance in the son of Jesse,' 1 King 12:16, their words were at once expressive of their sin, and prophetic of their doom. And hence the awful solemnity with which the sin of Jeroboam, the son of Nebat, whereby he made Israel to sin, is again and again pointed to, as the cause of the apostasy and overthrow of the kingdom of the ten tribes; 1 Kings 14:16; 15:26, 30; 16:19, &c. &c.

If men be sinners, as the Word of God and our own consciences testify, and if Jesus Christ be the seed of the woman who was to bruise the head of the serpent, Genesis 3:15, then no sin can be so great or so provoking to God as the rejection of this great Deliverer. Ought you not then, ye sons of Jacob, to inquire whether this be not the very sin lying upon you? Certain it is, that ever since you refused to own Jesus as your Saviour, the Lord has refused to own you as His people. You have often, it may be, said in your hearts, 'Wherefore have we fasted and thou seest not: Wherefore have we afflicted our soul, and thou takest no knowledge ?' Isaiah 58:3: 'Wherefore have we made many prayers, and still thou wilt not hear?' Isaiah 1:15. What if you should find that your hands are full of blood, Isaiah 1:15; and that blood the blood not of a fellow-creature, but of the man who is the fellow of the Almighty? Zechariah 13:7. What if you should discover that your King hath already come, just, and having salvation, Zechariah 9:9; but that you would have none of him-that the Messenger of the covenant, the Lord whom ye seek, has come to His temple, Malachi 3:1; but that you despised Him, and counted Him a liar?

It is the testimony of Scripture, that righteousness exalteth a nation, but sin is a reproach to any people; Proverbs 14:34. Is it not remarkable then, that while the fall of Israel has been contemporaneous with their rejection of Jesus, the rise of the Gentiles has run parallel with their faith in His name ? It was a wonderful sight, in the early age of the Church, to behold the gospel of Christ, wherever its power was felt, overturning the temples of the gods, and raising men to the character of holy and devout worshippers of Jehovah. The like effects have ever followed it, wherever it has been received, and just in proportion as it has been received, in truth. We speak it to the praise of Jehovah's grace, that through the knowledge of the Messiah our own country has risen to the rank which she occupies among the nations. It is simply, we believe, because he has here ordained a lamp for His Anointed, Psalm 132:17, that the King of nations, Jeremiah 10. 7, has rendered the name of Britain illustrious, her arms powerful, her arts flourishing, her people intelligent and free. These advantages, however, are as nothing, compared with those which the soul receives. There are many, indeed, among us, who, like those spoken of, Isaiah 48. 1, make mention of the God of Israel, but not in truth or righteousness; and for them, if they repent not, Tophet is ordained of old; Isaiah 30:33. But there are not a few of whom it can be said, 'Blessed is the people that know the joyful sound; they shall walk, O Lord, in the light of thy countenance;' Psalm 89:15. In Scotland, the land of our birth, Messiah has had a seed to serve him for generations past; Psalm 22:30; Isaiah 53:10. This wild and barren land has heard the Redeemer's call, Isaiah 49:1, 'Listen, O isles unto me, and hearken ye people from far. She has heard his voice; and the wilderness and the solitary place has been gladdened by it; and the desert has rejoiced and blossomed like the rose;' Isaiah 35:1. She has received the word of the Witness to the people, the leader and commander to the people, Isaiah 55:4, 11, and the promise has many a time been made good, verses 12, 13, 'Ye shall go out with joy, and be led forth with peace; the mountains and the hills shall break forth before you into singing, and all the trees of the field shall clap their hands. Instead of the thorn shall come up the fir-tree, and instead of the briar shall come up the myrtle-tree: and it shall be to the Lord for a name, for an everlasting sign that shall not be cut off.' The gospel of Jesus Christ, the proclamation of a free salvation through the death of Him who made His soul an offering for sin, Isaiah 53:10, 55:1, has, in innumerable instances, proved itself to be the Word of God, by changing, through the power of His Spirit, the heart of stone into a heart of flesh; and causing men to walk in Jehovah's statutes, and to keep His judgments, and do them; Ezekiel 36:25-27; Isaiah 52:13-15. The power of that mysterious name, The Lord our Righteousness, by the knowledge of which, we trust that Judah shall soon be saved, and Israel dwell safely, Jeremiah 23:6, has been felt in creating peace in the conscience which before was like the troubled sea, Isaiah 58:19-21, and love in the heart which before was at enmity with God and with man.

Ungodly sinners have been taught to fear that great and fearful name, the Lord our God; Deuteronomy 28:58. They have been made holy in their lives and their end has been peace; Psalm 37:37.

Fruits like these are not produced by a false religion. They can only grow in the field which has been sown with the sacred seed of the Divine Word; Psalm 19:7-14. And so it is here. The Scriptures of truth, the Old as well as the New Testament, are highly prized by everyone who believes in Jesus Christ. They are his meditation every day: the books of Moses and the Prophets, no less than the gospels and epistles. The histories of the Old as well as the New Testament furnish him with instruction, reproof, and comfort. The songs of Zion, the psalms of the sweet Singer of Israel, 2 Samuel 23:1, are most precious to every soul among us that seeketh after God. They are milk to our children, and meat to our strong men. They are sung in the tabernacles of the righteous, Psalm 118:15, by the families who call on the name of the Lord. They are sung in the assemblies of the upright, Psalm 111:1; at the meetings of the saints, Psalm 89:7; when they enter into His gates with thanksgiving, and into His courts with praise, Psalm 100:4.

It is impossible that these things could be, were we not worshippers of the God whom your fathers worshipped, and did we not expect to be saved as they were. Men and brethren, it is even so. Our faith is the same as that of Abel, who brought of the firstlings of the flock an offering to God, Genesis 4:4; as that of Enoch, who walked with God, chapter 5. 24; as that of Noah, who found grace in the eyes of the Lord, chapter 6:8, and offered burnt-offerings to Him on the altar which he built, chapter 8:20; as that of Abraham, with whom the covenant was made by sacrifice, chapter 15, and whose faith was counted for righteousness, verse 6; as that of Jacob, who declared himself unworthy of the least of all God's mercies, chapter 32:10; and who, when dying, said, he had waited for the salvation of God, chapter 49:18. These, and all other true worshippers of Jehovah, whose names are recorded in the Old Testament, had respect to the Redeemer who was to come : we have respect to the same Redeemer, now that he has come. It is by the faith of him who was to make reconciliation for iniquity, and to bring in everlasting righteousness, Daniel 9:24, that we read those

Scriptures, which you hold in your hands, with profit and delight. It is through him that we see the glory and understand the meaning of the daily sacrifice and the Passover, of the fast of atonement and the feast of tabernacles, of the year of release and the trumpet of jubilee, of the tabernacle in the wilderness and the temple at Jerusalem, with their sacred furniture and utensils: the candlestick, the altar of burnt-offering, and the show-bread, the holy of holies, the ark of the covenant, the mercy-seat, and the altar of incense. It is in Him whose name is Immanuel, Isaiah 7:14, that we discern the wisdom and the beauty of the laws of Moses; and not only so, but find in them that which gives life and salvation to our souls.

Come, then, O house of Jacob, and let us walk together in the light of the Lord; Isaiah 2:5. Why should you remain any longer in darkness and in sorrow? Century after century have you been looking for Messiah, but have looked in vain. The time of His coming has been often fixed by your learned men, and every time their calculations have failed. Meanwhile successive generations of your race have passed into eternity without knowing the answer to that all-important question, Job 25:4, 'How can man be justified with God, or how can he be clean that is born of a woman?' Why would ye be stricken anymore? Isaiah 1:5. Will it not suffice you, that for eighteen hundred years you have followed the traditions of your fathers, and have found them like the friends of Job in his affliction – miserable comforters? Job 14:2. What avail your Talleth or Tsitsith, to what purpose your Tephillin or Mezuzoth ? May it not truly be said of them, 'the bed is shorter than that a man can stretch himself upon, and the covering narrower than that he can wrap himself in it?' Isaiah 28:20. Would that you would listen to Jehovah's own words, Jeremiah 31:41, &c., 'Behold the days come that I will make a new covenant with the house of Israel, and with the house of Judah; not according to the covenant that I made with their fathers in the day that I took them by the hand to bring them out of the land of Egypt.' Would that you heard the voice of your redeeming God, saying, 'Behold me, behold me. Look unto me and be saved, all the ends of the earth;' Isaiah 65:1; 45:22. Would that the Lord Himself might be pleased to pour out upon you the spirit of grace and supplications promised, Zechariah 12:10;

and then would you be made to look on Him whom you have pierced, and to mourn for Him. Then would your eyes be opened to see the fountain which has been opened for sin and uncleanness, Zechariah 13:1; and which flows from the pierced heart of Him on whom the Lord laid the iniquity of us all; Isaiah 53:6.

Blessed will be the day when Jews and Gentiles together shall submit to Him who is to have dominion from sea to sea, and from the river to the ends of the earth; Psalm 72:8. Then shall be fulfilled to their utmost extent the words of prophecy, 'The wolf shall dwell with the lamb, and the leopard shall lie down with the kid; the sucking child shall play on the hole of the asp, and the weaned child shall put his hand on the cockatrice den. They shall not hurt or destroy in all my holy mountain; for the earth shall be full of the knowledge of the Lord as the waters cover the sea;' Isaiah 11:1-9. Then shall Jerusalem be a crown of glory in the hand of the Lord, and a royal diadem in the hand of your God; Isaiah 62:3. To her light the Gentiles shall come, and kings to the brightness of her rising; Isaiah 60:3. Then shall that song be sung in the land of Judah, and re-echoed from the ends of the earth, 'We have a strong city, salvation will God appoint for walls and bulwarks;' Isaiah 26:1. 'O Lord, I will praise thee; though thou wast angry with me, thine anger is turned away, and thou comfortedst me. Behold, God is my salvation; I will trust and not be afraid; for Jehovah, Jehovah, is my strength and my song; he also is become my salvation;' Isaiah 12.

May the Lord hasten it in His time; Isaiah 60:22.
In name and by appointment of the General Assembly,
ROBERT GORDON, *Moderator.*

Endnotes

INTRODUCTION

1. Sources for the life of Jane Haining include, David McDougall, *Jane Haining, 1897–1944* (Glasgow: Church of Scotland Jewish Mission Committee, 1949); Nicholas Railton, *Jane Haining and the Work of the Scottish Mission with Hungarian Jews, 1932–1945* (Budapest: Church of Scotland Jewish Mission Committee, 2007); Mary Miller, *Jane Haining: A Life of Love and Courage* (Edinburgh: Birlinn, 2015). Among other useful articles one stands out: D. F. Wright, 'Jane Haining' in *Oxford Dictionary of National Biography*.

2. For Grierson of Lag and his harrying of the Covenanters see: Robert Simpson, *Traditions of the Covenanters* (Edinburgh: Gall and Inglis, 1867); J. H. Thomson, Matthew Hutchinson, and David Hay, *The Martyr Graves of Scotland* (Edinburgh: Oliphant, Anderson and Ferrier, n.d.) Alex. Smellie, *Men of the Covenant: the Story of the Scottish Church in the Years of the Persecution* (London: London, A. Melrose, 1904).

3. *Band of Hope Blue Book: Manual of Instruction and Training* (no author, date, place or publisher given). A number of Blue Books are in the Livesey Collection at the University of Central Lancashire, Preston, Lancashire.

CHAPTER 1

1. See 'Scotland' in *The Standard Jewish Encyclopaedia* (London: W. H. Allen, 1959); Chaim Bermant, *Troubled Eden: An Anatomy of British Jewry* (London: Vallentine Mitchell, 1969), p. 54ff.

2. Unfortunately, Donald N. Panther-Yates and Elizabeth Hirschman, *When Scotland was Jewish: DNA Evidence, Archeology, Analysis of Migrations, and Public and Family Records Show Twelfth Century Semitic Roots* (Jefferson, NC: McFarland & Co Inc., 2013), is weak on solid evidence, but strong on chutzpah.

3. Adomnán, *De Locis Sanctis*, chapter 9, 'Concerning the shroud with which the Lord's head was covered when he was buried'.

4. W. C. Dickinson ed., *John Knox's History of the Reformation in Scotland* (Edinburgh: Nelson, 1949), p. 238.

5. See, Jack C. Whytock, *An Educated Clergy: Scottish Theological Education and Training in the Kirk and Secession, 1560–1850* (Milton Keynes: Paternoster, 2007), pp. 475-477; Hew Scott, *Fasti Ecclesiae Scoticanae* (Edinburgh: Oliver and Boyd), vol. 7, p. 386.

6. John Cosgrove, 'Scottish Jewry,' Stephen W. Massil ed., *The Jewish Year Book 5760–5761* (London: Valentine Mitchell, 2000), p. 12f.

7. For a recent evaluations of The Merchant of Venice and Shakespeare's depiction of the character of Shylock see, Steve Frank, '"The Merchant of Venice" Perpetuates Vile Stereotypes of Jews. So why do we still produce it?' in *Washington Post*, 28th July, 2016; David Jay, 'Is it Antisemitic? "Yes": How Jewish Actors and Directors Tackle The Merchant of Venice,' an interview with Tracy-Ann Oberman, in *The Guardian*, 22nd February, 2023.

8. John W. Osborne, 'William Cobbett's Anti-Semitism,' *The Historian*, vol. 47, no. 1 (1984), pp. 86-92.

9. For a brief summary of the depiction of Fagin in movies see Michael Joseph Gross, 'New "Oliver Twist" rejects old stereotype,' *New York Times*, 24 August, 2005. Polanski's Jewish parents Ryszard Mojżesz and Bula Liebling were both incarcerated in Auschwitz, where his mother died. His father survived, changing the family name to Polanski.

10. Chaim Bermant, *Troubled Eden* (London: Valentine Mitchell, 1969), p. 22.

11. Donald Meek, 'The Bible and Social Change in the Nineteenth Century Highlands' in *The Bible in Scottish Life and Literature*, David F. Wright ed. (Edinburgh: St Andrew Press, 1988), p. 180.

12. Alexander Smellie, *Men of the Covenant* (rpt. Edinburgh: Banner of Truth Trust, 1962), p. 15.

13. Thomas M'Crie, *The Story of the Scottish Church* (Glasgow: Free Presbyterian Publications, 1988), p. 70.

14. Andrew Bonar ed., *Letters of Samuel Rutherford* (Edinburgh: Oliphant Anderson and Ferrier, 1891), p. 122-123.

15. James Walker, *The Theology and Theologians of Scotland 1560–1750* (Edinburgh: Knox Press, 1982) p. 92.

16. J. A. Wylie, *Disruption Worthies: A Memorial of 1843* (Edinburgh: T & T Clark, 1881), p. 336.

17. Douglas S. Mack ed., James Hogg, *Memoirs of the Author's Life and Familiar Anecdotes of Sir Walter Scott* (Edinburgh: Scottish Academic Press, 1972), pp. 6-7.

18. See Henry A. Glass, *The Story of the Psalters* (London: Kegan, Paul & Trench, 1888), p. 48.

19. William Knight, *Colloquia Peripatetica* (Edinburgh: David Douglas, 1878), p. 128.

20. W. D. Killen, *The Ecclesiastical History of Ireland* (London: Macmillan & Co., 1875), vol. I, p. 38.

21. James Gilfinnan, *The Sabbath Viewed in the Light of Reason, Revelation and History* (Edinburgh: Andrew Elliot, 1863), pp. 158-160.

22. R. M. M'Cheyne, 'I Love the Lord's Day,' *Memoir and Remains of Robert Murray M'Cheyne*, A. A. Bonar ed. (Dundee: William Middleton, 1852), p. 543.

23. William Knight ed., *Colloquia Peripatetica: Deep-sea Soundings: Being Notes of Conversations by John Duncan* (Edinburgh: Edmonston and Douglas, 1870), p. 125.

24. Alexander Black, 'Statement Submitted to the Committee of the General Assembly on the Conversion of the Jews,' in *The Conversion of the Jews: A Series of Lectures Delivered in Edinburgh by Ministers of the Church of Scotland* (Edinburgh: John Johnstone, 1842), p. vii.

25. John G. Lorimer, 'The Duty of Christians Towards the Jews – Answer to Objections' in *A Course of Lectures on the Jews by Ministers of the Established Church in Glasgow* (Glasgow: Williams Collins, 1839), p. 441.

26. See Appendix 2.

CHAPTER 2

1. Andrew Bonar ed., *Letters of Samuel Rutherford* (Edinburgh: Oliphant Anderson and Ferrier, 1891), p. 59.

2. Samuel McMillan ed., *The Whole Works of the Late Rev'd Thomas Boston of Ettrick* (Edinburgh: George and Robert King, 1848), vol. III, p. 358-371.

3. Ibid., pp. 466-467.

4. Patrick Walker, *Six Saints of the Covenant* (Hodder and Stoughton, 1901), vol. II, p. 94.

5. For Whitefield's ministry and the revival at Cambuslang see D. Macfarlan, *The Revivals of the Eighteenth Century Particularly at Cambuslang* (Edinburgh: John Johnstone, n.d.); Arthur Fawcett, *The Cambuslang Revival* (Edinburgh: Banner of Truth Trust, 1971).

6. I. H. Murray, *The Puritan Hope* (Edinburgh: Banner of Truth Trust, 1971), pp. 48-55; Peter De Jong, *As the Waters Cover the Sea* (Kampem: Kok, 1970), pp. 119-121; David J. Bosch, *Transforming Mission* (Maryknoll: Orbis, 1995), p. 277f.

7. Jonathan Edwards 'A History of the Work of Redemption' in *The Works of Jonathan Edwards* (Banner of Truth Trust, 1974), p. 211.

8. Ibid., pp. 386-387.

9. Edwards, vol. I, p. 607.

10. For Buchanan see Hugh Pearson, *Memoirs of the Life and Writing of the Rev. Claudius Buchanan, D.D.* (Oxford: University Press, 1817).

11. Jonathan Aitken, *John Newton: From Disgrace to Amazing Grace* (London: Continuum, 2007), pp. 260-1.

12. For Thornton, see Standish Meacham, *Henry Thornton of Clapham, 1760–1815* (Harvard: Harvard University Press, 1964).

13. Pearson, p. 110.

14. John Sargent, *Memoir of the Rev. Henry Martyn* (New York: Seeley and Burnside, 1851), p. 369.

15. Pearson, p. 156.

16. Ibid., p. 153.

17. W. T. Gidney, *The History of the London Society for Promoting Christianity Amongst the Jews: 1809–1908* (London: London Society for Promoting Christianity Amongst the Jews, 1908), p. 55.

18. Pearson, p. 358.

19. Gidney, p. 115.

CHAPTER 3

1. J. H. S. Burleigh, *A Church History of Scotland* (Hope Trust, 1983), p. 313.

2. *Edinburgh Christian Instructor*, vol. 10 (April 1815), p. 282f. Cf. W. T. Gidney, *The History of the London Society for Promoting Christianity Amongst the Jews: 1809–1908* (London: London Society for Promoting Christianity Amongst the Jews, 1908), p. 46f.

3. Ridley H. Herschell ed., *Jewish Witnesses that Jesus is the Christ* (Aylott & Jones, 1848), p. 48f.

4. *ECI*, vol. 15 (Sept., 1817), p. 202f; cf. vol. 16, (March 1818), p. 198; vol. 16, (April 1818), p. 275.

5. *ECI*, vol. 1 (Nov. 1810), p. 285; *Home and Foreign Missionary Record of the Church of Scotland*, no. 1 (July 1839), p. 12.

6. *Scottish Missionary Review* (March 1820), p. 77.

7. David Brown, *Life of the Late John Duncan* (Edinburgh: Edmonston and Douglas, 1872), p. 232f.

8. Andrew A. Bonar and Robert M. M'Cheyne, *Narrative of a Mission of Inquiry to the Jews from the Church of Scotland in 1839* (Edinburgh: William Whyte, 1842, second edition), p. 307. After the formation of the Jewish Committee in 1838, Cerf continued to work but under the direction of the Glasgow sub-committee. The General Committee had limited confidence in him, especially his ability to handle finance. He incurred debts which he attributed partly to the costs of a recent illness and partly to the support he had disbursed to needy enquirers. The committee cleared his debts, forbidding him to apply for assistance on behalf of 'any stranger Jews'. The committee considered that the opportunities for work in Glasgow and Edinburgh 'were very circumscribed' and decided to send Cerf to Posen in Germany, but in 1841 he was still in Scotland. He was granted travel expenses to go abroad 'for his health' and to 'avail himself of every opportunity of Christian usefulness amongst his brethren of the Seed of Abraham'. Whilst abroad Cerf requested more money from the Committee. The Glasgow sub-committee was sympathetic, but the General Committee refused. After a joint meeting to resolve the matter all reference to Cerf ceases, until 26th August, 1844, when we read of a donation of £20 sent for him from Dr John Duncan. Duncan's generosity was characteristic of the man and the product of personal acquaintance with Cerf when Duncan had been a member of the Glasgow sub-committee. Cf. Minute book 1 of the Committee for the Conversion of the Jews (NLS Dep. 298/249), pp. 15; 64; 111-2; 115; 148; 292.

9. ECI, vol. 17 (July 1818), p. 56.

10. John J. Lorimer, 'Preliminary Essay' in Robert Wodrow, *The Past History and Future Destiny of Israel* (Blackie and Son, 1844), p. v.

11. Gavin Carlyle, *Mighty in the Scriptures: A Memoir of Adolph Saphir DD*. (John F Shaw, 1894) p. 2.; John Duncan, 'Assembly Address' in Sinclair ed., *Rich Gleanings from Rabbi Duncan* (Chas. J. Thynne & Jarvis, 1925) p. 371; David Brown, *The Life of Rabbi Duncan* (Free Presbyterian Publications, 1986) p. 295 fn.2; Gavin Carlyle, *Life and Work of Rev. William Wingate: Missionary to the Jews* (R. L. Alan, c.1900), p. 7.

12. 'Report of the Jew's Committee' in *HMFR* (1841), p. 348

13. Brown, p. 296.

14. Printed Papers of the General Assembly of the Church of Scotland, National Archives of Scotland, CH 1/2 174.

15. See Christiane Dithmar, *Zinzendorfs nonkonformistische Haltung zum Judentum*, dissertation for University of Jewish Studies Heidelberg, 2000; Peter Vogt, 'Count Zinzendorf's Encounter with Judaism and the Jews. A Fictitious Dialogue from 1739,' *Journal of Moravian History*, no. 6 (2009), pp. 101-19.

16. Kenneth Moody Stuart, *Alexander Moody Stuart DD: A Memoir* (Hodder and Stoughton, 1900), p. 145. Mrs Smith's name recurs in lists of subscriptions as a generous supporter of the work, where it is recorded that she subscribed £52.10.0 towards the expenses of the Deputation to Palestine and collected further funds to the amount of £14.3.0. See e.g. *HFMR* No. 3. September, 1838, p. 47, and No.5 November 1, 1839, p. 80.

17. The Principal Acts of the General Assembly of the Church of Scotland, 26th May 1838.

CHAPTER 4

1. 'It is not often that the world has seen men like Thomas Chalmers, nor can the world afford to forget them; or in its most careless mood, be willing to. Probably the time is coming when it will be more apparent than it is now to everyone, that here, intrinsically, was the chief Scottish man of his time – a man possessed of such massive geniality of intellect as belonged to no other man. What a grand simplicity, broad humour, blent so kindly with enthusiasm, ardour and blazing thought – a man of such noble valour, strength and piety – above all things, of such perfect veracity, I have not met with in these times. Honour to him, honour belongs to him, and to the essential work he did – an everlasting continuance among the possessions of this world.' Letter from Thomas Carlyle to William Hanna, Chalmers' son-in-law and biographer, cited by Norman L. Walker, *Chapters from the History of the Free Church of Scotland* (Edinburgh London: Oliphant, Anderson & Ferrier, 1895), pp. 20-21.

2. W. Y. Fullerton, *Charles Haddon Spurgeon: A Biography* (London: Williams and Norgate, 1920), p. 281.

3. John Brown, *Horae Subsecivae: Rab and his Friends and Other Papers* (Edinburgh: David Douglas, 1884), p. 115.

4. See Don Chambers, 'Prelude to the Last Things: The Church of Scotland's Mission to the Jews,' *Records of the Scottish Church History Society* XIX, no. 1 (1975); John Roxborogh, *Thomas Chalmers: Enthusiast for Mission* (Rutherford House, 1999); Stuart Piggin and John Roxborogh, *The St. Andrews Seven* (Edinburgh: Banner of Truth Trust, 1985).

5. William Hanna, *Memoirs of Thomas Chalmers D.D. LL.D.* (Edinburgh: Thomas Constable & Co, 1854), vol. 1, p. 479.

6. Ibid.

7. Thomas Chalmers, *Lectures on the Epistle to the Romans* (London: Thomas Constable & Co, 1854) vol. 2, p. 373.

8. Ibid., p. 370.

9. Thomas Chalmers, 'Sabbath Scripture Readings,' W. Hanna ed., *Posthumous Works of the Rev. Thomas Chalmers,* vol. IV (Edinburgh: Sutherland and Knox, 1858), p. 210.

10. Chalmers Papers in New College Library, CHA 6.25.12.

11. M'Cheyne's Papers in New College Library, Macch 1.9.

12. Thomas Chalmers, 'Lecture LXXXV' in *Lectures on the Epistle to the Romans* (London: Thomas Constable & Co, 1854), vol. 2, p. 377.

Chapter 5

1. Keith's *Evidence of the Truth of the Christian Religion Derived from the Literal Fulfilment of Prophecy; Particularly as Illustrated by the History of the Jews, and by the Discoveries of Recent Travellers* was published in Edinburgh by William Whyte and Co. in 1838; ten years later it had passed through thirty-six editions.

2. Alexander Keith, *Evidence of the Truth of the Christian Religion Derived from the Literal Fulfilment of Prophecy; Particularly as Illustrated by the History of the Jews, and by the Discoveries of Recent Travellers* (Edinburgh: William Whyte and Co. 1848, 36th ed.), p. 8.

3. Cf. John Calvin, *The Epistle of Paul the Apostle to the Romans* in, trans. Ross MacKenzie, *Calvin's Commentaries*, David W. Torrance ed. and Thomas F. Torrance (Edinburgh: St. Andrew Press, 1961), p. 4.

4. Keith, *Evidence*, p. 14.

5. Andrew A. Bonar, Robert M. M'Cheyne, *A Narrative of a Mission of Enquiry to the Jews from the Church of Scotland in 1839* (Edinburgh: William Oliphant, 1878 [3rd edition]), pp. 192-193. M'Cheyne appears to have understood *grammatical* in a manner similar to Karl A. G. Keil, as *grammatico-historical* which meant not so much 'the sense required by the laws of grammar' as, 'literal'; it was the 'simple, direct, plain, ordinary and literal sense of the phrases, clauses and sentences.' Cf. Walter C. Kaiser, Jnr., *Towards an Exegetical Theology* (Grand Rapids: Baker, 1981), pp. 87-88.

6. Jonathan Anderson, Alexander Somerville, and Robert Buchanan in *A Course of Lectures on the Jews by the Ministers of the Established Church in Glasgow* (Glasgow: William Collins, 1839), p. 373.

7. Ibid., p. 374. Emphasis mine.

8. *Edinburgh Christian Instructor*, no. CCXIII, April 1828, vol. XXVIII, no. IV, p. 292.

9. Ibid., p. 483.

10. Ibid., p. 604.

11. Andrew A. Bonar, 'The Hope of the Lord's Return' in *Sheaves After Harvest* (Glasgow: Pickering and Inglis, 1927), p. 44

12. William Hanna, *Memoirs of Thomas Chalmers D.D. LL.D.* (Edinburgh: Thomas Constable & Co, 1854), vol. 2, p. 172.

13. Ibid., pp. 173-4.

14. Mrs Oliphant, *The Life of Edward Irving* (London: Hurst and Blackett, 1862), vol. II, p. 23.

15. In view of M'Cheyne's early death and the lack of direct reference to his millennial views, either from his own pen or from those of his contemporaries, it is impossible to be dogmatic with regard to his eschatological views. It is significant, however, that Bonar, M'Cheyne's close friend and biographer, does not claim him as a premillennial ally, though he had no hesitation in asserting that Chalmers was premillennial.

16. A. Bonar, *Diary* (24 May 1829).

17. A. Bonar, *Sheaves After Harvest* (London: Pickering and Inglis, n.d), pp. 43-44.

18. John James Bonar, 'Note on Dr Bonar's Prophetical Views' in *Horatius Bonar D.D.: A Memorial* (London: James Nisbet & Co., 1889), p. 95.

19. Thomas Chalmers, *Posthumous Works*, vol. iii. p. 51, p. 69.

20. Bonar, *Sheaves*, p. 44.

21. Patrick Fairburn, *The Interpretation of Prophecy* (reprint London: Banner of Truth Trust, 1993), p. 286.

22. *The Free Church Magazine*, June to November, 1845. David Brown's magazine articles were published in book form the following year as *Christ's Second Coming: Will it be Pre-millennial* (Edinburgh: John Johnstone, 1846).

23. Horatius Bonar, *Prophetical Landmarks* (London: James Nisbet, 1847), p. v.

24. Andrew Bonar, *Redemption Drawing Nigh: A Defence of the Premillennial Advent* (London: James Nisbet, 1847), p. vii.

25. Ibid., p. 275.

26. Bonar warns of a utilitarian or pragmatic approach to a text by which its interpretation is influenced through a perception of what might be deemed the most edifying understanding; the comparative value of a spiritual or literal reading is irrelevant.

27. Cited by John James Bonar, op. cit., p. 102.

28. Bonar, H., *Prophetical Landmarks*, p. 280.

29. Ibid., p. 288.

30. Ibid., p. 297.

31. Ibid., p. 302.

32. Ibid., p. 307.

33. Ibid., p. 309-310.

34. Ibid., p. 310. Emphasis original.

35. Ibid., p. 310. Emphasis mine.

36. Ibid., pp. 311-313.

37. E.g. Louis Berkhof, *Systematic Theology* (London: Banner of Truth Trust, 1958), pp. 712-713.

38. Bonar, H., p. 389.

39. Bonar, A., p. 181.

40. Bonar, H., p. 388 Cf. RD, p. 186.

41. Bonar, A., p. 157.

42. Cf. I. H. Murray, *The Puritan Hope* (Edinburgh: Banner of Truth Trust, 1971), pp. 185-206.

43. Ibid., p. 205

44. Ibid., op. cit., p. 205, but see David B. Barrett, *World Christian Encyclopaedia* (Oxford: Oxford University Press, 1982), p. 3; Patrick Johnstone and Jason Mandryk, *Operation World* (Carlisle: Paternoster Lifestyle, 2001), p. 4.

45. David Brown, *Christ's Second Coming: Will it be Premillennial?* (Edinburgh: John Johnstone, 1846); David Brown, *The Restoration of the Jews* (Edinburgh: A. Strahan, 1861).

46. John Macleod, *Scottish Theology in Relation to Church History since the Reformation* (Edinburgh: Knox Press, 1974), p. 279.

47. In 1839, Arnold had published *Two Sermons on the Interpretation of Prophecy* which expounded the view that Israel had been superseded by the Church. For Anglican supercessionism, the forerunner of modern 'replacement theology', see Frances Knight, 'The Bishops and the Jews,' Diana Wood ed., *Studies in Church History vol. 29: Christianity and Judaism* (Oxford: Blackwell Publishing, for The Ecclesiastical History Society, 1992), p. 390.

48. David Brown, *The Restoration of the Jews* (Edinburgh: A. Strahan, 1861), p. 70. Henceforth RJ.

49. Ibid., p. 106.

50. Ibid., p. 117.

51. Ibid., p. 122.

52. Ibid., p. 147. Emphasis mine.

53. Brown in Jamieson, Fausset and Brown, *The Holy Bible and an Original and Copious Critical and Explanatory Commentary* (Glasgow: William Collins, 1863) vol. III., p. 119 ad. loc. (emphasis mine).

54. William Garden Blaikie, *David Brown* (Hodder and Stoughton, 1898), p. 354 (emphasis mine).

55. David Brown, *The Life of the Late John Duncan* (Edinburgh: Edmonston and Douglas, 1872), *second edition, revised*, p. 416.

56. Ibid., p. 489.

57. W. T. Gidney, *The History of the London Society for Promoting Christianity Amongst the Jews: 1809–1908* (London: London Society for Promoting Christianity Amongst the Jews, 1908), p. 35.

58. Summary of Printed Overtures in Printed Papers of Assembly. NAS CH 1/2 174.

59. Bonar, *Memoir*, p. 444.

60. John G. Lorimer, 'Immediate Duties of the Christian Church in Relation to Israel: Answers to Objections' in *A Course of Lectures on the Jews by Ministers of the Established Church in Glasgow* (Glasgow: William Collins, 1839), p. 409.

61. *The Conversion of the Jews: A Series of Lectures Delivered in Edinburgh by Ministers of the Church of Scotland* (Edinburgh: John Johnstone, 1842), p. vi.

62. Andrew A. Bonar, 'The First Captivity and Restoration of the Jews Viewed in Reference to the Coming of Messiah' in *The Conversion of the Jews*, p. 68.

63. Alexander Black, 'Statement Submitted to the Committee of the General Assembly on the Conversion of the Jews' in *The Conversion of the Jews*, p. xv.

64. John Wilson, *The Lands of the Bible* (Edinburgh: William Whyte, 1847), vol. 2, p. 292

65. Ibid., vol. 1. p. x.

66. Ibid., vol. 1. p. 2.

67. Ibid., vol. 2. p. 630.

CHAPTER 6

1. MacGill *et. al.*, *A Course of Lectures on the Jews: By Ministers of the Established Church* (Glasgow: William Collins, 1839), p. 447.

2. *The Conversion of the Jews: A Series of Lectures Delivered in Edinburgh by Ministers of the Church of Scotland* (Edinburgh: John Johnstone, 1842), p. 2

3. MacGill *et. al.*, p. 463.

4. Ibid., pp. 361-362.

CHAPTER 7

1. David McDougall, *In Search of Israel* (Edinburgh: Thomas Nelson, 1941), p. 25.

2. *Minute Book 1 of the Committee for the Conversion of the Jews* (NLS Dep. 298/249), p. 14.

3. MB1., p. 50; *Home and Foreign Missionary Record, 1840*, p. 348.

4. *HMFR* Advertising Sheet i–iii, vol. 1 (1839–1841).

5. Ian R. MacDonald, *Glasgow's Gaelic Churches* (Edinburgh: The Knox Press, 1995), p. 4. For Aberdeen see Ian R. MacDonald, *Aberdeen and the Highland Church* (Edinburgh: St Andrew Press, 2000), pp. 2f.

6. *The Inverness Journal*, 5th March, 1830. The Gaelic Church was established in the aftermath of the 1715 Jacobite Rebellion, reputedly for loyal Gaelic-speaking Government troops who could not attend worship at the Old High Church because they could not understand English. In 1958, the church became Greyfriars Free Church of Scotland, and when a new church building was established in a new housing area in 1994 the old building was sold and is now a large secondhand book shop. The author was minister of the congregation between 2002 and 2008.

7. *Inverness Courier*, 3rd March, 1830.

8. See, *HMFR* 1841, Highlands, p. 98; Skye, pp. 148f, Uists, Harris, Barra, Uig-Lewis pp. 123, 208f.

9. Donald MacDonald, *Lewis: A History of the Island* (Edinburgh: Gordon Wright Publishing, 1978), p. 142.

10. John Macleod, *By-paths of Highland Church History* (Edinburgh: Knox Press, 1965), p. 43.

11. Thomas Brown, *Annals of the Disruption* (Edinburgh: Macniven and Wallace, 1884), p. 509.

12. Kenneth Moody Stuart, *Alexander Moody Stuart DD: A Memoir* (London: Hodder and Stoughton, 1900), p. 146.

13. See Rowland S. Ward, *The Smith of Dunesk Mission: Forerunner of the Australian Inland Mission* (Melbourne: New Melbourne Press, 2014).

14. W. P. Livingstone, *A Galilee Doctor : Being a Sketch of the Career of Dr D. W. Torrance of Tiberias* (London: Hodder and Stoughton, n.d.), p. 9.

15. Elizabeth Grant Smith, *Memoirs of a Highland lady; the Autobiography of Elizabeth Grant of Rothiemurchus, Afterwards Mrs Smith of Baltiboys, 1797–1830* (London: J. Murray, 1911), p. 253. Elizabeth Grant ameliorated her rather acerbic earlier comments in a further description: 'Lady Huntly was an excellent woman ; she brought him a large fortune, a clear business head, good temper, and high principles. She soon set straight all that she had found crooked. She was not handsome, though she had a good figure, a good skin, and beautiful hands – the Brodie face is short and broad ; but she suited him, every one liked her, and she always liked me, so the fortnight I passed with her was very agreeable.' Ibid., p. 381.

16. See Alexander Moody Stuart, *Life and Letters of Elisabeth Last Duchess of Gordon* (London: James Nisbet and Co. 1866), p. 298.

17. Ibid., pp. 298-301

18. Gavin Carlyle, *Life and Work of the Rev. William Wingate Missionary to the Jews* (Glasgow: R. L. Allan & Son, n.d.), p. 141.

19. See, for example, *HMFR*, No.18 (Dec. 1st 1840), p. 259.

20. *HMFR*, No.27 (Sept 1st 1840) p. 377.

21. MB1, p. 30.

22. John Wilson, *Memoir of Mrs Wilson of Bombay* (Edinburgh, 1838), p. 515.

23. See HFMR (1841), p. 143, pp. 204f.

24. *Children's Missionary Record*, No. 6 (June 1845), p. 81.

25. *CMR* (January 1846), p. 4.

26. *CMR* (July 1845), p. 115.

27. *CMR* (October 1847), p. 206.

28. *CMR* (June 1845), p. 81.

29. William Hanna, *Memoirs of Thomas Chalmers*, vol. 1 (Edinburgh: Thomas Constable, 1854), p. 447

Chapter 8

1. Specimens of the questionnaires can be seen in the collection of the National Library of Scotland, Acquisition 11820: *Letters, papers and questionnaires, 1838–40, relating to the General Assembly of the Church of Scotland's Committee on the Conversion of the Jews.*

2. For correspondence on possible locations see MB1, p. 50; HFMR February 1839 to July 1841.

3. See e.g. numerous references in *Home and Foreign Missionary Record for the Church of Scotland*, vol. 8 (1853).

4. J. Rees, *List of Tombs of Europeans in the Nigiri District* (Ootacamund: Lawrence Asylum Press, 1893), p. 18.

5. MB1, p. 9.

6. For discussions of and correspondence relating to Aden see: *HFMR* (1 April, 1840); letter from John Wilson, *HMFR* (1 April, 1840), and letter from Alexander Duff, *HFMR* (1 May, 1841).

7. See Robert Sinker, *Memorials of the Hon. Ion Keith-Falconer* (Cambridge: Deighton, Bell, 1890).

8. MB1, p. 76.

9. For brief biographies of the ministers see entries in Hew Scott, *Fasti Ecclesiae Scoticanae* (Edinburgh: Oliver and Boyd, 1915–1928). For the committee's discussions see MB1, pp. 3, 4, 6.

10. Alexander Moody Stuart, *John Duncan LL.D.,* James L. Wylie ed., *Disruption Worthies* (Edinburgh: Thomas C. Jack, 1881), p. 236.

11. See, e.g. Lionel Gossman, *Thomas Annan of Glasgow: Pioneer of the Documentary Photograph* (Cambridge: Open Book Publishers, 2015), pp. 1-12; Mike Weaver ed., *British Photography in the Nineteenth Century: The Fine Art Tradition* (Cambridge: Cambridge University Press, 1989), p. 17; Charles Sinclair Minto, *Thomas Keith, 1827–1895, Surgeon and Photographer: The Hurd Bequest of Photographic Paper Negatives* (Edinburgh: Libraries and Museums Committee, 1972).

12. For M'Cheyne see: *Fasti*, 5.340; Andrew A. Bonar, *Memoir and Remains of Robert Murray M'Cheyne* (Dundee: William Middleton, 1852); Alexander Smellie, *Robert Murray McCheyne* (London: National Council of Evangelical Free Church, 1913); L. J. Van Valen, *Constrained by Love* (Tain: Christian Focus, 2003) and David Victor Yeaworth, *Robert Murray McCheyne (1813–1843): A Study of an Early Nineteenth Century Scottish Evangelical* (unpublished PhD thesis, University of Edinburgh, 1957). Ian Hamilton in DSCHT.

13. William Garden Blaikie, *The Preachers of Scotland* (Edinburgh: Banner of Truth Trust, 2001), p. 295.

14. Murdoch Campbell, *Diary of Jessie Thain: Friend of Robert Murray McCheyne* (private publication, 1955).

15. Bonar, *Memoir*, p. 5.

16. Thomas Guthrie, *Autobiography of Thomas Guthrie DD and Memoir by his Sons* (London: Daldy, Ibister, & Co., 1874), p. 174.

17. Bonar, *Narrative*, pp. 301-302, 461.

18. Gavin Carlyle, *Mighty in the Scriptures: A Memoir of Adolph Saphir D.D.* (John F. Shaw and Co., 1894), p. 3.

19. Andrew A. Bonar, *Memoir and Remains of Robert Murray M'Cheyne* (James Nisbet, 1844,) p. 13, see also pp. 17, 18.

20. NCL MACCH 2.1.19 M'Cheyne to J. M. Nairne of Collace inviting him, prior to Andrew Bonar's settlement, to consider becoming their minister.

21. Bonar, *Memoir*, pp. 17-18, 41.

22. MCL, MACCH 2.1.63. Alex. Flemming to M'Cheyne, n.d.

23. MACCH 2.1.67. St Peter's Kirk Session to M'Cheyne; the letter carries 25 signatures.

24. For Bonar's interest in the Jewish people see: Robert E. Palmer, *Andrew A. Bonar, 1810–1892: A Study of his Life Work and Religious Thought* (PhD thesis, New College, Edinburgh 1955).

25. Marjory Bonar ed., *Andrew A. Bonar, D.D., Diary and Letters* (London: Hodder and Stoughton, 1894), p. 7.

26. Bonar, *Diary and Letters*, pp. 54, 65.

27. Bonar to Alexander Sommerville: 11th December 1837 in Majorie Bonar ed., *Reminiscences of Andrew A. Bonar* (London: Hodder and Stoughton, 1895), p. 172.

28. Bonar, *Diary and Letters*, p. 334.

29. NCL MACCH 2.4.1 Somerville to M'Cheyne.

30. MACCH 2.1.64, Bonar to M'Cheyne.

31. MACCH 2.1.65, Grierson to M'Cheyne.

32. Bonar, *Diary and Letters*, p. 77.

33. Ibid., p. 78.

34. D. P. Thompson, *On the Slopes of the Sidlaws: On Some of the Ministers of the District* (Crieff: The Munro Press, 1953), p. 6.

CHAPTER 9

1. MACCH 1.9, M'Cheyne's small Black De La Rue leatherette note-book (approx. 2x4 inches), with a holder for a thin pencil, containing drawings and notes, addresses, and lists of names, items, etc.

2. MACCH 2.1.72. Adam M'Cheyne to R.M.M.

3. MACCH 1.11.

4. MACCH 1.4. M'Cheyne to parents, 9 April 1839.

5. Ibid.

6. MACCH 1.8. p. 1.

7. John Duncan was also inclined to steer clear of foods 'strangled and of blood'. David Brown recalls how hare-soup, enriched with the blood, was once served up for dinner, but Duncan would not taste it, quoting Acts xv. 20. When told it was excellent and pressed to take some, he refused, saying if he ate it his conscience would be violated. Brown recalled how Duncan 'retained this prejudice to his dying day.' John Brown, *Life of the late John Duncan* (Edinburgh: Edmonston and Douglas, 1872), p. 264. Moody Stuart adds that the experience disconcerted Duncan and depressed his spirits, which were only lifted after he read Isaiah 65:4, about those who 'eat swine's flesh, and broth of abominable things is in their vessels'. Thus cheered up, he remained in high spirits 'discussing poetry and all the poets'. Alexander Moody Stuart, *Recollections of the Late of John Duncan* (Edinburgh: Edmonston and Douglas, 1872), p. 122.

8. MACCH 1.8, p. 2.

9. Ibid., p. 2

10. Ibid., p. 3.

11. For Nisbet see: John A. Wallace, *Lessons from the Life of the Late James Nisbet, Publisher, London, a Study for Young Men* (Johnston and Hunter, 1867); William Arnot, *Life of James Hamilton* (James Nisbet & Co, 1870), pp. 431, 284, 320, 330, 332, 415; Philip A. H. Brown, *London Publishers and Printers, c.1800–1870* (London: British Library, 1982); ONBD; *Blackwell Dictionary of Evangelical Biography*.

12. For Regent Square National Scotch Church see William Arnot, *Life of James Hamilton* (London: James Nisbet & Co, 1870); John Hair, *Regent Square: Eighty Years of a London Congregation* (London: James Nisbet, 1898) and George G. Cameron, *The Scots Kirk in London* (Oxford: Beckett Publications, 1979).

13. Bonar, *Memoirs and Remains*, p. 27.

14. MACCH 1.4. The letter is handwritten, of course, and as the expression 'ignorant clowns' sounded to me very unlike M'Cheyne, I puzzled over it for days before concluding it did in fact say what I took it to say.

15. Ibid.

16. MACCH 1.8. For Baptist Noel see D. W. Bebbington, Donald M. Lewis ed., *Dictionary of Evangelical Biography* (Oxford: Blackwell Publishing, 1995).

17. Ibid.

18. Ibid.

19. Ibid.

20. Ibid.

21. See Anon, *The Correspondence Between Dr Chalmers and the Earl of Aberdeen in the years 1839 and 1840* (Edinburgh: David Douglas, 1893).

22. MACCH 1.8.

CHAPTER 10

1. MACCH 1.8, 12 April, 1839.

2. Bonar and M'Cheyne, *Narrative*, p. 4

3. Ibid., p. 32.

4. Ibid., p. 7f.

5. MACCH Notebook, April 14th, 1839.

6. *Narrative*, pp. 13-15.

7. Ibid., pp. 14-15.

8. Ibid., p. 31.

9. Ibid., pp. 20-32.

10. Ibid., pp. 36-37.

11. For David Roberts see James Ballantine, *The Life of David Roberts RA: Complied from his Journals* (Edinburgh: Adam and Charles Black, 1866).

12. The most accessible source of British Foreign Office papers relative to the establishment of the Jerusalem Consulate is the selection published by Albert M. Hyamson, *The British Consulate in Jerusalem in Relation to the Jews of Palestine, 1838–1914* (London: Jewish Historical Society, 1939–1942), pp. 19-24.

13. For a superb account of post-Grand Tour travel in the Levant, see Naomi Shepherd, *The Zealous Intruders: The Western Rediscovery of Palestine* (San Francisco: Harper and Row, 1987).

14. W. T. Gidney, *The History of the London Society for Promoting Christianity amongst the Jews, from 1809 to 1908* (London: London Society for Promoting Christianity amongst the Jews, 1908), pp. 119-121.

15. For a modern appraisal of Mehmed Ali see, Khaled Fahmy, *All the Pasha's Men: Mehmed Ali, his Army and the Making of Modern Egypt* (Cambridge: Cambridge University Press, 1997).

CHAPTER 11

1. *Narrative*, p. 50.

2. Edward Robinson, *Biblical Researches in Palestine* (London: John Murray, 1841), pp. 51-52.

3. *Narrative*, p. 252.

4. Ibid., p. 51.

5. Malcolm Shifrin, 'The Victorian Turkish Bath' in *The Gilded Lily: The Quarterly Publication of The Ladies' Tea Guild* (Summer 2002).

6. *Narrative*, pp. 75-76.

7. Ibid., p. 78. Maybe to avoid causing undue alarm, M'Cheyne's letters of 27 June and 5 July, 1839 to the Jewish Committee do not mention Black's accident, although it did allude to his fatigue, which he attributed largely to the climate.

8. *HFMR* 2 Sept. 1839, M'Cheyne's letter, p. 33.

9. *Memoirs*, p. 92.

10. *Memoirs*, p. 94.

11. *Narrative*, p. 125. Edward Robinson wrote: 'The feelings of a Christian traveller on approaching Jerusalem, can be better conceived than described. Mine were strongly excited. ... From the earliest childhood, I had read and studied the localities of this sacred spot; now I beheld them with my own eyes'. Robinson, op. cit. vol. I, p. 326.

12. Albert. M. Hyamson, *The British Consulate in Jerusalem in Relation to the Jews of Palestine, 1838–1914* (London: Edward Goldston, for the Jewish Historical Society of England, 1939), p. 2.

13. *Narrative*, p. 127.

14. Ibid., p. 129; *Memoirs*, p. 96.

15. 'Two teens to face charges for vandalizing Christian cemetery in Jerusalem' in *Times of Israel*, 16th January 2023.

16. *Narrative*, p. 130; *HMFR* (2 Sept, 1839), p. 34.

17. William T. Young letter to Viscount Palmerston, Jerusalem, 25th May, 1839, in Hyamson, op. cit., p. 7.

18. Lewis Loewe, *Diaries of Sir Moses and Lady Montefiore* (London: Jewish Historical Society of England, 1983), p. 179ff.

19. *HMFR*, M'Cheyne letter 2 Sept., 1839.

20. See Jobani, Yuval and Nahshon Perez, 'Introduction' in *Governing the Sacred: Political Toleration in Five Contested Sacred Sites* (New York, 2020; online edn, Oxford Academic, 21 May 2020), https://doi.org/10.1093/oso/97801909 32381.003.0001, accessed 19 Oct. 2023.

21. R. A. Stewart Macalister, 'The Garden Tomb' in *Palestine Exploration Fund: Quarterly statement* (1907), p. 229.

22. See Dan Bahat, 'Does the Holy Sepulchre Church Mark the Burial of Jesus?' in Biblical Archeology Review, May/June 1986.

23. *HMFR*, M'Cheyne letter, 2 September, 1839.

24. *Narrative*, p. 183.

25. Ibid., p. 192

26. Ibid., pp. 196-7.

CHAPTER 12

1. *Narrative*, p. 197.

2. John Wilson, *The Lands of the Bible* (Edinburgh: William White & Co., 1847), vol.II, p. 56f.

3. The Earl Marischal was the hereditary office of the bodyguard of the kings of Scotland and custodian of the Royal Regalia of Scotland. The title was forfeited in 1715 due to George Keith the 10th Earl's involvement in the Jacobite rebellion of that year.

4. Loewe, *Diaries*, p. 190.

5. *Narrative*, p. 232 The tarry taste they complained about suggests that the wine had been infused with Aleppo pine resin, as in a Greek *Retsina*.

6. Ibid., p. 238.

7. Ibid., p. 249.

8. MACCH 1.8, p. 7.

9. *Narrative*, p. 267.

10. Ibid., p. 284. Some weeks earlier the Tzfat community had been warned by Montefiore's men that the Scottish ministers were bent on making them Christians.

11. Ibid., pp. 312-314.

12. Ibid., p. 320; Loewe, *Diaries*, p. 197.

13. Ibid., p. 322.

14. For Cohen see Gidney, *The History of the London Society*, p. 173ff.

15. For Schauffler, see William G. Schaufler, *Autobiography of William G. Schaufler* (New York: Anson D. F. Randolf & Co, 1887).

16. *Narrative*, pp. 356-7.

17. Ibid., p. 351; Gidney, *The History of the London Society*, p. 177.

18. Ibid., pp. 412-418. For the Chabad movement see *Encyclopaedia Judaica*.

19. Ibid., p. 471.

20. Ibid., p. 438.

21. Ibid., p. 446.

22. Ibid., p. 461.

23. Ibid., p. 494.

24. For Johann August Wilhelm Neander as a Jewish Christian see Gidney's appreciation reprinted in Bernstein, *Jewish Witnesses*, p. 389ff.

25. For Moritz see Gidney, *The History of the London Society*, p. 168 and Berstein, *Jewish Witnesses*, p. 381f.

26. *Narrative*, p. 520.

ENDNOTES

Chapter 13

1. *Narrative*, p. 518.
2. See *Presbyterian Review* xi (October 1838), pp. 264-9; Stewart J. Brown, *Thomas Chalmers and the Godly Commonwealth* (OUP, 1982), pp. 324f.
3. MB1 (NLS Dep. 298/249), p. 12.
4. Islay Burns, *Memoir of the Rev. Wm. C. Burns, M.A., Missionary to China from the English Presbyterian Church* (London: James Nisbet, 1870), p. 98.
5. *Memoir*, p. 109.
6. The Corn Laws guaranteed farmers a price for their wheat and were thereby inflationary, putting up the price of bread and creating hardship and poverty. The meeting at which M'Cheyne spoke was reported by *The Dundee, Perth and Cupar Advertiser*, and is cited in, J. Harrison Hudson, Thomas W. Jarvie, and Jock Stein, *Let the Fire Burn: A Study of R. M. McCheyne, Robert Annan, and Mary Slessor* (Dundee: Handsel Publications, 1978), p. 8.
7. Ibid., p. 114.
8. *The Dundee Advertiser*, cited by *Perthshire Courier* – Thursday 29 August 1839.
9. John Kennedy, *The 'Apostle of the North.' The Life and Labours of the Rev. Dr M'Donald* (London: T. Nelson and Sons, 1866), p. 226.
10. *Dundee and Angus Advertiser*, 16 August, 1839.
11. Kennedy, pp. 227, 228
12. Ibid., p. 228
13. Burns, p. 104
14. Kennedy, p. 229.
15. Burns, pp. 123-4.
16. 'Evidence on Revivals', in *Memoir*, p. 545.
17. Kennedy, p. 229.
18. Ibid., p. 232.
19. Burns, p. 121.
20. Arnot, op. cit., pp. 238-239.
21. Horatius Bonar, *Life of Rev. John Milne of Perth* (London: James Nisbet, 1869), p. 52.
22. Burns, p. 62.
23. Ibid., p. 128.
24. Burns, p. 120.
25. See Burns, pp. 489-497.
26. Burns, p. 496.
27. Burns, p. 496.
28. Burns, p. 134.

343

29. Thomas Hamilton, *History of the Irish Presbyterian Church* (Edinburgh: T & T Clark, n.d.), p. 169.

Chapter 14

1. Gavin Carlyle, *Mighty in the Scriptures: A Memoir of Adolph Saphir D.D.* (John Shaw and Company, 1894), p. 4; Appendix A, pp. 430-431.

2. The modern name Budapest did not come into use until after the construction of the Széchenyi Chain Bridge across the Danube, linking the twin cities of Buda and Pesth. See: 'Szechenyi's Role from the Idea to the Passing of the Bridge Act,' Gall & Hollo eds., *The Széchenyi Chain Bridge and Adam Clark* (City Hall, 1999), p. 12ff.; Sandor P. Vac, 'William Tierney Clark and the Buda-Pesth Chain Bridge' in *Proceedings of the Institution of Civil Engineers – Engineering History and Heritage* (2011, 164:2), pp. 109-122.

3. Carlyle, p. 430.

4. Andrew Wheatcroft, *The Habsburgs* (Penguin, 1996), p. 251.

5. For Maria Dorothea see Georg Bauhofer, *The History of the Protestant Church of Hungary From the Beginning of the Reformation to 1850* (James Nisbet & Co, 1854), p. xxx; Anne Marie Kool, *God Moves In A Mysterious Way* (Zoetermeer: Boekcentrum, 1993), pp. 97-101.

6. Carlyle, p. 6.

7. Brown, *Duncan*, p. 307.

8. Alexander Keith, 'Origin of the Mission to the Jews at Pesth', in *The Sunday at Home* (1867), p. 432.

9. See ODNB 'Julia Pardoe'; Elizabeth Barrett Browning, *The letters of Elizabeth Barrett Browning to Mary Russell Mitford, 1836–1854*, vol. 1 (Waco: Armstrong Browning Library of Baylor University, 1983), pp. 54-55; 327; 329; 336-337; 343.

10. Alexander Keith, 'Origin of the Mission to the Jews at Pesth' in *The Sunday at Home* (6 April, 1867), p. 234.

11. Ibid., p. 234.

12. Ibid., p. 262.

13. Ibid., p. 261.

14. Brown, *Duncan*, p. 310.

15. Laurie to RMM, NCL MACCH 2.1.82.

16. Carlyle, op. cit., p. 436.

17. Alexander Keith 'The Origin of the Mission to the Jews at Pesth' in *The Sunday at Home*, 1867, in instalments from pp. 212ff; pp. 232ff; pp245ff; 261ff.

Chapter 15

1. MB1, p. 17. Cf. Advertisement in *The Scotsman* (23 November, 1839 and HFMR December 1839), p. 87.

2. MB1, p. 22.

3. MACCH 2.1.87 Wodrow to M'Cheyne (no date).

4. *HMFR* No. 8 (February 1840), p. 126. Emphasis original.

5. *The Record of the Free Church of Scotland* (1st March, 1864), p. 473.

6. Keith, *Sunday at Home*, No. 675, p. 212.

7. MB1, p. 22.

8. See, *HMFR* No. 13 (July 1840), pp. 190-191.

9. Ibid., p. 191.

10. *HMFR* No.13 (July 1840), p. 192.

11. *HMFR* No.13 (July 1840), p. 191.

12. *HMFR* No.15 (September 1840), p. 214

13. *HMFR* No.15 (September 1840), p. 215.

14. *HMFR* No.13 (September 1840), p. 215.

15. For Dalton's brief time in Jerusalem see, Gidney, *History of the London Society*, p. 178.

16. *HMFR* No.13 (September 1840), p. 216.

17. *HMFR* No.13 (September 1840), p. 217.

18. *HMFR* No. 13 (September 1840), p. 217. Friedrich August Gottreu Tholuck (1799–1877) was professor of theology in Halle from 1826. He had been influenced by Pietism and was involved with the revival movement, he staunchly opposed the intrusion of theological Rationalism. An enthusiastic advocate of Jewish missions, he assisted the LSPCJ as their representative in Germany. Cf. Gidney, *History of the London Society*, pp. 70, 125, 130, 155. The reference in the Assembly report was to an article written by Dr Tholuck for the *Jewish Intelligence* (1837), p. 97.

19. *HMFR* No. 13 (September 1840), p. 217.

20. *HMFR* No.13 (September 1840), p. 218. Emphasis original.

21. *Proceedings of the General Assembly of the Church of Scotland*, 22nd May, 1840.

CHAPTER 16

1. MACCH 1.8; 1.9 The following note books and sketch books belonging to M'Cheyne have survived: a plain page notebook, measuring 5"x 8", bound in marbled boards with a red cloth spine, containing notes and sketches of the expedition. Its opening entry, providing information on M'Cheyne's preparatory visit to London was written on 27th March, 1839; the following pages record details of the European stage of the journey up to 26th April in Leghorn. There follows twenty-three blank pages. The account of the journey was resumed on 30th May, somewhere near the Egyptian border, at El Arish and continues to 6th June when the Deputation was at Doulis, in Palestine. Another break follows, with no material relative to the Mission of Inquiry until close to the end where an appendix records information about Jewish

settlement in Palestine, as gleaned from Nicolayson, and similar information on some of the European communities, as given by Pieretz. There follows two lists of qualifications considered necessary for a missionary to the Jews; one is from Nicolayson, the other from Pieretz. Two other notebooks have been referred to in a previous chapter: the most interesting being the small black Del La Rue leatherette pocket notebook, which contains sketches and notes of the Mediterranean leg of the journey, with lists of names and addresses, covering the period from 18th March, to c.17th May, 1839.

2. Adam M'Cheyne to R.M.M, MACCH 2.1.72

3. MB1, p. 86; p. 142.

4. NCL Bon. 1 *The Church of Scotland's Care for Israel, being a narrative of enquiry into the present condition of the Jews in Palestine and other countries made by a deputation of ministers of the Church of Scotland in the year 1839, and drawn up by two of their number, Rev'd Robert M. M'Cheyne and Rev'd Andrew A. Bonar.* The finished work was published as *A Narrative of a Mission of Inquiry to the Jews from the Church of Scotland in 1839* (Edinburgh: William Whyte & Co, 1842).

5. S. G. Reif, 'A Mission to the Holy Land – 1839,' *Glasgow Oriental Society Transactions* vol. XXIV (1971–72), p. 6.

6. *Narrative*, p. 197.

7. Ibid., pp. 278-9. Cf. Reif, op. cit., p. 8.

8. Ibid., pp. 278-9.

9. Ibid., p. 130.

10. Alan H. Harman ed., *Mission of Discovery* (Christian Focus, 1996), p. 14; cf. Tudor V. Parfitt, 'The Use of Hebrew in Palestine 1800–1882,' *Journal of Semitic Studies* 17 (1972), pp. 237-252.

11. The Jewish Committee's treasurer's report states that the cost of production of the first edition was £349.13.8 and the income had been £388.15.5, turning a profit of £39.1.9, and so it continued throughout all subsequent reprints.

12. Robert Smith, *Early Days of the Mission to the Jews in Pesth* (Edinburgh: Oliphant, Anderson and Ferrier, 1893).

13. J. W. Alexander, 'Scottish Mission to the Jews,' *The Princeton Review*, No. III (July 1844), pp. 329-350.

14. Anon, 'Review of Narrative,' *The Jewish Missionary Herald*, vol.vi. no. i (May 1846), pp. 109-111.

CHAPTER 17

1. MB1, pp. 31, 35.

2. Ibid., p. 32.

3. Ibid., pp. 32-34.

4. Ibid., pp. 46-50.

5. Bernstein, *Witnesses*, p. 468.

6. *HFMRFCS* (1891), p. 75.

7. See Ritchie, *Daniel Edward*, p. 175.

8. MB1, p. 162.

9. Catherine Edward, *Missionary Life Among the Jews in Moldavia, Galicia and Silesia* (London: Hamilton, Adams and Co., 1867), p. 33. Any account of the Edwards' missionary work in Iaşi will depend heavily on this firsthand, though hardly objective, source.

10. Edward, pp. 34-43.

11. Misha Glenny, *The Balkans 1804–1999* (London: Granta Books, 1999), pp. 65, 448-449.

12. See, e.g. 'Rumania' in *Encyclopedia Judaica* (London: Macmillan, 1971), vol. 14, p. 387.

13. Edward, p. 35.

14. Ibid., pp. 56-57.

15. MB1, p. 372. Cf. William Ewing, *Annals of the Free Church of Scotland* (Edinburgh: T & T Clark, 1914), vol. 2, p. 34.

16. Edward, p. 57-62.

17. MB1, p. 437.

18. Edward, pp. 48-49.

19. Ritchie, *Daniel Edward*, citing Iaşi State Archives, Secretariul de Stat, file 1576 (1846-7), passim.

20. Mason frankly describes the problems he faced with the Iaşi *Comité Sanitaire* (Board of Health) who submitted him to very tedious examination and concluded he was incompetent to practice. The official finding was as follows (in translation): 'The Board of Health has just received the answer of the Medical Committee, No. 87, announcing that, having examined Doctor Mason, they have ascertained that his knowledge, both of surgery and medicine, is superficial, scarcely corresponding to the diploma produced. The Board, therefore, restrained by the law, cannot license Mr the Doctor Mason, and, therefore, the Board has renewed its order to the chief of police to seal up all the medicines in the doctor's house, expressly forbidding him to practise, for fear that he should injure human health. Informing the Honourable Consul of these circumstances, the Board have the honour to beg him himself to debar the doctor from practice.' It is not outside the bounds of possibility that the *Comité Sanitaire* made Mason's life difficult on account of his association with the mission. Cf. Mason, *Three Years in Turkey*, p. 84.

21. Personal email communication from Marianne Smith, College Librarian,The Royal College of Surgeons of Edinburgh, Nicolson Street, Edinburgh, EH8 9DW (26 July, 2012).

22. John Mason, *Three Years in Turkey: The Journal of a Medical Mission to the Jews* (London: John Snow, 1860).

23. Ibid., p. 1.

24. MB2, p. 4.

25. Ibid., pp. 4-10.

26. John Mason, *Three Years in Turkey: the Journal of a Medical Mission to the Jews* (London: John Snow, 1860), p. 208.

27. Wood to Mason. NLS MS 19000, p. 301.

28. Wigtonshire register of birth, marriages and deaths: 12/11/1849 Mason, John (OPR Marriages 821/00 0090 0114 Dumfries).

29. Case Book: Lunatic Department of the General Prison at Perth, page 33.

30. See *Dumfries and Galloway Standard and Advertiser*, 19 March, 1851; Kathryn Burtinshaw, John Burt, *Madness, Murder and Mayhem: Criminal Insanity in Victorian and Edwardian Britain* (Barnsley: Pen and Sword, 2018), Kindle ed., chapter 3. The Lunatic Department of the General Prison at Perth was established in 1846, predating Broadmoor in England (1863) and Dundrum, Ireland (1850); here 'offenders were admitted not for the crime committed, but for the threat presented by their insanity.' See *Prisoners or Patients: Criminal Insanity in Victorian Scotland*, National Records of Scotland.

31. *Edinburgh Evening News* (2 May, 1898), p. 2.

32. MB2, pp. 73-75.

33. Ibid., pp. 91-92.

34. Ibid., p. 156.

35. Ibid., p. 94.

36. Ibid., pp. 160-61.

37. Brown, *Duncan*, p. 292.

38. For further information about Philip see: Bernhard Pick, 'Hermann, Philip' in *Cyclopædia of Biblical, Theological and Ecclesiastical Literature* (New York: Harper and Bros, 1880), ad. loc.

39. MB2, pp. 230, 246-247, 278-280.

40. Edward, *Missionary Life*, pp. 65, 79.

41. Ibid., pp. 107-108.

42. Ibid., p. 109.

43. Ibid., p. 142.

44. Ibid., p. 84.

45. Ibid., pp. 91-95.

46. Ibid., pp. 100-101.

47. MB2, p. 27.

48. *HFMRFCS*, no. 482 (1848).

49. Edward, p. 127. Emphasis original.

50. Gavin Carlyle, *Life and Word of the Rev. William Wingate* (Glasgow: R. L. Allan & Son, n.d), p. 112.

51. Edward, pp. 119-120.

52. Ibid., p. 127.

53. *HFMRFCS* (1848), p. 521.

54. Edward, pp. 133-139.

55. For the work in Lviv and Breslau see Catherine Edward, op. cit. *passim*; Ritchie op. cit.

56. Edward, p. 158.

57. Christopher Clark, *The Politics of Conversion: Missionary Protestantism and the Jews in Prussia 1728–1941* (Oxford: Clarendon Press, 1995), p. 246.

CHAPTER 18

1. A. J. P. Taylor, *The Habsburg Monarchy: 1809–1918* (London: Hamish Hamilton, 1948), p. 47.

2. J. A. R. Marriot, *A History of Europe 1815–1939* (London: Methuen, 1931), p. 146f.

3. Brown, *Duncan*, p. 311.

4. Francis W. Newman ed., *Select Speeches of Kossuth* (London: Trübner & Co, 1852), p. 238.

5. See Andrew Wheatcroft, *The Habsburgs* (London: Penguin, 1996), p. 251ff.

6. Imre Revesz, *History of the Hungarian Reformed Church* (Budapest: Hungarica America, 1956), p. 111; Georg Bauhoffer, *The History of the Protestant Church of Hungary From the Beginning of the Reformation to 1850* (London: James Nisbet & Co, 1854), p. 431.

7. Raphael Patai, *The Jews of Hungary* (Detroit: Wayne State University Press, 1996), p. 22f.

8. For Reform Judaism see David Philipson, *The Reform Movement in Judaism* (New York: The Macmillan Company, 1907); Leo Trepp, *A History of the Jewish Experience* (Milburn NJ: Behrman House, 1962), pp. 297-298, 301-307; Dan Cohn Sherbok, *The Jewish Faith* (London: SPCK, 1993), pp. 6-7.

9. Patai, p. 242.

10. Patai, p. 252. Patai, who generally takes a cynical view of conversions, nevertheless argues that Habsburg prejudices 'motivated many talented Hungarian Jews either to convert to Christianity or emigrate and try their luck in other countries – or, in some cases, to take both steps .... Statistical data are lacking, but one gets the definite impression that both conversion and emigration were much more frequent among highly talented Hungarian Jews than in the Hungarian Jewish community as a whole.'

11. Szilvia Andrea Holló, 'Széchenyi's Role from the Idea to the Passing of the Bridge Act' in *The Széchenyi Chain Bridge and Adam Clark* (Budapest: City Hall, 1999), p. 12ff.

12. Judit Brody, 'William Tierney Clark: Civil Engineer' in *The Széchenyi Chain Bridge*, p. 63.

13. Gavin Carlyle, *Life and Work of William Wingate* (Glasgow: R. L. Allan & Sons, n.d.), p. 26.

14. For Immanuel Tremellius as a Jewish Christian, see Bernstein, *Some Jewish Witnesses for Christ* (Operative Jewish Converts Institute, 1909), ad loc.; W. T. Gidney, *The Jews and their Evangelisation* (Student Christian Movement, 1899) p. 88.

15. See A. I. Dunlop, *Burning Bush*, Nigel M. de S. Cameron ed., *Dictionary of Scottish Church History and Theology* (T & T Clark, 1993) ad. loc.; George C. Cameron, *The Scots Kirk in London* (Becket Publications, 1979), p. 210, fn. 1; G. D. Henderson, *The Burning Bush* (St. Andrews Press, 1957), chapter 1.

16. See Jack C. Whytock 'The History and Development of Scottish Theological Education and Training, Kirk and Secession (c.1560–c.1850)' (Ph.D. thesis: University of Wales, Lampeter 2001), pp. 475-477.

17. Graeme Murdock, *Calvinism on the Frontier 1600–1660: International Calvinism and the Reformed Church in Hungary and Transylvania* (Oxford: Oxford University Press, 2000), p. 83.

18. Bauhoffer, p. 322ff.

19. See Krisztina Fenyö, *Contempt, Sympathy and Romance* (Edinburgh: Tuckwell Press, 2000), p. 79.

20. László Kósa 'The Age of Emergent Bourgeois Society, from the Late 18th Century to 1920. I. Everyday Culture,' Kósa ed., *A Cultural History of Hungary* (Budapest: Corvina Books Ltd., 2000), pp. 93-95.

21. See Carlyle, *Wingate*, p. 10; Brown, *Duncan*, p. 350, also John Duncan *Assembly Address V.*, James S. Sinclair ed., *Rich Gleanings After the Vintage from 'Rabbi' Duncan* (Free Presbyterian Publications, 1984), p. 378. Mrs Daniel Edwards of Iaşi, Moldavia, wrote to her friend Miss Catherine Douglas saying, 'I had written what I should not about the truly excellent *lady on the hill* whom the Duchess [of Gordon] hopes to see, but I find it dangerous even to allude to her here.' Catherine Edward, *Missionary Life*, p. 37. Emphasis mine. The Duchess of Gordon and Dr Keith did meet with her in 1846, not in Buda, but at the Duchess' mother's palace in Kirkheim, Würtemberg. Carlyle, *Wingate*, p. 434.

22. Bauhoffer, p. 444.

CHAPTER 19

1. The standard biography of John Duncan is David Brown, *The Life of Rabbi Duncan* (Glasgow: Edmonston and Douglas, 1872), a book already referred to frequently.

2. Brown, *Duncan*, p. 76.

3. For one attempt at grappling with Duncan's intractable problems with Christian assurance see John E. Marshall, '"Rabbi" Duncan and the Problem of Assurance' in *Banner of Truth*, issue 201 (Edinburgh: Banner of Truth Trust, June 1980), pp. 16-27.

4. Anon, *In Memoriam: Maria Dorothea Duncan Spaeth* (Philadelphia: private publication, 1879), pp. 56f.

5. New College, Edinburgh, Mss.CM/D60 7/327/14.

6. Alexander Moody Stuart, *Recollections of the Late John Duncan* (Edinburgh: Edmonston and Douglas, 1872), p. 59.

7. A collection of correspondence between Maria Dorothea and her father and husband was posthumously published as *In Memoriam: Maria Dorothea Duncan Spaeth* (Philadelphia: private publication, 1879). The book is important not only as a memorial of Maria Dorothea, but because it contains the only extant collection of John Duncan's letters. For Spaeth see: J. C. Jensson, *American Lutheran Biographies* (Milwaukee: 1890), pp. 734-736.

8. Cited: Brown, *Duncan*, p. 295, fn. 1.

9. The standard biography is Gavin Carlyle, *The Life and Work of William Wingate, Missionary to the Jews* (Glasgow: R. L. Allan & Son, n.d.).

10. For Wingate's time in Berlin and his acquaintance with Daniel Edward, see Carlyle, *Wingate*, pp. 344f.

11. MB1, p. 48.

12. See *Fasti*, vol. 7, p. 714.

13. MB1, p. 65.

14. Copy minute of meeting of the Edinburgh subcommittee in MB1, p. 78.

15. Robert Smith, *Early Days of the Mission to the Jews in Pesth* (Edinburgh: Oliphant, Anderson and Ferrier, 1893), pp. 8-9.

16. Smith, p. 10.

17. Smith, ibid., see also Carlyle, *Wingate*, p. 42; Carlyle, *Saphir*, p. 440.

18. Moody Stuart, *Recollections*, p. 70.

19. See Ottó Vág, 'The Influence of the English Infant School in Hungary,' *International Journal of Early Childhood*, vol. 7, (1975).

20. Moody Stuart, p. 66-67.

21. Brown, *Duncan*, p. 317.

22. Carlyle, *Saphir*, pp. 11f.

23. Moody Stuart, p. 75.

24. Ibid., p. 73.

25. William W. Ewing, *Annals of the Free Church of Scotland, 1843–1900*, vol. 1 (Edinburgh: T. & T. Clark, 1914), p. 345.

26. Smith, p. 11; Anne Marie Kool, *God Moves In A Mysterious Way* (Zoetermeer: Boekcentrum, 1993), pp. 103f.

27. Brown, *Duncan*, p. 323.

28. Bauhoffer, p. 428.

29. Brown, *Duncan*, p. 319.

30. John Duncan with William Knight, *Colloquia Peripatetica* (Edinburgh: Edmonston and Douglas, 1873), p. 8. A modern collection of Duncan's sayings is John M. Brentnall, *Just a Talker: Sayings of John ('Rabbi') Duncan* (Edinburgh: Banner of Truth Trust, 1997).

31. Brown, *Duncan*, p. 348.

32. Thomas Brown, *Annals of the Disruption* (Edinburgh: Macniven and Wallace, 1893), p. 98.

33. *The Witness*, vol. 4, no. 353 (May 25, 1843).

34. *Fasti*, vol. 7, p. 686, for Ann Petrie as the wife of John Anderson of Coulter, see *Fasti*, vol. 1, p. 247.

35. MB1, p. 244.

36. Brown, *Duncan*, p. 432.

37. Ibid., p. 373.

38. Moody Stuart, p. 105.

39. See, J. S. Sinclair ed., *Rich Gleanings After the Vintage from 'Rabbi' Duncan* (London: Chas. J. Thynne & Jarvis, Ltd., 1925), pp. 359-388.

40. Moody Stuart, p. 165.

41. MB2, p. 151.

42. Ibid., p. 361.

43. *Correspondence Respecting the Expulsion of Messrs. Edward, Wingate and Smith from the Austrian Dominions* (Parliamentary Papers, June 22nd 1852; Item 32.

44. *The Independent* (New York, 23rd October, 1851).

45. See e.g. *The Witness* (July 31, 1852).

46. MB2, p. 389.

47. Ibid., p. 417.

48. Ewing, *Annals, ad. loc.*

49. Carlyle, *Wingate*, p. 183.

CHAPTER 20

1. Carlyle, p. 313. Emphasis original.

2. Carlyle, p. 435.

3. Moody Stuart, p. 70.

4. Carlyle, p. 24.

5. For Israel Saphir's baptism and 'denunciation' by his friend Rabbi Schwab in the Budapest synagogue see, Carlyle, *Saphir*, pp. 23-26.

6. Ibid., p. 24.

7. Clyde Binfield, *George Williams and the YMCA* (Sheffield Academic Press in association with YMCA England, 1994), pp. 16, 56ff; C. P. Shedd ed., *History of the World Alliance of Young Men's Christian Associations* (London, 1955), pp. 250, 263, 330 & 368.

8. Adolph Saphir ed., *Letters and Diaries of Philipp Saphir* (Edinburgh: Johnstone and Hunter, 1852).

9. Bernstein, p. 446, Cf. Carlyle, pp. 273-274.

10. Carlyle, p. 285.

11. See William D. Rubinstein 'The Secret of Leopold Amery,' *History Today* (February 1999), pp. 17-23.

12. For the detainment and release of Stern and other hostages by Tewodros II see Philip Marsden, *The Barefoot Emperor: An Ethiopian Tragedy* (London: Harper Perennial, 2008).

13. For Stern see, Albert Augustus Isaacs, *Biography of the Rev. Henry Aaron Stern, DD: For More than Forty Years a Missionary amongst the Jews* (London: James Nisbet, 1886).

14. See, Leo Amery, *My Political Life* (London: Hutchinson, 1953–55), in three volumes.

15. See, Leonard Stein, *The Balfour Declaration* (London: Valentine Mitchell, 1961).

16. For Orde Wingate see, Christopher Sykes, *Orde Wingate* (London: Collins, 1959).

17. Sir Ronald Wingate, *Wingate of the Sudan* (London: John Murray, 1955), pp. 225-226. Sir Reginald has been credited with laying the foundations of Orde's career. See Sykes, *Orde Wingate*, p. 57.

18. David Baron ed., *Christ and Israel: Lectures and Addresses on the Jews by Adolph Saphir* (London: Morgan and Scott, 1911), p. 10.

19. Bernstein, p. 330.

20. Dr Rich Robinson, personal communication, citing Efim Melamed's observation about life at the seminary in 'The Zhitomir Rabbinical School: New Materials and Perspectives,' Anthony Polonsky ed., *Studies in Polish Jewry Volume 14: Focusing on Jews in the Polish Borderlands* (Liverpool: Liverpool University Press, 2001), pp. 105-115.

21. Arthur James Muller, *Apostle of China, Samuel Isaac Joseph Schereschewsky, 1831–1906* (New York: Morehouse Pub. Co., 1937), p. 30.

22. Muller, p. 31.

23. Muller, p. 32.

24. K. S. Latourette, *A History of the Expansion of Christianity. Volume 6: The Great Century: North Africa and Asia 1800–1914* (Exeter: Paternoster Press, 1971), p. 319.

25. Michael Pollack, *Mandarins, Jews, and Missionaries: The Jewish Experience in the Chinese Empire* (Philadelphia: Jewish Publication Society of America, 1980), pp. 187-197.

26. James A. Muller, *Apostle of China: Samuel Isaac Joseph Schereschewsky 1831–1906* (New York: Morehouse Publishing, 1937), p. 254.

27. Personal interview. Since c.1985 Christian Witness to Israel has employed a number of Chinese missionaries to the Jews, see Staff Book of Christian Witness to Israel (now International Mission to the Jewish People).

28. MB2, pp. 15-18. He appears in William Wingate's list of converts for the year 1846.

29. Ibid., p. 21.

30. Ibid., pp. 19-22.

31. William Wingate, Report for the 1847 General Assembly of the Free Church of Scotland, MB2, p. 25.

32. Wayne Grudem, *Systematic Theology: An Introduction to Biblical Doctrine* (Leicester: Inter-Varsity Press, 1994), p. 709.

33. Knight, *Colloquia Peripatetica*, p. 86.

Chapter 21

1. Carlyle, p. 57.

2. W. Garden Blaikie, *After Fifty Years, 1843–1893* (Edinburgh: Thomas Nelson and Son, 1893), p. 110.

3. Gidney, p. 623.

4. Anon, 'The Findings of the Budapest Conference' in *The Christian Approach to the Jew: Being the Report of Conferences held in Budapest and Warsaw in April 1927* (Edinburgh: Edinburgh House Press, 1927), p. 18.

5. Sinclair, p. 378.

6. Adolph Saphir ed., C. A. Schönberger, 'Movements in Russia and Hungary' in *Israel Mine Inheritance: Being Addresses delivered at the Jewish Convention held at Mildmay Park, October 1st, 2nd, & 3rd, 1889* (London: John F. Shaw, n.d.), p. 221.

7. Randolph L. Braham, *The Politics of Genocide: The Holocaust in Hungary* (Columbia: Columbia University Press, 1981), vol. 1, pp. 1051-1053.

8. MB2, p. 26.

9. Kool, p. 104.

10. Imre Revesz, *History of the Hungarian Reformed Church* (Washington: Hungarian Reformed Federation of America, 1956), p. 147. English translation by George A. F. Knight.

11. Bauhoffer, p. 436.

12. Carlyle, p. 49.

13. Kool, p. 146.

14. McDougall, p. 163.

15. Randolph L. Braham, pp. 1052-3.

16. For allegations of bias, see Moshe Y. Herczel, *Christianity and the Holocaust of Hungarian Jewry* (New York: New York University Press, 1993), p. 191.

17. Personal interview.

Appendix 1

1. See *Belfast Newsletter* (15th May, 12th June 1840, 15th June 1841).

2. Thomas Hamilton, *History of the Irish Presbyterian Church* (Edinburgh: T & T Clark, 1887), p. 169.

3. *Belfast Newsletter* (13th July, 1841).

4. W. D. Killen, 'The Story of the Union' in *Jubilee of the General Assembly of the Presbyterian Church in Ireland* (Belfast: 1890), p. 71.

5. MB1, p. 278.

6. Leone Levi ed., *Digest of the Acting and Proceedings of the Synod of the Presbyterian Church in England 1836–1866* (London: R. K. Burt & Co, 1869), p. 91.

7. Anon. 'Incidents in the Life of Rev. Ridley Haim Herschell,' John Dunlop ed., *Memories of Gospel Triumphs of the Jews during the Victorian Era* (London: S. W. Partridge & Co., 1894), p. 40-41. Ridley Herschell was the father of Lord Herschell, Lord Chancellor of England. Cf. ODNB ad. loc.

8. MB1, p. 112.

9. Minute Book 1 of *BSPGJ*, p. 1.

10. MB1, pp. 157-8.

11. *Fasti*, vol. 7, p. 497.

12. *The Free Church Magazine* (June 1844), p. 191.

13. BJS, MB:1:189, letter introducing Cunningham from Dr W. Symington.

14. Matthew Hutchinson, *The Reformed Presbyterian Church in Scotland: Its Origin and History, 1680–1876* (Paisley: Parlane, 1893), p. 307.

15. Hutchinson, *The Reformed Presbyterian Church*, p. 307.

16. John Hughes Morris, *The History of the Welsh Calvinistic Methodists Foreign Mission* (Cardiff: Calvinistic Methodist Book Room, 1910), p. 272f.

17. *BSPGJ*, MB1, p. 187.

18. Bernstein, *Jewish Witnesses*, pp. 171-172.
19. *BSPGJ, MB1*, p. 219.
20. Morris, p. 272f.
21. Idem.
22. Morris, p. 278.

Bibliography

Manuscript Sources

International Mission to Jewish People, Witney, Oxfordshire.

Minute Book of British Society for the Propagation of the Gospel among the Jews, vol. I.

Free Church of Scotland, Edinburgh

M'Cheyne's Pastoral Letters.

Proceedings of the General Assembly of the Free Church of Scotland.

National Library of Scotland, Edinburgh

Ledger for Schemes (NLS MS 18927).

Letter Books of the Committee for the Conversion of the Jews of the Free Church of Scotland (NLS MS19000).

Minute Book of the Committee for the Conversion of the Jews of the Church of Scotland (NLS Dep. 298/249).

Minute Book of the Committee for the Conversion of the Jews of the Free Church of Scotland (NLS Dep. 298/250).

Minute Book of the Committee for the Conversion of the Jews of the Church of Scotland (NLS Dep. 298/203).

Nomina Eorum qui Gradum Medicinae Doctoris in Acedemia Jocobi Sexti Scotorum Regis Quae Edinburgi est, Adepti Sunt (Edinburgh: 1845).

Questionnaire from the Committee for the Conversion of the Jews to Ministers and Missionaries (NLS Acc 11820).

Treasurer's Accounts for the Committee for the Conversion of the Jews of the Church of Scotland (NLS MS 18999).

National Archives of Scotland, Edinburgh

Acts of the General Assembly of the Church of Scotland.

Summary of Printed Overtures (CH 1/2 174).

New College Library, Edinburgh

Chalmers Papers (NCL CHA).

M'Cheyne Papers (NCL MCCH).

The Church of Scotland's Care for Israel, being a narrative of enquiry into the present condition of the Jews in Palestine and other countries made by a Deputation of ministers of the Church of Scotland in the year 1839, and drawn up by two of their number, Rev'd Robert M. M'Cheyne and Rev'd Andrew A. Bonar (Bon.1).

United Reformed Church Historical Society, Cambridge

Minute Book of the Society of the Reformed Presbyterian Church in London.

Westminster College, Cambridge

Minutes of the Scots Presbytery in London, Vol. 2.

Government Records and Parliamentary Papers

Hansard's Parliamentary Debates.

The New Statistical Account of Scotland 1835–1845.

Parliamentary Papers 144: *Correspondence Respecting the Expulsion of Messrs. Edward, Wingate and Smith from the Austrian Dominions* (London: Harrison, 1892).

Newspapers

Belfast Newsletter
Children's Missionary Record
Edinburgh Christian Instructor
Free Church Magazine
Home and Foreign Missionary Record of the Church of Scotland
Home and Foreign Missionary Record of the Free Church of Scotland
High Peak News
The Inverness Journal
The Inverness Courier
Jewish Intelligence and Monthly Account
Jewish Missionary Herald
Monthly Missionary Herald

Palestine Exploration Fund Quarterly Statement, 1885
Presbyterian Review
Scottish Missionary Review
The Scotsman
The Sunday at Home
The Witness

Periodical Articles

Chambers, Don. 'Prelude to the Last Things: The Church of Scotland's Mission to the Jews,' *Records of the Scottish Church History Society*, XIX, 1 (1975).

Collins, Kenneth E. 'Jewish Medical Students and Graduates in Scotland, 1739–1862,' *Jewish Historical Studies*, vol. XXIX (1982–1986).

Marshall, John E. '"Rabbi" Duncan and the Problem of Assurance,' *Banner of Truth*, issue 201.

McCavery, Trevor. 'The Rev. William Stavely 1743–1825,' *Reformed Theological Journal*, Vol. 14 (November 1998).

Reif, S. G. 'A Mission to the Holy Land – 1839,' *Glasgow Oriental Society Transactions,* Vol. XXIV (1971/72).

Ritchie, Lionel Alexander. 'Daniel Edward (1815–1896) and the Free Church of Scotland Mission to the Jews in Central Europe,' *Records of the Scottish Church History Society*, vol. 31 (2002).

Ross, John S. 'Beyond Zionism: Evangelical Responsibility to Israel,' *Mishkan*, Jerusalem (1989).

Ross, John S. (ed.). 'A Family Correspondence: Letters of John Duncan and his daughter, Maria Dorothea and her husband, Adoph Spaeth, with extracts from Maria's Diary' in *Reformed Theological Journal*, Vol. 14 (November 1998).

Rubinstein, William D. 'The Secret of Leopold Amery,' *History Today* (February 1999).

Printed Sources

Primary sources

Anon. *The Christian Approach to the Jew: Being the Report of Conferences held in Budapest and Warsaw in April 1927.* Edinburgh: Edinburgh House Press, 1927.

Anon. *In Memoriam: Maria Dorothea Duncan Spaeth*. Philadelphia: private publication, 1879.

Anon. *Horatius Bonar D.D.: A Memorial*. London: James Nisbet & Co., 1889.

Anon. *'Far Above Rubies' Memoir of Helen S. Herschell by her Daughter*. London: Walton and Mabberly, 1854.

Bernstein, A. *Some Jewish Witnesses for Christ*. London: Operative Jewish Converts Institution, 1909.

Black Alex. et. al. *The Conversion of the Jews: A Series of Lectures Delivered in Edinburgh by Ministers of the Church of Scotland*. Edinburgh: John Johnstone, 1842.

Bonar. Andrew A. *Memoir and Remains of Robert Murray M'Cheyne*. Dundee: William Middleton, 1852 [2nd edition].

— *Diary and Life*. London: Banner of Truth, 1960.

— *Redemption Drawing Nigh: A Defence of the Premillennial Advent* (London: James Nisbet, 1847).

— *Sheaves After Harvest*. London: 1936.

Bonar, Andrew A. & M'Cheyne, R. M. *A Narrative of a Mission of Enquiry to the Jews from the Church of Scotland in 1839*. Edinburgh: William Oliphant, 1878 [3rd edition].

Brown, David. *The Restoration of the Jews* republished as Steve Schlissel (ed.) and David Brown. *Hal Lindsay and The Restoration of the Jews*. Edmonton: Still Waters Revival Books, 1990.

— *The Life of Rabbi Duncan*. Edinburgh: Edmonston and Douglas, 1872.

— *Christ's Second Coming: Will it be Pre-millennial*. Edinburgh: John Johnstone, 1846.

Carlyle, Gavin. *Mighty in the Scriptures: A Memoir of Adolph Saphir*. London: Shaw & Co., 1894.

— *Life and Works of the Rev. William Wingate: A Missionary to the Jews*. Glasgow: R. L. Alan, c.1900.

Chalmers, Thomas. *Lectures on the Epistle to the Romans*. Edinburgh: Thomas Constable & Co, 1854.

Church of Scotland, Principal Acts General Assembly of the. 1838, 1839.

Dunlop, J. *Memories of Gospel Triumphs among the Jews During the Victorian Era*. London: S. W. Partridge & Co, 1894.

Eber, Irene. *The Jewish Bishop and the Chinese Bible: S. I. J. Schereschewsky, 1831–1906*. Lieden: Brill, 1999.

Edward, Catherine. *Missionary Life Among the Jews in Moldavia, Galicia and Silesia* (London: Hamilton, Adams and Co., 1867).

Exley, Frank. *Our Hearts Desire*. London: British Society of the Propagation of the Gospel among the Jews, 1942.

Hanna, William. *Memoirs of Thomas Chalmers D.D. LL.D.* Edinburgh: Thomas Constable & Co, 1854.

— (ed.) *Posthumous Works of the Rev. Thomas Chalmers*. Edinburgh: Sutherland and Knox, 1858.

Hyamson, Albert. M. *The British Consulate in Jerusalem in relation to the Jews of Palestine, 1838–1914* (London: Jewish Historical Society, 1939–1942).

Keith, Alexander. *Evidence of the Truth of the Christian Religion Derived from the Literal Fulfilment of Prophecy; Particularly as Illustrated by the History of the Jews, and by the Discoveries of Recent Travellers*. Edinburgh: William Whyte and Co. 1848, [36th ed.].

M'Cheyne, Robert M. *Familial Letters*. Edinburgh: John Johnstone, 1848.

MacGill *et. al. A Course of Lectures on the Jews: By Ministers of the Established Church* (Glasgow: William Collins, 1839).

Moody Stuart, Alexander. *The Life of John Duncan* (Edinburgh: Banner of Truth Trust, 1991).

— *Life and Letters of Elisabeth Last Duchess of Gordon* (London: James Nisbet and Co. 1866).

Moody Stuart, Kenneth. *Alexander Moody Stuart* (London: Hodder and Stoughton, 1900).

Muller, Arthur James. *Apostle of China, Samuel Isaac Joseph Schereschewsky, 1831–1906* (New York: Morehouse Pub. Co., 1937).

Pearson, Hugh. *Memoirs of the Life and Writing of the Rev. Claudius Buchanan, D.D.* (London: Seeley and Burnside, 1834).

Philips, Abel. *A History of the Origins of the First Jewish Community in Scotland – Edinburgh 1816* (Edinburgh: John Donald, 1979).

Polonsky, Anthony. *Studies in Polish Jewry Volume 14: Focusing on Jews in the Polish Borderlands*. Liverpool: Liverpool University Press, 2001.

Robinson, Edward. *Biblical Researches in Palestine*. London: John Murray, 1841.

Saphir, Adolph (ed.). *Israel Mine Inheritance: Being Addresses delivered at the Jewish Convention held at Mildmay Park, October 1ˢᵗ, 2ⁿᵈ, & 3ʳᵈ, 1889*. London: John F. Shaw, n.d..

Saphir, Philip (ed.). Adolph Saphir. *Letter and Diaries of Philip Saphir*. Edinburgh: Johnstone and Hunter, 1852.

Scott, James. *A Catechism upon the Prophetical System of the Scriptures Evincing, by Scriptural and Historical Proofs, the truth of Pre-millennialism, the faith delivered to, and held by, the Jewish, Apostolic, and early Christian churches; and the heresy of Post-millennialism invented by the rise of the great apostasy, and still held by the Popish and Protestant churches*. Edinburgh: John Lowe, 1847.

Sinclair, J. S. (ed.). *Rich Gleanings After the Vintage from 'Rabbi' Duncan*. London: Chas. J. Thynne & Jarvis, Ltd. 1925.

Smith, Robert. *Early Days of the Mission to the Jews*. Oliphant, Anderson & Ferrier, 1893.

Wilson, James Hood and Wells, James. *The Sea of Galilee Mission of the Free Church of Scotland*. Edinburgh: T. Nelson & Sons, 1895.

Wilson, John. *Memoir of Mrs Wilson of Bombay*. John Johnstone: Edinburgh, 1838.

— *Lands of the Bible*. Edinburgh: William Whyte & Co. 1847.

Wilson, William. *Memorials of Robert Smith Candlish, D.D.* Edinburgh: Adam and Charles Black, 1880.

Wingate, William. *Reminiscences of Mission Work*. London: The Messenger of the English Presbyterian Church, 1878–79.

Wolff, Joseph. *Journal of the Rev. Joseph Wolff*. London: James Burns, 1839.

Secondary Sources

Addley, William Palmer. *A study of the Birth and Development of the Overseas Missions of the Presbyterian Church in Ireland up to 1910*. PhD. thesis, Queens University, Belfast, 1994.

Adomnan [Eng. Trans. Denis Meehan] *De Locis Sanctus.* Dublin: 1958.

Aitken, Jonathan. *John Newton: From Disgrace to Amazing Grace* (London: Continuum, 2007).

Allen, Robert. *Arnold Frank of Hamburg.* Cambridge: James Clark, 1966.

Amery, Leo. *My Political Life.* London: Hutchinson, 1953-55.

Arnot, William. *Life of James Hamilton.* London: James Nisbet & Co, 1870.

Baron, David (ed.). *Christ and Israel: Lectures and Addresses on the Jews by Adolph Saphir.* London: Morgan and Scott, 1911.

Bauhofer, Georg. *The History of the Protestant Church of Hungary From the Beginning of the Reformation to 1850.* London: James Nisbet & Co, 1854.

Bermant, Chaim. *Troubled Eden.* London: Valentine Mitchell, 1969.

Bibo, et. al. *The Szechenyi Chain Bridge and Adam Clark.* Budapest: City Hall, 1999.

Bicheno, James. *The Restoration of the Jews.* London: 1807.

Binfield, Clyde. *George Williams and the YMCA.* Sheffield: Sheffield Academic Press in association with YMCA England, 1994.

Black, Kenneth MacLeod. *The Scots Churches in England.* Edinburgh: William Blackwood, 1906.

Blaikie, W. Garden. *Thomas Chalmers.* Edinburgh: Oliphant Anderson & Ferrier, 1896.

— *David Brown. A Memoir.* London: Hodder and Stoughton, 1898.

— *After Fifty Years, 1843–1893.* Thomas Nelson and Son, 1893.

Bonar. Andrew A. (ed.). *The Letters of Samuel Rutherford.* Edinburgh: Oliphant, 1891.

Bonar, Andrew A. & M'Cheyne, R. M. (ed.). Allan Harman *Mission of Discovery.* Fearn: Christian Focus, 1996.

Bonar, Horatius. *Life of the Rev. John Milne of Perth.* London: James Nisbet, 1869.

— *The Desert of Sinai: Notes of a Journey from Cairo to Beersheba.* London: James Nisbet, 1857.

— *Prophetical Landmarks*. London: James Nisbet, 1847.

Bonar, Marjorie. *Reminiscences of A. Bonar*. London: Hodder & Stoughton, 1895.

Boston, Thomas. Sam. McMillan (ed.). *The Whole Works of the Late Rev'd Thomas Boston of Ettrick*. Edinburgh: George and Robert King, 1848–52.

Braham, Randolph L. *The Politics of Genocide: The Holocaust in Hungary*. Columbia: Columbia University Press, 1981.

Brown, David. *Christ's Second Coming: Will it be Pre-millennial?* Edinburgh: John Johnstone, 1846.

Brown, Thomas. *Annals of the Disruption*. Edinburgh: MacNiven & Wallace, 1884.

Brown, Stewart, Fry, Michael J. *Scotland in the Age of the Disruption*. Edinburgh: Edinburgh University Press, 1993.

Buchanan, Robert. *The Ten Years Conflict*. Glasgow: Blackie and Sons, 1852.

Burleigh, J. H. S. *A Church History of Scotland*. London: Oxford University Press, 1960.

Burns, I. *Memoir of the Rev. W. C. Burns MA*. London: James Nisbet, 1870.

Calvin, John. *The Epistle of Paul the Apostle to the Romans*. trans. Ross MacKenzie, Calvin's Commentaries (ed.), David W. Torrance and Thomas F. Torrance (Edinburgh: St. Andrew Press, 1961).

Cameron, George G. *The Scots Kirk in London* (Oxford: Becket Publications, 1979).

Chadwick, Owen. *The Victorian Church*. London: A & C Black, 1970.

Chambers, Don. *Mission and Party in the Church of Scotland, 1810–1843*. PhD. thesis, Cambridge University, 1971.

Cheyne A. C. *The Practical and the Pious: Essays on Thomas Chalmers, 1780–1847*. Edinburgh: St. Andrew Press, 1985.

Clark, Christopher. *The Politics of Conversion: Missionary Protestantism and the Jews in Prussia 1728–1941*. Oxford: Clarendon Press, 1995.

Cohen, Naomi (ed.). *Essential Papers on Jewish-Christian Relations in the United States: Image and Reality*. New York: New York University Press, 1990.

Cohen, Jeremy (ed.). *Essential Papers on Judaism and Christianity in Conflict*. New York: New York University Press, 1991.

Cohn Sherbok, Dan. *The Crucified Jew*. London: Harper Collins Religious, 1992.

— *Israel*. London: SPCK, 1992.

— *Messianic Judaism*. London: Cassell, 2000.

Collins, G.N.M. *The Heritage of our Fathers*. Edinburgh: Knox Press, 1976.

Cooke, Donnachie et. al. *Modern Scottish History 1707 to the Present*. East Linton: Tuckwell Press, 1998.

Crawford, Thomas Jackson. *An Argument for Jewish Missions, being a sermon, etc*. Edinburgh: Myles Macphail, 1847.

Crombie, Kevin. *For the Love of Zion*. London: Hodder and Stoughton, 1991.

Crozier, John A. *The Life of Henry Montogomery*. Belfast: W. H. Greer, 1875.

D'Aubigne, Merle. *History of the Church in Hungary*. London: James Nisbet, 1854.

Dallimore, Arnold. *George Whitefield*. Edinburgh: Banner of Truth Trust, 1970.

— *The Life of Edward Irving: The Forerunner of the Charismatic Movement*. Edinburgh: Banner of Truth Trust, 1983.

De Jong, P. *As the Waters Cover the Sea*. Kampem: Kok, 1970.

Devine, T. M. *The Scottish Nation 1700–2000*. London: Penguin Books, 1999.

Dickson, David. *A Commentary on the Psalms*, 1653-5 [reprint]. London: Banner of Truth Trust, 1959.

Dickinson, W. C. (ed.). *John Knox's History of the Reformation in Scotland*. London: Nelson, 1949.

Drummond, Andrew Lansdale. *Edward Irving and his Circle*. Cambridge: James Clarke & Co, n.d.

Drummond and Bulloch. *The Church in Victorian Scotland 1843–1874*. Edinburgh: St. Andrew Press, 1975.

Duff, Alexander. *Speech delivered in Exeter Hall ... at the anniversary of the Church of Scotland's Foreign Missions*. Edinburgh, 1837.

— *Missions the Chief End of the Christian Church … being the substance of Services held on 7th March, in St Andrew's Church, Edinburgh, at the Ordination of the Rev. Thomas Smith, as one of the Church of Scotland's Missionaries to India.* Edinburgh, 1839.

Duncan, John. *Pulpit and Communion Table* (Inverness: Free Presbyterian Publications, 1969).

Edwards Jonathan. *Works.* Edinburgh: Banner of Truth Trust, 1974.

Eichhorn, David Max. *Evangelizing the American Jew.* Middle Village: Jonathan David, 1978.

Endelman, Todd M. (ed.). *Jewish Apostasy in the Modern World.* New York: Holmes and Meir, 1987.

Ewing, William. *Annals of the Free Church of Scotland.* Edinburgh: T & T Clark, 1914.

Faber, George Stanley. *A General and Connected View of the Prophecies.* London, 1809.

Fairburn, Patrick. *The Interpretation of Prophecy.* Edinburgh: Banner of Truth Trust, 1993.

Fawcett, A. *The Cambuslang Revival.* Edinburgh: Banner of Truth Trust, 1971.

Fenyö, Krisztina. *Contempt, Sympathy and Romance.* Edinburgh: Tuckwell Press, 2000.

Gadkar, E. M. Jacob. *The Religious and Cultural Heritage of the Bene-Israels of India.* Bombay: Gate of Mercy Synagogue, 1984.

Gáll, Imre & Holló, Szilvia. *The Szechenyi Chain Bridge and Adam Clark.* Budapest: City Hall, 1999.

Ganzfried, Solomon R. *Kitzur Shulhan Arukh* [English translation Godlin, Hyman E. *Code of Jewish Law*]. New York: Hebrew Publishing Company, 1961.

Gidney, W. T. *The History of the London Society for Promoting Christianity Amongst the Jews: 1809–1908.* London: London Society for Promoting Christianity Amongst the Jews, 1908.

— *The Jews and Their Evangelisation.* London: Student Volunteer Missionary Union, 1899.

Gilfinnan, James. *The Sabbath Viewed in the Light of Reason, Revelation and History.* Edinburgh: Andrew Elliot, 1863.

Glass, Henry Alexander. *The Story of the Psalters*. London: Kegan Paul, Trench & Co, 1888.

Glenny, Misha. *The Balkans 1804–1999*. London: Granta Books, 1999.

Goold, W. H. *The Reformed Presbyterian Church in Scotland: Its Origin and History, 1680–1876*. Edinburgh: Parlane, 1893.

Grudem, Wayne. *Systematic Theology*. Leicester: Inter Varsity Press, 1994.

Guthrie, Thomas. *Autobiography of Thomas Guthrie* DD *and Memoir by his Sons*. London: Daldy, Ibister, & Co., 1874.

Hamilton, James. *A Memoir of Lady Colquhorn*. London: James Nisbet, 1849.

Hamilton, Thomas. *History of the Irish Presbyterian Church*. Edinburgh: T & T Clark, 1887.

Herschell, Miss. *Memoir of Helen S. Herschell*. London: Walton and Maberley, 1854.

Herschell, Ridley H. (ed.). *Jewish Witnesses that Jesus is the Christ*. London: Aylott & Jones, 1848.

Herczel, Moshe Y. *Christianity and the Holocaust of Hungarian Jewry*. New York: New York University Press, 1993.

Howie (ed.). *Sermons in Times of Persecution*. Edinburgh: Johnstone, Hunter & Co., 1880.

Holmes, R. F. G. *The General Assembly of the Presbyterian Church in Ireland 1840–1990: A Celebration of Irish Presbyterian Witness During a Century*. Belfast: Presbyterian Historical Society, 1990.

Hudson, J. Hamilton. *Let the Fire Burn*. Edinburgh: Handsel, 1978.

Hunter, Henry. *The Rise, Fall, and Future Restoration of the Jews*. London, 1806.

Hyamson, Albert. M. *A History of the Jews in England*. London: Methuen and Co. 1908.

Innes, A. Taylor. *Studies in Scottish History, Chiefly Ecclesiastical*. London: Hodder and Staughton, 1892.

Jamieson, Fausset and Brown. *The Holy Bible and an Original and Copious Critical and Explanatory Commentary*. Glasgow: William Collins, 1863.

Johnson, Paul. *A History of the Jews*. London: Weidenfeld and Nicholson, 1987.

Kennedy, John. *The Days of the Fathers in Ross-shire*. Inverness: Northern Chronicle, 1897.

— *The 'Apostle of the North' The Life and Labours of the Rev. Dr M'Donald*. London: T. Nelson and Sons, 1866.

Killen, W. D. *The Ecclesiastical History of Ireland*. London: Macmillam & Co., 1875.

— *Reminiscences of a Long Life*. London: Hodder & Stoughton, 1901.

— *The Story of the Union* in *Jubilee of the General Assembly of the Presbyterian Church in Ireland*. Belfast: Mullan, 1890.

Kool, Anne Marie. *God Moves In A Mysterious Way*. Zoetermeer: Boekcentrum, 1993.

Kósa, László (ed) A. *Cultural History of Hungary*. Budapest: Corvina Books Ltd. 2000.

Knight, William. *Colloquia Peripatetica*. Edinburgh: David Douglas, 1879.

— *Some Nineteenth Century Scotsmen*. Edinburgh: Oliphant, Anderson and Ferrier, 1908.

Knight, Frances. 'The Bishops and the Jews 1828–1858' in *Christianity and Judaism: Studies in Church History*, vol. 29. Oxford: Ecclesiastical History Society & Blackwells, 1992.

Knox, John. *The Works of John Knox*. New York: AMS Press, 1966 [reprint].

Lachman, David C. *The Marrow Controversy*. Edinburgh: Rutherford House, 1988.

Lambert, Richard S. *For the Time is at Hand*. London: Andrew Montrose, 1947.

Latourette, K. S. *A History of the Expansion of Christianity: vol. 6, The Great Century*. Exeter: Paternoster Press, 1971.

Levi, Leone (ed.). *Digest of the Acting and Proceedings of the Synod of the Presbyterian Church of England 1836–1866*. London: R. K. Burt & Co., 1869.

Lightfoot, J. B. *Saint Paul's Epistles to the Colossians and to Philemon*. Grand Rapids: Zondervan, 1978 reprint of 1879 ed.

Lindsay, T. M. *History of the Reformation*. Edinburgh: T & T Clark, 1906.

Lord, J. H. *The Jews in India and the Far East*. Bombay: S.P.C.K., 1907.

Loewe, Lewis (ed.). *Diaries of Sir Moses and Lady Montefiore*. London: Jewish Historical Society of England, 1983.

Lukas, Lajos. *The Vatican and Hungary 1846–1878*. Budapest: 1981.

M'Crie, C. G. *The Confessions of the Church of Scotland: Their Evolution and History*. Edinburgh: MacNiven & Wallace, 1907.

M'Crie, Thomas. *The Story of the Scottish Church*. Glasgow: Free Presbyterian Publications, 1988.

— *The Life of John Knox*. Edinburgh: William Blackwood and Sons, 1855.

MacDonald, Ian R. *Glasgow's Gaelic Churches*. Edinburgh: The Knox Press, 1995.

— *Aberdeen and the Highland Church*. Edinburgh: St Andrew Press, 2000.

MacDonald, Lesley A. Orr *A Unique and Glorious Mission: Women and Presbyterianism in Scotland 1830–1930*. Edinburgh: John MacDonald, 2000.

McDougall, David. *In Search of Israel. A Chronicle of the Jewish Missions of the Church of Scotland*. London: T. Nelson & Sons, 1941.

Macfarlan, D. *The Revivals of the Eighteenth Century*. London: Johnson, n.d.

MacFarlane, John. *Good Will to Israel*. Edinburgh, 1845.

MacGill, et. al. *Course of Lectures on the Jews by Ministers of the Established Church in Glasgow*. Glasgow: William Collins, 1839.

Macleod, John. *Scottish Theology in Relation to Church History*. Edinburgh: Knox Press, 1974.

— *By-paths of Highland Church History*. Edinburgh: Knox Press, 1965.

MacNaughton, Colin. *Church Life in Ross and Sutherland*. Inverness: Northern Counties Newspaper and Printing and Publishing Company, 1915.

Marriot, J. A. R. *A History of Europe 1815–1939*. London: Methuen, 1931.

Maxwell, William D. *An Outline of Christian Worship*. Oxford: Oxford University Press, 1936.

Mayer, Lewis. *Restoration of the Jews*. London, 1806.

Meirs, John. *Short Treatise Composed and Published by John Meirs Formerly a Jew Now by the Signal Mercy of God in Christ Converted to the Christian Faith as Own'd and Ackowledg'd by the Church of Ireland*. Dublin: Andrew Cook, 1709.

Menasseh Ben Israel. *The Hope of Israel*. Oxford: Oxford University Press for The Littman Library, 1987.

Moore, Prof. *Mission to the Jews* in *The Challenge of our Heritage*. Edinburgh: Free Church College, 1932.

Morris, John Hughes. *The History of the Welsh Calvinistic Methodists Foreign Mission*. Cardiff: C.M. Book Room, 1910.

Moule, H. C .G. *Charles Simeon*. London: Intervaristy Fellowship, 1948.

Murdock, Graeme. *Calvinism on the Frontier 1600–1660: International Calvinism and the Reformed Church in Hungary and Transylvania*. Oxford: Oxford University Press, 2000.

Newton, John. *Works*. Edinburgh: The Banner of Truth Trust, 1988.

Oliphant, Benjamin. R. *Horatius Bonar, 1808–1889. A Study of his Religious Thought and Activity* (PhD. thesis – New College, Edinburgh 1951).

Oliphant, Mrs. *The Life of Edward Irving*. London: Hurst and Blackett, 1862.

Orr, J. Edwin. *The Light of the Nations*. Exeter: Paternoster Press, 1965.

Owen, John *The Works of John Owen*. Edinburgh: Banner of Truth Trust, 1966.

Padwick, Constance. *Henry Martyn Confessor of the Faith*. Leicester: Intervarsity Fellowship, 1953.

Palmer, Robert. E. *Andrew A. Bonar 1810–1892. A Study of his life, work, and religious thought*. PhD. thesis, New College, Edinburgh 1955.

Patai, Raphael. *The Jews of Hungary*. Detroit: Wayne State University Press, 1996.

Patrick, Millar. *The Story of the Church's Song*. Edinburgh: The Scottish Churches Joint Committee on Youth, 1927.

— *Four Centuries of Scottish Psalmody*. Oxford: Oxford University Press, 1949.

Philipson, David. *The Reform Movement in Judaism*. London: Macmillan Co., 1907.

Piggin, Stuart and Roxborogh, John. *The St. Andrews Seven*. Edinburgh: Banner of Truth Trust, 1985.

Poliakov, Leon. *The History of Anti-Semitism*. London: Routlege, Kegan and Paul, 1975.

Pollack, Michael. *Mandarins, Jews, and Missionaries: The Jewish Experience in the Chinese Empire*. Philadelphia: Jewish Publication Society of America, 1980.

Porter, J. L. *The Life and Times of Henry Cooke*. Belfast: William Mullan, 1875.

Pragai, Michael J. *Faith and Fulfilment*. London: Valentine Mitchell, 1985.

Revesz, Imre. *History of the Hungarian Reformed Church*. Washington: Hungarica America, 1956.

Roxborogh, John. *Thomas Chalmers, Enthusiast for Mission: The Christian Good of Scotland and the Rise of the Missionary Movement* (Edinburgh: Rutherford House, 1999.

Schaufler, William G. *Autobiography of William G. Schaufler* (New York: Anson D. F. Randolf & Co, 1887).

Scott, Hew. *Fasti Ecclesiae Scoticanae*. Edinburgh: Oliver and Boyd, [3rd Ed. 1915–1928].

Shedd, C. P. (ed.). *History of the World Alliance of Young Men's Christian Associations* (London: n.p. 1955).

Shepherd, Naomi. *The Zealous Intruders*. San Franciso: Harper & Row, 1987.

Smellie, Alexander. *Men of the Covenant*. Edinburgh: Banner of Truth, 1962.

— *Robert Murray McCheyne*. London: National Council of Evangelical Free Church, 1913.

Smith, Robert. *Quiet Thoughts of a Quiet Thinker*. Edinburgh: 1896.

Stephen, W. *History of the Scottish Church*. Edinburgh: David Douglas, 1896.

Stevens, George. *Go Tell My Brethren: A Short History of the Church's Mission to the Jews*. London: CMJ, 1959.

Steel, Judy. *The Nithsdale Martyr of Auschwitz* in *Discover Scotland*, no.38. n.d.

Stein Leonard. *The Balfour Declaration*. London: Valentine Mitchell.

Stewart, James Haldane. *The Destiny of the Jews and their Connection with the Gentile Nations*. London: John Hatchard & Son, 1841.

Sykes, Christopher. *Orde Wingate*. London: William Collins, 1959.

Thomas, J. Llewellyn. *The Restoration of Israel*. London: Marshall Bros., 1922.

Thomson, D. P. *On the Slopes of Sidlaws*. Edinburgh: The Munro Press, 1953.

Toon, Peter (ed.). *Puritans, The Millennium and the Future of Israel: Puritan Eschatology 1600–1660*. Cambridge: James Clark, 1970.

Torrance, David (ed.). *The Witness of the Jews to God*. Edinburgh: Handsel, 1982.

Trepp, Leo. *A History of the Jewish Experience*. New York: Berhman House, 1962.

Tuchman, Barbara. *Bible and Sword*. New York: Ballantine, 1984.

Walker, James. *The Theology and Theologians of Scotland, 1560–1750*. Edinburgh: Knox Press, 1981.

Walker, Norman. *Chapters From the History of the Free Church of Scotland*. Edinburgh: Oliphant Anderson & Ferrier, 1895.

Walker, Patrick. *Six Saints of the Covenants*. London: Hodder and Stoughton, 1901.

Warren, Max. *To Apply the Gospel: Selections from the Writings of Henry Venn*. Grand Rapids: W. B. Eerdmans, 1971.

Weller, Robert W. *Worship Old and New*. Grand Rapids: Zondervan, 1994.

Wheatcroft, Andrew. *The Habsburgs*. London: Penguin, 1996.

Wodrow, Robert. *The Past History and Future Destiny of Israel*, includes *To the Children of Israel in all the Lands of their Dispersion*. Glasgow: Blackie, 1844.

Wood, Diana (ed.). *Studies in Church History: vol. 29. Christianity and Judaism*. Oxford: Blackwell, 1994.

Wright, David F. (ed.). *The Bible in Scottish Life and Literature*. Edinburgh: St Andrew Press, 1988.

Wylie, James A. *Disruption Worthies: A Memorial of 1843*. Edinburgh: Thomas C. Jack, 1881.

Yapp, M. E. *The Making of the Modern Near East 1792–1923*. London: Longman, 1987.

Yeaworth, David, V. *Robert Murray McCheyne (1813–1843): A Study of an Early Nineteenth Century Scottish Evangelical*. PhD. thesis, New College, Edinburgh, 1957.

Also available from Christian Focus Publications …

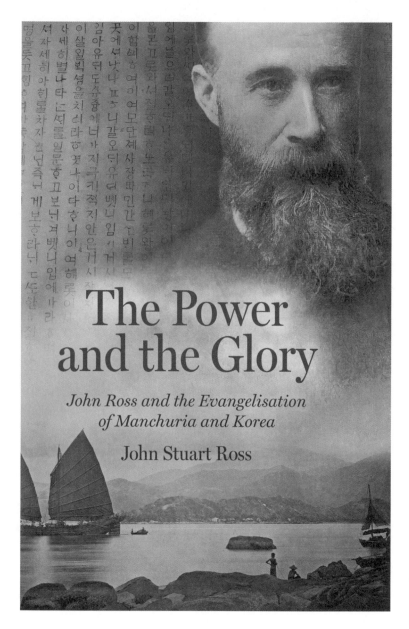

The Power and the Glory

*John Ross and the Evangelisation
of Manchuria and Korea*

John Stuart Ross

978-1-5271-0891-2

The Power and the Glory

*John Ross and the Evangelisation
of Manchuria and Korea*

Born in the northeast of Scotland, John Ross arrived in Manchuria in 1872 and spent 40 years of his life there. He left behind an amazing legacy of culturally sensitive evangelism, established presbyterian churches, innovative missionary principles, valuable publications, and a rich vein of translations, including the first version of the New Testament in Korean.

John S. Ross's riveting biography tracks not only his life, but also the social, political and spiritual influences which shaped his life and work. God is still using John Ross's labours to grow his Kingdom in South and North Korea today.

Christian Focus Publications

Our mission statement –

STAYING FAITHFUL

In dependence upon God we seek to impact the world through literature faithful to His infallible Word, the Bible. Our aim is to ensure that the Lord Jesus Christ is presented as the only hope to obtain forgiveness of sin, live a useful life and look forward to heaven with Him.

Our books are published in four imprints:

CHRISTIAN FOCUS

Popular works including biographies, commentaries, basic doctrine and Christian living.

CHRISTIAN HERITAGE

Books representing some of the best material from the rich heritage of the church.

MENTOR

Books written at a level suitable for Bible College and seminary students, pastors, and other serious readers. The imprint includes commentaries, doctrinal studies, examination of current issues and church history.

CF4•K

Children's books for quality Bible teaching and for all age groups: Sunday school curriculum, puzzle and activity books; personal and family devotional titles, biographies and inspirational stories – because you are never too young to know Jesus!

Christian Focus Publications Ltd,
Geanies House, Fearn, Ross-shire,
IV20 1TW, Scotland, United Kingdom.
www.christianfocus.com